SPENSER STUDIES

XXIII

SPENSER STUDIES

A Renaissance Poetry Annual

XXIII

EDITED BY
William A. Oram
Anne Lake Prescott
Thomas P. Roche, Jr.

AMS PRESS, INC.
New York

SPENSER STUDIES
A RENAISSANCE POETRY ANNUAL

edited by Anne Lake Prescott, William A. Oram, and Thomas P. Roche, Jr.

is published annually by AMS Press, Inc. as a forum for Spenser scholarship and criticism and related Renaissance subjects. Manuscripts must be double-spaced, including notes, which should be grouped at the end and should be prepared according to *The Chicago Manual of Style*. Authors of essay-length manuscripts should include an abstract of 100–150 words and provide a disk version of the article, preferably in a Windows-compatible format. One copy of each manuscript should be sent to Thomas P. Roche, Jr., Program of Liberal Studies, 215 O'Shaugnessy Hall, University of Notre Dame, Notre Dame, IN 46556; one copy to Anne Lake Prescott, Department of English, Barnard College, Columbia University, 3009 Broadway, New York, NY 10027–6598; and one copy to William A. Oram, Department of English, Smith College, Northampton, MA 01063.

Please send inquiries concerning subscriptions or the availability of earlier volumes to AMS Press, Inc., Brooklyn Navy Yard, 63 Flushing Ave., Unit 221, Brooklyn, NY 11205–1073, USA.

ISSN 0195–9468

International Standard Book Numbers

Set ISBN-10: 0-404-19200-9
Set ISBN-13: 978-0-404-19200-6

Vol. XXIII ISBN-10: 0–404–19223–8
Vol. XXIII ISBN-13: 978–0–404–19223–5

AMS PRESS, INC.
Brooklyn Navy Yard, 63 Flushing Avenue–Unit #221
Brooklyn, NY 11205-1073, USA
www.amspressinc.com

Contents

Gleanings
275

Illustrations

Index

This volume of *Spenser Studies* is dedicated to the memory of Richard Helgerson, 22 August 1940 to 26 April 2008.

F. W. BROWNLOW

The British Church in
The Shepheardes Calender

The dialogues in the ecclesiastical eclogues of *The Shepheardes Calender (February, May, July, September)* reflect discussions of Church history and government in Pembroke College, Cambridge, during Spenser's time there as a student. The ideal Church in the collegiate debaters' minds seems to be the legendary "British Church" founded by Joseph of Arimathæa, among others, and reinvented for Henry VIII as a rationale for his royal supremacy and the consequent separation of the English provinces from the rest of the Western Church. This romantic ecclesiastical fiction was powerfully influential in the development of the Protestant Church of England under Elizabeth I, and provided the historical basis for Spenser's approach to British history, as well as Arthur's role in it as a Protestant warrior.

*T*HE SHEPHEARDES CALENDER proper begins with an engraving of a shepherd boy, Colin Clout, rather raggedly dressed as suits his name, looking up to the sign of the zodiac (Aquarius, which the sun entered about mid-January in Spenser's time). He stands in the center of the picture between his flock and the "neighbour" town where he would rather be because he has fallen in love with a girl who lives there called Rosalinde, who will have nothing to do with him and his poems. His broken pipe, which lies on the ground before him, implying a necessary and accepted break with his former ways, suggests that the world waiting for Colin, like his uncooperative Rosalind (who is in some way a figure for that world), has no use for shepherd boys' songs.[1] So there Colin stands, caught between a happy, peaceable, unstressed life behind him, and an unavoidably dangerous life of aggressive competition that lies ahead for all shepherd boys who leave home.

In the eclogues that follow, the pastoral landscape and the shepherds and shepherd boys who inhabit it are figures—as they are in

1

Lycidas—of sociable, safe collegiate life as opposed to the urbane, "real" life of court and town. Cambridge, and specifically Spenser's college, Pembroke, where he matriculated in 1569, provides the location and the themes of the *Calender*'s debates. [2] It probably provided the personnel as well. We know that Colin is Spenser, and that Colin's older friend Hobbinol is Gabriel Harvey, fellow of Pembroke from 1570 until 1578; and it would not be at all surprising if other Pembroke fellows, scholars, sizars, and gentlemen commoners were concealed among the Calender's shepherds and shepherd lads. Everyone knows that Algrin, whom Thomalin in the July eclogue reports badly hurt when an eagle drops a shell-fish on his head from a great height, is Edmund Grindal, Elizabeth I's sequestered archbishop of Canterbury. What is not so well known is that Grindal was a Pembroke man who served as master of the college from 1559 until 1562. Colin's employer, Roffy, is another Pembroke man, John Young, master during Spenser's time from 1567 to 1578. He resigned after his consecration as bishop of Rochester, which entitled him to sign himself, "Roffensis." Hence his poetical name, "Roffy." Spenser was briefly his secretary.

It will be noticed that there is no attempt to conceal these identities. They would have been obvious to any member of Pembroke College, or, probably, of Cambridge University. Similarly, the religious discussions in which these names figure would have been familiar to the fellows and scholars of Spenser's Pembroke; and since the college housed and educated some of the most distinguished churchmen of the period, these discussions were not trivial.

To illustrate the point, one can begin by turning to the second eclogue, *February*, in which Cuddie, a figure for shallow, know-it-all, self-absorbed youth, is feeling sorry for himself because winter (i.e., seniority and old gentlemen) is keeping him cold, that is to say inactive and unemployed. So Thenot, one of the old shepherds—he's really old, too, over 90—tells Cuddie a story to put him in his place. This is the fable of the oak and the briar, and it is meant to warn Cuddie that without the protection of the old, he will come to no good;[3] but besides doing that, the fable offers a monitory reading of recent religious history as a contest between youth and age: the oak is the old Church in England displaced by the young Protestant Church represented as the upstart briar.

In this allegory, the "husbandman" who plants the briar, and takes down the oak, associated with, but older than, "fancies, "fooleries," and the "priestes crewe," is the Crown: the briar's colors, red, green, and white, are the Tudor colors. Nonetheless, the oak proves right in the end. Without his shelter, the briar—presumably the new state

Church—dies, blasted by winter and trampled by the herd. The fable's even-handed ambiguity continues into the concluding emblems, though the weight of meaning seems to be more on Thenot's side than Cuddie's. The implication of Thenot's fable and emblem is that God and the Church, like the oak, are both old and to be revered. On the other hand, it seems to be undeniable that some old things need renewal from time to time.

Similar ambiguities appear whenever the shepherds discuss religion in the *Calender*. E. K.—whoever he is[4]—tells us that Palinode in the fifth eclogue, *May*, represents the Catholic priest, Piers the Protestant minister. Now it is true that the fable of the Fox and the Kid deceived by a crafty pedlar attacks the Catholic missionary priests, but in the eclogue it has no connection with anything Palinode actually says. It seems to be a warning to Palinode to be wary of the company he keeps rather than a warning-off to Palinode himself; and though Piers wins the argument on points, Palinode's approach is by no means contemptible. He enjoys ordinary people's amusements, and sees no reason why shepherds should not enjoy any prosperity that comes their way. As he says, there's misery enough to go round: "Sorrowe ne neede be hastened on:/For he will come without calling anone" (152–53).[5] We hear of Palinode again, in *July*'s debate between Morrell and Thomalin about the relative virtues of proud hill-dwellers and humble valley-men.[6] According to Thomalin, Palinode has now been to Rome, and strongly disapproves of what he has seen there; therefore, whatever Palinode is, he is no Romanist. Thomalin, moreover, who seems to represent a straightforward Protestant position in that eclogue, specifically says that he reverences and adores—surprisingly strong language—the hills where the holy saints lived; and these lines occupy the central position in the eclogue, which is significant because central accent is important in the forms of the *Calender*.[7]

In the ninth eclogue, *September*, another dialogue—this time between Hobbinoll and Diggon Davy—discusses corrupted shepherds and neglected sheep. The eclogue divides into two parts, the first dealing with Protestantism's self-betrayal by idle, greedy clergy, the second focused upon the threat from Catholics, that is, wolves in sheeps' clothing. The eclogue's central twelve lines attack powerful people, presumably the queen and her most important courtiers—Burghley and Leicester among others come to mind—as "bulles *of Basan*" who enrich themselves at the expense of the Church: the passage is so strongly worded that Hobbinoll is worried about the openness of Diggon's remarks (136–37).

What then, by implication, is the ideal, longed-for Church debated and spoken for in these eclogues and—we may suspect—in Pembroke College? Apparently, it is old, but reformed; it is hospitable to tradition, including religious traditions centered upon saints and holy places, but it is anti-Roman, and its proponents object strongly to the alienation of its endowments. Yet it cannot simply be the state Church of England as it existed in 1579, because that Church is implicitly criticized in all these eclogues, and especially in the September eclogue; nor is it a Protestant Church set up independently of the state, as many Cantabrigians—especially of "the younger sort" —desired, because the historical Roffy and Algrin, both treated admiringly in the *Calender*, were bishops of the state Church. To explain this implied Church, as many do, as a compromise between Geneva and Rome by invoking the Victorian terminology of the *Via Media* is an anachronism. These Cantabrigian debaters were not interested in compromise: they were looking for the true Church and a true church polity; those were the terms of debate at Cambridge. We need to remember that during Spenser's undergraduate years at Pembroke, Thomas Cartwright, fellow of Trinity, and appointed Lady Margaret Professor in 1569, challenged the whole basis of the current ecclesiastical establishment, and that when he did so, he encountered the unanimous opposition of John Whitgift, master of Trinity, William Chaderton, the Regius Professor, and Edmund Grindal, then archbishop of York, and soon to be one of the heroes of the *Calender*. Cartwright was deprived of his professorship and his fellowship, and forbidden to preach in the university.[8]

The answer, I want to suggest, is that in the *Calender* Spenser appears as a proponent of what George Herbert called "The British Church," an invention now long-forgotten, though fully described by—among others—Foxe in *Actes and Monuments*, by the eccentric historian William Harrison in his *Historicall Description of the Island of Britain*, and by Camden in his *Remaines*. This version of British Church history, one of the more outlandish products of the English Reformation, entailed a wholesale rewriting of Church history, and—ironically—derived from just the kind of "monkish" forgery for which Elizabethan Protestants usually had nothing but loud mockery. Nonetheless, it provided necessary comfort for Protestants under Catholic attack on charges of novelty and schism; and as a significant by-product, it authorized Spenser's approach to English—or rather British—history in *The Faerie Queene*, including his treatment of Arthur as a Protestant prince.

The actual invention of this version of Church history occurred in the days of England's prototypical divorcé, Henry VIII, when his urgent need for historical as well as theological arguments that would enable him to separate his kingdom from Papal jurisdiction without provoking too much scholarly laughter led him to appoint a carefully picked committee to research the early history of British Christianity. The members of this committee, Thomas Cranmer, Edward Foxe, Edward Lee, Nicholas de Burgo, and John Stokesley (Cuthbert Tunstall's successor as bishop of London), were all advocates of the king's view of his marriage to Catherine of Aragon. Cranmer and Foxe, though, seem to have been the chief authors of the committee's report. This was a treatise, *Collectanea satis copiosa,* completed by September 1530[9] that, predictably enough—given the circumstances and the actors—gave Henry all the arguments he had asked for, even though it took some inventive scholarship to produce that result. By taking their history mostly from Geoffrey of Monmouth and a fake thirteenth-century legal text, the *Leges Anglorum*, Cranmer and Foxe succeeded in writing the jurisdiction of the Roman Church right out of British history, and the story they told remained the received version of Church history in England until well into the seventeenth century.[10]

Camden's *Remaines* provides a succinct epitome of this now mostly forgotten story:

> The true Christian Religion was planted heere most auntiently by *Joseph* of *Arithmathia*, *Simon Zelotes*, *Aristobulus*, yea by saint *Peter*, and saint *Paul*, as may be prooved by *Dorotheus*, *Theodoretus*, *Sophronius*, & before the yere of Christ 200. it was propagated, as *Tertullian* writes to places of *Britaine inacessa Romanis*, whither the *Romans* never reached, which can not be understoode, but of that parte which was afterward called *Scotland.* [11]

Foxe's similarly brief version included in his "Protestation to the whole Church of England" prefacing *Actes and Monuments* received a wide circulation,[12] but the most complete, detailed brief narrative version appeared in William Harrison's *Historicall Description* prefixed to the 1577 edition of Holinshed.[13] Harrison began by thinking it just possible that St. Paul came to Britain, but preferring to deal only with what he considered certainties, went on to tell how Philip the Apostle, having withdrawn into France during the Neronian persecution (64 A.D.) with "diuers of the godlie" sent no less a person than Joseph of Arimethæa, accompanied by Simon Zelotes "to preach vnto the Britons." Joseph then set up his first episcopal see in Avalon, now called Glastonbury (Not that this was actually the first coming of the gospel to a Briton: Harrison claims as British a Christian Roman lady, Claudia Ruffina, mentioned by both St. Paul and Martial). The next important event occurred in the second century, when a British king called Lucius sent two philosophers to Pope Eleutherius, "not to promise any subiection to his sea, which then was not required," but to be instructed in the faith, and to bring back preachers in order that "the foundation of the gospell might surelie be laid ouer all the portion of the Ile, which conteined his kingdome." One of the king's messengers was a man called Elvanus Avalonius, "a man borne in the Ile of *Aualon*, and brought up there vnder those godlie pastours and their disciples, whom *Philip* sent ouer." This King Lucius built churches, including one in London which was the metropolitan church of the kingdom until "it was remoued to Canterburie by *Austine* the monke." Finally, when Lucius sent again to Eleutherius for further instructions, that good Pope turned down his request in a long letter, written in terms that Richard Hooker would have strongly approved, telling him that "all nations are not of like condition," and that practices suitable to one will not suit another. The Pope also told Lucius that "Christ had left sufficient order in the scriptures for the gouernment of his Church." Britain thus became "the first prouince that generallie receiued the faith, and where the gospell was freelie preached without inhibition of hir prince."[14]

After this apostolic and evangelical beginning, though, things went badly wrong. Pelagius brought heresy and monasticism to Britain. Then, encouraged by St. Patrick, the British even began to pray for the dead. As a punishment for their backsliding, therefore, God afflicted them with the Saxons, for whom Harrison has no good thing to say. They were barbarians "who left no idoll unhonored, no not their filthie *Priapus*, unto whom the women builded temples, and made a beastlie image (*Cum pene intenso*, and as if he had beene circumcised)."[15] Then Pope Gregory—known to history, of course, as Gregory the Great—sent Augustine and his forty monks from Rome, and "they were drowned altogither in the pits of error digged up by Antichrist." Even though Harrison concedes that Augustine converted the Saxons from paganism, he insists that he "imbued them with no lesse hurtfull superstition, then they did know before," and that their conversion was from "grosse to subtill treacherie, from open to secret idolatrie." And he concludes:

Thus we see what religion hath from time to time beene receiued in this Iland, and how and when the faith of Christ came first into our countrie. Howbeit as in processe of time it was ouershadowed, and corrupted with the dreames and fantasticall imaginations of man, so it daily waxed worse & worse, till that it pleased God to restore the preaching of his gospell in our daies, whereby the man of sinne is nowe openlie reuealed, and the puritie of the worde once againe brought to light, to the finall ouerthrow of the Romish Sathan, and his popish adherents that honour him daie and night. . . ."

The core of this story is traceable to St. Bede, who tells the story of King Lucius and the Pope in the fourth chapter of his *History*.[16] Bede found Pope Eleutherius amd King Lucius in the sixth-century *Liber Pontificalis*, a collection of papal biographies. Pope Eleutherius is genuine enough, but the compiler of *Liber Pontificalis*, it is now thought, mistook *Britio* (the name of the fortress of Edessa) for *Britannio;* and thus by this mistake turned the Syrian ruler Lucius Ælius Septimus Megas Abgar IX into a Briton called Lucius. Geoffrey of Monmouth added his own inventions freely to Bede's version of Lucius, and the authors of the thirteenth-century *Leges Anglorum* even improved upon Geoffrey, producing a version of the Pope's letter to Lucius that will have proved very exciting to Henry VIII:

For you are vicar of God in your kingdom. . . . A king is named by virtue of ruling not for having a realm. You shall be king while you rule well, but if you do otherwise the name of king shall not remain upon you, and you will lose it. The omnipotent God grant you so to rule the kingdom of Britain that you may reign with him eternally, whose vicar you are in the said realm.[17]

As for Joseph of Arimathæa, whose legend still lives on at Glastonbury: he first appears in British or English history in a mid-thirteenth-century addition to William of Malmesbury's *De Antiquitate*, which also first credited St. Philip with the sending of preachers to Britain. The actual origin of the Joseph story seems to have been a fake charter of St. Patrick, supposed to have been found in St. Michael's Chapel on Glastonbury Tor, c.1195. At about the same time, the French poet Robert de Boron, in his romance, *Joseph d'Arimathie* "echoes very faintly the early claim that the first preachers of Christ had visited Glastonbury."[18] The Welsh, among whom we should probably include England's Welsh king, Henry Tudor, took these

legends seriously. Geoffrey of Monmouth, who expanded enormously—and unscrupulously—upon Bede's brief notice of King
Lucius, is the source of William Harrison's anti-Saxon, anti-Roman
attack on St. Augustine's mission to King Ethelbert of Kent in 597.
Harrison's contemporaries, the Welsh scholars William Salesbury,
Humphrey Llwyd, Thomas Huet, and Richard Davies all used Geoffrey's legends to justify the Protestantism of the reformed Welsh
Church. Davies—who may be Spenser's Diggon Davy—included
them in the preface to the Welsh translation of the New Testament.[19]

Astonishing—not to say nonsensical—though this story is, it provided a historical foundation for the national and Protestant enterprise of England in the later sixteenth century. As a myth of origins,
it had everything needed. Like the wider Protestant and humanist
movement itself, it invited English reformers to go searching for the
primitive Church, but it encouraged them to look for it in their
own island, not in the world at large; and when they accepted the
invitation, they found, first, a Church brought to Britain by apostolic
preachers who had known Christ himself, and second, a British king
confirmed in full authority over that Church and his kingdom by
the Pope himself. It was then a short step to argue that St. Augustine's
mission of 597 was the first of many Roman intrusions on British
self-sufficiency. Perhaps most important of all, the legend of an independent, apostolic British Church provided a religious complement
to the growing political insularity of sixteenth-century England. It
laid down the historical premise of Hooker's definition of the Catholic Church as a federation of national churches, of which the English
Church is one. It gave spiritual validity to the supra-national idea of
Britain, encompassing the three kingdoms of England, Scotland, and
Ireland, plus the principality of Wales, united under one crown
claiming both secular and spiritual authority. It also provided the
Welsh Tudors with a better mandate to govern Britain than descent
from intrusive Saxons or Normans.

Moreover, and most fascinatingly, it made primitive Britain, and
with it, King Arthur, Protestant; and because of its peculiar interpretation of Augustine's mission to the Saxons, it made Arthur into a
prototype of the Elizabethan anti-Catholic soldier, as well as the
prophetic founder of a British Empire destined to eclipse Rome.
Consequently, when taunted by their Catholic opponents for dis-
carding a thousand years of history and inventing a Church with
no past, Elizabethan Protestant controversialists could reply—with
straight faces—that the English had recovered and rejuvenated a
church older and more Catholic than the Church of Rome itself. In
1571 William Fulke, then a fellow of St. John's, but later a very

popular master of Pembroke in 1578 in succession to John Young, made just that reply when John Feckenham, the deprived Abbot of Westminster, charged the new, Protestant Church of England with novelty and schism. In effect, Fulke answered the abbot by citing Geoffrey of Monmouth against Bede. First, he disposed of the argument that St. Augustine brought the Church to England in 597. On the contrary, he wrote, St. Augustine was no saint; he was an ignorant monk sent to England to corrupt the true faith which the Britons had received from the Apostles; and in any case, just as Augustine's religion was younger than the Apostles' so Abbot Feckenham's religion was even younger than his:

> But to consider your groundes particularly, that Augustine, whom you call saincte Augustine, was an vnlearned Monke, as appereth by his questions, propounded to Pope Gregorie, that came into this land, to corrupte the sinceritie of faithe, which the Britons had receiued, euen from the Apostles, about fiue hundred yeres after Christe; and liued twoo hundred yeres at the least, after the aunciente father sainct Augustine bushoppe of Hippo in Affrica; of whose pride and folie, you maie reade in *Galfridus Monumeth. Matheus Westmin.* and others. And truthe it is, that muche superstition, and false doctrine, he brought in, and by tyrannie mainteined, as our stories witnesse, but not all that you holde at this tyme, for your religion, in all pointes, is nothing so old. And as for Beda, he lived longe after Augustine.[20]

This ancient British church, then, is the true church that Spenser has in mind as his shepherd lads and shepherds talk about religion in their academic Arcadia: a wonderful institution that is simultaneously old and new, Catholic and Protestant, universal and local, and thoroughly British. Of course, what it really is, is that curious Tudor creation the Church of England in the process of its transformation in the imaginations of young Cambridge dons from the dead letter of parliamentary legislation and bogus scholarship into a real, livable institution. It proved to be a powerfully attractive conception, too. Under its influence, two of the most distinguished younger clergy at Pembroke, Lancelot Andrewes (exactly contemporary with Spenser) and Samuel Harsnett, both of them to serve as masters of the college, became founders of the High Church movement. It is

not generally known that Andrewes, considered the founder of high
Anglicanism, began his career at Pembroke as a strict Protestant under
Walsingham's patronage. As for Harsnett, his younger protégé, he
entered Pembroke as a Calvinist from Colchester, and as a newly
ordained priest was even disciplined by Whitgift for refusing to wear
the surplice. He too, experienced a change of mind, and when he
made his will as archbishop of York in 1631 he not only defined
himself as a priest of the "Primitive Church"—

> I dye in the auncient faithe of the true Catholicke and Apostol-
> icke Churche called the Primative Churche, that Faithe as it
> was professed by the auncient Holy Fathers next after the blessed
> Apostles the greate Renowned Pillars of the same, and signed
> and sealed with theire Bloude: Renowncinge from my harte
> all modern Popishe Superstitions and alsoe all novities of *Ge-
> neva* not concordant with the *maxims* of the Primative Re-
> nowned Churche.[21]

—but left detailed instructions for the depiction of himself as one on
a remarkable memorial brass which survives in St. Mary's Church,
Chigwell, Essex, showing him as a fully-vested bishop with mitre
and crozier—and Book of Common Prayer.[22] As for Pembroke's
poet, the dream of the primitive British Church, apostolic, royally
governed, militantly defended, and newly restored gave him not just
his hero, Prince Arthur, but the whole animating conceit of *The
Faerie Queene* as a religious and national epic with roots in a deep
and British past.

Ecclesiastically speaking, the Primitive British Church's restoration proved short-lived. Serious ecclesiastical history had no place
for the materials of which it was made, but it was not easy to criticize
such an attractive, romantic story under the Tudors. Polydore Vergil,
writing his *Anglica Historia* for Henry VII, had disposed of Geoffrey
as a serious historian. Yet even he, "to avoid ill-will," as he put it,
and under protest, allowed Geoffrey's British kings into his narrative,
and when he came to deal with Britain under the Romans, included
the stories of Joseph of Arimathæa and King Lucius.[23] Nor is it hard
to understand why, in the cultural wreckage of the mid-sixteenth
century, the story of the British Church proved such a compelling
narrative for the students of Elizabeth I's Pembroke.

Mount Holyoke College

NOTES

1.   Richard Peterson and Lin Kelsey, "Rereading Colin's Broken Pipe: Spenser and the Problem of Patronage" (*Spenser Studies* 15 [2001]: 233–72), show that the broken pastoral pipe is a figure with invariably satirical implications, usually signifying the poet's difficulty in finding an understanding audience and patron.

2.   Gary M. Bouchard, *Colin's Campus: Cambridge Life and the English Eclogue* (Selinsgrove: Susquehanna University Press; London; Cranbury, NJ: Associated University Presses, 2000) is a study of the academic presence in the *Calender*, though Bouchard does not discuss the *Calender*'s religion.

3.   The theme was academically topical in Spenser's Cambridge. Under the Elizabethan statutes of 1559, by the later 1560s, owing to a dramatic increase by about a third in the number of dons at Cambridge, the younger fellows, or "regent masters" (M.A.'s of up to three years' standing) held decisive power in the university senate. The senior members of the university fought back, imposing new statutes in 1570 during John Whitgift's vice-chancellorship which shifted power in the university and the colleges alike from the younger dons to the heads of colleges and the doctors. Subordination of the young by the old, therefore, was a theme of Cambridge life in the 1570s: as Whitgift wrote (November 1570), thanking Chancellor Burghley for "procuring of the late statutes," "the younger sort for the restraint of their liberty much murmur and grudge at them" (H. C. Porter, *Reformation and Reaction in Tudor Cambridge* [Cambridge: Cambridge University Press, 1958], 108–09, 163–67). Whitgift's statutes remained in force until 1856. John Whitgift was another Pembroke man, matriculating in 1550 and briefly master (1567).

4.   If Spenser himself, or Spenser and his friends, wrote the epistle and commentary, then its attribution to "E. K." will have been a joke among the college's literary inner circle. There was an Edward Kirke at Pembroke, two years junior to Spenser, entering as a sizar in 1571. Perhaps he had literary and social aspirations that Spenser and his friends found funny.

5.   Quotations are from *The Yale Edition of the Shorter Poems of Edmund Spenser*, ed. William A. Oram, Einar Bjorvand, Ronald Bond, Thomas H. Cain, Alexander Dunlop, and Richard Schell (New Haven: Yale University Press, 1989.)

6.   Paul E. McLane, *Spenser's Shepheardes Calender: A Study in Elizabethan Allegory* (Notre Dame: Notre Dame University Press, 1961), 188–215, who attempts to identify the speakers, argues that Morell and *July*'s (but not *March*'s) Thomalin are John Aylmer and Thomas Cooper respectively, bishops of London and Lincoln. There is no convincing evidence for this suggestion in the content of the eclogue, and splitting the character of Thomalin into two further weakens the argument.

7.   In the *Calender*'s numerical construction, eight out of twelve eclogues are deployed about a central accent: 1, 2, 3, 4, 6, 7, 9, 10.

8.   Porter, 178–79.

9.   Identified by Graham Nicholson in his unpublished Ph.D. dissertation "The Nature and Function of Historical Argument in the Henrician Reformation" (Cambridge, 1977).

10.   For a dryly elegant account of Henry VIII's remaking of English history, see John Guy, "Thomas Cromwell and the Intellectual Origins of the Henrician

Revolution," available online at http://www.johnguy.co.uk/history.php?&content =intellectual.html.

11. William Camden, *Remaines of a Greater Worke, Concerning Britaine* (London, 1605; STC 4521), sig. B2–2v.

12. *Actes and Monuments* (1583; STC 11225), sig. ★iiij: "In the time of these Emperours, God raysed vp then in this Realme of Britaine diuers worth teachers and witnesses. . . . In whose time the doctrine of fayth without mens traditions was sincerely preached. . . . All this while about the space of foure hundred yeares, Religion remayned in Britayne vncorrupt and the word of Christ truely preached, till about the comming of Austen and of hys companions from Rome, many of the sayd Britayne preachers were slayne by the Saxons. After that began Christen fayth to enter & spring among the Saxons, after a certayne romish sort, yet notwithstanding some what more tollerable, then were the times, which after folowed."

13. The extracts following are taken from *The First and Second Volumes of Chronicles* (1587; STC 13569), 23–28.

14. Foxe tells the story of Lucius in detail in *Actes and Monuments*, "The Second Booke," 106–18 (sigs. I5v–I6v), where his main purpose is to make sure that no one misinterprets the story to mean that Lucius (and Britain) *received* the faith from the Pope.

15. This could be a reference to the hill-figure known as the Cerne Abbas giant. If so, it would be the earliest known reference to it.

16. Thomas Stapleton, trans., *The History of the Church of Englande. Compiled by Venerable Bede, Englishman* (Antwerp, 1565; STC 1778), sig. D4.

17. Cited by Guy, op. cit. According to John Guy, a draft version of the preamble to the Act of Appeals (1533) actually referred to King Lucius's "letter," but the reference came out of the final version, Guy thinks, because, "To have left King Lucius unexpurgated would have been to proclaim to the world the poverty of the Henrician political alphabet—a schism which rested on pro-baronial propaganda cooked in the reign of King John."

18. *Catholic Encyclopedia* (now available online at http://www.newadvent.org/cathen/index.html), s.v. "Pope St. Eleutherius (Eleutheros)"; R. S. Loomis, ed., *Arthurian Literature in the Middle Ages* (Oxford: Clarendon Press, 1959), 284–85; J. Armitage Robinson, *Two Glastonbury Legends: King Arthur and St. Joseph of Arimathea* (Cambridge: Cambridge University Press, 1926), 15.

19. Davies, of course, may be the "Diggon Davy" of the September eclogue. Perhaps the most surprising aspect of the whole episode is the English Protestants' enthusiastic acceptance of Geoffrey's unscrupulous manipulation of Bede's text to implicate Augustine of Canterbury in the pagan king Ethelfrith's slaughter of the Bangor monks at the battle of Legacester. Cf. Geoffrey of Monmouth, *Historia regum Britanniae*, Book 11, ch. 12, and Bede, Book 2, ch. 2 (*op.cit.*, N2v—N3).

20. William Fulke, *An answere to a popishe and slaunderous libell in forme of an apologie* (London, 1572; STC 11426.7), 8. The comical irony of Fulke's position in this skirmish is that he considered himself, with some justice, to be a champion of reason against superstitious fantasy.

21. Harsnett's will (Prerogative Court of Canterbury 78 St. John), cited in F. W. Brownlow, *Shakespeare, Harsnett, and the Devils of Denham* (Newark: University of Delaware Press, 1993), 162. For Harsnett's own account of his prosecution by Whitgift, see ibid., 40.

22. Harsnett was the first Church of England bishop to be depicted wearing a miter.

23. *Anglica Historia*, I.21, II.7, 11.

STEVEN K. GALBRAITH

"English" Black–Letter Type and Spenser's *Shepheardes Calender*

Modern studies of books as material objects have neglected the fact that in sixteenth- and seventeenth–century England black-letter type was called "English." Consequently, they have neglected the implications of such a designation. Returning black-letter type to its original context as "English" type demonstrates how it signified the English language. The relation between type and language expanded beyond black letter and the English language. Reflecting Continental typographic trends, English printers set modern European languages other than English in the typefaces in which they normally appeared in their native countries. In this way, typefaces represented a visual expression of language and nationality. The use of black-letter type in the first edition of Edmund Spenser's *Shepheardes Calender* was a deliberate typographical deviation from its bibliographic model, a 1571 edition of Jacopo Sannazaro's *Arcadia*. This deviation superimposed the English vernacular, represented by black-letter or "English" type, onto the Italian vernacular, represented by italic and roman type. The choice of "English" type supported the book's overarching promotion of English literature and language, along with Spenser's self-promotion as an English poet.

> I suspect that the use of black letter in the *Shepheardes Calender* of 1579 was an intentional bit of antiquarianism.
> —Ronald McKerrow[1]

ONE COULD EASILY INTERPRET the use of black-letter type in *The Shepheardes Calender* as intentional antiquarianism. After all, an archaic type would complement the old-fashioned spellings and the crudely-designed woodcut illustrations that accompany each eclogue.

13

These aesthetic elements highlight the text's archaic language, which the book's enigmatic commentator, E. K., emphasizes and defends in the poem's "Epistle." Nevertheless, it seems just as likely that the use of black-letter type had no significance at all. Perhaps it was simply a convention of the contemporary print trade. Perhaps the book's printer, Hugh Singleton, was making do with what type he had available.

A reexamination of black-letter, or "English" type as it was called in the sixteenth and seventeenth centuries, presents an alternative possibility: that the choice of type for *The Shepheardes Calender* embodied a nationalist significance. In physical appearance, the *Calender* followed its bibliographic model, a 1571 edition of Jacopo Sannazaro's *Arcadia*, nearly to the letter. The conspicuous exception was Singleton's substitution of black-letter type in the *Calender's* main body of text for *Arcadia's* roman and italic. In this essay, I argue that this typographic deviation represented a deliberate choice, one that superimposed the English vernacular, as embodied in black-letter or "English type," onto the Italian vernacular, as embodied in roman and italic. Furthermore, I will demonstrate how this typographical shift supported the book's promotion of English language and literature. Returning black-letter type to its original context as "English" type informs this conclusion. The essay begins, therefore, with a reexamination of black-letter type.

AN "ENGLISH" TYPE

There being diuers Impressions of the Fruteful Sermon, it is to be obserued, that al the Quotations are taken out of the Booke printed in the English Pica, not in the Romane letter.

John Windet set this curious printer's note on the verso side of the title page of his 1590 edition of Thomas Rogers's *A Sermon Vpon the 6.7. and 8. Verses of the 12. Chapter of S. Paules Epistle Vnto the Romanes Made to the Confutation of So Much of Another Sermon, Entituled, A Fruitful Sermon &c.* (fig. 1).[2] The note uses typefaces to differentiate between editions of Laurence Chaderton's *A Fruitfull Sermon, Vpon the 3.4.5.6.7. and 8. Verses, of the 12. Chapiter of The Epistle of S. Paul to the Romanes* (1584).[3] The meaning of "Romane letter" is clear enough, but the reference to "English Pica" may puzzle modern scholars. In modern bibliographic terms, "English" and "pica" refer

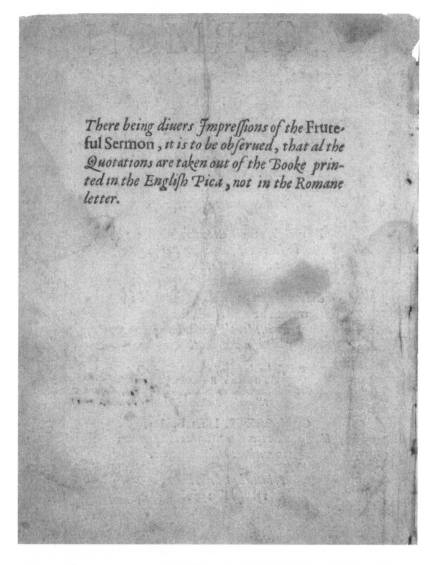

Fig. 1. This printer's note differentiating previous editions of Laurence Chaderton's sermon by typeface is found on the verso of the title page of Thomas Rogers's *A Sermon Vpon the 6.7. and 8. Verses of the 12. chapter of S. Paules epistle vnto the Romanes* (1590). By permission of the Folger Shakespeare Library.

to type sizes. In the sixteenth and seventeenth centuries, however, "English" described both a type size and a typeface. More specifically, "English" referred to the typeface that is more commonly known today as "black letter." In Windet's note, therefore, "Pica" represents the size of the type and "English" the typeface. "Pica English" is what modern bibliographers call "pica black letter."

Samples of typefaces printed in Charles Butler's *Oratoriae Libri Dvo* (1629) help contextualize Windet's note (fig. 2).[4] The first samples found in figure 2, "Primier," "Pique [Pica]," "English," "Great Primier," and so forth, are various sizes of roman type. After these, Butler lists the types used "pro sermone Anglico" (i.e., "for English discourse"): "English Roman," "English Italicke," and "English English." The "English" used in all three of these examples refers to the size of the type, while "Roman," "Italicke," and "English" refer to the typeface. "English English," is what modern bibliographers call "English black letter."

Curiously, modern studies of books as material objects have neglected the fact that in the sixteenth and seventeenth centuries black-letter type was referred to as "English." Consequently, they have neglected the implications of such a designation. Harry Carter, one the twentieth century's preeminent historians of typography, notes that "Englishmen called black letter 'English' just as 'Dutchmen and Flemings called it 'Duyts' meaning 'Deutsch' or Germanic."[5] Although Carter does not explicitly say it, he tacitly acknowledges that black letter represented the vernacular language in the Germanic regions and in England. Simply put, black-letter or "English" type signified the English language.

The use of black-letter type in England began with its first printer, William Caxton. Having learned the print trade in Cologne and Bruges, Caxton conformed to the use of black letter in those regions and brought the practice to England when he established the first English press at Westminster in 1476. Thus, the black-letter style of Cologne and Bruges became the style of England.[6] Had Caxton traveled elsewhere on the continent to learn the trade, the style of English printing could have been radically different:

It is interesting to speculate how the style of English and American print might have developed if Caxton had learned to work type, and print from it, in Italy or France. Had he done so, there might have been an earlier release from the thralldom of the black letter, not to mention an initial appreciation of the full resources of roman.[7]

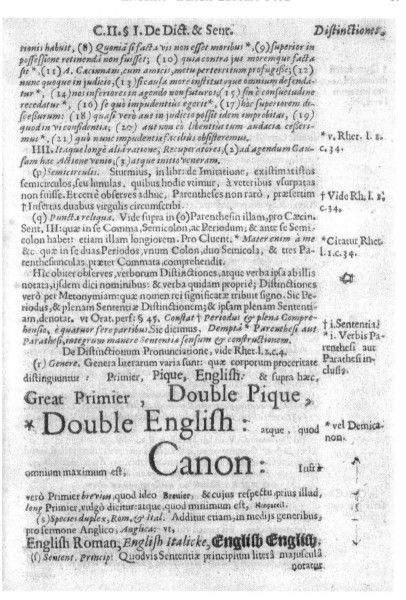

Fig. 2. Samples of type from Charles Butler's 1629 *Oratoriae Libri Dvo* (A4ʳ). "English English," is what modern scholars call "English black-letter." Beinecke Rare Book and Manuscript Library, Yale University.

Prolific printers such as Wynkyn de Worde and Richard Pynson carried on Caxton's black-letter style, forging a typographical standard that carried across most of the sixteenth century. During this time, printers and readers associated black-letter type with the English vernacular language.

Multilingual sixteenth-century books best exemplify the use of type to represent vernacular language. The text block of *An Exposition of Certaine Difficult and Obscure Words, and Termes of the Lawes of This Realme, Newly Set Foorth and Augmented, Both in French and English,* printed by Richard Tottell in 1579, affords a good example (fig. 3).[8] Tottell divided the bilingual text into two columns, one for the French, the other for the English. Appropriately, he set each language in its own distinct type: French in roman, English in black letter. This was not simply a case of two typefaces used to distinguish two different bodies of texts. That same year, Thomas Vautrollier printed Philippe de Mornay's *Traicte, de l'eglise auquel sont disputees les principalles questions, qui ont esté meues sus ce point en nostre temps.*[9] Later that year, Christopher Barker printed an English translation of this text.[10] Following the same typographical standards that guided Tottell in the previous example, Vautrollier prints the French edition in roman, while Barker prints the English edition in black letter.

The works of printer John Wolfe further demonstrate the association of type with language. After cutting short an apprenticeship with the English printer John Day, Wolfe appears to have completed his training in Italy.[11] Afterward, he returned to England, where he was very much involved in printing Continental works both in their original languages and in translation. In doing so, he normally assigned type by language: roman for French and Latin, italic for Italian, and black letter for English.[12] A page from his 1588 edition of Castiglione's *The Courtier of Count Baldessar Castilio* (i.e., *The Book of the Courtier*) provides a telling example (fig. 4).[13] Wolfe divided the pages of this polyglot edition into three columns for the languages of Italian, French, and English, and set each language in its corresponding type: Italian in italic, French in roman, and English in black letter.

The publication strategy used to disseminate *The Execution of Justice in England* further establishes the vital connection between type and language.[14] Written in response to the growing influence of Jesuit missionaries in England, William Cecil, Queen Elizabeth's right-hand man, argued that missionaries were not coming to England to spread Catholicism peacefully, as argued by figures such as William Allen, but rather were preparing for a future revolt against Elizabeth.[15] Cecil maintained, therefore, that the English government was prosecuting Catholic missionaries not simply because of their faith, but because

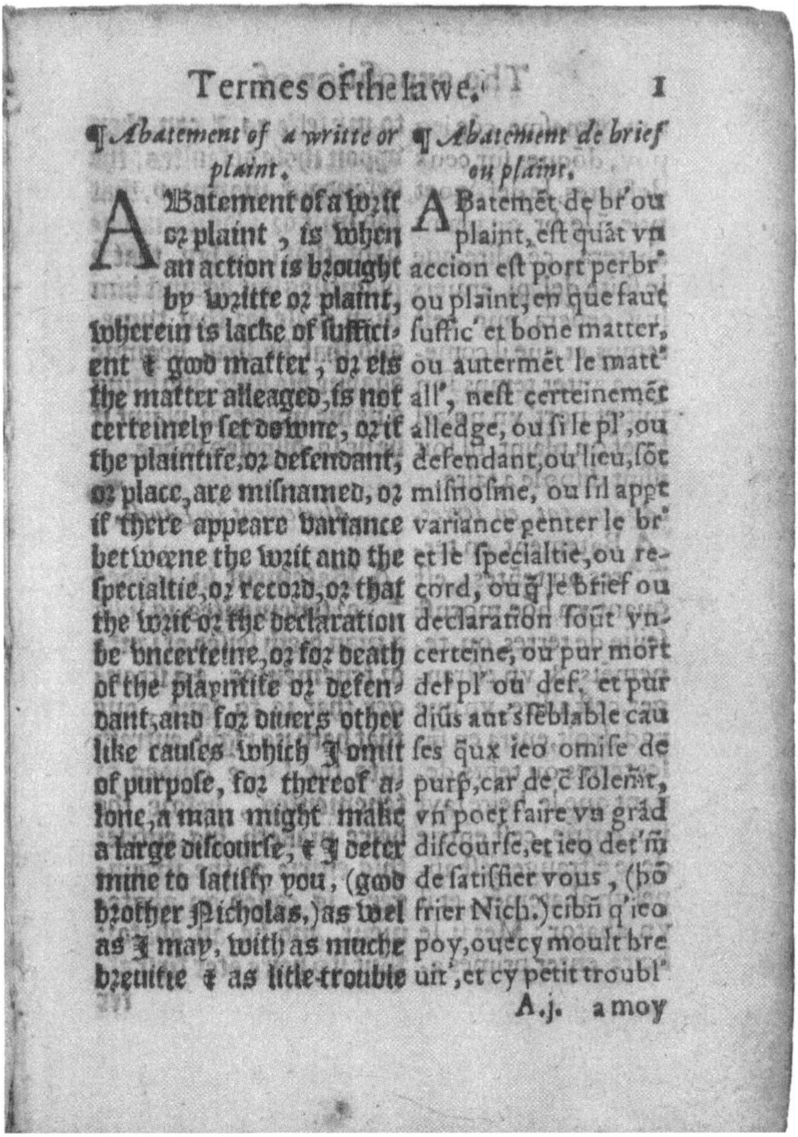

Termes of the lawe. I

¶ Abatement of a writte or ¶ Abatement de brief
plaint. ou plaint.

ABatement of a writ A Batemēt de br'ou
oz plaint, is when plaint, est quāt vn
an action is bzought accion est port perbr'
by writte oz plaint, ou plaint, en que faut
wherein is lacke of suffici- suffic' et bone matter,
ent & good matter, oz els ou autermēt le matt'
the matter alleaged, is not all', nest certeinemēt
certeinely set downe, oz if alledge, ou si le pl', ou
the plaintife, oz defendant, defendant, ou lieu, sōt
oz place, are misnamed, oz mis̄os̄ne, ou s'il appt
if there appeare variance variance pēnter le br'
betweene the writ and the et le specialtie, ou re-
specialtie, oz recozd, oz that cord, ou q̃ le brief ou
the writ oz the declaration declaratiō sout vn-
be vncerteine, oz foz death certeine, ou pur mort
of the plaintife oz defen- det pl' ou def. et pur
dant, and foz diuers other diůs aut's feblable cau
like causes which I omit ses q̃ux ieo omise de
of purpose, foz thereof a- purp, car de c̄ solēnt,
lone, a man might make vn poet faire vn grād
a large difcourse, & I deter difcourse, et ieo det'm̃
mine to satisfy you, (good de satiffier vous, (bō
bzother Nicholas,) as wel frier Nich.) cibñ q'ieo
as I may, with as muche poy, oue cy moult bre
bzeuitie & as litle-trouble uit', et cy petit troubl'
A.j. a moy

Fig. 3. A page from Richard Tottell's *An Exposition of Certaine Difficult and Obscure Words, and Termes of the Lawes of This Realme, Newly Set Foorth and Augmented, Both in French and English* (1579, A1ʳ). Tottell set the English text in "English" or black-letter type, and the French in roman. By permission of the Folger Shakespeare Library.

Fig. 4. A page from Wolfe's 1588 edition of Castiglione's *Book of the Courtier* (A1ʳ). Wolfe sets each language in its corresponding type: Italian in italic, French in roman, and English in black letter. By permission of the Folger Shakespeare Library.

they were committing acts of treason. His *Execution of Justice* was first
printed by the queen's printer Christopher Barker in late 1583. In
an effort to circulate the tract internationally, the text was also printed
the following year in Latin, Dutch, French, and Italian.[16] Here is a
case where the choice of type was unmistakably used to help disseminate official English policy or propaganda. The English edition appeared in black-letter type. The Latin and French editions appeared
in roman, the Italian appeared in italic, and the Dutch in black letter.
In this way, each edition appeared in the type that readers in their
corresponding nations were most accustomed to reading. It wasn't
enough to translate the *language*; they also had to *translate* the *type*.

As these examples demonstrate, type and language were inextrica-
ble for English readers. To be literate in black letter was to be literate
in English. In other words, black-letter literacy and English-language
literacy were basically the same thing. If you could only read English,
then you were virtually only reading it in black letter or English
type. Likewise roman-type literacy was a higher form of literacy,
because it likely meant that the reader could read the languages most
commonly set in roman type, namely, Latin and French.

The relation between type and language extended further into an
association between type and national identity, as explained in a 1567
text entitled, "Dialogues François pour les Jeunes Enfans," which was
published and perhaps written by Christopher Plantin, the famous
Antwerp printer. The dialogue, a conversation between the unidentified G., H., and E.,[17] sets out to explain the arts of calligraphy and
printing:

> G. Is it your opinion that, through being accustomed to make a
> book in a certain kind of type they have called such type
> after it?
>
> E. I understand it so, as in the composition of missals they called
> some missal types *canon* and *petit canon de messel, glose de messel;
> letter de Cicero, letter de S. Augustin,* because they had been used
> to printing such authors with these types.
>
> G. Where did the others get their names?
>
> E. Some have taken them from nations which have used them
> commonly. Of this sort are some we call *romain* and *gros romain*
> or *texte,* ordinary *romain, petit romain,* and the italics, *letter fran-
> coise,* and Greek type.[18]

While "English" does not appear among his examples, the naming
of roman, italic, and Greek indicates that type reflected, and perhaps

symbolically represented, nationhood. The use of "English" type for the English language concurs with the dialogue's examples.

What becomes abundantly clear in looking at these examples is that type conveyed a cultural significance that, in the case of black-letter type, modern scholars have overlooked. According to the *Oxford English Dictionary*, the term "black letter" originated around 1600. Yet, when Joseph Moxon examined type founding and printing in his *Mechanick Exercises on the Whole Art of Printing* (1683–4) over three-quarters of a century later, he referred to black letter as "English" or "black English letter."[19] Moreover, a specimen sheet displaying type fonts donated to the Oxford University Press in 1693 suggests that "English" was still a term for black letter at the close of the seventeenth century.[20] Therefore, when modern scholars use the term "black letter" for sixteenth- and early seventeenth-century books, they impose retrospective nomenclature and ignore the contemporaneous cultural and political significance of "English" type.

As scholars grow increasingly interested in the book as a material object and in its possible effect on its readership, typography must play a key role. Certainly there are many occasions when type is just type, when printing customs or the ownership of type determines its use. Nevertheless, the choice of type may often have a greater significance. Windet's aforementioned note on "English Pica" and "Romane letter" shows that both printers and readers were aware both of the use and nomenclature for different typefaces. This awareness becomes significant when the chosen type speaks to issues of language and nationhood. With the cultural significance of "English" type in mind, I return to the first edition of Spenser's *Shepheardes Calender* in order to demonstrate how its typography supported a greater nationalist argument.

An "English" Text

Let us begin with a brief description of the typography of *The Shepheardes Calender*.[21] Hugh Singleton employed a sophisticated layout when he printed the first edition of the *Calender* in 1579.[22] The most striking typographical feature is the inclusion of twelve original woodcut illustrations that correspond to each of the eclogues, because "no new poetry had been so illustrated in England . . . within at least two decades and would not be for at least two centuries."[23] The title page, however, is fairly stark for a book of its era. This is mostly due to the lack of a decorative border, an element added to subsequent editions.[24] Black-letter, italic, and roman type all appear on the title page, which is "characteristic of many English books of the time and typical of Singleton's house style."[25] Following on the verso side of the title page, the envoy, "To His Booke," is set in a striking italic type. Next comes E. K.'s dedicatory "Epistle" and the "General Argument of the Whole Book," of which both are set in a roman type. The preliminaries end here, and the body of the text begins. Reflecting the arrangement of a calendar, the main text undergoes division into twelve eclogues corresponding to each of the twelve months. Each eclogue contains the following elements: a woodcut illustration, the "Argument," the text of the eclogue, an emblem, and a "Glosse." Each of these elements appears in its own particular type: the "argument" is in italic, the text of the eclogue in black letter, the emblem most often in italic, and the gloss in roman. English printers commonly used different typefaces to differentiate among different sections of text.[26] In the case of the *Calender,* different type-faces help distinguish the various elements of each eclogue.[27] This typographical pattern repeats itself through the rest of the book until we reach the colophon page, which, like the title page, uses black-letter, italic, and roman types.

This essay began with McKerrow's suspicion that the use of black letter for the *Calender's* main body of text was a deliberate attempt at antiquarianism. He bases his argument on a perceived shift in the English book trade from a predominant use of black-letter type to roman, which he believes was well underway in 1579.[28] If McKerrow were correct, then Singleton's use of black letter would certainly be archaic or, at the very least, "old fashioned." In order for the use of black letter to be considered archaic, however, one must posit that someone involved in the printing made a deliberate choice to employ a type that was out of style or going out of style.

Contrary to McKerrow's suspicion, black letter had not gone out of style by 1579. Approximately 78% of English books published in 1579 were set in black letter, whereas 18% were set in roman, and 4% in italic.[29] Black-letter type continued to dominate English printing.[30] Most generally this is due to the enduring influence of black letter in England—the long arm of Caxton. On a more localized level, it surely had everything to do with the availability of type in the posses-sion of individual printers. Therefore, to determine Hugh Singleton's type supply and house style, we must examine his output.

Singleton was almost exclusively a black-letter printer.[31] Neverthe-less, he used roman and italic types quite often. He would frequently set the main body of text in black letter, using roman and italic types for preliminary materials and paratext such as marginal notes. In this way, *The Shepheardes Calender* tends to follow Singleton's house style, as do other books that he produced during the same year. For example, in *A Reply with The Occasion Thereof, To a Late Rayling, Lying, Reprochful and Blasphemous Libel, of The Papists*, he set the main body of text in black letter, marginal glosses in roman, section titles in italic, sections of verse in both italic and roman, and concluding blocks of prayer in roman.[32] This book exemplifies the breadth of Singleton's type supply. His *A Necessary Instruction of Christian Faith and Hope for Christians to Holde Fast* features a similar breadth of type fonts, whereby, in addition to the black-letter type of the main text, the book contains a dedication set in italic, a preface in roman, and marginal glosses in roman.[33]

The anomaly among Singleton's imprints is the single text set entirely in roman type: John Stubbs's *The Discouerie of a Gaping Gulf Whereinto England is Like to Be Swallovved by Another French Marriage* (1579). This scandalous text argued against Queen Elizabeth's proposed marriage to François, duc d'Anjou. When it came to the attention of the queen, she issued a proclamation dated 27 September in order to punish those involved with producing such a "lewde seditious booke."[34] Arrested and imprisoned on 13 October, both Singleton and Stubbs would be tried on 30 October.[35] Stubbs suffered the punishment of having his right hand cut off, but Singleton appears to have received a pardon due to his old age.[36]

The circumstances concerning the *Gaping Gulf* controversy are helpful in constructing a chronology for the printing of *The Shepheardes Calender*. The *Calender's* "Epistle" written by E. K. is dated 10 April 1579, whereas Singleton entered the text into the *Stationers' Register* on 5 December of that same year.[37] At this point in his career, Singleton likely owned only one press.[38] The *Gaping Gulf* tied up Singleton's lone press during most of August,[39] and Singleton spent most of October in jail. This suggests a few windows for the production of *The Shepheardes Calender*: the months preceding the printing of the *Gaping Gulf* in August, the month or so between the completion of the *Gaping Gulf* and Singleton's arrest, and the months following his October imprisonment. He may have printed part of the *Calender* before the *Gaping Gulf* and before his imprisonment, but the bulk of the printing probably occurred in and around its 5 December entry in the *Stationers' Register*.

Because Singleton had only one press, we may assume that he had the type available to print the whole of *The Shepheardes Calender* in roman, as he had done with the *Gaping Gulf*. We also may assume that he could have used his italic types as well. It is important to keep this in mind as we shift to an examination of Francesco Sansovino's 1571 printing of Jacopo Sannazaro's *Arcadia*. The first edition of *The Shepheardes Calender* faithfully followed this bibliographic model, or very nearly so, the only exception being the choice of type.

Sannazaro's *Arcadia*

S. K. Heninger has convincingly demonstrated that Sansovino's edition of Sannazaro's *Arcadia* was the bibliographic model for the 1579 edition of *The Shepheardes Calender*.[40] Sannazaro's text is arranged into twelve eclogues containing the following elements: an illustration, "Argomento," "Prosa" (a prose introduction), "Annotatione," an additional illustration, the text of the eclogue, and further annotations. With only slight alterations, the *Calender* mirrors this arrangement: "Argument," text, emblem, and "Glosse." Sansovino set *Arcadia*'s "Argumento," "Prosa," and "Annotiatione" in roman type, and the verse of the eclogue in italic. Setting the body of an Italian text in italic type was appropriate, because italic and roman were the most popular typefaces in Italy, their country of origin.[41] Moreover, as the aforementioned 1567 dialogue attributed to Plantin demonstrates, type often took the names of the nations "which have used them commonly" as in the example of "*romain* . . . and the italics." Thus, the use of italic for each eclogue's verse signified the Italian vernacular. So, too, did the roman type, which Sansovino used for the prose sections and for the supporting sections of arguments and annotations.

Although *The Shepheardes Calender* follows the model of Sannazaro's *Arcadia* quite closely, it deviates typographically by substituting black-letter for roman type in the prose and italics in the verse. Singleton could have set *The Shepheardes Calender* in roman type, just as he had done with *Gaping Gulf*. Singleton's *A Reply with the Occasion Thereof, To a Late Rayling, Lying, Reprochful and Blasphemous Libel, Of The Papists* demonstrates a supply of both roman and italic types and their previous use for verse. If Singleton, or anyone else involved in the production of the *Calender*, wanted thoroughly to imitate the 1571 edition of Sannazaro's *Arcadia* they had the means of doing so. Nevertheless, someone reached the decision to set the main text in type other than italic or roman. But to what end?

OUR "ENGLISH TONGUE"

If we think about typography within its historical context, the choice of black-letter, or "English" type, for *The Shepheardes Calender* begins to take on a new cultural significance. The imposition of black-letter or "English" type in place of italic and roman connotes the imposition of the English vernacular onto Italian. Had Spenser's *Shepheardes Calender* explicitly followed the typography of Sannazaro's *Arcadia*, it would have remained Italianate. Instead, we find a conscious move to *English* (i.e., translate) an Italian literary model.[42]

This typographical move is mirrored in E. K.'s "Epistle" by the construction of a literary heritage that foregrounds the English literary tradition over the classical and Continental:

> Uncouthe unkiste, sayde the olde famous Poete Chaucer: Whom for his excellencie and wonderfull skil in making, his scholer Lidgate, a worthy scholler of so excellent a maister, calleth the Loadstarre of our Language: and whom our Colin Clout in his Aeglogue calleth Tityrus the God of Shepheards, comparing hym to the worthines of the Roman Tityrus Virgile.[43]

Although Virgil's eclogues are perhaps the primary literary influence on Spenser's *Calender*, E. K. focuses first on the English lineage of Chaucer, Lydgate, and "our new Poete" Spenser. In this way, E. K. highlights Englishness by focusing on English authors and by promoting the English vernacular, as suggested in his description of Chaucer as "the Loadestarre of our Language." As E. K. notes, Spenser compares Chaucer to Virgil through the name "Tityrus," a name under which Virgil "secretly shadoweth himself."[44] Thus, in another layer of "Englishing," Chaucer, the English "Tityrus," supplants "the Roman Tityrus Virgile."[45]

The types in which the works of Chaucer and Virgil appeared at this time physically exemplify the distinction between the English and Roman Tityrus. Predictably, editions of Chaucer from the years 1561 and 1598, the last editions of the sixteenth century, appear in black letter.[46] In fact, with the exception of an edition of the apocryphal *Plough-mans Tale* printed in 1606 that appeared in roman type,[47] Chaucer's works appeared in black letter across the seventeenth century.[48] The Latin editions of Virgil's work printed in England through the years 1570–1590 are all set in italic, a type often used for Latin verse.[49] In contrast, the editions of Virgil's works that have been "Englished" (i.e., translated into English) appear in black letter.[50] The only exception is an edition that appeared in italic, which, as the choice of type suggests, was not printed in England, but rather "at Leiden in Holland" by John Pates.[51] Thus, translation into English was only part of "Englishing"; in order to "English" Virgil completely, the translation also had to appear in "English" type. Similarly, *The Shepheardes Calender* "Englishes" the Virgilian pastoral typographically, while subordinating the "roman" Virgil to the "English" Chaucer.

This cultural move was vital, for Spenser's literary project was as much about the promotion of the English language and a native literary tradition as it was about the promotion of the author.[52] The two were inseparable. Before an English poet could situate himself among his classical and Continental predecessors, the English language had to be accepted as a viable vehicle for literature.[53] E. K.'s naming of Chaucer as "the Loadstarre of *our* Language" [my emphasis] is an inclusive move, referring not only to Chaucer, Lydgate, Spenser, and himself, but also to the book's vernacular readers.

Throughout the "Epistle," E. K. articulates a nationalist argument centered on the vernacular language. For example, his defense of Spenser's archaic English implies a linguistic reformation: "For in my opinion it is one special prayse, of many which are dew to this Poete, that he hath laboured to restore, as to theyr rightful heritage such good and naturall English words, as have ben long time out of use and almost cleare disherited."[54] To "restore" England's "rightful heritage" of language is to return to a "disherited" purer form of English. E. K. argues that Spenser's language, though archaic, is a form of English unadulterated by the assimilation of foreign languages, unlike more hybridized usage: "Which default when as some endevoured to salve and recure, they patched up the holes with peces and rags of other languages, borrowing here of the French, there of the Italian, every where of the Latin. . . . So now they have made our English tongue, a gallimaufray or hodgepodge of al other speches."[55] The assimilation of foreign languages into English was unnecessary: "our Mother tonge, which truly of it self is both ful enough for prose and stately enough for verse, which hath long time ben counted most bare and barrein of both."[56] E. K. makes good rhetorical use of the magisterial first person plural: "Our English tongue," "Our Mother tonge." This brings to mind the words written by Spenser in a letter to Gabriel Harvey: "For, why a Gods name may not we, as else the Greekes, haue the kingdome of oure owne

Language."[57] Written in April of 1580, shortly after the printing of *The Shepheardes Calender,* Spenser echoes E. K.'s defense of the English vernacular. Also apparent is the enduring influence of Richard Mulcaster, Spenser's schoolmaster at Merchant Taylors' School, whose championing of the English language surely set a powerful example on his young pupil. As Mulcaster writes in the *Elementarie* (1582), "our tung nedeth not to giue place, to anie of her peres."[58]

"Our Mother tongue" and "our English tonge" are represented typographically by the "English" typeface; the choice of this type for *The Shepheardes Calender* is a part of an overarching promotion of Englishness.[59] To have fully imitated Sannazaro's *Arcadia* typographically would have produced a text that was, in appearance, Italianate or, at the very least, Continental. The decision to replace the italic and roman type with black letter emphasized the *Calender*'s embodiment of Englishness. But whose choice was it?

In the Printing House

Scholars are increasingly recognizing the working relationships between authors and printers. Indeed, authors may have had more input into the physical appearance of their printed works than previously thought. Two primary documents shed light on this subject. The first is an advertisement from a specimen broadsheet printed in 1592, which displays type produced by the foundry of Conrad Berner:

> Specimen and print of the finest and most beautiful types ever yet seen, assembled at great labor and cost at first by the late Christian Egenolff himself, the first printer in Frankfurt, and then by his widow, thereafter by his successors Jacob Sabon and Conrad Berner. Published for the benefit of all who use a pen, but more especially for the advantage of authors of printers' copy, so that they may judge in what type their work may best be done, but equally useful to type-casters and printers as showing what may be of service in every printing-office and business.[60]

Most likely produced for display at the Frankfurt book fairs, this advertisement is aimed specifically at authors to help them better decide which type their work should be set in. This suggests that authors were making typographical decisions.

Moxon's *Mechanick Exercises* supports this notion. His discussion of "the Compositor's Trade" quite explicitly acknowledges that authors should play a role in the printing process:

> Although I have in the precedent *Excercises* shew'd the Accomplishments of a good Compositer, yet will not a curious Author trust either to his Care or Abilities in Pointing, Italicking, Capitalling, Breaking, &c. Therefore it behoves an Author to examine his Copy very well e're he deliver it to the Printer, and to Point it, and mark it so as the Compositer may know what Words to Set in Italick, English Capitals, &c.[61]

In Moxon's experience, "curious" (i.e., attentive or careful) authors did make decisions concerning the appearance of their printed work, including the choice of type.

One such "curious" author was Sir John Harington. Written communication from Harington to printer Richard Field survives in British Museum Additional 18920, the holograph manuscript that served as the copy text for most of Harington's translation of *Orlando Furioso*, printed by Field in 1591.[62] This manuscript provides an informative example of an author directing the physical appearance of the printed text. For instance, Harington specifically tells Field how he wants the end of his book to appear:

> Mr. Feeld I dowt this will not come in in the last page, and thearfore I wowld have immedyatly in the next page after the fynyshinge of this last booke, with some pretty knotte to [*ileg.*] set down the tytle, and a peece of the Allegory as followeth in this next page—I wowld hav the allegory (as allso the appollogy and all the prose that ys to come except the table in the same printe that Putnams book ys.[63]

In response to Harington's request for a "pretty knotte" to separate the end of canto 46 and the title of the following section, Field inserted a large printer's ornament. By "the allegory," Harington refers to the "Briefe Allegorie of Orlando Furioso," the section that follows the final canto. Following Harington's instructions, Field set

this section and the "Apologie of Poetrie" that begins the book in
pica roman type, the "same print" Field had previously used in Put-
nam's 1589 *Arte of English Poesie*.[64] Both of Harington's instructions
to "Mr. Feeld" in this example concern typography. Clearly this
"curious" author chose how his book would appear typographically.

Could Spenser or another agent outside of the printing house have
contributed to the design of *The Shepheardes Calender*? The material
text of the *Calender* suggests that there were agents other than Singleton involved in its design. The first evidence is the text's use of
archaic English language. As Ernest de Selincourt observes, "the spelling of Q1 [1579 edition] is definitely archaic, dialectical, experimen-
tal, of a piece with the general character of the poem; and in every
succeeding edition, especially in every succeeding edition . . . it tends
to become more normal."[65] As E. K. makes clear in his "Epistle," it
was the author's decision to use archaic language in the *Calender*:
"Framing his words: thewhich if many thinges which in him be
straunge, I know will seeme the straungest, the words them selves
being so auncient, the knitting of them so short and intricate."[66] That
the choice of archaic language was the author's own and that it was
carried through the press without the normalization that begins to
affect "every succeeding edition" implies that someone had instructed the compositor to keep the copy-text as-is.[67]

The use of woodcut illustrations affords further evidence of outside
contribution. Woodcut illustrations were an anomaly for Singleton,
who had not been involved in the production of an illustrated book
in over twenty years.[68] Procuring woodcuts was costly, so printers
tended to make the most of the woodcuts they already owned by
reusing them in various books. Yet, the woodcut illustrations in *The
Shepheardes Calender* appear to be made to order, and largely reflect
the content of Spenser's eclogues. Singleton's continued struggle with
poverty makes it unlikely that he would have commissioned original
woodcut illustrations for the book.[69] Similarly, neither Spenser nor
Harvey appear to have been in a financial position to serve as the
publisher of the text and, therefore, probably did not commission the
woodcuts. This suggests that a third party, perhaps Spenser's patron,
Robert Dudley, Earl of Leicester, provided the funds for the literary
project. Noting the use of "his honor" in the *Calendar*'s "To his His
Booke," William Ringler argues that Leicester was the book's original
dedicatee rather than Sir Philip Sidney. "The Elizabethans were
punctilious in their use of terms of address and used 'his honor' only
when referring to a nobleman or person of equivalent dignity, 'his
worship' when referring to a knight or a gentleman."[70]

It also seems unlikely that Singleton would have chosen Sannazaro's *Arcadia* as a model for *The Shepheardes Calender*. A reference to Sannazaro in Sidney's *Defense of Poesy* (composed c.1579–80) suggests that the Sidney circle, with which both Spenser and Harvey were associated, had access to *Arcadia* around the time of the printing *Calender*.[71] Heninger believes that Harvey chose the model of *Arcadia* in an attempt to flatter Sidney indirectly.[72] He further contends that Harvey is E. K. and that his influence permeates the "Epistle" and glosses.[73] While Harvey's influence is apparent in the paratext of the *Shepheardes Calender*, Heninger's overarching argument is a difficult one to prove, particularly because, as he also argues, Spenser appears to incorporate Sannazaro's use of the sestina into his "August" eclogue.[74] This raises the possibility that it was Spenser who selected Sannazaro's *Arcadia* as a bibliographic model.

Lastly, Singleton's scattered use of Greek type, a practice that is not continued in the next three editions of the *Calender*, suggests involvement from outside the print shop. Thomas East, who printed the second edition for John Harrison II, transliterated the Greek into the Roman alphabet and did a poor job of it.[75] In the third edition, the printer John Wolfe followed East's example and, despite being a rather savvy printer of Continental works, managed to mangle the Greek. Taken in the context of the work of his successors, Singleton's use of Greek type in the first edition becomes an interesting anomaly, particularly because his own print history reveals no use of Greek type prior to *The Shepheardes Calender*.[76] In fact, in his 1574 printing of *The Hope of the Faithfull*, much like East and Wolfe, Singleton opts to transliterate a portion of Greek into the Roman alphabet.[77] Singleton may have owned Greek type without using it, but this seems improbable. Type was expensive, and Singleton was not in the financial position to own fonts that he would not use. Singleton either borrowed the type, or someone else involved in the *Calender* bought it specifically for the project. This evidence suggests that someone other than Singleton made the decision to use Greek type in the *Calender*.

The idea of an outside agent participating in the choice of Greek type for Greek text is significant because it suggests an influence other than Singleton's on the choice of type. Here, Stubbs's *Gaping Gulf* provides a telling example, for the decision to print the book in roman type appears not to have been Singleton's and most likely came from Stubbs himself or the book's publisher, William Page.[78] Might someone other than Singleton have been responsible for the choice of type in *The Shepheardes Calender*? Here, Spenser becomes a strong candidate, because he may have been already familiar with

the relation between type and language through his participation in
the publication of the English translation of Jan van der Noot's *A
Theatre Wherein Be Represented As Well the Miseries and Calamities that
Follow the Voluptuous Worldlings* in 1569.[79]

Spenser's contribution to the *Theatre for Worldlings,* as modern
scholars more commonly call it, was his first published work. As a
young student about to set off for Cambridge from the Merchant
Taylors' School, he contributed English translations of the epigrams
and sonnets that had appeared in the Dutch and French editions of
the *Theatre* published by John Day during the previous year.[80] Spenser
based his translations on the French edition.[81] Similarly, Henry
Bynneman, the printer of the English edition of the *Theatre,* used
Day's French edition as his bibliographic model. Specific examples
of agreement include the use of an ornamental, floral border for the
title page (the Dutch version has an elaborately illustrated title page
border), the inclusion of a dedication to Elizabeth (absent in the
Dutch version), and similarly designed colophon pages.

Typographically, Bynneman followed Day's precedent of setting
the text of the epigrams and sonnets in italic, but deviated from Day
by setting the English translation of the prose section that follows
the verse in black-letter type rather than roman (figs. 5a and 5b). As
we have seen in figures 3 and 4, both Tottell and Wolfe assigned
black-letter type to English and roman to French. Likewise, Bynneman's choice of black letter for English and Day's choice of roman
type for French followed English printing conventions, which associated type with language. As many scholars have observed, Spenser's
participation in the *Theatre* would greatly influence his later works.[82]
He learns "a way of transmuting Continental models into his own
English voice; he learns to narrate and domesticate 'the world' as it
comes to him in contemporaneous poetry."[83] Bynneman, too, do-
mesticated the *Theatre.* Not only did he superimpose an English translation onto the French, he superimposed black-letter or "English"
type onto the roman in the prose section. This change could not
have been lost on Spenser. Deeply familiar with both the French and
English editions of the *Theatre,* he surely was aware of this typographic shift and the relation between type and language that it embodied. Perhaps, then, it was Spenser who decided that his text
should appear in black letter. Ultimately, it appears that he did contribute to the design of his book in collaboration with Singleton
and Harvey.

A Return to "English" Type

Spenser's *Shepheardes Calender* was a literary project that promoted English language and literature. Its Englishness represented a distinctive component of the text. Therefore, Spenser, Harvey, E. K., and Singleton took measures to ensure that it looked like an English book. First, Spenser wrote in a consciously archaic style that embodied a purer form of English. Second, E. K., whom most scholars see as a persona for Spenser, defended this archaism and further promoted the use and viability of the English vernacular in his dedicatory "Epistle" and glosses. Finally, the person or persons responsible for printing the *Calender* chose Sannazaro's *Arcadia* as their bibliographic model, but *Englished* the text by superimposing English printing styles onto the Continental. The English vernacular represented by black-letter type had to replace the Italian vernacular represented by italic and roman, or the book would have appeared to be Continental or, above all, Italianate. Thus, the culture of Englishness promoted so heavily in the text of *The Shepheardes Calender* carried through to the material text. The choice of black letter was indeed intentional as McKerrow proposed, but those intentions worked more in the service of a growing nationalism than in that of a "bit of antiquarianism."

The Folger Shakespeare Library

Notes

1.   Ronald Brunlees McKerrow, *An Introduction to Bibliography for Literary Students* (Oxford: Clarendon Press, 1967), 297n.

2.   Thomas Rogers, *A Sermon vpon the 6.7. and 8. Verses of the 12. Chapter of S. Paules Epistle vnto the Romanes Made to the Confutation of So Much of Another Sermon, Entituled, A Fruitful Sermon &c.* (London: Printed by Iohn Windet, 1590; *STC* 21240).

3.   The edition printed in "English Pica" is Laurence Chaderton, *A Fruitfull Sermon* (London: Printed by Robert Walde-graue, 1584; *STC* 4926.5). The edition in "Romane letter" is Laurence Chaderton, *A Fruitfull Sermon* (London: Printed by Robert Walde-graue, 1584; *STC* 4926).

4.   Charles Butler, *Oratoriae libri duo quorum alter ejus definitionem, alter partitionem explicat: in usum scholarum recèns editi* (Oxford: Turner, 1629; *STC* 4194.5.), A4^r.

5.   Harry Graham Carter, *A View of Early Typography up to about 1600* (Oxford: Clarendon Press, 1969), 65.

6.   For more on Caxton, see Norman Blake's *Caxton: England's First Printer* (London: Osprey, 1976).

7.   Warren Chappel, *A Short History of the Printed Word* (New York: Knopf, 1970), 74.

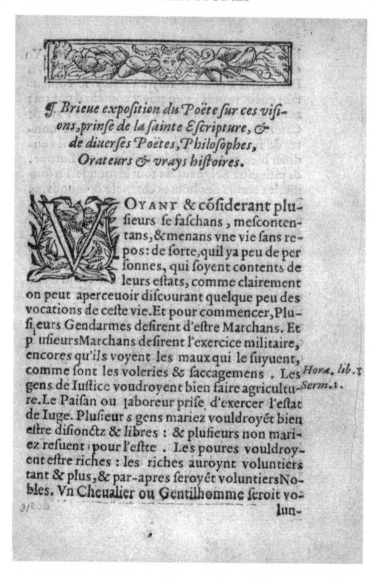

Fig. 5a. The French edition of *Theatre for Worldlings*, set by John Day in roman type.

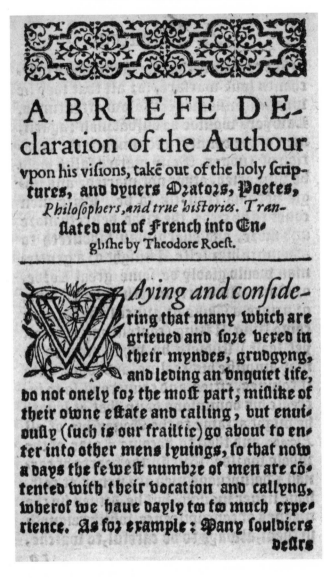

Fig. 5b. The English edition of *Theatre for Wordlings,* set by Henry Bynneman in black letter. Note the typographic similarities; Bynneman used Day's French edition as a bibliographic model. Both images by permission of the Folger Shakespeare Library.

8. John Rastell, *An Exposition of Certaine Difficult and Obscure Words, and Termes of the Lawes of this Realme, Newly Set Foorth and Augmented, Both in French and English, for the Helpe of Such Younge Students as Are Desirous to Attaine the Knowledge of Ye Same* (London: Richard Tottell, 1579; *STC* 20706.5).

9. Philippe de Mornay, seigneur du Plessis-Marly, *Traicte, de l'eglise auquel sont disputees les principalles questions, qui ont esté meues sus ce point en nostre temps / par Philippes de Mornay* (Imprimé à Londres: Par Thomas Vautrollier, 1579; *STC* 18157).

10. Philippe de Mornay, seigneur du Plessis-Marly, *A treatise of the church in which are handled al the principall questions, that haue been mooued in our time concerning that matter* (Imprinted at London: By Christopher Barker, Printer to the Queenes Maiestie, Anno. Dom[ini] 1579; *STC* 18158).

11. In the dedicatory epistle to *Una Essortatione al timor di Dio* printed by Wolfe in 1579, the book's editor, Giovan Battista Castiglioni, explains that he was prompted to print the book by Wolfe's return from Italy, where he had "learned the art of printing." See John Leon Lievsay, *The Englishman's Italian Books, 1550–1700* (Philadelphia: University of Pennsylvania Press, 1969), 15–16.

12. I base this on my examination of almost all of Wolfe's imprints from 1580 through 1592.

13. Baldassarre Castiglione, *The Courtier of Count Baldessar Castilio Deuided into Foure Bookes. Verie Necessarie and Profitable for Young Gentlemen and Gentlewomen Abiding in Court, Pallace, or Place, Done into English by Thomas Hobby* (London: John Wolfe, 1588; *STC* 4781).

14. William Cecil, Baron Burghley, *The execution of iustice in England for maintenaunce of publique and Christian peace, against certeine stirrers of sedition, and adherents to the traytors and enemies of the realme, without any persecution of them for questions of religion, as is falsely reported and published by the fautors and fosterers of their treasons xvii. Decemb. 1583* (Imprinted at London: [By Christopher Barker], 1583; *STC* 4902).

15. Although the book identifies no author, most scholars believe it to be William Cecil.

16. *STC* 4904, 4905, 4906, and 4907.

17. As the modern editor, Ray Nash, notes, "The initials of the dramatis personae . . . are not identified in the long introductory verses written by Christopher Plantin, or elsewhere in the text." Christophe Plantin, *An Account of Calligraphy & Printing in the Sixteenth Century, from Dialogues Attributed to Christopher Plantin, Printed and Published by Him at Antwerp in 1567*, trans. Ray Nash (Cambridge, MA: Dept. of Printing and Graphic Arts, Harvard College Library, 1940), 23.

18. Ibid., 13–14.

19. Joseph Moxon, *Mechanick Exercises on the Whole Art of Printing (1683–4)*, ed. Herbert Davis and Harry Carter (New York: Dover Publications, 1978), 19, 123.

20. *A Specimen of the Several Sorts of Letter Given to the University by Dr. John Fell Late Lord Bishop of Oxford to which Is Added the Letter Given by Mr. F. Junius* (Oxford: Printed at the Theater, 1693; Wing F622), C2^r.

21. Edmund Spenser, *The Shepheardes Calender Aeglogues Proportionable to the Twelue Monethes. Entitled to the Noble and Vertuous Gentleman Most Worthy of All Titles Both of Learning and Cheualrie M. Philip Sidney* (London: Printed by Hugh Singleton, dwelling in Creede Lane neere vnto Ludgate at the signe of the gylden Tunne, and are there to be solde, 1579; *STC* 23089).

22. For a complete descriptive bibliography of this and of other early Spenser editions, see Francis Johnson, *Critical Bibliography of the Works of Edmund Spenser Printed Before 1700* (Baltimore: Johns Hopkins University Press, 1933).

23. Ruth Samson Luborsky, "The Allusive Presentation," *Spenser Studies* 1 (1980): 30.

24. *STC* 23090 (1581), 23091 (1586), and 23092 (1591).

25. Luborsky, "The Allusive Presentation," 33.

26. An example of this printing practice dates as far back as Richard Pynson's 1509 edition of Sebastian Brant's *Stultifera Navis* (London: Printed by Richard Pynson; *STC* 3545). In this book, Pynson used roman type to set the preliminaries apart from the black letter of the main text.

27. Mark Bland observes that the typography deployed in *The Shepheardes Calender* indicated "the different character of the constituent parts." See "The Appearance of the Text in Early Modern England," *TEXT* 11 (1998): 100.

28. McKerrow claims "about 1580 the use of black letter in plays and the higher kinds of English verse, as well as Latin books, had almost ceased" (*An Introduction*, 297).

29. I base this conclusion upon a detailed examination of the types used in English books printed in 1579. Using as a guide the chronological index in the third volume of the Pollard and Redgrave's *Short-title Catalogue of Books Printed in England, Scotland, & Ireland and of English Books Printed Abroad, 1475–1640* (London: Bibliographical Society, 1976), I examined 175 of the 243 titles printed in 1579, approximately 72% of the texts from that year (not including variants, issues, etc). Of interest was the type chosen for the main body of text. Of the 175 titles, 139 (79%) were set in black letter, twenty-eight (16%) in roman, and eight (5%) in italic.

30. A more exhaustive census that I conducted of the years 1579–92 demonstrates that roman type did not overtake black letter until 1590/1591.

31. I base this on my examination of twenty-nine of the thirty-eight books that Singleton printed between 1555 and 1579. In the early part of his career, 1548–55, Singleton worked primarily as a publisher, rather than a printer. Of these books, Singleton set the main text of only one in a type other than black letter, namely John Stubbs's *Gaping Gulf* (*STC* 23400), which he set entirely in roman type.

32. *A Reply with the Occasion Thereof, to a Late Rayling, Lying, Reprochful and Blasphemous Libel, of The Papists Set Vpon Postes, and Also in Paules Church in London: Against God, His Truth, His Annointed, the Whole State, and Vniuersall Church Of Christ* (London: Printed by H. Singleton, 1579; *STC* 19179).

33. Urbanus Rhegius, *A Necessary Instruction of Christian Faith and Hope for Christians to Holde Fast, And to be Bolde Vp on The Promise of God, & Not To Doubt of Their Saluation in Christ* (London: By Hugh Singleton, 1579; *STC* 20848).

34. *Although Her Maiestie hath had So Good Proofe of Gods Singular Goodnes, in the Continual Preseruation of Her from His First Setting of Her in the Crowne* (London: Christopher Barker, printer to the Queenes Maiestie, 1579; *STC* 8114).

35. John Stubbes, *Gaping Gulf, with Letters and Other Relevant Documents,* ed. Lloyd E. Berry (Charlottesville: Published for the Folger Shakespeare Library by the University Press of Virginia, 1968), xxiv. See also, Anne Lake Prescott's essay documenting annotations written in a 1579 almanac by an unidentified barrister connected

with Lincoln's Inn. Near the date 30 October, he notes, "Jo. Stubbes, page et Syngleton arraynd et le judgment done per Justice Sowthcot en bank de royne" (137). Prescott, "Getting a Record: Stubbs, Singleton, and a 1579 Almanac," *Sidney Journal* 22.1–2 (2004): 131–37.

36.   Natalie Mears, "Stubbe [Stubbs], John (*c.*1541–1590)," in *Oxford Dictionary of National Biography* (Oxford University Press [Cited 3 July 2005]), <http://www.ox-forddnb.com.proxy.lib.ohio-state.edu/view/article/26736>.

37.   Edward Arber, ed., *A Transcript of the Registers of the Company of Stationers of London, 1554–1640* (New York: P. Smith, 1950), 2.362.

38.   H. J. Byrom, "Edmund Spenser's First Printer, Hugh Singleton," *The Library* 14.2 (1933): 154. "Singleton ceased to own a press in 1581 or 1582: his name does not occur in the list of London printers drawn up in May 1583, by order of the Bishop of London, and in September of that year he was employing a deputy to print for him" (ibid., 131).

39.   Byrom fixes "the date of publication between 17 and 29 August" (ibid., 138).

40.   S. K. Heninger, "The Typographical Layout of Spenser's *Shepheardes Calender*," *Word and Visual Imagination: Studies in the Interaction of English Literature and the Visual Arts*, ed. Karl Josef Holtgen, Peter Daly, and Wolfgang Lottes (Erlangen: Universitatsbibliothek Erlangen-Nurnberg, 1988), 35.

41.   Carter, 117; A. F. Johnson, *Type Designs: Their History and Development* (London: Grafton, 1959), 102.

42.   "English" as a verb denotes translation into English. See the title pages to *STC* 13494 and 19809 for instances of its use.

43.   Edmund Spenser, *The Yale Edition of the Shorter Poems of Edmund Spenser*, ed. William A. Oram et al. (New Haven: Yale University Press, 1989), 13.

44.   Ibid., 13.

45.   Ibid., 13, 171.

46.   *STC* 5075, 5076, 5077, 5078, 5079.

47.   *STC* 5101.

48.   *STC* 5097 is a bilingual edition of *Troilus and Criseyde* printed in black letter for English and italic for Latin (1635). The others editions are of Chaucer's *Workes*: *STC* 5080 (1602), 5081 (1602), and Wing C3736 (1687).

49.   *STC* 24788, 24788a, 24789, 24790.

50.   *STC* 24801, 24802, 24806, 24807, 24816, 24817.

51.   *STC* 24806.

52.   Adding to the promotion of the native tradition is the invocation of *The Shepheardes Calender's* namesake, *The Kalender of Shepherdes*. As E. K. reports in his "Epistle," Spenser titles his work "the *SHEPHEARDS CALENDAR*, applying an olde name to a new worke" (Spenser, *The Yale Edition*, 19). *The Kalender of Shepherdes*, an English translation of the French *Compost et Kalendrier des Bergiers* first published in Paris in 1493, went through at least nineteen editions in England from 1503 through 1656. The book first appeared with the title *The Shepardes Kalender* in 1570. Not only does the use of black-letter type in Spenser's *Shepheardes Calender* correspond to the vernacular calendar tradition exemplified by the *Kalender of Shepherdes*, the *Calender's* woodcut illustrations invoke the *Kalender of Shepherdes* and its French cousin *Le Grant Kalendrier et Compost et Kalendrier des Bergiers*. See Ruth

Samson Luborksy "The Illustrations to *The Shepheardes Calender,*" *Spenser Studies* 2 (1981): 3–53.

53. The promotion and defense of vernacular English appears throughout the evolution of English literature. For a helpful overview, see *The Idea of the Vernacular: An Anthology of Middle English Literary Theory, 1280–1520,* ed. Wogan-Browne et al. (State College: Pennsylvania State University Press, 1999).

54. Spenser, *The Yale Edition,* 16.

55. Ibid.

56. Ibid.

57. Richard Helgerson uses this quotation as a touchstone for his book *Forms of Nationhood: The Elizabethan Writing of England* (Chicago: University of Chicago Press, 1992).

58. Richard Mulcaster, *The first part of the elementarie vvhich entreateth chefelie of the right writing of our English tung, set furth by Richard Mulcaster* (Imprinted at London: By Thomas Vautroullier dwelling in the blak-friers by Lud-gate, 1582; *STC* 18250), 80.

59. The responses of early readers of *The Shepheardes Calender* suggest the power of its nationalist English message. For example, see William Webbe, *A Discourse of English Poetrie Together, with the Authors Iudgment, Touching the Reformation of Our English Verse* (London: By Iohn Charlewood for Robert Walley, 1586; *STC* 25172), B3ʳ; Thomas Nashe, *Works, Edited from the Original Texts,* ed. F. P. Wilson (Oxford: B. Blackwell, 1958), A2ᵛ; and, of course, Philip Sidney, *An Apology for Poetry,* ed. J. A. Van Dorsten (Oxford: Oxford University Press, 1966), 64.

60. Qtd. in Carter, 99.

61. Moxon, 250.

62. The manuscript contains canto 14 through the "Briefe Allegorie of Orlando Furioso" that, along with a life of Ariosto and a table of the principal characters, concludes the book. See Lodovico Ariosto, *Orlando Furioso, Translated into English Heroical Verse by Sir John Harington,* ed. Robert McNulty (Oxford, Clarendon Press, 1972), 557n.

63. Qtd. in Aristoso, 557n.

64. Continuing to follow Harington's instructions, Field did not set the text of "the table" in pica roman as he did with the "Apologie" and "allegorie" section, but in the smaller long primer roman. Further signs of Field's interaction with the manuscript are printer's notes that organize the text by marking signatures and pagination. See W. W. Greg, "An Elizabethan Printer and His Copy," *The Library* 4 (1924): 105–06.

65. Edmund Spenser, *Spenser's Minor Poems,* ed. Ernest De Selincourt (Oxford: Clarendon Press, 1910), viii.

66. Spenser, *The Yale Edition,* 14.

67. Unless, of course, the copy text had many more archaisms, which the compositor normalized. This strikes me as unlikely.

68. Luborsky, "The Allusive Presentation," 41.

69. See Byrom, 129–31.

70. See William Ringler, "Spenser, Shakespeare, Honor and Worship," *Renaissance News* 14 (1961): 160.

71. Sidney, 42, 74.

72. Heninger suggests "a tribute to Sannazaro would be construed as a compliment to the young aristocrat turned poet [Sidney] who chose to present himself as the English Sincero" (41).

73. Ibid., 47.

74. Ibid., 37. Heninger argues that the absence of a gloss in the "August" eclogue indicates that it was completed after E. K. had written all of his glosses. Therefore, Sannazaro's *Arcadia* had a late influence on the *Calender*. Hence, the choice of the *Arcadia* as a model text for the printing of the *Calender* would also have come later in the process.

75. Spenser, *Spenser's Minor Poems*, xii.

76. I base this on my examination of twenty-nine of the thirty-eight books that Singleton printed between 1555 and 1579, none of which use Greek type.

77. Heinrich Bullinger, *The hope of the faithfull. Declaring breefely and clearly the resurrection of our Lord Iesus Christ past, and of oure true essentiall bodies to come* (Printed at London: In Crede Lane, by Hugh Singleton, at the signe of the Golden Tunne, Anno. 1574; *STC* 25250), M8^v.

78. Using records of the Stubbes's trial, Berry reconstructs the events preceding the book's publication: "Stubbes wrote the book at his room in Lincoln's Inn on various dates before August 4. A Francis Chamberlain, 'late of the city of London, gentleman,' took the book on August 6 and 7 to Hugh Singleton and ordered him to print one thousand copies" (Stubbes xxvi). A fourth man, William Page, was cited in the trial as the book's publisher. As the publisher, Page would have had financial responsibility for the book and may have also made decisions on its printing. Both Stubbs and Page might have wanted the book printed in roman type to reflect a more up-market audience, geared perhaps to a more learned international audience. Indeed, there is some speculation that Francis Walsingham may have been involved in its publication. See John King, *Spenser's Poetry and the Reformation Tradition* (Princeton, N.J.: Princeton University Press, 1990), 235.

79. Jan van der Noot, *A Theatre Wherein be Represented as Wel the Miseries & Calamities that Follow the Voluptuous Worldlings* (London: By Henry Bynneman, 1569; *STC* 18602).

80. See Jan van der Noot, *Het theatre oft Toon-neel waer in ter eender de ongelucken ende elenden die den werelts gesinden ende boosen menschen toecomen* (London: John Day, 1568; *STC* 18601); and Jan van der Noot, *Le theatre anquel sont exposés & monstrés les inconueniens & miseres qui suiuent les mondains & vicieux* (Par le Seigneur Iean Vander Noot. London: John Day, 1568; *STC* 18603).

81. "Spenser appears to have translated all 22 poems from the French, checking them against an English draft translation from the Dutch" (Jan van Dorsten, "*A Theatre for Worldlings*." *The Spenser Encyclopedia*, ed. A. C. Hamilton [Toronto: University of Toronto Press, 1990], 685). Also see Leonard Forster, "The Translator of the 'Theatre for Wordlings,'" *English Studies* 48 (1976): 27–34, and W. J. B. Pienaar, "Edmund Spenser and Jonker Jan van der Noot," *English Studies* 8 (1926): 33–44.

82. On the impact of the *Theatre*'s use of the Book of Revelation on Spenser's *Faerie Queene*, see King 72–85. On the influence of the *Theatre's* visual poetics, see Ernest B. Gilman, *Iconoclasm and Poetry in the English Reformation: Down Went Dagon* (Chicago: University of Chicago Press, 1984), 63–64.

83. Roland Greene, "Spenser and Contemporary Vernacular Poetry," *The Cambridge Companion to Spenser*, ed. Andrew Hadfield (Cambridge: Cambridge University Press, 2001), 241.

CATHERINE NICHOLSON

Pastoral in Exile: Spenser and the Poetics of English Alienation

This essay argues that Spenser's *Shepheardes Calender* invents a poetics of deliberate estrangement, capitalizing on the unpromising fact of England's remoteness from the classical world. Although it is understood both in the Renaissance and in modern criticism as the natural starting point for a poetic career, pastoral is a singularly inhospitable genre for an English poet: in Virgil's first eclogue Britain appears as the antithesis of pastoral contentment, a place of exile and colonial abjection. By treating English as a quasi-foreign tongue—and adopting the errant and alienated persona of Colin Clout—Spenser repeats this marginalizing gesture, discovering in distance itself a means of reinvigorating vernacular poetry. Ultimately, his insistence on the virtues of estrangement allows Spenser to find a place for pastoral and for Colin Clout in England's own abject colonial sphere, beyond the Irish pale.

E. K.'S INTRODUCTION TO *The Shepheardes Calender* (1579) represents pastoral as the logical birthplace of poetic excellence, the "nest" of literary ambition:

> So flew Theocritus, as you may percieue he was all ready full fledged. So flew Virgile, as not yet well feeling his winges. So flew Mantuane, as being not full somd. So Petrarque. So Boccace; So Marot, Sanazarus, and also diuers other excellent both Italian and French Poetes, whose foting this Author euery where followeth, yet so as few, but they be well sented can trace him out.[1]

Because the *Calender* was quickly recognized as a signal achievement
not only for the anonymous "new poete" but for the hitherto undis-
tinguished canon of English poetry, E. K.'s analysis of its generic
orientation has remained persuasive. It has become, as Anne Lake
Prescott observes, "a scholarly commonplace" that by "mask[ing] in
lowly shepherds' weeds . . . Spenser was gesturing at a laureate Virgilian career."[2] Pastoral is the "inaugural phase" in what Patrick Cheney
dubs "the New Poet's flight pattern";[3] it serves, in Louis Montrose's
words, as "a vehicle for the highest personal aspirations and public
significance a poet can claim" and "demonstrate[s] the capacity of
the vernacular to produce a poetry 'well grounded, finely framed,
and strongly trussed up together.' "[4] But if pastoral is a logical generic
locus for the expression of literary ambition, it is a rather more
vexed starting point for an *English* poet—or for an English poetic
renaissance—than E. K. and most subsequent critics acknowledge.[5]
After all, the most influential poems in the tradition, Virgil's eclogues,
establish their vision of the genre on the assumption that Britain is
no place for pastoral. Indeed, as the first English translation of the
eclogues makes clear, only a few years before *The Shepheardes Calender*, England may be no place for poetry at all.

Certainly, such a dismal conclusion is not the intended message
of Abraham Fleming's *The Bucoliks of Publius Virgil* (1575). Rather,
Fleming undertakes his translation in order to remove the barriers
between English readers and what he regards as an unnecessarily
remote poetic tradition. By rendering Virgil's elegant Latin into "ye
vulgar and common phrase of speache," amplified by an abundance
of marginal notes and glosses, Fleming hopes to foster a new sense
of "familiaritie and acquaintance with Virgils verse": to guarantee
"readie and speedie passage" across the distances imposed by geographic, historical, and linguistic difference.[6] This desire to domesticate Virgilian pastoral takes its most literal form in the compilation
of marginal glosses defining all place names and geographical features
cited in the poems. Like a map of a foreign country, Fleming writes,
his glosses will prevent "the ignorant" from "wander[ing] wyde" by
erroneously "applying . . . the name of a mountaine to a man, the
name of a fountaine to a towne, the name of a village to a floud, the
name of a citie to a riuer" (sig. A3v).[7] Thus freed from all "stoppes
and impediments" to understanding, the reader may find in Fleming's
translation "stiles" or "bridges to passe ouer into the plaine fields of
the Poets meaning" (sig. A2v).

But if Fleming's translation, and especially his glossary, is meant
to help readers traverse an unfamiliar poetic landscape, it also exposes
England's own place in—or displacement from—that landscape. It is

not only that the glosses highlight precisely those aspects of Virgil's diction—namely, the "proper names of gods, goddesses, men, women, hilles, flouddes, cities, townes, and villages &c." (sig. A1r)—least amenable to vernacular translation, since by definition, proper names cannot be rendered "plaine and familiar Englishe" (sig. A1r). More importantly, the focus on strange place names and geographic features foregrounds the fact that Virgilian pastoral is emphatically—and literally—*topical*, rooted in the particular place and time of its composition. Critics of the genre rarely identify pastoral with a language of geographic and historical specificity; indeed, its landscape is associated with an allegorical conventionality that would seem to exclude proper names. As one critic asserts, contingencies of time and place are precisely what the pastoral poet must eschew in his pursuit of "a world of his own, a cleared space counterfeited from tradition and his own inventive wit," a "green world" crucially and definitively "distant from our own."[8] But Fleming's readers do not have the luxury of subsuming Virgil's landscape into such amorphous generalities: the challenges of translation, and the compensatory labor of Fleming's assiduous glosses, force attention to the fact that pastoral abounds in local particularity.

The problem is more pointed—and painful—than this. Virgil's eclogues locate pastoral existence firmly within the world of Augustan Rome in order to make a claim about the interdependence of poetry and place.[9] The eclogues begin by contrasting the circumstances of two pastoral poets: Tityrus (a figure, Fleming informs us, "represent[ing] *Virgilles* person" [C1r]) and his neighbor, Meliboeus. Tityrus attributes his poetic success to his happy proximity to "the Citye . . . call'd Rome," whose "God . . . hath graunted these my beastes to grase, and eake my selfe with glee / To playe vpon my homelye pipe such songes as liked mee" (C1v). He laments the fate of less fortunate foreigners—the "Parthian banisht man" and the "German stranger"—who, if they would seek Rome, are condemned to "wandring others ground" (C2r). Meliboeus concurs in praising Rome: although "in fieldes abroade such troubles bee," in Roman pastures a shepherd "lying at [his] ease, vnder the broad beeche shade, / A countrye song does tune right well" (C1r–v).

But Meliboeus's associations with the city and its ruler have proved less fortunate: his land has just been confiscated to pay one of Caesar's imperial mercenaries, and he therefore faces an imminent departure from Rome: "Our countrey borders wee doe leaue, and Medowes swete forsake" (C1r). Anticipating an end to his pastoral contentment, Meliboeus bids his sheep "[d]epart . . . a[nd] Cattell once full happye goe and flytt, / I shall not see you after this, in greene caue

where I sytt" (C2r). He and his fellow exiles must seek refuge on
the outskirts of the Roman empire, whose territories he enumerates
in a grim litany: "[S]ome of vs to droughte Affrike land hence wyll
go, / To Scythia and to Candy, where Oaxis scarce doth flowe"
(C2r). But he saves the worst for last: some, perhaps he himself, will
be sent "[a]s farre as Britan Ile, cut of from the wide world" (C2r).[10]
Just in case any of his English readers should have missed the point,
Fleming drives it mercilessly home: "Britan," he notes, "is an Ilande,
compassed about with the sea, . . . called also Anglia because it stan-
deth in a corner of the world alone" (C2r–v, note n). In such a place,
Meliboeus glumly concludes, "no sonnets will I syng" (C2r).[11]

This assumption—that to go to Britain is to abandon poetry—poses serious difficulties for Fleming and his readers. After all,
what kind of "familiaritie" or "speedie passage" can be fashioned in
relation to a poem that locates England—and English readers—on
the far side of an apparently unbridgeable divide? Tityrus's response
to Meliboeus in the eclogue's final lines, the offer of a final night's
rest in his cottage, tacks on a consolatory ending and temporarily
forestalls the threat of exile.[12] But for the English reader, there is no
reprieve: in the poem that inaugurates the career of Rome's greatest
poet, Britain remains the sign of all that is antithetical to poetry. The
somewhat fanciful claim Fleming makes on behalf of his translation—that it carries Virgilian pastoral out of Rome and into England—turns out, on the poem's own terms, to be impossible.

I have dwelt at some length on Fleming's translation, admittedly
a very minor entry in the canons of late sixteenth-century classical
scholarship and vernacular poetry, because it provides an especially
concrete demonstration of the challenges facing all those who sought
to use classical texts and forms as vehicles for importing poetic excellence into England. "[I]n the process of retrieving from Antiquity
the terms and concepts that introduced new distinctions to the field
of English writing," as Sean Keilen has argued, "vernacular writers
were obliged to confront the radical alterity of England to the ancient
world, and of English to the languages and aesthetic canons they
wanted to assimilate."[13] Of course, the challenge of bridging the gap
created by this "radical alterity" was not unique to English poets:
vernacular authors on the Continent struggled under similar burdens
of belatedness and distance from the classical world, and as E. K.
himself points out, Spenser's efforts are inspired by the successes of
such poets as Marot and Sannazaro.[14] And yet, as my reading of
Fleming's translation suggests, would-be authors of English pastoral
encounter the difficulties (and, perhaps, the opportunities) of alienation from antiquity in more literal shape, for no other form insists so

strongly on the interdependence of poet and place, song and setting. It is therefore crucial that we not forget what E. K.'s survey of pastoral poets and poetry conveniently overlooks: that in the form's preeminent incarnation, the Virgilian eclogue, English readers find their own native place located beyond poetry's pale. This inescapable fact invites us to reconsider Spenser's choice of pastoral as the generic locus of his own ambitious foray into vernacular poetics: "the best and most Auncient Poetes" may, as E. K. claims, have valued pastoral for its "homely" qualities, but for Spenser, the pastoral tradition has more to say about the "unhomely"—about alienation, exclusion, and the paradoxical virtues of exile.[15]

The ironies and incongruities of Fleming's English Virgil may therefore help us to appreciate in a new way how and why Spenser's vernacular pastoral embraces linguistic estrangement and geographic dislocation as the emblems, and engines, of English poetry.[16] For if alienation is the defining characteristic of Colin Clout, with his neglected flocks and his shattered pipe, it is also the central strategy of Spenser's poetry, the process of occlusion and defamiliarization through which his readers are forced to reencounter their native tongue. In the world of Virgilian pastoral, exile to Britain marks the limits of geographic and poetic possibility; in the world of *The Shepheardes Calender*, distance and disability become the necessary conditions of writing and reading English verse. "Cut off from the wide world" by virtue of its Englishness, but also by virtue of its willfully difficult language, Spenser's *Calender* finds in the rudeness and rusticity of the mother tongue the materials of its own peculiar eloquence.

*

The reader's experience of estrangement begins on the *Calender*'s title page, which, although it names the poem, offers a brief description of its contents, and announces its dedication to Philip Sidney, makes no mention of an author. Turning the page, one learns that this omission is deliberate: a verse *envoi* instructs the poem to present itself "[a]s child whose parent is vnkent" and cautions, "if that any aske thy name,/Say thou wert base begot with blame,/For thy thereof thou takest shame."[17] The poem is famously signed "*Immerito*" (24)—the unworthy one. The following page introduces a new character, the equally mysterious E. K.,[18] whose introductory epistle

claims as its goal to "commendeth the good lyking . . . and the patronage of the new Poete" (25), but who proves a rather jealous guard
of the privileges of his own "familiar acquaintance" (29) with both
poet and poem. He boasts, for instance, of having been "made priuie
to [*Immeritô's*] counsel and secret meaning" in writing the *Calender*,
but unhelpfully adds that, "[t]ouching the generall dryft and purpose
of his Aeglogues, I mind not to say much, him selfe labouring to
conceale it" (29). As Lynn Staley Johnson observes, E. K.'s remarks
frequently afford *Immeritô* an "opaque cover" not unlike the pseudonym itself, as the commentator "interposes himself between *Immeritô*" and his public.[19] In his epistle's final paragraph, therefore, when
E. K. addresses the mystery of *Immeritô's* identity, he does so simply
to declare himself an accessory to the poet's desire to keep himself,
for the time being, "furre estraunged": "worthy of many, yet . . . k-
nowen to few" (30).

The peculiarities of E. K.'s relation to the poem sharpen when he
turns to the issue of *Immeritô's* language. As he acknowledges, his
own "maner of glosing and commenting" must "seeme straunge and
rare" (29) when applied to a poem ostensibly written in the reader's
"own country and natural speech," his very "mother tongue" (27).
In fact, these glosses and commentary seem more suited to an edition
of classical verse—like Fleming's translation of Virgil—or the work
of a celebrated modern poet such as Petrarch or Sannazaro. Both
Fleming and E. K. offer prefatory essays on the history of pastoral and
the etymology of the word "eclogue," provide prose "arguments"
summarizing each eclogue, and surround the poems with an abundance of editorial notes and glosses. Fleming can justify such an elaborate apparatus by appealing to the distance separating his English
readers from the language and landscape of Virgil's poetry. As he
himself confesses, E. K.'s interventions are less easily accounted for:
why should an English reader require a gloss or commentary to assist
his comprehension of a work set in his own time, place, and native
tongue? Rather, such commentary as E. K. does provide seems calculated to *intensify* the reader's sense of remove from the poem he is
about to read, to function, that is, as the very sort of "stoppes and
impediments" (sig. A2) Fleming is so eager to remove from his own
reader's path.

Certainly a scholarly apparatus would have seemed out of place in
earlier English pastorals, whose authors tend to apologize for the
straightforward and uncomplicated nature of their verses rather than
offer any aid in understanding them. Indeed, poets like Alexander
Barclay and George Turbervile worry that the language of their pastorals will seem all *too* familiar to the average reader. Urging readers

of his *Egloges* (1530) "not to be grieved with any playne sentence / Rudely conuayed for lacke of eloquence," Barclay reminds them that "[i]t were not fitting a heard or man rurall / To speak in termes gay and rhetoricall."[20] Turbervile, whose *Eglogs* (1567) mimic those of Mantuan, apologizes for "forcing" that poet's Latin-speaking shepherds "to speake with an English mouthe" and cautions that "as ye conference betwixt Shephierds is familiar stuffe and homely: so haue I shapt my stile and tempred it with suche common and ordinarie phrase of speech as Countrymen do vse in their affaires."[21]

E. K. mentions the homely style of pastoral verse, but he also declares that *Immeritô*'s "words" are "the straungest" of "many thinges which in him be straunge" (25). When he insists on the need for a gloss for those words, or feels constrained to point out that they are "both English, and also vsed of most excellent Authors and most famous Poetes" (25–26), he redefines the limits of both pastoral and the vernacular: neither will be confined to the familiar or homely. Although he begins by asserting an equivalence, or at least a dependence, between familiarity and admiration, he ultimately advances a more complicated understanding of that relationship. Just as his avowed longing to make *Immeritô* familiar to all conflicts with his wish to protect his own "familiar acquaintance" with the poet's "secret meanings," his observations on Spenser's language seem poised between the impulse to demystify and a desire to highlight its peculiarities. His glosses, for instance, serve a double purpose: added "for thexposition of old wordes and harder phrases," they are necessary lest the "excellent and proper devises" of Spenser's verse "passe in the speedy course of reading, *either as vnknowen, or as not marked*" (29, emphasis added). The gloss is a corrective, that is, against two equal and opposite dangers: that Spenser's language will strike readers as so remote as to be incomprehensible, or that it will fail to strike them at all. Where Fleming sought a "readie and speedie passage" into Virgil's poem, E. K. aims to slow his readers down—to function, in Fleming's terms, as both pathway *and* impediment, both stop *and* stile, champion of the poem's "seemely simplicity" *and* gatekeeper of its "graue . . . straungenesse" (25).[22]

The seemingly paradoxical claims E. K. makes on behalf of Spenser's poetic diction—that it is a function of both "custome" and "choyse" (26), that its archaisms are both a source of "great grace and . . . auctoritie" and a "rough and harsh" foil to more "glorious words" (26–27), and that it generates a style both "straunge" (25) and "homely" (29)—are hard to reconcile with the straightforward equation of pastoral and plainness found in the prefaces to so many other vernacular poems, but they do reflect the complicated and at

times contradictory interpretive practices of another important literary genre of sixteenth-century England: biblical translation. That
Spenser's *Calender* is a profoundly Protestant text is a critical commonplace, but most accounts of the poem's religious affiliations re-
strict themselves to questions of content, to analyses of the eclogues'
satirical and allegorical engagements with doctrinal and ecclesiastical
controversies.[23] I want to suggest that Protestantism also provides a
matrix for understanding the poem's language and the way that language is represented and mediated by E. K. Among the translators
of scripture, we find an approach to the vernacular like that of E. K.,
precariously poised between the values of simplicity and strangeness—and here, as in *The Shepheardes Calender*, the practice most likely
to disturb this equilibrium is glossing.

As Lynne Long has established, glossing was the original point of
contact between the vernacular and sacred writing, an essential and
often controversial precursor to full-fledged biblical translation.[24] The
vernacular notes that appeared, as early as the eighth century, in the
margins and between the lines of English biblical texts served as an
important aid to readers whose Latin was weak or nonexistent, but
they also forced translators and editors to think carefully about the
relative values of accessibility and difficulty. Of his vernacular edition
of the *Lives of the Saints*, the Anglo-Saxon translator Aelfric writes
that his desire to render his text "into the usual English speech [*ad
usitatem Anglicam sermocinationem*]" conflicted at times with his wish
to preserve the challenges and mysteries of his source-text as guards
against an unfit readership: "I do not promise however to write very
many in this tongue, . . . lest peradventure the pearls of Christ be
had in disrespect."[25]

The sixteenth century, and especially the decades preceding the
publication of *The Shepherd's Calender*, witnessed an explosion of
English translations of the Bible and a corresponding rise in both the
estimation of the vernacular and the anxiety about its adequacy as a
vehicle for divine wisdom and eloquence. Like Aelfric, the translators
and editors of these texts often seem torn between a desire to promote
the plain and homely virtues of their vernacular scriptures and to
insist upon the salutary challenges posed by correct interpretation.
Thus, although the title page to the 1560 Geneva Bible promises
readers "the holy Scriptures faithfully and playnely translated" into
their own native tongue, the translators later note that "we moste
reuerently kept the proprietie of the [original Greek and Hebrew]
wordes" and "in many places reserued the Ebrewe phrases, notwithstanding that thei may seme somewhat hard in their eares that are
not well practiced" because the preservation of such interpretive

challenges accords with the practice of the Apostles themselves, "who spake and wrote to the Gentiles in the Greke tongue, [but] rather constrained them to the liuely phrase of the Ebrewe, then enterprised farre by mollifying their langage to speake as the Gentils did."[26] The English of the Bible, it appears, must seem both familiar and strange in order to elicit the proper readerly response—like E. K., these commentators are eager both to assist and impede the "speedy course" of their reader's understanding, to engender a sense of connection and proximity to the text even as they retain a sense of its distance and difficulty.

The English Bible translators also anticipate E. K. in that they must justify the deployment of often elaborate explanatory apparatuses alongside texts ostensibly written in plain English. Indeed, the desire to eliminate obtrusive and potentially misleading glosses was a primary impetus for translating scripture into the vernacular in the first place: in the preface to his 1534 *New Testament*, William Tyndale assails the obscurantism and elitism of the Catholic Church, whose mystique depends on the labor of those "false prophets and malicious hypocrites, whose perpetual study is to leaven the scripture with glosses." But Tyndale's concern for the proper reception of his own translation prompts him "in many places" to "set light in the margin to understand the text by": as he admits, due to allegorical figuration or theological complexity "the scripture and word of God, may be so locked up, that he which readeth or heareth it, cannot understand it" unless it is "dress[ed]" and "season[ed]" for "weak stomachs."[27] So, too, the Geneva translators, who chastise those (Catholic) scholars who "pretend" that ordinary readers "can not atteine to the true and simple meaning" of the scriptures even as they admit "how hard a thing it is to vnderstand the holy Scriptures."[28] Indeed, it is precisely because such understanding is so elusive that their translation comes equipped with a complex apparatus of "brief annotations," "figures and notes," even "mappes of Cosmographie," to guide the reader through Scripture's "hard" and "darke . . . places" and its "diuers . . . countries."[29]

Is the vernacular Bible easy or difficult to read? Are its "places," whether textual or geographic, accessible to or remote from the understanding and experiences of the English reader? The translators of the English Bible leave such questions largely unresolved, and they resonate with E. K.'s contradictory descriptions of the "new Poet's" simple yet strange verses. Indeed, the similarities between the presentation of the Geneva Bible and of *The Shepheardes Calender*—the prefatory essays, prose arguments, marginal annotations and glosses, and woodcut illustrations—suggest that Spenser's pastoral is designed to elicit a reading practice like that promoted by the authors of the English Bibles, in which the value of accessibility is in constant, productive tension with the value of alienation. We might further note that the *Calender's* affinity with England's vernacular Bibles affords the poem and its readers a very different view of Rome, and of classical antiquity, than that associated with the pastoral tradition. If, for Virgil's shepherds and their English heirs, eloquence must be anchored in Rome and Britain remain forever beyond the pale, within the context of the Protestant Reformation, this geography could be wholly reversed.[30]

When the Geneva Bible translators proclaim in their dedication to Queen Elizabeth that "the eyes of all that feare God in all places beholde your countreyes as an example to all that beleue,"[31] they are, of course, making a calculated appeal to the vanity of a monarch whose support was crucial to the success, indeed the survival, of their text. But they also invoke England's historic importance to the Protestant cause in general and Bible translation in particular. In this one area, thanks to a long tradition of vernacular homiletics and scriptural translation from Aelfric through Wycliffe, England could position itself in the vanguard of linguistic progress and cultural achievement, even as it anchored itself to a past more authentically antique than that of Rome: as the title page to the Geneva Bible states, it was "[t]ranslated according to the Ebrue and Greke," "the languages wherein [the scriptures] were first written by the holy Gost," and not, pointedly, according to the Latin Vulgate edition used by the Church of Rome. Far from being the sign of a privileged antiquity, as it is in Virgil's pastorals and in the rest of the secular literary tradition, for the translators of English scriptures Latin is the language of a belated and debased tradition, itself remote from the true origins of divine wisdom and Christian eloquence. The distance between the vernacular and Latin is thus touted as an advantage by Tyndale, who defends his own early sixteenth-century scriptural translations on the grounds that English is closer to the truly biblical languages: "For the Greek tongue agreeth more with the English than with the Latin. And the properties of the Hebrew tongu agreeth a thousand times more with the English than with the Latin."[32] Tyndale's rationale upends the linguistic hierarchy assumed by secular translators like Abraham Fleming and brings the vernacular into desirable proximity with a religious history and geography in which Rome (and Latin) is more peripheral than privileged.[33]

The complex, even contradictory, attitudes towards the vernacular evinced by E. K.'s epistle to *The Shepheardes Calender* produce a similarly radical reworking of linguistic and literary values. E. K.'s epistle does more than simply characterize *Immeritô*'s peculiar poetic voice; like the prefaces to English Bibles, it also reflects upon the peculiar position of the English language at the end of the sixteenth century. That is, if E. K. seeks to characterize *Immeritô*'s voice as simultaneously rare and unremarkable, he also seeks to characterize English as a paradoxical blend of the foreign and the familiar, a language which may appear most alien and inaccessible precisely when it hits closest to home.

As the epistle draws to a close, E. K.'s argument thus shifts from the particular case of *The Shepheardes Calender* to that of the vernacular as a whole. Those who "will rashly blame [*Immeritô*'s] purpose in choyce of old and vnwonted words," he writes, are themselves to be "more iustly blame[d] and condemne[d]" for failing to appreciate one of the chief beauties of his poetry, which aims "to restore, as to theyr rightfull heritage, such good and naturall English words as haue ben long time out of vse and almost cleane disherited" (27). This disregard for the origins of the language has deprived the vernacular of its own best resources and "is the onely cause, that our Mother tonge, truely of it self is both ful enough for prose and stately enough for verse, hath long time ben counted most bare and barrein of both" (27). Even worse than those who neglect English's roots are those who, "endeuour[ing] to salue and recure" the language's perceived deficits, have "patched vp the holes with peces and rags of other languages, borrowing here of the French, there of the Italian, euery where of the Latine, not weighing how il those tongues accord with themselues, but much worse with ours" (27). Over time, E. K. argues, the very concepts of foreign and familiar have been so confused that, while the adoption of alien terms has "made our English tongue, a gallimaufray or hodgepodge of al other speeches," the "very naturall and significant" words on which the tongue was founded are rejected as "no English, but gibberish" (27). Thanks to such linguistic promiscuity,[34] England has become estranged from itself, a nation "whose first shame is, that [its inhabitants] are not ashamed, in their owne mother tonge strangers to be counted and alienes" (27). If it is "straunge and rare" for a vernacular author to require the mediation of an editor in order to be understood by a native readership, that very peculiarity is, in E. K.'s view, what marks Immerito's work as truly and properly English.

In Virgil's first eclogue, and in Fleming's translation, distance is inimical to poetry: Meliboeus's exile threatens to end his song, and the unguided reader, "wander[ing] wyde" of Virgil's meaning, loses both the pleasure and the profit of his labor. Familiarity, whether it appears in the guise of a fellow shepherd's hospitality or a helpful

translator's marginal glosses, becomes the only defense against an
alienation that threatens to dissolve the pastoral landscape into a foreign wasteland, to turn eloquent Rome into mute and barren Britain.
In pre-Spenserian English pastorals, by contrast, familiarity and proximity—"homeliness"—are qualities that threatened to deny the vernacular poet his bid to participate in a more elevated literary
tradition; without the sponsorship of remote authorities, English
verse has no value. E. K.'s epistle reformulates these dilemmas—and
offers *Immeritô* a way out of the impasse—by refusing to admit an
opposition between familiarity and strangeness. Instead, he makes
familiarity (such as that he claims between himself and Spenser) an
excuse for secrecy and identifies the strangeness of Spenser's language
with its most native and homely virtues.

★★

Spenser's pastoral narrative itself performs a similarly complex rereading of the literary significance of exile. For most sixteenth-century
English rhetorical and poetic theorists, exile functions as a metaphor
for the exclusion of the vernacular from the company of learned and
eloquent tongues, and for the hardships vernacular speakers endure
as a result of this exclusion. In *The Pastime of Pleasure*, Stephen Hawes
identifies "elocucyon" with a process of purification that consigns
the homely vernacular "to exyle": separating "the dulcet speech /
from the langage rude," "the barbary tongue / it doth ferre exclude."[35] In *The Boke named the Governour*, Thomas Elyot makes the
more literal point that, if they wish to learn how to speak and write
well, Englishmen themselves must endure exile, being "constrained
. . . to leave our owne countraymen and resorte vs vnto strangers."[36]
   But for England's Bible translators, who endured unpredictable and
often violent reversals of fortune under the Tudors, exile bore a
more complicated relation to eloquence, as it was often the necessary
condition of writerly survival. William Tyndale concluded as a young
man that "there was no place . . . in all England" for someone who
believed as strongly as he did in the virtues of an English Bible, and
the very name of the Geneva Bible betrays that fact that, well into
the sixteenth century, this continued to be the case.[37] Striking, too,
is that Bible's curious gloss of Psalm 137, whose well-known opening
lines recall the Israelites' refusal to sing during their exile from the
promised land: "By the rivers of Babylon, there we sat down, yea,

we wept, when we remembered Zion. / We hanged our harps upon
the willows in the midst thereof. / For there they that carried us
away captive required of us a song; and they that wasted us [required
of us] mirth, [saying], Sing us [one] of the songs of Zion." The
Israelites' insistence that "the songs of Zion" belong to Zion alone
would seem to make Psalm 137 a kind of sacred precursor to the
lament of Meliboeus in Virgil's first eclogue, with the same melancholy alignment of poetry and place, exile and silence, but the Geneva
translators interpret it rather differently, as a mournful comment on
the necessity of self-imposed exile from a people who have lost their
way. Its opening plaint is glossed as a response not to the insults of
foreign captivity, but to the disappointments of home: "Even though
the country [of Babylon] was pleasant," the translators remark, "yet
it could not stay [the Israelites'] tears" when they recalled "[t]he
decay of God's religion in their country," which "was so grievous
that no joy could make them glad, unless it was restored."[38] In other
words, the roots of the Israelites' silence lie not in Babylon, but in
Zion; exile is simply the literal expression of—or even a consolation
for—a more profound and painful internal alienation. There is little
in the psalm itself to support such a reading. On the contrary, the
psalmist emphatically identifies his own ability to sing with his attachment to his native land, vowing, "let my tongue cleave to the
roof of my mouth, if I prefer not Jerusalem above my chief joy."[39]
But the gloss perhaps articulates the translators' own experiences, as
writers whose preference for English meant leaving England behind.

Spenser's poem both invokes and recasts these associations: while
acknowledging the loneliness of the poet severed from his native land,
it also embraces alienation as the paradoxically enabling condition of
a truly native eloquence. Like Tyndale and the Geneva translators,
Spenser follows the "barbary tongue" and "langage rude" into exile,
finding there the materials for renovating and replenishing an impov-
erished tradition. *The Shepheardes Calender* thus transforms Meliboeus,
Virgil's unwilling victim of exile, into Colin Clout, a poet whose
exile from the pastoral community is both self-imposed and strangely
productive. Like Meliboeus, Colin enters the pastoral world on the
verge of departing from it, breaking his pipes at the end of the
"Januarye" eclogue and quitting himself of the "rurall musick" to
which his "vnlucky Muse" has called him (lines 64, 69). His break
with pastoral poetry, we learn, is the consequence of infidelity to the
pastoral landscape, a fatal "long[ing]" to see "the neighbour towne"
(line 50). This wanderlust leads to an unrequited passion for Rosalind,
a town-dwelling lady who loathes "shepheards devise" (line 65),
"laughes" (line 66) at shepherds' songs, and infects Colin with a

similar disdain. Although he returns to his flocks and farm, he remains
alienated from the pleasures they once provided: neither his own
verses nor the "clownish giftes and curtsies," "kiddes," "cracknelles,"
and "early fruits" of his rustic companion Hobbinol please Colin
any longer.

In his gloss of this passage, E. K. observes that "[n]eighbour town
. . . express[es] the Latine Vicina" (38, n. 50), a clarification many
critics have cited as characteristically egregious—why bother to
translate a perfectly clear English phrase into its Latin equivalent? But
if the note violates the usual function of a gloss, its estranging effect
captures perfectly the paradox inherent in both E. K.'s apparatus and
Spenser's diction. Indeed, the very word "vicina" is suggestively apt,
as it denotes a locale that is at once elsewhere and close-at-hand,
remote and proximate. And when Hobbinol himself appears in the
"April" eclogue, he characterizes Colin's defection in similar terms:
"now his frend is changed for a frenne" (line 28). The latter word,
E. K. informs us, is a term "first poetically put, and afterward vsed
in commen custome of speech for forenne" (66–67, n. 28). Colin's
rejection of his familiar friend in favor of Rosalind—who, like the
"neighbour towne" or *vicina* in which she dwells, is both "forenne"
and familiar—casts him into a state of self-division that, as Hobbinoll
reports, alienates him from the sources of his poetic inspiration:

> Shepheards delights he doth them all forsweare,
> Hys pleasaunt Pipe, which made vs merriment,
> He wylfully hath broke, and doth forbeare
> His wonted songs, wherein he all outwent.
>
> (lines 13–16)

The measure of this loss to the pastoral community becomes clear
when, at his companion's request, Hobbinol recites one of the songs
Colin composed in happier days, when "by a spring he laye" and
"tuned" his music to the rhythm of "the Waters fall" (lines 35–36).
The reader is invited to compare such domestic harmony to the
frigid sympathy between poet and place Colin expresses in "January,"
when the frozen barrenness of the wintry fields merely encourages
the poet to forsake his pipes and regard his own youth as similarly
wasted. The song itself presents Colin as master of both a local and
a classical poetics: he invokes the "dayntye Nymphes" of his own
"blessed Brooke" (line 37) to join the Muses "that on Parnasse dwell"
(line 41) and help in the fashioning of his praise for Elisa, whose

glory is likened to that of *"Phoebus"* (line 73) and *"Cynthia"* (line 82). The two-part Latin tag with which the eclogue concludes—Aeneas's *"O quam te memorem virgo,"* *"O dea certe"*—casts Spenser as a second Virgil, even as it presents Elisa, England's queen, as "no whit inferiour to the Maiestie" of the goddess Venus and England, perhaps, as the fertile ground of a new poetic and political imperium.

Such sympathetic affinities—between poet and place, local and classical, vernacular and Latin, England and Rome—are, however, the stuff of the past, as Hobbinol regretfully notes: "But nowe from me hys madding minde is starte . . . " (line 25). The breach between Colin and his "clownish" friend signals a more pervasive state of alienation. A disinclination to sing, in fact, is the inauspicious starting point of nearly all of the *Calender*'s eclogues, whether it be the consequence of cold or age ("February"), the afflictions of love ("March," "August"), the disapproval of one's fellow shepherds ("Maye," "Julye"), or the lack of a patron to support the poet's efforts ("October"). This last circumstance leads the shepherd Cuddie to despair of the future of English pastoral: Virgil, "the Romish *Tityrus*" ("October," line 55), had both matter and means for his art, but now "Tom Piper" (line 78) with his "rymes of rybaudrye" (line 78) is the only poet who thrives. Once inspiration, like the Roman empire itself, seemed boundless; the muse "stretch[ed] her selfe at large from East to West" (line 44). Now, with neither empire nor Caesar to sustain it, it lies "pend in shamefull coupe" (line 72). "O pierlesse Poesye," Piers exclaims, "where then is thy place?" (line 79). Its place, Cuddie replies, is with Colin Clout; with his departure, poetry too has been "expell[ed]" (line 99).

The apparent solution, then, is to woo Colin back to the place (and time) in which his poetry flourished, to the domesticity and community represented and advocated by homely, humble Hobbinol, who becomes the voice of what Harry Berger has dubbed the poem's "paradisal" imperative: the call to a kind of "literary withdrawal" that is also "characteristically a 'return to' . . . a set of *topoi*, of 'places' as well as conventions, authenticated their durability."[40] Reunited with Colin in the "June" eclogue, Hobbinol does his best to woo his friend from his errant existence:

Lo *Colin*, here the place, whose pleasaunt syte
From other shades hath weand my wandring mynde.
Tell me, what wants me here, to worke delyte?
The simple ayre, the gentle warbling wynde,
So calme, so coole, as no where else I fynde.

(lines 1–5)

Colin concurs with Hobbinol's evaluation of his own happy lot, but insists that such domestic bliss is not for him:

> O happy *Hobbinoll*, I blesse thy state,
> That Paradise hast found, whych *Adam* lost . . .
> But I unhappy man, whom cruell fate,
> And angry Gods pursue from coste to coste,
> Can nowhere fynd, to shroude my lucklesse pate.[41]
>
> (lines 9–10, 14–16)

Hobbinol responds with an obvious solution—Colin must come home:

> Forsake the soyle, that so doth the bewitch:
> Leaue me those hilles, where harbrough nis to see,
> Nor holybush, nor brere, nor winding witche:
> And to the dales resort, where shepheards ritch,
> And fuictfull flocks bene every where to see.
> . . .
> Such pierlesse pleasures haue we in these places.
>
> (lines 18–22, 32)

But Colin counters that his dilemma is not situational, but existential: "since I am not, as I wish I were" (line 105)—that is, since he is exiled from Rosalind's affections—no place, "[w]hether on hylls, or dales, or other where" (line 107), can do more than "[b]eare witnesse" (line 108) to his suffering.

The aptness of Hobbinol's advice is cast into further doubt by his encounter with Diggon Davie in the September eclogue. In many ways, Diggon is a clear surrogate for Colin, another wayward prodigal, "a shepheard," as E. K. describes him, "that in hope of more gayne, droue his sheepe into a farre countrye" (116). Like Colin, who "curse[s]" the "carefull hower" of his departure from his pastoral home ("Januarye," line 49), Diggon comes to regret his waywardness, "curs[ing] the stounde / That euer I caste to haue lorne this grounde" (lines 56–57). He eventually makes his way back home, but errancy has marked his speech, which Hobbinol professes not to understand: "speake not so dirke" (line 102), he urges. Diggon acknowledges that "this English is flatt" (line 105), and E. K. comments that the peculiar "Dialecte and phrase of speache in this Dialogue," which "seemeth somewhat to differ from the comen," reflects Diggon's travels: having "bene long in foraine countries, and there seene many disorders," his very speech has become alien and disordered (125).

Diggon would appear to represent an extreme case of the dangers facing Colin Clout, whose defection from the pastoral world also threatens to divorce him from its poetry. But the September eclogue takes on a more ambiguous meaning in light of the *Calender*'s own departures from linguistic and pastoral convention. After all, one of the expressions which E. K. singles out as foreign and disorderly is the word "uncouthe" (line 60), which Diggon uses to disparage his decision to leave home, but which E. K. himself used in his epistle to describe the poem's author and which he attributed to England's own "olde" and "famous" poet, Chaucer (25). The moral of the "September" eclogue is further complicated by Diggon's choice of a Latin tag, "*Inopem me copia fecit*" (line 261), a phrase drawn, as E. K. observes, from Ovid's version of the tale of Narcissus. Diggon uses it, he hypothesizes, to show that "by tryall of many wayes, [he] founde the worst," but this is, he admits "to other purpose" than "fyrste Narcissus spake it" (127). And indeed, Narcissus is an odd figure for Diggon: while Diggon's desire for "chaunge" (line 69) displaces him, leading him to abandon the "grounde" (line 57) he knows best, Narcissus's self-love engrafts him in one place—if anyone could be said to be "[c]ontent [to] liue with tried state" (line 70), as Hobbinol urges Diggon to be, it is Narcissus. If both Narcissus and Diggon ultimately find cause to mourn that "plenty has made me poor," they seek for plenty in very different places: one in the too-close circuit formed by his own person and its reflection and the other by "measur[ing] much grownd, . . . wandr[ing] the world rounde" (lines 21–22). They are linked perhaps, by their inability to judge distances rightly: for Narcissus, distance from the object of his desire is both unattainable and inescapable; for Diggon, whose very name proclaims his homely, earthbound calling, distance is a false lure, an invitation to riches that vanish when seen up close.

Ultimately, Narcissus is perhaps a less apt figure for Diggon (of whom he is, at best, an inverted or mirror image) than he is for Colin Clout—not as he is, but as Hobbinol wishes him to be. The self-love and stasis that waste Narcissus are not so different from the paradisal pleasures Hobbinol urges upon Colin in the "June" eclogue, pleasures of proximity, familiarity, and sameness. And indeed, when the reader first encounters Colin, in "Januarye," his condition is perilously Narcissus-like. The icy sheen of the frozen ground, he claims, had been "made a myrrhour, to behold my plight" (line 20), and his own self-absorbed reflection threatens to consume him. The very syntax of his verse seems governed by a logic of reflexivity, replete with chiastic echoes, parallel structures, and insistent repetitions.[42] When he falls to the ground after breaking his pipe, it seems possible that he, like Narcissus, will never get up again. It is only by rousing himself to abandon the pastoral place, rejecting home and its comforts, that Colin rediscovers his poetic voice—although it is no longer the same voice that once delighted his fellow shepherds with its sweetness. Thus, when Hobbinol pleads "to heare thy rymes and roundelays, / Which thou were wont on wastfull hylls to singe" (lines 49–51), Colin announces that "such delights . . . amongst my peeres" no longer entice him (line 35). His exile has taught him "newe delightes" (line 40), "play[ing] to please my selfe, all be it ill" (line 72). These new songs, he says, do not imitate or emulate the songs of others, "to winne renowne, or passe the rest" (line 74); instead, they are fitted to the peculiar demands of his situation: "I wote my rhymes bene rough, and rudely drest," but "[t]he fitter they, my carefull case to frame, / Enough is me to paint out my vnrest" (lines 77–79).

In making the case for his songs of "vnrest," Colin does not claim to have abandoned his roots altogether. Instead, he argues, he follows the example of his master, "[t]he God of shepheards *Tityrus* . . . / Who taught me homely, as I can to make" (lines 81–82). This "homely" art is, nevertheless, as remote and inaccessible as any of the prospects Hobbinol has described: "*Tityrus* . . . is dead" (line 81), and "all hys passing skil with him is fledde" (line 91). Colin's own song is thus defined by relationships of proximity and likeness—to Chaucer, to Virgil—that perpetually fall away into distance and alienation, just as his "place in [Rosalind's] heart" ("Argvment" to "June," 87) turns out to be no place at all—indeed, turns out to spoil and evacuate all places.

Chaucer and Virgil share the role of Tityrus, Colin's poetic mentor, with an unacknowledged third poet: Ovid, the "poet . . . of exile and complaint" who, as Syrithe Pugh argues, through "an accumulation of mostly covert allusions" becomes the *Calender*'s silent "presiding genius."[43] One such allusion may be found in the song Colin sings in the "Nouember" eclogue, a dirge in honor of one Dido, "dead alas and drent" (line 37)—a passage which long puzzled Spenser's readers since the Virgilian Dido dies a famously fiery death.[44] Patrick Cheney solves the conundrum by pointing to the "March" section of the *Fasti*, Ovid's never-completed calendrical poem celebrating Rome's mythic and imperial history, which recounts the fate of Dido's lesser-known sister, Anna. Exiled from Carthage after her sister's death, Anna is driven across the sea to Italy, where she seeks help from Aeneas and, then, fearing his wife's jealousy, casts herself into the river Numicius.[45] In fact, the parallels between this sister of Dido and the figure mourned by Colin are even more striking than Cheney allows: like Ovid's Anna, Colin's Dido is remembered for her generosity to the rustic poor (*Fasti*, 3.670–71; "Nouember," lines 95–96), memorialized in the bawdy songs of young girls (*Fasti*, 3.675–76; "Nouember," lines 77–79), and transcends her watery death to achieve immortality (*Fasti* 3.653–54; "November," line 175). Ultimately, however, Colin's Dido surpasses her Ovidian model; "raign[ing] a goddesse now among the saintes" (line 175), she achieves a glory inaccessible to the pagan Anna.[46]

The Spenserian Dido's supercession of her classical predecessor reflects her creator's supercession of his own classical predecessor, whose calendrical poem has no "November" section—indeed nothing at all past "June." *The Shepheardes Calender* may follow Ovid's "ensample," as E. K.'s final note observes (156), but it also succeeds where Ovid failed, simply in arriving at an end.[47] The significance of this implicit contest with Ovid deepens if we recall the reason Ovid's calendar lacks an ending: his banishment from Rome. The fate of the *Fasti*'s author recalls that of Virgil's Meliboeus: Ovid abandons the poem when, accused of some obscure offense to Caesar, he is forced to abandon Rome and take up residence in Tomis, on the Black Sea—like Britain, a desolate colonial outpost on the frontier of the Roman empire.[48] Instead of completing his calendar, a project he now regarded with bitterness, Ovid began the series of poems known as the *Tristia*, in which he bemoans the cultural and linguistic impoverishment of his new home "at the world's end."[49] The *Tristia* is haunted by Ovid's fear that, cut off from other native speakers of Latin, he will lose his poetic voice, descending to the barbarous accents of those around him. He obsessively charts the decline of his once-eloquent tongue, complaining that, surrounded by "Thracian and Scythian voices, I've unlearned the art of speech" (3.14.46). "If some phrases sound un-Latin," he apologizes, "remember / They were penned on barbarian soil" (3.1.17–18). His poetry has become a mass of "barbarous solecisms," for which, he insists, "you must blame the place, not the author" (5.7.60–61).

Ovid's mournful insistence that it is "the place," the non-Roman North itself, which stops his once eloquent tongue, resonates with many sixteenth-century accounts of the English language: for instance, Thomas Elyot's argument that the "infilicitie of our time and countray . . . compelleth"[50] the English to labor in the study of classical tongues, and Gabriel Harvey's claim that a "revolution of the

heavens" was needed to bring eloquence "to these remote parts of
the world."[51] By completing the poetic project left unfinished by
Ovid in his *Fasti*, and by rooting it in the unpromising locale of
the rude vernacular, Spenser thus challenges, yet again, the classical
tradition's equation of exile—especially to the barbarous
North—with poetic impotence. The rocks on which Ovid's calendar
founders become the soil on which Spenser's *Calender* thrives. Thus,
when begged by Hobbinoll to "forsake the soyle" that stifles his once
fluent song—soil identified by E. K. as "the Northparts" ("Glosse"
to "June," 91)—Colin Clout refuses to do so, embracing alienation
and distance as inspirations for his "rough, and rudely drest" verses
("June," line 77): he is, as Colin Burrow has noted, the "poet of
loss, exile, and solitude."[52]

In the epilogue to the *Calender*, Spenser also embraces the distance
between himself and other poets, claiming that his poem has earned
"a free passeporte" to "followe" from "farre off" the works of earlier
authors ("Epilogue," lines 7, 11). The claim sustains a conventional
gesture of modesty—he "dare[s] not match [his] pipe" (line 9) with
those greater—but it also identifies distance, whether linguistic, temporal, cultural, or geographic, with an expansion of literary possibility
and with a challenge to the hierarchies that had kept vernacular poets
in their place. The strangeness that, for E. K., makes *Immeritô*'s English truly and virtuously homely works its way through the narrative
of Colin Clout's poetic development, which emerges out of the same
paradoxical play of distance and proximity, foreignness and familiarity, exile and return.

★ ★ ★

For all the admiration that *The Shepheardes Calender* garnered from
contemporary readers, not all of Spenser's peers appreciated the
poem's embrace of strangeness.[53] William Webbe, author of *A Discourse of English Poetrie* (1586), proclaims Spenser "the rightest English
Poet, that euer I read" (35), but his praise of *The Shepheardes Calender*
betrays a certain strain. Spenser's "trauell in that peece of English
Poetrie," he writes,

> I think verily is so commendable, as none of equall iudgement
> can yeelde him lesse prayse for hys excellent skyll, and skyllful
> excellency shewed foorth in the same, then they would to

eyther *Theocritus* or *Virgill*, whom in mine opinion, if the
coursenes of our speeche (I meane the course of custome which
he woulde not infringe) had beene no more let vnto him, then
theyr pure natiue tongues were vnto them, he would haue (if
it might be) surpassed them. (53)

High praise, undoubtedly—the highest, for a critic who longs to see
English poetry converted to quantitative measures "in imitation of
the Greekes and Latines" (20). But Webbe's punning admission that
"the coursenes of our speeche" or "the course of custome which he
would not infringe" have prevented Spenser from surpassing his classical models introduces a rather serious qualification, especially since,
earlier in the treatise, he identifies "the canckred enmitie of curious
custome" (19) as the single most pernicious influence on modern
vernacular poets, the chief cause of England's persistent linguistic and
poetic backwardness. Moreover, as readers of *The Shepheardes Calender* know, far from being unwilling to "infringe" upon the "course
of custome," according to E. K. Spenser's diction is the result of a
deliberately "curious" poetic practice, his "choyce of old and
vnwonted words."[54]
    Philip Sidney, the poem's dedicatee, expresses a similar unease
about this choice in his *Defence of Poesy* (1595), granting that Spenser
"hath much *Poetrie* in his Egloges, indeed worthie the reading" but
insisting that he "dare not allow" the "framing of his style to an olde
rusticke language."[55] If it is difficult for a modern reader to understand how one might commend the pastoral conceit of Spenser's
Calender—what Sidney calls its "*Poetrie*"—while disapproving of the
rustic language that seems so central to that conceit, the strain the
Calender placed on its early modern readers is nonetheless plain: in
Sidney's treatise, as in Webbe's, admiration for the *Calender*'s unmis-
takable genius wars with the perception that there is something
flawed, even self-defeating, at work in the poem. Such ambivalent
responses reproduce, almost uncannily, the tensions within the poem
between the admiration expressed for Colin Clout and the irritation
at his refusal to occupy a place commensurate with his talents: like
Colin, Spenser is hailed by peers such as Sidney and Webbe as an
exemplary genius even as he is reproached for what seems to be a
posture of willful self-estrangement. Certainly Ben Jonson sounds
rather Hobbinol-like when he warns readers of medieval poetry
against "falling too much in love with antiquity," lest "they grow
rough and barren in language only" and holds up Spenser as an example of one overcome with an unwise and immoderate affection for

things remote from his experience. If antiquity—specifically, England's antiquity—is Spenser's Rosalind in this allegory of misplaced affection, his archaic diction is an instrument as fractured and self-indulgent as Colin's shattered pipe: "Spenser, in affecting the ancients," Jonson famously concludes, "writ no language."[56]

The judgments of Webbe, Sidney, and Jonson have shaped many later accounts of the poem, but it is possible that they exaggerate the strangeness and difficulty of Spenser's diction. The eighteenth-century critic Thomas Warton sounded an early note of skepticism:

> The censure of Jonson, upon our author's style, is perhaps unreasonable. . . . The groundwork and substance of his style is the language of his age. This indeed is seasoned with various expressions, adopted from the elder poets; but . . . the affectation of Spenser in this point, is by no means so striking and visible, as Jonson has insinuated; nor is his phraseology so difficult and obsolete, as it is generally supposed to be.[57]

Warton's argument has encouraged a few twentieth-century critics to reconsider the prevailing view of the language of *The Shepheardes Calender*, especially when it is placed alongside lesser-known works of the mid-sixteenth century. Certainly Spenser embraces an array of archaic and dialect terms to ornament his shepherds' speech, but so, too, as Roscoe Parker points out, did most earlier writers of English pastoral, and Spenser's antiquated, rustic-sounding shepherds are not so different from those found in the eclogues of Barclay, Turbervile, and Barnabe Googe.[58] Veré Rubel adds that "it is interesting to note how many of the archaisms, poetic borrowings, and poetic constructions which distinguish the language of *The Shepheardes Calender* are to be found in *Tottel's Miscellany* as well."[59] To argue, as W. L. Renwick does, that "[t]he solemn Introduction and Notes contributed by E. K. are evidence that the [linguistic] innovation was acutely felt and required explanation; further, that it claimed serious consideration; and again, that it was deliberate,"[60] may be to acquiesce too much to E. K.'s own commentary, which, as I have argued, is at least as invested in emphasizing the innovative strangeness of Spenser's language as it is in dispelling that strangeness.[61]

Perhaps most intriguing in this regard is Megan Cook's observation that sixteenth-century editions of Chaucer were not glossed for "hard words" until *after* the publication of *The Shepheardes Calender*; until Thomas Speght's 1598 edition of Chaucer's poems, readers apparently were not expected to require assistance in decoding Chaucer's

English or to experience that English as substantially different from their own.[62] Speght's claim that his edition has "restored [Chaucer] to his owne Antiquitie"[63] makes plain the double impulse behind his gloss, at once to facilitate the reader's encounter with poetry deemed too remote for easy comprehension and to guarantee that this remoteness is recognized and appreciated. It is a mode of annotation Speght might well have learned from E. K.

Such observations help to contextualize Spenser's language and encourage us to adopt a more skeptical view of E. K.'s claims on its behalf. They also allow us to conceive of Spenser's collaboration with E. K. as an attempt—bolstered by the mystery surrounding Immerito's identity and by the archaizing effect of the blackletter type in which the poem was printed[64]—to generate a kind of "alienation effect" for *The Shepheardes Calender*, to cultivate remoteness as a deliberate mode of relation to readers.[65] Readers of *The Shepheardes Calender* have observed that Colin Clout's gestures of alienation and abandonment—his broken pipes, his exile to the North, his refusal to sing—are rarely permanent or wholehearted. Colin and his songs are, in fact, everywhere in the world of the *Calender*, if often at a remove, present only through the mediating influence of his fellow shepherds. The same might be said of Spenser's language, which, if it is "the straungest" of "many thinges which in him be straunge," is also the aspect of the poem most insistently present to its readers, thanks to the mediating influence of E. K.

I began this essay by noting that the pastoral tradition, especially Virgil's eclogues, posed difficulties for English authors and readers who wished to assert a greater affinity between their own language and culture and that of the Rome. Because Virgilian pastoral acknowledges Britain only as an emblem of distance, deprivation, and barbarism, it frustrated, or at least complicated, the efforts of English translators and imitators to use literature as a vehicle for overcoming their geographic, temporal, and linguistic remoteness from classical Latinity. *The Shepheardes Calender* seems to have frustrated readers like Webbe, Sidney, and Jonson—all equally, although differently, invested in the project of classicizing English poetry—for a similar reason, by both appealing to and resisting their desire for proximity to the classical world. The very aspects of the *Calender* that most clearly advertise its affiliation to the classical tradition, its genre and its scholarly apparatus, are also precisely the elements that most challenge that affiliation. E. K.'s epistle and notes habitually conflate foreignness with familiarity and estrangement with identification, insisting on such paradoxes as the necessary attributes of a truly English poetics; likewise, Spenser's pastoral plot fashions itself around a figure whose perpetual departures and returns challenge any effort to fix the place of pastoral and so lay claim to it for England. To write (or read) vernacular poetry may mean estrangement from one's native tongue; to locate pastoral in Britain, "cut of[f] from the wide world," may mean leaving the community of shepherd-poets behind.

★ ★ ★ ★

From 1580 on, of course, Spenser spent virtually his entire life in a state of literal proximity to and alienation from his native land and fellow English poets: as a functionary of Ireland's colonial administration, he watched from afar the dissolution of his hopes for a reform-minded Protestant court, a court that would nurture the kind of poetic community the language deserved. Ireland is thus a crucial figure for Spenser's ambivalent engagement with English vernacular poetry; it is the site of his own unwilling but productive displacement, the barren and rude prospect from which he, like Meliboeus or Ovid, must reenvision his native land. It is also, as Willy Maley and Andrew Hadfield have argued, the place where Spenser encountered a version of the vernacular, that spoken by members of the "Old English" colonial community, purified of modern corruptions by virtue of having been "preserved in the colonial margins rather than the cosmopolitan center."[66] Finally, Ireland is where Colin Clout reappears in Spenser's poetry, in a 1595 pastoral whose title—*Colin Clouts Come Home Againe*—invokes a "home" that turns out to be preserved in these same colonial margins.

This late work both intensifies and seeks to resolve the dynamics of displacement and estrangement that Spenser and E. K. negotiate in *The Shepheardes Calender*. It begins in what is for readers of the *Calender* a familiar vein, with Hobbinol hailing Colin's return from recent wanderings and begging him not to leave again: "*Colin* my liefe, my life, How great a losse / Had all the shepheards nation by the lacke?"[67] For the moment it appears that we are right back in the "June" eclogue, and that the intervening years have been occupied with more unhappy departures from and fretful returns to the place of pastoral. The discourse of departure and return is given an unexpected twist, however, when Colin's "late voyage" (line 34) abroad turns out to have taken him, of all places, to England: the shepherd's nation has been transplanted, like Spenser himself, beyond the Irish Pale.

The rest of the poem elaborates this ironic inversion of home and abroad, what Julia Reinhardt Lupton refers to as "the *unheimlich* contradictions and displacements implicit in the pastoral foundations of the Spenserian home."[68] When his fellow shepherds ask him to describe his exotic journey, ascribing their interest to a love of "forreine thing[s]" (line 162), Colin obliges by describing a country "farre away, / so farre that land our mother vs did leaue, / and nought but sea and heauen to vs appeare" (lines 225–27). At first, this England appears as an ideal home for poets, where "shepheards abroad . . . may safely lie" (line 316), where "learned arts do florish in great honor, / And Poets wits are had in peerlesse price" (lines 320–21), and where a gracious queen "enclin[es] her eare" to "take delight" in the "rude and roughly dight" music of Colin's pipe (lines 360–63). As Colin enumerates the fortunate poets who enjoy this happy place, however, his descriptions betray a darker view: Harpalus is "woxen aged / In faithfull service" (lines 380–81), Corydon is "meanly waged" (line 382), "sad *Alcyon*" is "bent to mourne" (line 384), Palin is "worthie of great praise" but consumed by "envie" (lines 392–93), Alcon requires "matter of more skill" (line 395), Palemon "himself may be rewed, / That sung so long vntill quite hoarse he grew" (lines 398–99), Alabaster is "throughly taught" but "knowen yet to few" and not "knowne . . . as he ought" (lines 400–402), Amyntas "quite is gone and lies full low" (line 435), and the best of them all, Astrofell "is dead and gone" (lines 449). By the time the litany ends, Colin's remark that "[a]ll these do florish in their sundry kind" (line 452) can only be read as bitter irony, and when Thestylis asks, "Why didst thou euer leaue that happie place?" (line 654), the answer seems self-evident: "[S]ooth to say, it is no sort of life, / For shepheard fit to lead in that same place" (lines 688–89).

There is more at stake here than the usual pastoral satire of courtly life. Colin redefines the terms of his own apparent alienation so that exile becomes the necessary condition of poetic excellence and the paradoxical guarantee of a higher home. He and his fellow Irish swains may live on "barrein soyle / Where cold and care and penury do dwell" (lines 656–57), but he anticipates a final reckoning at which the poets whose cunning has earned them proximity to power will suffer a worse fate: "Ne mongst true louers will they place inherit / But as exuls out of [Love's] court be thrust" (lines 893–94). For Colin—and perhaps for Spenser himself—the very extremity of Irish colonial existence becomes an ideal, and bracingly material, figure for the displacement and alienation that has always characterized, indeed made possible, his peculiar inhabitation of the pastoral world.

The University of Pennsylvania

NOTES

1. "Epistle," 29. This and all subsequent quotations from *The Shepheardes Calender* are taken from Edmund Spenser, *The Shorter Poems*, ed. Richard A. McCabe (New York: Penguin, 1999).

2. Anne Lake Prescott, "The Laurel and the Myrtle: Spenser and Ronsard," in *Worldmaking Spenser: Explorations in the Early Modern Age*, ed. Patrick Cheney and Lauren Silberman (Lexington: University Press of Kentucky, 2000), 63.

3. Patrick Cheney, *Spenser's Famous Flight* (Toronto: University of Toronto Press, 1993), 19.

4. Louis Adrian Montrose, " 'The Perfecte Paterne of a Poete': The Poetics of Courtship in *The Shepheardes Calender*," *Critical Essays on Edmund Spenser*, ed. Mihoko Suzuki (New York: G. K. Hall, 1996), 8.

5. My interest here is in the generic problems encountered if we take pastoral, especially Virgilian pastoral, as the normative locus of poetic birth or rebirth. For a related consideration of *The Shepheardes Calender*'s appropriation of and negotiations with Virgilian poetics, specifically the trope of "ruin," see Rebeca Helfer, "The Death of the 'New Poete': Virgilian Ruin and Ciceronian Recollection in Spenser's *The Shepheardes Calender*," *Renaissance Quarterly* 56.3 (Autumn 2003): 723–56.

6. Abraham Fleming, *The Bucoliks of Pvblivs Virgilius Maro, with Alphabeticall annotations vpon proper names of Gods, Goddesses, men, women, hilles, flouddes, cities, townes, and villages orderly placed in the margent* (London: John Charlewood, 1575), sigs. A2r–A3r.

7. Fleming's second translation of Virgil's eclogues, published in 1589 along with his version of the *Georgics*, dispenses with the glosses of proper nouns and place names, substituting fewer and more general marginal notes. Indeed, although the preface to this later edition reiterates Fleming's desire to provide "weake Grammarians" with Virgil "in a familiar phrase," the new translation is less obviously positioned to orient and assist the unlearned vernacular reader; it repudiates, for instance, the "foolish" rhymed couplets of the 1575 translation in favor of an English line approximating the "due proportion and measure" of classical verse (*The Bucoliks of Publius Virgilius Maro . . . Together with his Geogiks or Ruralls* [London: Thomas Orwin, 1589], sigs. A2r, A4v).

8. Richard Mallette, *Spenser, Milton, and Renaissance Pastoral* (Lewisburg: Bucknell University Press, 1981), 21. In his work on English pastoral, Patrick Cullen offers a similar interpretation of the genre's geography, arguing that while that the urban spaces from which pastoral figures flee—Virgil's Rome, Dante's Florence, or Sannazaro's Naples—may differ, the place to which they retreat—Arcadia—is eternally the same (*Spenser, Marvell, and Renaissance Pastoral* [Cambridge, MA: Harvard University Press, 1970], 99.

9. As Julia Reinhardt Lupton observes, "the pastoral genre, in this brilliant commencement of the Latin tradition, is instituted as performing the necessary yet often violent cultural work of finding a home," and this home, "the paradigmatic object of nostalgia, is a category of experience only fashioned in the alienated desiring distance from it" ("Home-Making in Ireland: Virgil's Eclogue I and Book VI of *The Faerie Queene*," *Spenser Studies* 8 (1987): 119–45; 120–21). Lupton's remark reminds us that, in the early modern period, nostalgia retained its etymological

significance as an essentially *geographic* affliction: to feel nostalgia is to be, literally, homesick. Her argument, which anticipates this essay's interest in the paradoxical interdependence of home and exile in the pastoral mode, identifies the Meliboee episode in Book VI of *The Faerie Queene* as a revision of the first eclogue that allows Spenser to "accommodate the positions of both exile and home-maker" (119).

10.   The Latin reads: *At nos hinc alii sitientis ibimus Afros, / pars Scythiam et rapidum cretae veniemus Oaxen / et penitus toto divisos orbe Britannos.*

11.   In Virgil's equally blunt phrase, *"carmina nulla canam."*

12.   And, in fact, Meliboeus reappears in Eclogue VII, no longer in any apparent danger of losing his land, his flocks, or his poetic identity.

13.   *Vulgar Eloquence: On the Renaissance Invention of English Literature* (New Haven: Yale University Press, 2006), 78.

14.   Although this essay seeks to articulate why, given Britain's pointed exclusion from the world of Virgil's *Eclogues*, pastoral might have posed a particular challenge—and opportunity—to a poet such as Spenser, whose relationship to his own native land is one of ambivalence and alienation, one might profitably pursue a similar line of argument with regard to either Marot or Sannazaro, each of whom suffered exile from his homeland. For more on the impact of political exile on Sannazaro's poetic career, see William Kennedy, *Jacopo Sannazaro and the Uses of Pastoral* (Hanover: University Press of New England, 1983), 21–27; for a discussion of Marot's experiences as a religious exile, as well as an account of his influence on Spenser and other sixteenth-century English poets, see Anne Lake Prescott, *French Poets and the English Renaissance* (New Haven: Yale University Press, 1978), 3–15.

15.   It seems to me (and also, I believe, to Spenser) particularly significant that Meliboeus should identify exile to Britain with the loss of his ability to sing. A recent essay by Stewart Mottram argues for a more politically oriented reading of the relationship between Meliboeus and Colin Clout, suggesting that "Spenser's task in the *Calender* . . . was to turn Virgil's place of exile into a place of empire – to identify England as an empire, not in spite of, but precisely because of its boasted isolation from Rome and the rest of the world" ("Empire, Exile, and England's 'British Problem': Recent Approaches to Spenser's *Shepheardes Calender* as a Colonial and Postcolonial Text," *Literature Compass* 4.4 (2007): 1059–77; 1066).

16.   *Contra* Nancy Jo Hoffman's assertion that Spenser "frees pastoral . . . from attachment to real geographic place" and "is the first to sense that pastoral can become an integral, inclusive landscape" (*Spenser's Pastorals:* The Shepheardes Calender *and* Colin Clout [Baltimore: Johns Hopkins University Press, 1977], 11), I would argue that Spenser forces pastoral to reckon with its attachment with real geographic place, and in particular, with the limitations and exclusions incumbent upon England (and English) itself. In this regard, my reading of the poem is akin to that offered by Paula Blank in *Broken English: Dialects and the Politics of Language in Renaissance Writings* (New York: Routledge, 1996), which highlights Spenser's use of English rural dialects to construct a fragmented and alienated pastoral landscape.

17.   "To His Booke," lines 2, 13–15.

18.   Among many theories propounded as to the identity of the mysterious E. K., Louis Waldman has proposed a deliberately veiled and estranged version of Spenser himself: Edmundus Kedemon, with the Greek κηδεμων, meaning "procurator" or

"spencer," substituting for the poet's English surname ("Spenser's Pseudonym 'E. K.' and Humanist Self-Naming," *Spenser Studies* 9 [1988]: 21–31). Louise Schleiner has similarly proposed that the initials be deciphered "Edmund Kent," a double pun signaling "of Kent" and "kenned" ("Spenser's 'E. K.' as Edmund Kent (Kenned/ of Kent): Kyth (Couth), Kissed, and Kunning-Conning," *ELR* 20 [1990]: 374–407). Such conjectures jibe nicely with my own understanding of E. K.'s obfuscatory relation to the *Calender* and of Spenser's alienated and alienating mode of authorship, but for the purposes of this essay, I'm content to take E. K. at face value—as the poem's first reader and critic.

19.   Lynn Staley Johnson, *The Shepheardes Calender: An Introduction* (University Park: Pennsylvania State University Press, 1990), 31.

20.   *The Egloges of Alexander Barclay* (Southwark: P. Traveris, c. 1530), sig. [A3]r.

21.   *The Eglogs of the Poet B. Mantuan Carmelitas* (London: Henry Bynneman, 1567), sigs. A2r, A3v.

22.   The word "gloss" itself distills this tension between familiarization and estrangement, since it comes from a Greek word meaning "strange" or "foreign" but is used in English to describe practices whereby a word or passage is clarified or made more plain.

23.   Robert Lane's *Sheheards Devises: Edmund Spenser's* Shepheardes Calender *and the Institutions of Elizabethan Society* (Athens: University of Georgia Press, 1993) is an exception: Lane considers both how Spenser's rustic diction might signal opposition to the elitism of contemporary homiletic practice and how E. K.'s often unhelpful glosses reflect the self-protective strategies of reformist authors in response to an increasingly centralized state religion (see esp. pp. 28–35, 56–73).

24.   For a history of vernacular glosses of scripture, see Long's *Translating the Bible: From the Seventh to the Seventeenth Century* (Burlington, VT: Ashgate, 2001).

25.   Qtd., Long, 47.

26.   *The Geneva Bible: A Facsimile of the 1560 Edition*, with an introduction by Lloyd E. Berry (Madison: University of Wisconsin Press, 1969), sigs. ★★★i[r] and ★★★iiii[r].

27.   *Tyndale's New Testament*, ed. David Daniell (New Haven: Yale University Press, 1989), 3–4.

28.   *Geneva Bible*, sig. ★★★iiii[v].

29.   *Geneva Bible*, sig. ★★★iiii[v].

30.   Not just geography, of course, but temporality as well: however innovative their approach to biblical translation might seem from the perspective of Catholic tradition, Protestant translators (and Protestants more generally) insisted that their labors were in fact more consistent with the practices of the early church, and that their version of Christian revelation simply returned the faith to its true origins. Such a claim obviously also resonates with E. K.'s insistence that Spenser's apparently newfangled diction restores to English poetry a long lost dignity and richness of expression.

31.   *Geneva Bible*, sig. ★★★i[r].

32.   From the preface to *Obedience of a Christian Man*; qtd., Long, 148.

33.   Indeed, in the Geneva Bible, Paul's Epistle to the Romans is preceded by a map illustrating just how belated and marginal Rome's place was in the world of biblical antiquity: purporting to represent the spread of the gospel outward from

Jerusalem, the map includes Rome barely at all, relegating it to the far northwest corner of the world—precisely where English readers would have been accustomed to finding their own remote island. Such a map literalizes the ambitions of England's sixteenth-century Bible translators, whose insistence on the more-than-adequate character of the English vernacular was simply one aspect of their effort to displace Rome from the center of Christianity, restoring a more antique and authentic Church whose home was, properly, everywhere—and perhaps especially in England.

34.   A promiscuity enacted in E. K.'s own words, since both "gallimaufray" and "hodgepodge" are borrowings from French: see *OED*, s.vv. "gallimaufry" and "hotchpot."

35.   Qtd., Veré L. Rubel, *Poetic Diction in the English Renaissance from Skelton through Spenser* (London: Oxford University Press, 1941), 6.

36.   Thomas Elyot, *A Critical Edition of Sir Thomas Elyot's The Boke named the Governour* (1531), ed. Donald W. Rude (New York: Garland Publishing, 1992), 34.

37.   "W.T. to the Reader," *Tyndale's Old Testament*, ed. David Daniell (New Haven: Yale University Press, 1992), 5.

38.   *Geneva Bible*, Psalm 137, notes a and e.

39.   *Geneva Bible*, Psalm 137:6.

40.   Harry Berger, *Revisionary Play: Studies in the Spenserian Dynamics* (Berkeley: University of California Press, 1988), 288. Roland Greene's reading of the poem also focuses on the shepherds' desire to restore Colin to a dialogic model of poetic creativity: the "hypothetical discourse . . . associated since 'Januarye' with Colin's lost expression and defined by its absence . . . lies just beyond the circumscription of the poem" and is "hypostasize[d] as a kind of *place*. . . . It is invoked, one might say, as a pastoral within the general pastoral landscape of the *Calender*, a particularly ideal 'here'. . . . [T]o entice Colin 'here' would be to reinstall the common voice of those shepherds and so to cancel the curse of isolation and divergence" ("*The Shepheardes Calendar*, Dialogue, and Periphrasis," *Spenser Studies* 8 (1987): 16–17; emphasis added).

41.   These lines, which cast Colin as Aeneas, suggest that Spenserian pastoral already incorporates the geographic restlessness usually identified with epic.

42.   For more on the narcissistic pleasures and perils of "Januarie," see Berger's essay on "The Mirror Stage of Colin Clout" in *Revisionary Play*, 325–46.

43.   Syrithe Pugh, *Spenser and Ovid* (Burlington, VT: Ashgate, 2005), 12. Pugh does not discuss the "Nouember" eclogue, which is my focus here, but her chapter on *The Shepheardes Calender* as a "New *Fasti*" shares many of this essay's preoccupations, especially with regard to Spenser's emphasis on exile and alienation as the defining experiences of the English pastoral poet.

44.   Colin's song is a translation of Clément Marot's "Eclogue sur le Trespas de ma Dame Loyse de Savoye, Mere du Roy Francoys," the first French eclogue, written in 1531, and also framed within a dialogue between two shepherds named Colin and Thenot, but the name "Dido" is Spenser's innovation.

45.   Donald Cheney, "Spenser's Currencies," in *Edmund Spenser: Essays on Culture and Allegory*, ed. Jennifer Klein Morrison and Matthew Greenfield (Burlington, VT: Ashgate, 2000), 42. See also Donald Cheney, "The Circular Argument of *The Shepheardes Calender*," in *Unfolded Tales: Studies in Renaissance Romance*, ed. G. M. Logan and Gordon Teskey (Ithaca: Cornell University Press, 1989), 137–61.

46. This message is driven home by the eclogue's emblem, "*La mort ny mord*" (line 210), which, as E. K. explains, serves as a reminder that "death biteth not" since "being ouercome by the death of one, that dyed for all, it is now made (as Chaucer sayth) the grene path way to life" (147). For more on the "Nouember" eclogue's reworking of classical narratives of female suffering, see John Watkins, *The Specter of Dido: Spenser and Virgilian Epic* (New Haven: Yale University Press, 1995), 79–82, although Watkins does not cite the Ovidian parallel.

47. The *Calender*'s verse coda seems to advertise this triumph by beginning in words that echo—and overgo—the famous boast at the end of the *Metamorphoses*: where Ovid brags of a poem that will last as long as Rome itself, Spenser declares, "I haue made a Calender for euery yeare, / That steele in strength, and time in durance shall outweare," a poem made to endure not to the end of an empire, but to the very limits of the Christian eschaton, "to the worlds dissolution" (156).

48. For more on the murky circumstances surrounding Ovid's exile to Tomis, see the foreword and introduction to Peter Green's translation of Ovid's *Poems of Exile* (Berkeley: University of California Press, 2005), vii–xii, xxiv–xxxv.

49. *Tristia*, 1.1.128. This and all subsequent citations from the *Tristia* are from Green's translation.

50. Elyot, *The Boke named the Governour*, 31.

51. Gabriel Harvey, *Pierce's Supererogation, or A New Praise of the Old Asse* (London: John Wolfe, 1593), sig. B4v.

52. Colin Burrow, *Edmund Spenser* (Plymouth: Northcote House Publishers, 1996), 9.

53. For the full range of responses to *The Shepheardes Calender*, see R. M. Cummings, *Spenser: The Critical Heritage* (London: Routledge and Kegan Paul, 1971), which contains a section devoted to comments on Spenser's language.

54. E. K., "Epistle," 27.

55. Philip Sidney, *The Defence of Poesie* (London: William Ponsonby, 1595), sig. H3v.

56. Ben Jonson, *Discoveries: A Critical Edition.*, ed. Maurice Castelain (Paris: Librairie Hachette, 1906), 90.

57. Thomas Warton, *Observations on the Fairy Queen of Spenser*, 2 ed., enlarged and corrected (London: 1762), 1:133.

58. Roscoe E. Parker, "Spenser's Language and the Pastoral Tradition," *Language* 1 (1925): 80–87.

59. Veré L. Rubel, *Poetic Diction in the English Renaissance from Skelton through Spenser* (London: Oxford University Press, 1941), 145.

60. Qtd., Rubel, 136n11.

61. Lynn Staley Johnson notes, furthermore, that E. K. encourages a kind of linguistic disorientation in his own readers, when, for instance, he categorizes the *Calender*'s eclogues as "moral," "plaintive," and "recreative": "His tone implies that he speaks of what everyone knows, that the terms he uses are standard critical usage. . . . But 'moral,' 'plaintive,' and 'recreative' are in no dictionary of rhetorical terms, no handbook of poetic forms. . . . [T]hey exist only within the closed world and language of *The Shepheardes Calender*" and "are defined [only] in terms of what they define," so that the reader "seems to have stumbled into a particularly zany world [of] unknown but familiar-sounding words" (*The Shepheardes Calender*, 38).

62. I am grateful to Megan Cook for sharing with me her unpublished essay on Speght and E. K., " 'The Hard Words of Chaucer, Explained': Glossing Archaic Language in Spenser's *Shepheardes Calendar* and Speght's Chaucer." Cook identifies a number of suggestive parallels between Speght's editorial practice and that of E. K., including the identification of Chaucer with an exemplary and purified form of the vernacular and the application of classical rhetorical theory to the use of vernacular archaisms. She points out that E. K.'s gloss has been marshaled as a key piece of evidence in tracing the evolution of attitudes toward Chaucer's language, but that critics have failed to consider that the gloss might affect that trajectory as much or even more than it reflects it. And in fact, most of the sixteenth-century comments on Chaucer's English that emphasize its difference from contemporary usage postdate *The Shepheardes Calender*.

63. Qtd. in Cook, 14.

64. Such type "would have looked decidedly old fashioned in 1579," notes Colin Burrow (*Edmund Spenser*, 12). For a broader discussion of typographical archaism in the sixteenth century, see Zachary Lesser, "Typographic Nostalgia: Play-Reading, Popularity, and the Meanings of Black Letter," *The Book at the Play: Playwrights, Stationers, and Readers in Early Modern England*, ed. Marta Straznicky (Amherst: University of Massachusetts Press, 2006).

65. I'm being wildly anachronistic, of course—and playing fast and loose with genre—in borrowing Bertolt Brecht's term (*verfremdungseffekt*) for the strategy of the self-conscious metatheatricality employed by his dramatic productions. I don't mean to suggest any larger parallel between Brecht's Marxist socioeconomic ideals and whatever poetic or linguistic aspirations might have motivated Spenser or E. K., but I do think that a similar attitude toward the illuminating and even liberating effects of distance is at work.

66. Willy Maley, "Spenser's Languages: Writing in the Ruins of English." *The Cambridge Companion to Spenser*, ed. Andrew Hadfield (Cambridge: Cambridge University Press, 2001), 169. See also Andrew Hadfield, *Shakespeare, Spenser, and the Matter of Britain* (New York: Palgrave Macmillan, 2004), esp. pp. 32–33.

67. Edmund Spenser, *Colin Clout's Come Home Againe* (1595), lines 16–17; in *The Shorter Poems*, ed. Richard A. McCabe (New York, Penguin Books, 1999). All subsequent citations are from this edition of the poem.

68. Lupton, 141.

DANIEL MOSS

Spenser's Despair and God's Grace

Focusing on Una's delay in repudiating Despair in *Faerie Queene* I.ix, this article reads the critical impulse to answer for Redcrosse as a theologically flawed mitigation of Spenser's allegorical rigor. Given the reader's incapacity to anticipate or to ventriloquize grace, the only sufficient answer to Despair must come from without, by means of a fully divine prerogative. Despair's temptation is expressly designed to transmute all potential response—especially the sort of recourse to Scriptural citation on display in the Geneva Bible's margins—into fuel for his rhetorical machine: we can offer no sufficient reply however much we look to Scripture as the one sufficient text by which to answer him. The agency of answering is no more the reader's than it is the knight's. When not fallen to its damnable nadir, despair may be salutary—both Luther in his theological argumentation and English pastors in their prescripted homilies promote it as the prelude to grace—but it must nevertheless seem damnable to the sufferer, becoming manifest as spiritual health only later or from an outside perspective unavailable in Spenser's allegorical cave. Despair's ability to confound all mortal response renders him invincible in the mutable world, but because God's grace—invoked and enacted by Una in her allegorical capacity as the true church—is an infinite blessing, Una alone may nullify this most terrible of the devil's temptations, pending Christ's triumphant return at the end of time, when Despair "should die his last, that is eternally."

DESPAIR'S CAVE IS A DARK PLACE.[1] Spenser's erring knights find it increasingly difficult to see once inside, and Redcrosse in particular loses sight of Una, who must save him despite himself. Despair's own vision, however, seems to have adjusted to the absence of light; although "his hollow eyne / Lookt deadly dull, and stared as astound"[2]—the result of peering through the darkness at knight after knight—he is nonetheless able to identify Una, so as to include her in his temptation:

Is not enough, that to this Ladie milde
Thou falsed hast thy faith with periurie,
And sold thy selfe to serue *Duessa* vilde,
With whom in all abuse thou hast thy selfe defilde?

(I.ix.46.6–9)

Despair's vision, then, extends to clairvoyance, to knowledge of
Redcrosse's secret sin with a woman not in the cave; in a sense,
Despair sees through his victim's eyes, while conversely Redcrosse
now sees erroneously or not at all with his foe's "hollow eyne." The
demon reminds those who have ventured inside the cave of what
remains outside, and then replaces that which is desired but absent
with his own presence—with what he tells us we see in the darkness,
which is always himself.

If Despair's temptation relies thus on a trick of the eye, the demon
also exploits Redcrosse's poor sense of hearing, or more properly the
knight's inability to recall what he has heard, ever since he first erred
into Error's archetypal cave. Redcrosse's continued failure to process
Una's original admonition—"Add faith vnto your force, and be not
faint" (I.i.19.3)—constitutes what Richard Mallette has termed the
hero's "gravel deafness,"[3] which is itself less a failure to hear than a
failure to learn. Deafness to Una in the cave translates allegorically
as the obtuseness of the wayfaring Christian in the world—well-
intentioned, perhaps, but inherently sinful and numb to the Word,
however much he hears it with his own ears, however often he reads
it with his own eyes. The intention is in any case irrelevant, for the
deafness of Spenser's hero is continuous with Book I's larger allegory:
fallen man's utter incapacity to secure his own salvation from correct
doctrine alone, without the intervention of an external grace. It matters less that Redcrosse does not heed Una's words than that he *cannot*
do so; hence her decisive action, complementing her speech: "Out
of his hand she snatcht the cursed knife" (I.ix.52.4).

Redcrosse's paralysis itself constitutes Spenser's narrative exploration of an intractable anxiety at the heart of Reformed theology and
epistemology. In his seminal article on the Despair episode, Harold
Skulsky has identified the source of this anxiety as the endlessly debated doctrine of *fiducia*, or the palpable assurance among the Elect
of a predestined salvation. Skulsky writes:

[T]he Reformation account of *fiducia* turns out to undermine
itself: how does one distinguish, at any given moment, between

a temporary and permanent calling, between the confused sense of grace of the Reprobate and the imperfect faith of the Elect? . . . I conclude that if the assurance that rallies Redcrosse from despair has less force as evidence than he ascribes to it, the poem is all the more candid and penetrating as an insider's exploration of the Protestant religious temper.[4]

Skulsky's reading helps explain the narrative problem of Redcrosse's sensory deprivation, his failure to see or hear Una in the funhouse/echo-chamber of Despair's cave. But the paradox of *fiducia*—the omnipresent danger of substituting self-reliance for faith in God—also augments our sense of the blessedness and superlative power of grace, as the only legitimate way around the central disconnect of despair.

For Andrew Escobedo, arguing from the perspective of Kierkegaard's uncompromising analysis of the problem in *The Sickness unto Death*, "despair functions simultaneously as a transparent manifestation of God's dispensation and as a kind of joint or pivot between paradoxes inherent in Protestant Christianity."[5] As this kinetic imagery implies, despair not only finds a place in Reformed theology at large and in Spenser's allegory in particular, but becomes the very fulcrum of the process by which the individual Protestant negotiates the obstacles to his own faith in the fallen world: "The sinner's relation to the world emerges from the necessary incommensurability between the sinner's obduracy and the extension of grace, between the human soul and the calculus of divine wrath and mercy."[6] As a sin, despair must be damned—Spenser's Despair is thoroughly evil—and yet he may also be necessary to the Christian's salvation, a salutary consequence of the Fortunate Fall, or as Kierkegaard writes:

Precisely because the sickness of despair is totally dialectical, it is the worst misfortune never to have had that sickness: it is a true godsend to get it, even if it is the most dangerous of illnesses, if one does not want to be cured of it . . .

[T]he person who without affectation says that he is in despair is still a little closer, is dialectically closer, to being cured than all those who are not regarded as such and who do not regard themselves as being in despair.[7]

Taken together, Skulsky's identification of Despair as a recalcitrant theological enigma and Escobedo's analysis of the villain's potentially salutary impact on the Protestant reader make for a powerful reading of the episode, but they do not quite account for a further element of the allegorical narrative: Una's long silence during the exchange between her knight and his demon. As Redcrosse can boast no agency despite his good will, the central difficulty of Spenser's allegory of Despair remains Una's delay; for fourteen stanzas she permits the temptation to unfold, and does not interject when Redcrosse answers their common foe with lethal insufficiency, nor even when Despair introduces her as evidence against him. A speaking witness for the defense, rather than the prosecution's exhibit, Una's power over Despair should be absolute, for she cannot be tempted and has only to contradict him to repudiate him, much as she will contradict "Fidessa" and Archimago in the final canto of Book I, deciding a similar trial (I.xii.33).

Because the delay of Una's fully sufficient answer to Despair itself enables the full articulation of the demon's temptation—the unfolding of the episode as narrative—any critical effort to interpret Spenser's allegory without reference to this delay must fall short. There is a hermetic quality, too, to Una's response; her authority is not only divinely inspired, but rhetorically self-contained. Thus, to anticipate her answer (on a first reading), to embellish it with further evidence, to gloss it with citations from Scripture or any other text, even to paraphrase it—all are understandable critical impulses, yet every one of them avoids the central issue: that there is no agency by which to repudiate Despair, save the grace for which Una as the true church is the only vector within narrative, and for which Christ is the sole agent overseeing any Protestant narrative, allegorical or otherwise. If we are to read Spenser's allegory with interpretive rigor, we must suffer its terms; we cannot remain outside the cave with Sir Trevisan. Rather, we must follow Redcrosse inside, even if we are better advised not to do so, even if we know that to follow him into this extreme temptation is to approximate his role, to come as close as any reader can come to being the next knight, intent on revenge and self-vindication—and thus the next victim. As that readerly error appears increasingly inevitable in retrospect, Despair's power over Redcrosse and over us will only grow, until Una—"One"—alone can answer him.

I. THE TEMPTATIONS OF KNIGHTS, READERS, AND CRITICS

Too often, this assumption of "readerly error" is no more than a critical convenience, but not in this poem, and least of all in this cave. Throughout the Legend of Holiness, and most acutely in its darkest places, Spenser propagates not only the errancy of his hero, but that of his readers as well, until our very act of describing what Redcrosse *should* have done (what we *would* have done in his stirrups) ironically becomes tantamount to his pride. At times we learn from our experience of Faerieland at the knight's slow pace—as when we follow him into Error's Den or Archimago's "little lowly Hermitage" (I.i.34.1); at times we foresee the danger into which he errs—as when he enters the "goodly" House of Pride, which only we (and the narrator, and perhaps Pride herself) know to be "ruinous and old" (I.iv.5.1,9). In either case, however, we adventure with Redcrosse and end up where he does, exiting the House of Pride behind him and through the same unsavory portal. The discomfort of the notion that we can never be rid of Redcrosse as we read his tale is amply counterbalanced by our share in his triumph, the hero's comic transmutation from Arthurian bumpkin to English St. George. Precisely because Redcrosse is Spenser's "Fall guy"—always testifying to the magnitude of our universal orginal sin through the dependability of his personal failure—his election notwithstanding communicates the hopefulness of the allegory, helping us by "ensample" (I.iv.1.9) to embrace real salvation outside the poem and beyond its fictions.

Perhaps surprisingly, the allegorical hero's bifurcation into plowman and saint unifies the poem's readership, rather than polarizing it, because Redcrosse experiences Faerieland over time, just as we live and read in time. Time, of course, has nothing to do with predestined salvation. The curse of despair and the gift of hope—twinned consequences of original sin and the fortunate Fall—are equally temporal phenomena stemming from the same catastrophic event, such that to read for the one is generally to read for the other, but never simultaneously. It is not possible to see the New Jerusalem from inside the cave of Despair, a perspectival malfunction reflecting the theological "scandal" of *fiducia* so aptly described by Skulsky. Redcrosse, we can be sure, will survive Despair's temptation—the Legend of Holiness, after all, is more than nine cantos long—but the hero's peril nonetheless triggers suspense in the reader. The episode is an allegorical emergency, during which the hero's self-doubt merges with our own skepticism, linking his fictional experience to our fallen condition.

Spenser plays thus with his reader's shifting perspective throughout Book I, but we are rarely if ever as close to merging with Redcrosse as we are here and now, for although the hero has been in dark places before, they were not quite our places. Despair's cave differs from Orgoglio's dungeon, for example, primarily insofar as we ourselves were not in any direct sense Orgoglio's victims; we looked down into the dungeon through Arthur's eyes, never perceiving it from the terrifying perspective of Redcrosse's solitary confinement.[8] When we enter Despair's cave, on the other hand, it is as if we stand next to the knight or immediately behind him, coming as close as we ever will to inhabiting the hero's body and suffering from his false or blind perspective (an instance of *trompe l'oeil* inverted into clairvoyance once we ascend Contemplation's peak with Redcrosse).[9]

Una's long silence in Despair's cave thus functions as the inaudible complement to her invisibility, not only to Redcrosse, but to all the readers who enter the cave behind him. Until Despair identifies her, there is no way for us to read her back into the narrative, to look to her for help while Redcrosse continues to stare blindly at his foe. Hence there is an ironic dimension to the readiness and confidence with which many of Spenser's critics have claimed to refute his villain's arguments. Perhaps because Redcrosse's own response to Despair's temptation is so feeble, readers too are tempted to respond with superior claims, to answer for Redcrosse with appropriate Scriptural citations, or to ventriloquize Una's answer to Despair with their own timing and on their own terms.

As a result, Despair seems to have become less lethal over time, as Spenserians have probed the rhetorical disjunctions in his argument, proposing various passages from the New Testament in order to facilitate the reader's escape from the allegorical cave. Thus Ernest Sirluck, in his ground-breaking 1949 article on "the basic device governing Despair's rhetoric," insists upon the *simplicity* of that device:

> Like most really effective rhetorical tricks, it is as simple as it is bold. . . . One ventures to think that it was instantly recognized by those generations of readers who, like Spenser's contemporaries, were accustomed to thinking of last things in terms of Christian theology.
>
> It consists quite simply in the suppression of one of a pair of essential terms (mercy) in the Christian equation of judgment, and the representation of the other (justice) as constituting the whole relation of God to human conduct.[10]

Even as he argues cogently for the centrality of this rhetorical device to the demon's sophistical program—his *enthymeme* has become a critical *donnée*—Sirluck's constant emphasis on the trope's simplicity undercuts the seriousness of the episode. This harrowing allegory of fallen humanity's fundamental vulnerability to the mishearing and misrepresentation of the saving Word is thus recast as mere catechism.[11]

In general, critical esteem for Despair's rhetorical prowess has only grown since Sirluck's article, yet there has been little movement away from the notion that Despair's sermon can easily be recognized as parody by the reader, and almost as easily refuted with reference to any number of outside texts espousing correct doctrine.[12] Aside from the efforts of Skulsky and Escobedo, the original distinction between the villain's accomplished style and empty content persists, and while Despair is now understood to pose a serious danger to Redcrosse and even to the Protestant reader he represents, it is still a critical commonplace that the better one reads the *Faerie Queene* and its allegory, the more apparent will be the falsity of the villain's sophistical claims. Judith Anderson, recommending the episode to instructors of undergraduates new to Spenser's poetry, identifies the young reader's conquest of Despair's rhetoric as an early benchmark for measuring his or her progress toward critical aptitude. Citing her "own familiarity with the sophistries and fallacies in Despair's argument," and relying on the episode's "Christian context" to correct "unexpectedly hesitant" students too easily persuaded by the demon's "Senecan" rhetoric, Anderson asserts, "We can see through such reasoning [as Despair's], if we remember to look hard at it, but the catch lies in the conditional *if*."[13] In other words, the closer we read Spenser, the more readily we will read through Despair.

Such straightforward critiques are hardly in keeping with the intricacies of Spenserian allegory, which rarely if ever rewards reading directly—lest, like Error, we devour books only to vomit them up. Put another way, there seems little in keeping here with this poet's obsessive tendency to interrogate and to castigate every kind of "ease" (Despair's favorite word), his readiness to punish overconfident readers. Indeed, I suspect that our very presumption that we can read around Despair's rhetoric—read through to his insubstantiality, read him away—represents his greatest threat.[14] The episode allegorizes, among other epistemological disasters, the limitations and vulnerabilities of reading Spenser; when Despair claims that "he, that once hath missed the right way, / The further he doth goe, the further he doth stray" (I.ix.45.8–9), his admonition is directed not only at Redcrosse but at the reader behind him, at us, insofar as we have followed the knight all the way from the opening stanza's empty plain to this grotesque cave. From this perspective, perhaps the most circumspect among Anderson's "unexpectedly hesitant" students are reading Despair best after all, as they may be willing to listen to his

arguments until they have been persuaded, like Redcrosse, of their
veracity. Such readers will most appreciate the miracle of Una's intervention, for the more lost they become, the more dramatic and
indeed full of grace will be the agency that finds them.

Such an inverse relationship—between the reader's arithmetically
deeper descent into Despair's cave, overbalanced by the Christian's
geometrically increasing and finally infinite sense of the blessedness
of God's grace—is fully in keeping with Reformation theology at
large. But Protestant doctrine does not provide for any interpretive
shortcut to this knowledge; while the allegory of grace requires the
continuous presence of truth, the allegory of despair entails a counter-
active moment (or lifetime) of self-deception, a forgetting of truth.
It is not the reader's role to remind Redcrosse of his salvation, but
Una's, and Una herself is only partly the poet's creature; for Spenser,
the theological truths embodied in her, and the grace she relays,
derive from God. Were the poet to deny Redcrosse Una's intervention, the hero would simply be damned by his creator to suicide—would become an allegory for the reprobate man in the absence
of grace—but when Spenser narrates Redcrosse's salvation through
Una's intervention, he celebrates a divine prerogative, testifying to
an absolute power not his own. The problem of Una's more-than-
momentary vanishing act, then, reflects the rigor of the *Faerie
Queene*'s allegory at this critical narrative juncture; indeed, her disap-
pearance to all but Despair himself is not primarily a matter of narrative convenience or inconvenience, but constitutes the negative
allegorical corollary to the personified sin presently expostulating
with Redcrosse. Because Redcrosse stands for any English Protestant,
his loss of Una is also our loss and Spenser's own loss.

Overall, of course, Spenser's allegorical articulation of religion involves much more compromise than this; Book I ranges an especially
wide gamut between the poet's satirical repudiation of Archimago's
Ave-Mary (I.i.35.9) on the one hand, and his encomiastic accommo-
dation of the House of Holinesse's rather papistic beadmen
(I.x.36–45) on the other. Not only does the *Faerie Queene*'s genre—its
romantic range and intricacy—moreover frustrate any reductive allegorical account of Spenser's personal orthodoxy,[15] but the poem's
status as a fiction renders any straightforward identification between
poet, reader, and Redcrosse finally untenable. Yet it does not follow
from this—from a reader's fundamental distance from fiction—that
Spenser's Protestant audience is entitled to part ways with Redcrosse
whenever the hero's allegorical path becomes especially narrow or
dark. For all the euphemistic solace of poetry and allegory, Redcrosse—as the patron saint of the Protestant everyman—may still

command our readerly rigor, most insistently in his climactic encounter with Despair, within the cave into which the critic's bird's-eye vantage cannot penetrate.

This does not mean that we should not criticize the Despair episode at all; on the contrary, reading this allegory involves the recognition that we are bound to do so. But it does mean that we should know when we have lost the argument, at which point Book I's greatest allegory—that of God's grace—will become manifest. We should see, in other words, why it is to the reader's advantage to listen to Despair, for Una cannot put on or embody grace in all its potency until Redcrosse has been tempted in full, until Despair has brought Holiness to the brink of suicide, and done his utmost to justify his own diabolical existence and persistence.

II. LISTENING TO DESPAIR

Article VI of the Thirty-Nine Articles assures English Protestants as to the ease of salvation by emphasizing the sufficiency of the Word of God: "Holy Scripture conteyneth all things necessary to saluation: so that whatsoeuer is not read therein, nor may be proued thereby, is not to be required of any man, that it shoulde be beleeued as an article of the Faith, or be thought requisite or necessary to saluation."[16] In other words, the righteous Christian need know only one book. Nevertheless, Cranmer and company proceed to divide this one text into an itemized canon, including a comprehensive list of the twenty-four official books of the Protestant Old Testament and "All the bookes of the Newe Testament, as they are commonly receiued" (the absence of a list presumably reflects the absence of widespread debate within England over the canonicity of New Testament books). Between the Old and New come the Apocryphal texts—like the Book of Judith or "the rest of the booke of Hester"—which, "(as Hierome saith) the Church doeth read for example of life and instruction of manners; but yet doth it not applie them to establish any doctrine."[17] The central section of this single book, then—on the authority of an extratextual source (St. Jerome)—is merely supplemental to the discrete halves of the sufficient Word preceding and following it.

But after the sixth article's division of the sufficient text into units and elements, the seventh stages a recovery of the Bible's coherence, insisting that: "The Old Testament is not contrary to the newe: for

both in the olde and newe testament euerlasting life is offered to
Mankind by Christ, who is the onely mediatour betweene God and
man, being both God and man. Wherefore they are not to be heard,
which faine that the old fathers did looke onely for transitorie promises."[18] Whatever the polemical content of the articles, the basic rhetorical movement between these two contiguous texts is clear
enough, from the initial insistence on sufficiency to the disorienting
subdivision into parts in the sixth article, followed by the seventh's
recuperative language of coherence—"not contrary," "both in the
olde and newe," "both God and man." The coherence of the parts
complements the sufficiency of the whole, and the heretic, "not to
be heard," is precisely the one who would insist on the irrelevance
of part of the text. It is the Christian's duty to know—that is, to
remember—the whole Word, even its killing letters.

By which logic at the heart of English Protestant theology, Spenser's Despair must be heard, for it is the old man's pastime to hold
forth on the continued relevance of portions of the Bible that, for
all their renovation by Christ's advent, are still indispensably reso-
nant, still required reading. In essence, Despair exploits not the Bible
itself, but its fallen readership. It is not after all Redcrosse's knowledge
of the Bible (assuming he has read the book he presents to Arthur
at I.ix.19.6–9) that saves him from Despair, but Una's externalized
intervention, not the Protestant's reading but his faith. Far from
tempting the knight away from the truths he knows as a Christian,
Despair appeals to Redcrosse as a reader of the Bible, just as he has
already exploited the reader of Petrarchan love-poetry in the hapless
Terwin, by emphasizing and amplifying the fully Petrarchan trope of
unrealized and unrealizable desire:

> Which when he knew, and felt our feeble harts
> Embost with bale, and bitter byting griefe,
> Which loue had launched with his deadly darts,
> With wounding words and termes of foule repriefe,
> He pluckt from vs all hope of due reliefe,
> That earst vs held in loue of lingering life. . . .
>
> (I.ix.29.1–6)

It seems without once mentioning (though never contradicting) the
prospect of this unseen Laura's pity—indeed without ever referring
to her directly—Despair has heightened Terwin's awareness of her
scorn to such an intolerable degree that the lover elects to kill himself.

Terwin's suicide parodies the mordancy of the Petrarchan motif of amorous despair, precluding the possibility of the despairing lover's ever enjoying his beloved's meliorative pity, a worldly prototype for the denial of God's grace, with which Despair will soon threaten Redcrosse.[19] As the demon turns Terwin's Petrarchan reading against him, so he turns Redcrosse's own Protestant reading against him, always arguing from within his victim's conceptual apparatus, never outside it.[20] His rhetoric is indeed false, but not because it alters the listener's terms of ideological reference, but instead because it misrepresents the proportions by which the paradoxes generated by any ideology can be tolerated.[21] And just as the Petrarchan tropes Despair exploits against Terwin can be found in any amatory sonnet sequence, so the elements of Christian doctrine the demon employs against Redcrosse could be heard in any English church of the period, or derived from any Protestant Bible.[22] Despair is so dangerous a villain—and so difficult an allegory—not because we cannot see through to his pagan lies or Jewish half-truths, but because his Christian truths are so apparent.

The casual reader's temptation to relegate Despair to the status of Old Testament guru, while applauding Una for her New Testament solution to the demon's obsolete conundrums, persists in some of the best-known Spenser criticism; James Nohrnberg argues, "what [Despair] contemplates is the old covenant to the exclusion of the new one," and declares that, "Essentially, Despair urges that Redcross cut his losses to the Law, and Una must intervene with the promises of the New Testament."[23] Yet Nohrnberg, also the most venturesome explorer of Spenser's biblical allusions, goes on to emphasize the New Testament provenance of much of Despair's argument. He writes:

> Spenser's sinner "that once hath missed the right way' shares in the general condemnation: "They haue all gone out of the way . . . there is none that doeth good, no not one' (Rom. 3:12, Ps. 14:3). The "righteous *sentence* of th'Almighties law', under which Redcrosse is prepared to die, is Pauline too, for Paul at one point 'all to gether douted, euen of life . . . ' According to the Geneva gloss on this place, Paul, in his 'infirmity,' was utterly resolved to die; he exposes himself so that 'it might appeare how wonderfully Gods graces wrought in him,' and Spenser draws the same conclusion in the opening stanza of the following canto.[24]

At the close of this intricately wrought analysis, we should notice how Nohrnberg saves himself from simply echoing Despair by citing the Geneva Bible's gloss on the temporary and integral nature of the Apostle's own encounter with despair, and then drawing our attention to Spenser's similar recuperative movement at the beginning of the tenth canto, right before the knight's emergency refresher course in holiness.

But the reader of Spenser's poem—rather unlike the reader of the Geneva Bible—reads the text over time, stanza by stanza, canto by canto. There is no gloss in the margins of canto ix directing the despairing reader to the beginning of canto x, no critic or commentator present in that lonely cave to provide a cross-reference to Una's salvific stanza even as Redcrosse accepts Despair's knife. Nor, presumably, would Paul's own despair have been persuasive and exemplary had the Geneva editors been present to gloss it with the promise of grace, which it was incumbent upon Paul to remember, and which in any event is only God's to give. The act of glossing the hyperallusive biblical text—as an attempt to supplement one part of Scripture with disparate others, with the reader forging his or her own links between multiple discrete portions of a sufficient whole—bespeaks the insufficiency of the reader, even as it emphasizes the coherence of the Bible.[25] As in the sixth article, the Protestant reader divides the unitary Word into fragments by glossing, while depending upon scriptural coherence—the seventh article—for the authority to do so.[26]

But this pragmatic allusivity is easily distorted: even in the recuperative seventh article, we are admonished to remember not the New Testament but the Old, echoing the way in which the sixth article itemizes the relevant books of the Law and the supplementary Apocrypha, while cramming the unnamed Gospels and epistles into a single line. And as Nohrnberg's meticulous analysis makes clear, Despair creates the illusion of wholeness by alluding precisely to those New Testament passages that themselves allude to the Old. Nohrnberg writes:

> In Spenser, 'the day of wrath' awaiting the sinner whose 'measure' is 'High heaped vp with huge iniquitie' is the Pauline *dies irae* of Zephaniah 1:15, as it is invoked in Romans 2:5f. ('But thou, after thine hardnes and heart that can not repent, heapest vnto thy self wrath against the day of wrath and of the declaration of the iuste iudgement of God, Who wil reward euerie man according to his workes.')[27]

Citing Paul, Despair refers simultaneously to both Testaments, to the prophecy before Christ's advent as well as to the judgment after his return; what we lose—what goes uncited—is the presence of Christ himself. We should note moreover that the Geneva gloss on Romans 2:5 fails to point the reader to the echoed verse in Zephaniah, referring us instead to James 5:3, which describes in gruesome detail the "reward" awaiting the avaricious, and which is accompanied only by a gloss directing us back to Romans 2:5.[28] Like Despair's words re-echoing on the walls of his cave, the two glosses bounce us back and forth between these terrifying biblical pronouncements. By identifying the line's prophetic source in the Old Testament, Nohrnberg amplifies the Pauline condemnation; his gloss, at least in this case, only pulls us deeper into the fallen world.

The problem becomes worse, not better, as cross-references proliferate, and as the reader comes to rely increasingly on the editors' signposts, compounding the lingering difficulty of reconciling the popular Geneva editions with the Thirty-Nine Articles.[29] Article XX cautions, "it is not lawfull for the Church to ordayne any thing that is contrary to Gods word written, neither may it so expound one place of Scripture, that it be repugnant to another."[30] Here the Church of England seems at odds with the Geneva editors, who evince a mania for glossing. In Despair's condemnation of him "that once hath missed the right way," for instance, Nohrnberg finds an allusion to Romans 3:12, which itself echoes the beginning of the fourteenth Psalm, but the Geneva editors include for this and adjacent verses cross-references to Psalms 5, 10, 53, 140, Proverbs 1, Isaiah 59, and—lest we forget the New Testament—Galatians 3.

Although Despair exploits only portions of the Bible, most effectively the epistles of Paul and the Psalms of David—those two archetypal victims of salutary despair—we should remember that this emphasis was exactly the norm in Elizabethan England. Patrick Collinson writes, "The Bible, or parts of it, especially, as [John] Foxe reports, the epistles, but also the Psalms, were memorized . . . as an essential component and reinforcement of religious education and conduct at all educational levels."[31] When Redcrosse argues, "The souldier may not moue from watchfull sted, / Nor leaue his stand, vntill his Captaine bed," his words echo Psalm 130:6—"My soule waiteth on the Lord more then the morning watche watcheth for the morning"—triggering Despair's retrieval and insidious distortion of the scriptural reference:

Who life did limit by almightie doome,
(Quoth he) knowes best the termes established;
And he, that points the Centonell his roome,
Doth license him depart at sound of morning droome.

$$(I.ix.41.4–9)^{32}$$

The "license" to "depart at . . . morning"—the demon's unsubstanti-
ated, ostensibly divine permission to end life early—expressly contra-
dicts the psalmist's metaphor. Despair's "Centonell" is here
misidentified and falsely equated with the soul (Redcrosse's "souldier"), whereas, in the psalm, soul and watchman are decisively differ-
entiated, in that the soul waits for the Lord *more* than the watchman
watches for morning. Once Despair has collapsed soul into sentinel,
the original metaphor, taken literally, abbreviates life to a single night.
Despair has perverted a scriptural testimony of the soul's endurance
into an advertisement for his own hollow ideal of "Ease after
warre" (I.ix.40.9).

In terms of larger social and economic scales, too, Despair's approach to the text is eminently Protestant. Collinson writes that for
Reformation editors of the Bible, the advent of the printing press
meant "the propagation on a liberal scale of the biblical text in its
entirety, in the vernacular and in standard formats, a work of constant
reference and cross-reference which dedicated Bible readers had at
their ready command, and by which their life was commanded."[33]
Again, if we detect a slippage between the sufficiency of a unified
whole and the necessity of an exhaustive apparatus of cross-reference,
we can easily perceive Despair's strategy: to defend a truncated text
with a heavily-annotated concordance, to hide incompletion behind
a pyrotechnic allusive display.[34] The demon's famous rhetoric—his
virtuosity in the employment of chiasmus, isocolon, climax, and all
the rest—makes reading masquerade as oratory, but we should be
clear what signifying work is performed by this rhetorical machine.
Despair here applies his ad hoc eloquence—just as serviceable for
ensnaring Petrarchan lovers—in order to shadow forth the illusory
wholeness of a constantly fragmenting text.[35] Because his foe's many
citations are accurate and his sequence of allusions coherent, Redcrosse can momentarily forget the lethal insufficiency of only half
the Word.[36]

The demon's temptation in fact depends upon the Christian reader's knowledge of Scripture and on his or her ability to move through
it referentially—not only forward, but also backward, like the Geneva
editors citing the Old Testament in the margins of the New. Since

the two Testaments are "not contrary," as the seventh article insists, Despair assumes that Redcrosse can be induced into a retrograde admission of the validity of the Law, so long as his citational process refers his hapless auditor in one direction—that is, from the New Testament to the Old—until Christ's supercession of the Law is buried beneath an avalanche of equally sufficient (if much less reassuring) Scripture. Nor is this diabolical strategy of over-citation some novel instance of casuistry, but is rather as old as Christ's own temptation in the wilderness. In the Gospels, when Satan tempts Christ to advertise his assurance of salvation by leaping from the Temple, the temptation is not to physical suicide but to spiritual presumption, accessed through seemingly innocent citation—the devil dares Jesus to cite Scripture like the devil:

> Then he broght him to Ierusalem, and set him on a pinacle of the Temple, and said vnto him, If thou be the Sonne of God, cast thy self downe from hence, For it is written, [Ps. 91.18] That he wil giue his Angels charge ouer thee to kepe thee: And with *their* hands they shal lift thee vp, lest at anie time thou shuldest dash thy fote against a stone.[37]

Jesus responds with his own citation to an even older portion of the Old Testament: "And Iesus answered, and said vnto him, It is said, [Deuter. 6.16] Thou shalt not tempt the Lord thy God" (Lk. 4.9–12)." But the reader of the Geneva Bible cannot necessarily find reassurance in the readiness of Christ's response, for its superlative authority is clearly vested in his divinity, not in the common Scriptural source to which both God and devil refer. Were Redcrosse to respond with sufficient citational authority,[38] it could only be by the grace of God, who alone can out-cite the devil. Unassured of that grace (as the knight undoubtedly is until Una's intervention), to contradict Despair by citing Scripture is tantamount to taking up the devil's ultimate temptation on our own illusory authority.

Another way to put all this is that it does not matter how or with what text Redcrosse responds; his words prove—and without grace will always prove—as useless here as his sword has already fared against Orgoglio. Although between the cave of Error and the cave of Despair Redcrosse has wandered all over Faerieland, he has made exactly no progress, yet all the while has compounded his original sin. Essentially, the hero has *returned* to his point of errant departure, only to find it occupied by a more dangerous foe, an Error who vomits only one book—the only one, including the *Faerie Queene*, worth reading. Spenser moreover inserts Despair's lethal reading of the text between the two Bibles of Book I—Redcrosse's gilded Bible and Fidelia's bloody one—figuring forth the act of reading the Word as the shedding of blood, and not Christ's blood.

Worse than this, the demon offers himself as the supplementary agent through whom the fallen reader can recognize the coherence of the fully sufficient text; he uses New Testament and Old Testament allusions alike to supplement the Law with death, instead of completing it with grace. He substitutes himself, in other words, for Christ, after ventriloquizing only God's curse and not Christ's promise. Thus, when he offers Redcrosse "eternal rest, and happie ease," he offers the first half of Christ's own formulation in the Gospel of Matthew: "Come vnto me, all ye that are wearie & laden, and I wil ease you" (Mt. 11:28). What he does not offer is the following verse, the qualification and completion of the saving arc of the Gospel's argument: "Take my yoke on you, and learne of me, that I am meke and lowlie in heart: & ye shal finde rest vnto your soules" (Mt. 11:29). Buried beneath the demon's plenteous rhetoric is the nullification of the Gospel's promise by his careful elision of the final three words of the verse. Again, when Despair asks rhetorically, "Is not his lawe, let euery sinner die . . . ?", he acts the part of the Apostle, ventriloquizing Paul, who declared to the Romans that "the wages of sinne is death . . . " (Rom. 6:23), but he refuses to finish Paul's sentence, which continues "but the gifte of God *is* eternal life, through Iesus Christ our Lord." Indeed, so much of Despair's general argument depends upon the first half of another memorable line from Paul's Epistle to the Romans—"Moreouer the Law entred thereupon that the offence shulde abunde . . . " (Rom. 5:20)—that we might easily be tempted to neglect the spiritual work of finishing that thought with Paul's own, "neuertheles, where sinne abunded, *there* grace abunded muche more" (Rom. 5:21).[39]

So we may work by glossing to answer Despair, but our work can never refute him, for by answering his fragments of the Bible with our own fragments of the Bible, we merely parrot his rhetoric and re-enact his sin. However much the Christian reads, writes, or re-members the letter, the spirit remains God's free gift. Paul himself became an authority on grace only by that same grace (Rom. 1:5); without its inspiration on the road to Damascus, there would have been only despair—only Saul, persecutor of Christians, named for the Old Testament's most notorious suicide.

III. DESPAIR AS SPIRITUAL HEALTH

We must never forget that despair is a sin—the worst of them all—and Spenser's Despair is the greatest villain of the whole poem,[40] but however terrible his visitation, at least for the Elect his presence can nonetheless become a sign of spiritual health. Before permitting Una to intervene with her superlatively allusive grace, it is worth considering the potentially salutary nature of Despair's divisive referentiality. By leading Redcrosse into Despair's cave, Spenser is not simply condemning his tormented knight to another spiritless dungeon like that of Orgoglio, but is rather illuminating allegorically the darkest and most difficult mile of the Christian's path toward salvation. Martin Luther, after all, referred continually to his own despair and rendered it paradigmatic; Susan Snyder writes:

> Luther found the experience of despair so necessary a part of holiness that he extended it to Christ himself. According to traditional Catholic dogma, Christ's sufferings did not affect the higher powers of his soul. But Luther declares that Christ suffered in every sense as a man, not in show only but in reality, and furthermore his spiritual torments were greater and more terrible than his fleshly ones.[41]

Despair, then, even for the elect, could constitute an imitation of Christ, but Luther also emphasizes the sin's proximity to grace; referring to the supposed "injustice" of predestination, Luther confesses: "I myself have been offended at it more than once, even unto the deepest abyss of despair, so far that I wished I had never been made a man. That was before I knew how healthgiving that despair was and how near it was to grace."[42] Instead of explaining away Despair as some anomalous, phantom image of Redcrosse's depression or that of his biographer, we are better served to locate him at the center of the Protestant paradigm of a diachronic approach to the Word's sufficiency, precariously located between unlimited humility and absolute grace.[43]

The second of the Elizabethan homilies represents this balance rhetorically, demonstrating that the continental Reformation's view of despair—as potentially beneficial and in any case as contiguous with the doctrine of grace—had long since entered England and been disseminated. The pastor declares:

Thus we haue heard how euill we be of our selues, how of our
selues, and by our selues, we haue no goodnes, helpe nor saluation, but contrariwise, sinne, damnation, and death euerlasting:
which if we deeply weigh and consider, we shall the better
vnderstand the great mercie of GOD, and how our saluation
commeth onely by Christ.[44]

Here the impeccably balanced, elemental construct of Pauline Christianity—itself a revision of the Old Testament's parallelistic verse—is
evident in microcosm, as a colon marks the preacher's *caesura* between
"sinne, damnation, and death euerlasting" one moment and "the
great mercie of GOD" the next. This elemental paradigm thereupon
reproduces itself and extends outward, for following this composite
and complete sentence comes a litany of pure indictments of human
worthlessness and irredeemable sinfulness, which itself is followed by
repeated assurances of God's unadulturated perfection. The homily
ends with the guarantee of a cheerier sermon the next week:

Hitherto haue we heard what we are of our selues: very sinfull,
wretched, and damnable. . . . Again, we haue heard the tender
kindnesse and great mercy of GOD the Father towards vs. . . .
Now, how these exceeding great mercies of GOD, set abroad
in Christ Iesu for vs, be obtayned, and how we be deliuered
from the captiuity of sinne, death, and hell, it shall more at
large (with GODS helpe) bee declared in the next Sermon. In
the meane season, yea, and at all times let vs learne to know
our selues, our frailty and weakenesse, without any craking or
boasting of our owne good deedes and merits. . . , as GOD
himselfe sayth by the Prophet Osee, O Israel, thy destruction
commeth of thy selfe, but in me only is thy helpe and comfort.[45]

It is characteristic of this text, at every discursive level, to divide
the complete theological arc—of human imperfection succeeded by
divine perfection—into halves, according to which the second term's
wholeness cancels the first term's emptiness.

This rhetorical strategy is further manifested in the overall order of
the homilies, by the complementarity between this dark, accusatory
sermon and the strident gratitude of its successor, *A Sermon of the
Saluation of Mankind, by only Christ our Savior, from sin and death euerlasting.*[46] Thanks to the periodic adumbrations of grace throughout the

first, miserable sermon, the penitent Christian can presumably avoid despair during the "meane season" of self-accusation, via the proleptic reproduction of the whole paradigm. There is no danger of perdition, so long as the frail balance—epitomized in the easily-remembered line from Hosea—is maintained. Next week's sermon will tip the scales decidedly in favor of redemption through Christ's agency, the New Testament loading the shinier pan of Hosea's balance with the inestimable weight of grace. The subsequent, positive sermon works to counteract any overemphasis on the harsh truths brought to the listener's attention by the earlier harangue, thereby preventing any contradiction between the cogency of Christian humility on the one hand and God's grace through the agency of Christ on the other. For in that contradiction—the elevation of humility over grace—is the birth of that pride which Protestants understood as despair. Failure to heed the second sermon—that is, failure to complete the paradigm—leaves the penitent sinner subject to the deadliest sin of all.[47]

Spenser's Despair parodies the homiletic voice,[48] successfully dismantling the intricate proportionality of the second and third homilies; too much of the latter sermon's recuperative work is left for the cleaning ladies of the House of Holinesse, whom we will meet the next time we open the book to read the poem, only after a "meane season" of contemplating the Despair episode. But Book I of the *Faerie Queene* is an allegory meant to reflect the lifelong experience of the Protestant pilgrim, not a homily designed to admonish churchgoing subjects into contemplative obedience, and indeed, as rigorous allegory, Spenser's Despair episode parodies the ease of the homilist's confident about-face from damnation to salvation. Despair may "conceptually oscillate between irremediable sin and moral awareness," as Escobedo notes,[49] but for the knight or reader in despair, the diabolical assurance of eternal damnation cannot appear as the temporally limited movement of half an oscillation. Far beyond a systematically premeditated week's-worth of melancholy, for Spenser, as for Luther, the reality of the righteous man's pilgrimage follows a descent into an atemporal kind of humility that the Christian must identify with despair, upon which pivot only grace may begin to act. Hence, Escobedo rightly emphasizes the absence of a reassuring sequentiality in the state of despair, even after the House of Holinesse, and especially after the Mount of Contemplation, with its recognizably short-sighted old denizen:

Redcrosse's continued despair does not represent only a necessary phase in a sequence whose conclusion will determine that

despair's meaning, but also signals the extent to which Redcrosse remains unable to find an appropriate relation to a world
that he recognizes as sinful but from which he cannot simply
depart.[50]

Despair, then, may well be salutary, but not in any way recognizable
to the Christian presently in despair, and for all that, the sin might
simply be a sign of reprobation.

IV. SUFFICIENT GRACE

A century after Spenser, in *Grace Abounding to the Chief of Sinners*,
John Bunyan recalls the advent of grace precisely as the Lord's completion of a scriptural passage that, while still incomplete in his fallen
memory, spelled only despair:

> But one morning when I was again at prayer and trembling
> under the fear of this, that no word of God could help me, that
> piece of a sentence darted in upon me, *My grace is sufficient.* [2
> Cor. 12:9] . . .
>   Therefore I still did pray to God, that he would come in
> with this Scripture more fully on my heart, to wit, that he
> would help me to apply the whole sentence, for as yet I could
> not . . . *My grace is sufficient* . . . yet, because *for thee* was left out,
> I was not contented, but prayed to God for that also: Wherefore,
> one day as I was in a Meeting of Gods People, full of sadness
> and terrour, for my fears again were strong upon me . . . these
> words did with great power suddainly break in upon me, *My
> grace is sufficient for thee, my grace is sufficient for thee, my grace is
> sufficient for thee*; three times together.[51]

However anachronistic, this rich passage from Bunyan's conversion
narrative can help identify Una's role in the scene, for if Spenser's
Despair embodies the incomplete Word, then grace, accessible only
through faith, will take the form of the completion of Scripture, not
by the efforts of any fallen interpreter, but through Christ and his
True Church. Thus, Una's redemptive argument at the end of the
Despair episode functions not merely by reminding Redcrosse of

hope and grace in general, but by offering coherent and complete scriptural citations to supercede the demon's incomplete and insufficient ones. Her speech is notably brief, lasting only a stanza and a half to Despair's eighty-five lines of rhetoric, but its upshot, the penultimate stanza of the canto, is dense with authentic scriptural allusions uncorrupted by substantive elision. A. C. Hamilton's gloss identifies in this stanza no fewer than eight specific New Testament echoes—significantly, six of them Pauline—including "Where iustice growes, there grows eke greter grace" (I.ix.53.6 and n.), a deft paraphrase of Rom. 5.20, echoed earlier by Despair but left unfinished.[52] The brevity of Una's rebuttal has often troubled me, but from this perspective anyway, the proportions are apt enough, make more sense than the precarious balance of the Articles or the Homilies. After all, less than an ounce of God's grace can counterbalance a lifetime of human sinfulness, and this is best represented, almost onomatopoeically, as brevity, or as Bunyan briefly puts it, "My grace is sufficient for thee." But the speech's brevity also reflects the urgency of grace—its immediacy given the fallen condition—implying that this is all Una has time to say, as well as all she needs to say.[53]

Yet Spenser's Despair episode is more than the poetic expression of a theological paradox; it is also an allegorical tour de force. For Spenser—for his Protestant saint—this is how grace functions: briefly and decisively as the perfection of the fully sufficient Word; first a lifetime of sin, and then, for the elect, an instant of grace, presented to us by one outside ourselves, accessing us through our faith. Our despair is our own, but grace is God's alone to give. Thus, this greatest of Book I's allegories does not look like an allegory at all, looks nothing like the slow-moving denizens of the House of Holinesse, nothing like Zeal, Faith, Hope, Charity, Contemplation, Patience, seven beadmen, and so on. Indeed, how could grace ever have walked and talked like a human being? Facing that rhetorical question, Spenser refused to relegate the divine function to a place in the same mimetic category as the entirely fallen state of despair; God's grace defies anthropomorphic representation. Instead, the allegory of grace in Redcrosse's story is sudden and purely textual: God's perfection of the Word left incomplete by our own divisive and insufficient reading of the coherent and wholly sufficient Scripture.

Even this perfect moment of grace may not finally be sufficient, for despair—theological or psychological—is partly defined by the dependability of its own recurrence. Satan tempted Christ not once but three times in the wilderness, and even then, "when the deuil had ended all the tentacion, he departed from him for a litle season"

(Lk. 4:13).[54] That "litle season" could be the months that the church-
goer enjoys between hearing "A Sermon of the Saluation of Mankinde" and yet another rendition of "A Sermon of the Miserie of
All Mankinde," or it could be the turning of any given page in
Bunyan's conversion narrative,[55] but either way we can depend upon
Despair to return in new forms, citing new passages from Scripture.
He will haunt Redcrosse even in the House of Holinesse, where
the hero longs "to end his wretched dayes" (I.x.21.8),[56] and he will
challenge Guyon from the outset of his quest, through Amavia's
suicide. He will return as dragon, witch, and enchanter, and six years
later he will drive justice from Ireland, and elude courtesy in order
to end the poem itself with "venemous despite" (VI.xii.41.2).

But it is not finally necessary to scan the entire *Faerie Queene* for
instances of the devil's return in various guises, for Spenser's intricate
allegory of Despair's cave already provides for this eventuality in its
final stanza:

> So vp he [Redcrosse] rose, and thence amounted streight.
> Which when the carle beheld, and saw his guest
> Would safe depart, for all his subtill sleight,
> He chose an halter from among the rest,
> And with it hong him selfe, vnbid vnblest.
> But death he could not worke himselfe thereby;
> For thousand times he so him selfe had drest,
> Yet nathelesse it could not doe him die,
> Till he should die his last, that is eternally.
>
> (I.ix.54)

The initial irony here—that the tempter tempts himself to suicide—appears sufficient, as the poet not only seems to impose the
justice Redcrosse failed to effect, but to avenge his humiliated hero
as well. The stanza's first eight lines, however, record yet another
failure to end Despair's life; that Despair himself has no more agency
in this project than Redcrosse only testifies to his invincibility in the
fallen world. The alexandrine, on the other hand, does announce the
tempter's "last" death, permitting stanza and canto to close with
certain victory. Yet that satisfaction will come only at the end of
time, and the oblique quality of Spenser's final line—its lack of specificity, the absence of Christ as the expected agent, the modal verb
"should"—registers the absolute distance of the event: whenever it
will come, by whomever it must be, it is not now, nor thanks to
any of us.

There is a further irony, then, in Spenser's choice to remain in the cave once his hero has departed, to linger over Despair's suicide attempt, while knowing that "it could not doe him die, / Till he should die his last, that is eternally." Because the only agency is that of the unmentioned Christ—because Despair will never die within a time-bound allegory, but only at the end of time and allegories—there is an uncomfortable continuity between Redcrosse's attempt to punish Despair, Despair's attempt to destroy himself, and the poet's attempts to portray both acts of futility. The demon's compulsive reiteration of suicide attempts, without any capacity to complete the task, has its corollary in Spenser's choice to represent repeated encounters with him—first Trevisan/Terwin's, then Redcrosse's, then his own (or at least his narrator's). Unlike Orgoglio, who deflates with finality, Despair is most akin to Error, insofar as both continue to function within the allegory, even as the narrator leaves their bodies behind. But Despair is also the deepest, most recalcitrant body of Error, who was after all beheaded (for what her head was worth); nobody in or around the poem—not the knights, not even Una, nor Despair himself, certainly not the reader—is capable of killing this creature. Here even the poet seems to undergo the same temptation to try.

What are we to make of his effort? It would be too much to claim, from our experience of the poem's fictions, that Spenser here verifies his own despair by condemning his narrator to eight more lines of the villain's longevity. It remains possible, nonetheless, that Spenser is confessing that he *might* be in despair, that we cannot finally trust a poet so aware of his own potential faithlessness. Only a few allegories, like Una, are immune to this one temptation, whereas the poet, like everyone else, must simply pray for grace. In the dark cave, Redcrosse was blessed, through Una's words and deeds, with a full stanza of that light, but we must wait for our own experience of grace, whenever we are tempted. At the beginning of the next canto, in the daylight outside the cave, the poet teaches his hard lesson—that we can learn nothing from Despair save faith alone—one last time, but with a new clarity:

What man is he, that boasts of fleshly might,
And vain assurance of mortality,
Which all so soone, as it doth come to fight,
Against spirituall foes, yeelds by and by,
Or from the field most cowardly doth fly?
Ne let the man ascribe it to his skill,

That thorough grace hath gained victory.
If any strength we haue, it is to ill,
But all the good is Gods, both power and eke will.

(I.x.1)

Much of the stanza—in particular the damning rhetorical question—reminds us of the rhetoric of Despair; that Spenser is able to
write its sufficient final line at all is his testimony to God's grace.

Southern Methodist University

Notes

1.   A much earlier version of this paper was presented at the 2005 Renaissance
Society of America's conference in San Francisco. I am grateful for the advice and
support of Anne Prescott, Bill Oram, Tom Roche, James Nohrnberg, Oliver Arnold,
Jeff Dolven, Abby Heald, J. K. Barret, David Urban, Ken Moss, and the anonymous
readers of *Spenser Studies*.
2.   Edmund Spenser, *The Faerie Queene*, I.ix.35.6–7. All Spenser citations are from
the Longman edition: *The Faerie Queene*, ed. A. C. Hamilton et al. (Harlow, New
York: Pearson Education, 2001), and hereafter will be provided parenthetically.
3.   Richard Mallette, *Spenser and the Discourses of Reformation England* (Lincoln:
University of Nebraska Press, 1997), 40.
4.   Harold Skulsky, "Spenser's Despair Episode and the Theology of Doubt,"
Modern Philology 78.3 (February 1981): 237. Skulsky compares the views of an array
of early modern authorities—including Calvin, Chemnitz, and Hooker—on the
problem of *fiducia*, arguing that "the result of insisting on assurance was to create a
scandal for believers by making a duty out of an impossibility" (235). For Skulsky,
Spenser has designed his allegory to defeat all compromise on even the most faithful
Christian's assurance of Election. Whereas Calvin, for example, compares the self-
doubt of the Elect—nearing or approximating despair—to the desperate situation
of a prisoner in a dungeon only illuminated by a glimmer of light "from a slit,"
Spenser has previously condemned Redcrosse to Orgoglio's utterly lightless dungeon.
In the terms of Calvin's metaphor, then, Redcrosse has already despaired—already
sinned irredeemably against the Holy Spirit—*before* he is tempted by Despair himself.
The competing Reformation authorities Skulsky cites are no less eloquent or insightful than Calvin on the issue of *fiducia*, but their compromises are no more
sufficient as solutions to the epistemological glitch at the heart of this indispensable doctrine.
5.   Andrew Escobedo, "Despair and the Proportion of the Self," *Spenser Studies*
17 (2003): 77.
6.   "Proportion," 80. Escobedo further notes that "Spenser uses despair as a recurring sign of the slippage within a system trying to coordinate divine wrath and divine

grace" (78), before extending his argument revealingly to the poet's treatment of Malbecco and Contemplation, though these latter analyses actually leave him little opportunity to discuss Spenser's Despair episode itself in much detail. In keeping with the paradigm of despair/grace, however, Escobedo's article is the first of a pair: Beth Quitslund's "Despair and the Composition of the Self" (*Spenser Studies* 17 [2003]: 91–106) balances Escobedo's appropriately disheartening reading with a highly original study of how "writers operating within a generally Calvinist frame-work took advantage of medical rhetoric and the ambiguous relationship between physical and spiritual concerns to understand and enable their own interventions in what was, strictly speaking, a preordained transaction between God and the individual soul" (94). The thetic convolutions here are the apt critical reflection of a confused and overcompensatory metaphorical strategy on the parts of Reformed writers trying to disentangle the fundamental paradoxes of their own theology. Accordingly, Quitslund's article reads like the House of Holinesse after the Cave of Despair—that is, it cannot settle nearly as much as its predecessor unsettled. These linked articles are perhaps most revealing when read in reverse order.

7.   Søren Kierkegaard, *The Sickness unto Death: A Christian Psychological Exposition for Upbuilding and Awakening*, trans. Howard V. Hong and Edna H. Hong (Princeton: Princeton University Press, 1980), 26.

8.   In this regard, Error is the prototype of Despair, as she is the original in various senses for all of Book I's sins and failures. But again there is the problem of Una's delay; in Error's den, she intervened promptly and in a loud voice, while in Despair's cave she remains silent and inactive until the penultimate stanza.

9.   Our proximity to the hero, of course, is never quite identity. We do enter the cave with Redcrosse, so far as a reader can follow any fictional character; we do see Despair, to the extent that any reader can see a poetic conceit; and we too may be tempted by Despair's words, or have been before, or will be again. Each such temptation nonetheless takes place in stifling solitude. Redcrosse's despairing thoughts are his own, even if his experience is common and his exemplary actions can be observed by all. I do not want to ignore the basic problem of the pilgrimage allegory: that any easy identification of the reader's experience with that of the hero can be as illusory as the apparent identifications between characters within the narrative itself (that red cross on Archimago's armor, for example). But over-literal identification with the allegorical hero has never been much of a problem for Spenser's critics (nobody reads this poem in armor). The problem has rather been the opposite fallacy: the maintenance of an exaggerated critical distance from the allegorical hero's experience. On these questions, and at the risk of comparing Spenser too closely to Bunyan as an allegorist, see Stanley Fish's "Progress in *The Pilgrim's Progress*," in *Self-Consuming Artifacts* (Berkeley: University of California Press, 1972), 224–64.

10.   Ernest Sirluck, "A Note on the Rhetoric of Spenser's 'Despair,'" *Modern Philology* 47.1 (August 1949): 8–11. Katherine Koller makes a similar claim in "Art, Rhetoric, and Holy Dying in the *Faerie Queene* with Special Reference to the Despair Canto" (*Studies in Philology* 61 [1964]: 128–39): "The sixteenth century reader would have recognized Red Cross's situation, and known exactly what he should have done when confronted by Despair" (134).

11. See Tamara A. Goeglein, "Utterances of the Protestant Soul in the *Faerie Queene*: The Allegory of Holiness and the Humanist Discourse of Reason" (*Criticism* 36.1 [Winter 1994]: 1–10) for an excellent recent analysis of Despair's *enthymeme*, revisiting Sirluck's conclusions.

12. James Nohrnberg, *The Analogy of 'The Faerie Queene'* (Princeton: Princeton University Press, 1976) calls Despair "a manipulator of words unmatched anywhere else in the poem" (152). See Michael F. N. Dixon, *The Polliticke Courtier* (Montreal: McGill-Queen's University Press, 1996), 37–42, for a detailed technical account of the episode's rhetorical significance. Dixon's treatment complements Skulsky's fine article in *The Spenser Encyclopedia*, ed. A. C. Hamilton et al. (Toronto: University of Toronto Press, 1990), 213–14, which identifies, categorizes, and close-reads many of Despair's rhetorical tactics. See also Goeglein, "Utterances," 1–4. With regard to outside texts, see Ann E. Imbrie, " 'Playing Legerdemaine with the Scripture': Parodic Sermons in *The Faerie Queene* (*ELR* 17.2 [Spring 1987]: 142–55), especially 146–50, and Richard Mallette, *Spenser and the Discourses of Reformation England* (Lincoln: University of Nebraska Press, 1997), 37–41 on the importance of sermon manuals to Spenser's Despair episode. Both treatments are excellent and persuasive, and I do not intend here to deny the relevance of the manuals to Book I, but I would argue that such pastoral guides function in this canto more as Despair's raw material than as Redcrosse's way out. See also Samuel R. Kessler, "An Analogue for Spenser's Despair Episode: Perkins's 'Dialogue . . . betweene Sathan and the Christian," *Notes and Queries* 47.245.1 (March 2000): 31–34. Nohrnberg (*Analogy*, 153) proposes Thomas Becon's *The Christian Knight* as an analogue. Koller provides a helpful corrective to critical overemphasis on these analogues as aids to refutation: "A sixteenth-century audience would appreciate not only Despair's skill as an orator but also his effective use of the very material which the Church used to teach a man not to fear death" ("Holy Dying," 137). Patrick Cullen, *Infernal Triad: The Flesh, the World, and the Devil in Spenser and Milton* (Princeton: Princeton University Press, 1974) deftly analyzes several analogues without under-reading Spenser: "Spenser employs the conventions of the pilgrimage genre to expose his hero's and indirectly our own oversimplification of both human nature and the rigors of Christian life" (57–58).

13. Judith H. Anderson, "What I Really Teach When I'm Teaching Spenser," *Pedagogy* 3.2 (Spring 2003): 177–83, at 182. Anderson's article, of course, is not directly intended as criticism, and I agree wholeheartedly with her approach to teaching Spenser via Book I and Despair's cave, so long as students are also taught that the Despair episode may well demonstrate the danger to Spenser's reader of an over-reliance on reading itself. Like Escobedo, Anderson also testifies to the usefulness of teaching excerpts of Kierkegaard's *Sickness unto Death* alongside Spenser's text.

14. So, for example, Goeglein argues that "the semantics of despair must first be expurgated from the godly idiom" before the reader can approach the Mount of Contemplation ("Utterances," 3). But as I argue in this essay, the "expurgation" might not be for the fallen knight (nor the reader, nor the poet) to perform, and in any case, Despair's arguments are themselves couched in the "godly idiom."

15. There are a great many studies of Spenser's religious convictions as they are allegorized in his poetry. For a recent survey with extensive, useful commentary, see

Anne Lake Prescott, "Complicating the Allegory: Spenser and Religion in Recent Scholarship," *Renaissance and Reformation* 25.4 (2001): 9–23. Prescott writes, "What distinguishes a number of recent books from many earlier studies [of Spenser's religiosity] is both an increased sense of Spenser's own slipperiness . . . and a sharper awareness of the Reformation's dynamic instability" (11).

16. Church of England, *Thirty-Nine Articles* (London, 1590), A2[ʳ].

17. *Articles*, A3[ʳ].

18. *Articles*, A3[ᵛ].

19. Spenser would reverse the paradigm he parodies here in his *Amoretti* (1594).

20. Thomas P. Roche discusses the psychological claustrophobia of the episode in "The Menace of Despair and Arthur's Vision, *Faerie Queene* I.9," *Spenser Studies* 4 (1983): 71–92: "It is . . . as if the dialogue between Redcross and Despair were taking place only in Redcross's mind" (72).

21. Thus Escobedo rereads Spenser's villain through Kierkegaard's contention that "despair arises out of a misrelation between ourselves and the world" ("Proportion," 81), noting that "Despair manifests itself on the one hand as a *reduction* of self to world—what Kierkegaard calls an excessive 'finitude'—wherein we identify ourselves only with the material things before us and with an [*sic*] self-defeating understanding of the ways of the world. Conversely, despair may emerge as an *abstraction* of self from world—what Kierkegaard calls excessive 'infinitude'—wherein the 'fantastic' power of the imagination overlooks the necessary limitations on human life" (81–82). I would add that Spenser's Despair episode, by provoking our easy condemnation of Redcrosse's *reductive* despair, implies our own potential for *abstracted* despair, because we tend to forget that Redcrosse's human limitations are meant to reflect precisely our own.

22. Koller also draws the link between the rhetoric Despair employs against the Petrarchans and that which he uses against Redcrosse: "Despair's argument, subtly insinuated in their [Terwin and Trevisan's] unhappy minds, had removed their hope and offered death as an escape from present misery. This is the precise method of the devil which the religious writers describe" ("Holy Dying," 134).

23. Nohrnberg, *Analogy*, 152.

24. Nohrnberg, *Analogy*, 153.

25. On contemporary controversies over the Geneva annotations, see Maurice S. Betteridge, "The Bitter Notes: The Geneva Bible and its Annotations," *Sixteenth Century Journal* 14.1 (Spring 1983): 41–62, citing Archbishop Matthew Parker's admonishment to the translators of the officially sanctioned Bishop's Bible of 1568: "Item: to make no bitter notis uppon any text, or yet to set downe any determinacion in places of controversie." Betteridge emphasizes that "no section of the book can be treated in isolation. Nor can this Bible be separated from the books and supplements which were bound in with it" (44); he further notes that, while the Old Testament notes remain unchanged throughout the various editions, the New Testament notes fluctuate depending on the relative puritanical radicalism of each edition.

26. Citing Article XII, Skulsky ("Theology of Doubt," 230) identifies a related difficulty: "The authors of the Thirty-nine Articles . . . assure their flock that by good works 'a lively Faith may be as evidently known as a tree discerned by its

fruit,' but the indispensable doctrine of solifidianism requires the harsher view, stated nearly in the same breath, that such works 'cannot take away our sins, and endure the severity of God's judgment.' " As part of the English Protestant's supplemental theological apparatus, the Articles are just as vulnerable to Despair's divisive exploitation as any other doctrinal text, if not moreso, given their paradoxical and self-fragmenting rhetorical strategies. For a more traditional and positive account of Spenser's engagement with the Articles' salient theological claims, see Virgil Whitaker, "The Theological Structure of *The Faerie Queene*, Book I," *ELH* 19 (1952): 151–64.

27.   Nohrnberg, *Analogy*, 153.

28.   All biblical references are to *The Geneva Bible: A Facsimile of the 1560 Edition* (Madison: University of Wisconsin Press, 1969), and will be given parenthetically with the standard abbreviations or, if cited in the margins of the Geneva edition, in brackets with its own abbreviations. Carol V. Kaske demonstrates why the glosses of the Berry facsimile remain "insufficient for Spenser studies . . . because they do not include many [glosses] . . . added by Tomson in his revision of 1576" ("Bible," *Spenser Encyclopedia*, ed. A. C. Hamilton et al. [Toronto: University of Toronto Press, 1990], 90). Although I have also consulted a 1587 edition, which includes very different glosses, I have continued to use the Berry, not only for convenience, but also because so far as I know there is no clear indication that Spenser used a later and not an earlier edition of the Geneva Bible. Pending a properly synoptic edition of the Geneva glosses, the issue will continue to vex Spenser scholars.

29.   The Church of England, however, required the Bishop's Bible in this period; reconciling the Geneva editions with officially sanctioned texts was always a problem. See Betteridge, "Bitter Notes," *passim*.

30.   Article XX B2[ᵛ].

31.   Patrick Collinson, "The Coherence of the Text: How It Hangeth Together: The Bible in Reformation England," in *The Bible, the Reformation and the Church*, ed. W. P. Stephens (Sheffield: Sheffield Academic Press, 1995), 91.

32.   The Longman editors identify these lines as part of Redcrosse's argument (see I.ix.41.8–9n. and I.ix.42n.), but the speech tag at 41.7 indicates the change in speaker.

33.   Collinson, "Coherence," 85.

34.   Mallette (*Discourses*, 37–41) focuses on Despair as a corrupt preacher and false prophet who "suppresses half the text." In a variation on Sirluck's *enthymeme*, Mallette writes, "Despaire's performance . . . parodies sermons of the age not so much by distorting them (he actually mirrors them—or elements of them—quite accurately) as by simply omitting what normally follows fulminations against sin, namely assurance of salvation for the righteous" (38–39). I would also emphasize the episode's sense of solitude and claustrophobia; Despair's "chiding" sermon might be less an allegory for actual corrupt preaching from "Roman Catholic forces threatening to undo the godly work of the English church" (41) than an exposition of how even (or especially) one of the faithful of that church might listen himself into despair, might mishear or misremember the preaching of the Reformation Word, all the way to Hell.

35.   The Geneva editors identify rhetoric with the diabolical; see for example the sidenote to Satan's offer of temporal power to Christ at Lk. 4:6: "*By this worde,*

power, are the kingdomes themselues meant, which haue the power: and so it is spoken by the figure Metonymie."

36.   Thomas A. Dughi cites Luther: "[A]lthough it is good to preach and write about penitence, confession, and satisfaction, our teaching is unquestionably deceitful and diabolical if we stop with that and do not go on to teach about faith" ("Redcrosse's 'Springing Well' of Scriptural Faith," *SEL* 37.1 [Winter 1997]: 27).

37.   Luke makes this temptation the last of Christ's three temptations in the wilderness, though Matthew places it second. Nohrnberg (*Analogy*, 152) calls Despair's words "a little like Satan tempting Christ to throw himself from the temple."

38.   Redcrosse does not cite Scripture, however; his insufficient response to Despair alludes instead to Pagan authority—primarily to Cicero's *Tusculan Disputations*—and I do not wish to underestimate our hero's theological stupidity. Skulsky ("Theology of Doubt," 240) notes that, in his doubting of Una, the knight "has not acted on the best available evidence, inherently tentative as that best would have been. Moreover, he has not responded correctly to the circumstances *even as he interprets them.*" On the other hand, as Sirluck ("Rhetoric," 9) and Koller ("Holy Dying," 138) note, Redcrosse's Ciceronian reference is not so much unchristian as inadequate as a refutation. That conclusion, of course, does not suggest the availability of a better refutation according to better citation, and in general Redcrosse's exemplary unreadiness to answer Despair does not affirm by contrast the reader's citational aptitude; on the contrary, his failure admonishes us not to rely on our own resources when afflicted with similar spiritual doubt.

39.   Cullen (*Infernal Triad*, 59–61) identifies an impressive array of echoes of the Epistle to the Romans in Despair's speech, each in effect echoing only the first half of a Pauline sentence.

40.   Dixon (*Polliticke Courtier*, 43) offers a similar view in specifically rhetorical terms.

41.   Susan Snyder, "The Left Hand of God: Despair in the Medieval and Renaissance Tradition," *Studies in the Renaissance* 12 (1965): 27. Luther does, however, differentiate between salutary and mortally sinful despair (see Skulsky, "Despair," 1990, 214) and between melancholy and despair (see Douglas Trevor, "Sadness in *The Faerie Queene*," in *Reading the Early Modern Passions*, ed. Gail Kern Paster et al. [Philadelphia: University of Pennsylvania Press, 2004], 250–51).

42.   Martin Luther, "The Bondage of the Will," in *Discourse on Free Will by Erasmus and Luther*, trans. Ernst F. Winter (New York: Continuum, 2002), 131.

43.   See Dughi, "Springing Well," 27.

44.   Thomas Cranmer, "A Sermon of the Miserie of All Mankinde, and of his Condemnation to Death Euerlasting, by his own Sinne," *Certaine Sermons Appointed by the Queenes Maiestie* (London, 1587), B4[ʳ]. Skulsky ("Despair," 1990, 214) cites from elsewhere in this sermon, to corroborate Spenser's skeptical view of salvific assurance.

45.   Cranmer, "Miserie," B5[ʳ⁻ᵛ].

46.   Cranmer, *Certaine Sermons*, B6[ʳ]. John N. Wall, Jr. notes that "the clergy were instructed to read [the Homilies] 'in suche ordre as they stande in the boke' " ("The English Reformation and the Recovery of Christian Community in Spenser's *The Faerie Queene*," *Studies in Philology* 80.2 [Spring 1983]: 153). The 1559 Act of Uniformity, moreover, required all Elizabethan subjects to attend church each Sunday or

suffer a fine. The average congregation would therefore hear both sermons in the proper order. My thanks to Anne Prescott for reminding me of this last point.

47.   Dughi writes: "The basic rhetorical structure of the Bible as Luther understands it . . . teaches the doctrine of justification by faith alone by producing in the reader first the experience of his own innate corruption, then the joyful relief aroused by the promise of God's freely given grace ("Springing Well," 24–25).

48.   See Mallette (*Discourses*, 40): "[Despair's] speech is larded with homiletic idiom. . . . A number of his sentences would be quite at home in *The Book of Homilies*. . . . "

49.   Escobedo, "Proportion," 77.

50.   Escobedo, "Proportion," 87.

51.   John Bunyan, *Grace Abounding to the Chief of Sinners*, ed. Roger Sharrock (Oxford: Clarendon Press, 1962), ¶ 204, 206.

52.   See also Mallette (*Discourses*, 41) on Una as superlative homilist: "In one stanza [I.ix.53] . . . she delivers all five major types of homily, as classified by the sermon manuals."

53.   See Dixon, *Polliticke Courtier*, 42.

54.   The 1560 Geneva gloss reads, "It is not ynough, twise or thrise to resist Satan: for he neuer ceaseth to tempt: or if he relent a litle, it is to the end, that he maye renewe his force & assaile vs more sharply" (Lk. 4:13, n.f).

55.   Bunyan's account of the alternation of despair and grace is paradigmatic and elemental: "I have continued with much content through grace, but have met with many turnings and goings upon my heart both from the Lord, Satan, and my own corruptions . . . " (*Grace Abounding*, ¶ 320).

56.   See Skulsky, "Theology of Doubt," 233–34. Trevor ("Sadness," 242) does not adequately defend his claim that "after his treatment in the House of Holiness, Redcrosse is no longer vulnerable to the kind of melancholy embodied by Despair."

JUDITH H. ANDERSON

Flowers and Boars: Surmounting Sexual Binarism in Spenser's Garden of Adonis

Recent experiences teaching Spenser's Book III inform my skepticism regarding binaristic assumptions about sex and gender in the Garden of Adonis. The Garden Mount is ambiguously, or doubly, sexed. This doubleness is not that of the hermaphrodite or the androgyne, of visual, humanized forms belonging to the fixity of statues and to the landscape of quest beyond the Garden gates. The Garden is preeminently symbolic and mythic, rather than realistically anatomical or human in the quotidian sense, and it further resists full or consistent visualization for good reason. Like other features of the Garden, the flowers of poetic metamorphosis, of death and life and mutability and perpetuity, that grow in the Garden signal its earthly rather than heavenly nature. At the same time, however, the distance of the Garden from everyday life is vital to its regenerative vision. The coincidence of art with nature participates in the Garden's depiction of conjunctive generations that at once contain and surmount doubleness and difference. The punning senses of *contain* and *generations* (physical, cultural, and historical) begin to capture the simultaneities and complexities of this mythic place. The boar encaved beneath its Mount is at once a bisexual figure and a culminating emblem of *containment* in every sense of this fertile word. An attribute at once of Venus and Adonis, the boar conclusively depicts their ambisexuality.

*M*Y STORY STARTS WITH TWO recent classroom experiences: the first concerns a class of Honors undergraduates whom I was trying to persuade to read and think more figuratively and mythically. After receiving a set of papers on sex and gender in Spenser's third book, I took a leaf, as well as a tusk, from my own past and posed for discussion the difference between an analysis of Book III

103

in terms of male and female attributes and in terms of the flower and
the boar, two symbolic referents that variously weave through the
fabric of this book.[1] The students were on to the difference immediately: our class poet somewhat cryptically declared, "the allegory dis-
appears," by which I think he meant the figural dimension; then the
class queen of sex and gender surprised even herself with the discov-
ery that flower and boar are less fixed, looser, potentially more open
terms, and another bright woman suggested that there are female
boars and male poets. I hasten to add, as I did in class, that I am not
implying the categories *male* and *female* are not useful in reading
Spenser. They are essential, if you'll pardon the word, but as we all
know, they lead too easily to an offensive spinning of essence and a
premature closing of possibilities.

My second experience, which occurred in the same class, dealt
specifically with the Garden of Adonis.[2] When I made a point of the
mons veneris there, noting that this term is still a familiar one, my
students were incredulous. Mounts (not to mention points) and other
things that go up, they knew, are male.[3] I returned to the class with
a modern desk dictionary to let them see for themselves. There,
indeed, was the entry *mons veneris* and, several entries above it, *mons
pubis*: belonging to the adult abdomen of either sex.[4] When we
looked again at Spenser's Garden Mount, which certainly represents
a *mons veneris*, it began to be clear that it also has features that could
be related to either sex. Put another, better way, it appeared ambiguously, or doubly, sexed.

Spenser's "stately Mount" suggests more than a majestic ("stately")
protuberance, since punningly it is also something mounted,
horselike, as Adonis may well be. Myrtles, which grow on the mount,
are traditionally associated with Venus and at least by one mythogra-
pher with the female pudendum, but what *is* Venus in the Garden?[5]
John Hankins concludes that within the physical allegory, Venus sig-
nifies the masculo-feminine coital fluid, a conclusion that lines in
Colin Clouts Come Home Again support: "Venus selfe doth soly couples
seeme, / Both male and female through commixture joynd."[6] Similarly in Hesiod, Venus arises when the seed of (castrated) Uranus
meets the sea that his mother-wife Gaea (Earth) has brought forth of
herself.[7] Trees, as my students were quick to recall, have much to do
with Redcrosse's sexual fleshiness in Book I, from the grove of Fra-
dubio to Orgoglio's oak club and beyond, and the gloominess of
Spenser's Venerean myrtle grove glances at the darkness and deathli-
ness associated with the boar. Anyway, my students had me wondering, "Why should the traditionally female garden of the body have
been attributed by name to Adonis, rather than to Venus?" What

does "of" mean in the name "*Gardin of Adonis*": connected to, composed of, deriving from, possessed by (III.vi.29)? Should we think of Adonis, passive as he is at the climactic point in the Garden, as a tiller of its soil? *Soil*, of course, can signal sexual intercourse, and no one tills without sharp implements. But my speculative punning becomes digressive and calls for return to the Garden Mount.

Like steely sharpness, those "wicked beastes" of the *mons pubis* stanza also suggest the boar, a figure whose detailed treatment I defer for now, except to repeat that boars come in both sexes and in both genders in Spenser's third book, for that matter (vi.43). These boarish attributes may be explicitly excluded from the first stanza describing the Mount, yet by their mention they are actually also in some sense included, or accounted for, and thus as *contained* in both senses of this word-concept as is the pun on dying throughout Spenser's account of the Garden Mount. You will recall that "sharp steele" does not lop boughs on the Mount, and beasts do not crop tender tree buds. At least in the poetry of Donne and Herbert, buds and budding are delicately and poignantly associated with male sexuality and arousal, as well as with writing: in Donne, "Gentle love deeds, as blossomes on a bough, / From loves awaken'd root do bud out now," and less openly in Herbert, "now in age I bud again, / After so many deaths I live and write; / I once more smell the dew and rain, / And relish versing."[8] Sexual puns are notoriously long-lived and deep-rooted; in any case, Donne's life overlapped Spenser's for roughly twenty-seven years. Sweetness and gentleness, often associated with buds and flowers, is not exclusively feminine in the context of sex. This is especially and characteristically true of Spenser's poetry and specifically of the stanza in question, where the "sweet gum" of the myrtle produces "sweet delight."

I have little trouble finding male as well as female suggestions in lines after the one mentioning tree buds. The first of these sequels likens the trees to "a girlond compass[ing] . . . the hight" (vi.43). If circular garlands carry female associations; heights, things that stick up, continues to carry male ones, and either sex is implied by the next two lines, particularly if Hankins's conclusion is right that in terms of the physical allegory Venus represents a mixture of coital fluids: "And from their [the trees'] fruitfull sydes sweet gum did drop, / That all the ground with pretious deaw bedight, / Threw forth most dainty odours, and most sweet delight." My interest in recognizing the extraordinary extent of bisexuality on the Mount derives from my own recent work on Britomart as an androgynous figure.[9] Androgyny need not be bisexuality, and vice versa, but the middle books of *The Faerie Queene* are intensely concerned with both

and further concerned with their relation, and the Garden is central
to these concerns.

   In employing the term *bisexuality* to describe the pubic Mount, I
should make clear, however, that I am not referring to human behavior. To do so would be a rush to premature personification in the
Garden. By *bisexuality*, I refer to the defining features of a fictive
Mount that is ambiguously, or doubly (ambi-), sexed. Moreover, as
my discussion of mounts, budding, sweetness, and boarish traits might
already have suggested, I am not simply referencing Galen's notion
that the female organs of sex inversely and recessively mirror the male
ones but instead describing a true, if fictive, doubleness—one that is
fulfilled and positive, not failed, lesser, undeveloped, or arrested.[10]
Yet this doubleness is neither that of the hermaphrodite nor of the
androgyne, which is that of visual, humanized forms, although even
to mention these is to recognize the relevance of the Garden to them
by extension. While the Garden may glance at hermaphrodites and
androgynes, these belong to the visual fixity of statues and to the
landscape of quest outside its gates.[11] The Garden is symbolic and
mythic, not realistically anatomical or human in the quotidian sense.
Variously drawing on many, often contradictory traditions, which
have been traced to Aristotle, Plato, Galen, the Encyclopedists, the
Neoplatonists, Lucretius, biblical translation and commentary, my-
thography, earlier poetry, and elsewhere, the poet is not unimagina-
tively, ungeneratively, and unpoetically versifying an anatomical
textbook, any other single source, or even any one kind of source.[12]
The early modern poet at his Spenserian best is truly a maker, not
simply a copier.

★

The initial stanza describing the pubic Mount, on which I have
lingered, leads into a second artful stanza that focuses on the Mount's
pleasant arbor. This is made "not by art" but by an arboreal inclina-
tion that extends to the *knitting* of branches and the *fashioning* of vines,
and thus through its very diction signals a human presence in nature.
It concludes that neither sun nor wind—"*Phoebus* beams" nor Aeo-
lus's blasts—can harmfully penetrate "them," momentarily an elusive
pronoun in line 8 that recurs in line 9 and references the interweaving
boughs and entwining vines earlier in this stanza (vi.44). Two stanzas
later, looking back at this pronoun from lines that situate Venus and

Adonis on the Mount, with a retrospective regard that is typically Spenserian, we might suppose "them" to anticipate this mythic couple. Also in retrospect, the masculine potential of the "trees" —indeed, of the tree, since in Spenserian orthography the plural "trees" could always pun on a singular possessive—and the traditional feminine potential of the clinging vines comes to life. This landscape is everywhere imbued with bisexuality.

Even the two successive stanzas I have touched on so far also indicate that any stage of the Garden, not just the early ones commonly remarked, can be difficult to visualize consistently and fully, taking account of multiple dimensions and perspectives. I consider this difficulty functional and brilliantly so.[13] Visualization, on the eve of modern science, can readily imply the simple materialist's belief that seeing is believing, a notion limiting even in secular terms, as the reasoning of Milton's Satan has suggested long since. Although Spenser's art is typically imagistic, sometimes emblematic, and in such senses visual, its defining features are, when read, equally narrative, successive, and temporal. The latter, diegetic feature is what specifically and repeatedly challenges full or consistent visualization in the Garden. On occasion, I have compared the succession of perspectives ranging from mystical to scientific to fleshly in the Spenserian myth-making of Chrysogone's conception on the threshold of the Garden canto to the multicolored facets of a revolving disco ball: here is at once variousness and wholeness, difference and continuity, forward movement and, punningly, still-ness. Comparison to a disco ball is imperfect, of course, but it is less so if the ball is imagined also to progress in space. My comparison can begin to suggest something of the experience of reading not only the initial stage of the Garden canto, but also the second stage treating the rapprochement of Venus with Diana, and finally the three major stages of the Garden of Adonis itself. As stages, those within the Garden numerically recapitulate those in the whole Garden canto: first, the myth of Chrysogne's conception, with its all-inclusive perspectives; next, Venus's Actaeon-like surprisal of the disarrayed Diana, which, in transferring the role of mythic male hunter to Venerean goddess, aptly and anticipatively mixes sexes/genders in approaching the Garden; and finally, the mythic Garden itself.

A third stanza describing the pubic Mount within the Garden concerns the flowers resulting from the metamorphosis of hapless human lovers. To these male lovers, we read, "*sweet* Poets verse hath giuen endlesse date," thus conferring on them a form of immortality symbolized by recycling plants but at once formally and materially different, neither poems nor their readers being vegetables (vi.45: my emphasis).[14] The immortality within this stanza, like the nature of the Garden's arbor, exists as nature within art and as art within nature in much the senses that Sidney speaks of the poet as a maker of fictive nature and as one himself made by the God of all nature.[15] These flowers of metamorphosis—of *transformation* in Spenser's word and therefore of metaphor—imply the traditional flowers of rhetoric and, via the Greek word for flower, *anthos*, the idea of an anthology, or gathering, of flowers, which relates to the broadly encompassing nature of the Garden as a gathering of natural, cultural, and specifically verbal generations. Appropriately, the flowers of metamorphosis, at once of death and life, of mutability and perpetuity, on the Mount also *contain*—again in the punning sense—the jealousy, self-enclosure, grief, and despair variously found in the culturally fertile myths of Hyacinthus, Narcissus, Amaranthus, and all other sorts of floral metamorphees, as well as notably in the landscape of quest outside the Garden in Book III. Like many another figure in the Garden, the flowers of metamorphosis attest to its earthly, rather than perfect or heavenly, nature.

Art is thus conspicuous on the Mount, both as theme and as method, a juncture that can hardly be overemphasized. The coincidence of art with nature is another dimension of the Garden's inclusive commitment to conjunctive generations that at once contain and surmount doubleness and difference. I pun shamelessly with *surmount*, as well as with *generations* (physical, cultural, and historical procreation) and once more with *contain*. The very fact that an effort to discuss the Garden generates one pun after another (more in these pages than I flag) is worth further pondering. In the simultaneity of a pun, as I have observed elsewhere, the crossing of boundaries, disruption of the everyday, and doubling of reference can *trans-figure* the world that we know, rather than merely reflecting, refusing, or rising above it. By punning, we approach the nature of the Garden more nearly.[16]

★

The central stanzas of the Mount, 45 to 48, focus on Venus and Adonis and, not surprisingly, further illuminate the limits of sexual binarism in the everyday world, as distinct from the Garden. Before I proceed to them, an explanatory sidebar is needed, however: back in stanza 33, which belongs to the first substage of the cyclic garden, the stage of seed-forms, lines referring to Old Genius tell us that he reclothes the recycling babes "Or [they are] sent into the chaungefull world agayne."[17] Hamilton's indispensable second edition encourages a problem here by taking "Or" to express a "puzzling" alternative, since, Hamilton worries, we should logically expect "and." But "Or" is actually an abbreviated form of "before" well known to the *OED*, and, in a familiar version of Spenserian compression, the phrase "they are" is understood from earlier lines to precede the participle "sent."[18] The line in question thus affords a dubious basis on which to conclude that Garden and world are the same, a proposition Harry Berger has suggested. Although the mythic Garden is earthly, its distance from everyday life is vital to its regenerative vision. The difference between its glancing at realistic worldly anxieties, such as male fear, and giving full rein to them belongs to this distance.[19] Herein paradoxically lies, yet no more than Sidneyan fiction lieth, the difference between recognizing and transcending, or including and controlling, threats, on the one hand, and on the other, ceding authority to them.[20] In short, this is containment in its richest sense, with which conceptual pun, I return to the stanzas that focus on Venus and Adonis.

In the first of these, Venus is the reaper, or happy, productive, life-sustaining harvester, of "sweet pleasure" with Adonis. She reverses the destruction of the Saturnian scythe-bearer Time, whose *dis-semination* of Uranus in the familiar myth, taken by itself, intends only waste and death. True to Venus's mythic origin as *alienated*, irreparably *othered*, seed, "Born without Syre," Spenser's Venus defies both the Stygian gods of death and the saturnine scythe-bearer.[21] From them, she protects Adonis, "the wanton[, or 'lusty,'] boy" (46). Etymologically, he is the "unruly," "lacking" boy and punningly, the "wanting" boy in both senses of this word, since he lacks and desires what she offers.[22] She possesses him, taking her fill of his "sweetnesse," seemingly an obvious reference at this point to seminal fluid. Yet in this stanza, which initially stresses Venerean pleasure and joy, twice compounded, it is particularly difficult to keep various dimensions of allegory distinct. If we read in terms of character, the relation of Venus to Adonis is odd, even somewhat Acrasian, as many readers have noted. In this stanza, Spenser's relatively humanized forms, and I stress *relatively*, begin actually to invite more individualized, gendered, binary readings. If Venus and Adonis are read as female and male characters, her possessing him, however wanton this boy may be, carries a whiff of exploitation and incest. Besides, since *wanton* basically means "unruly," or "self-indulgent," it anticipates the other, less cooperative aspects of Shakespeare's more fully and dramatically individualized Adonis, a figure whose relation to Shake-speare's Venus in their eponymous epyllion recurrently looks back to Spenser's third Book.[23]

More than any other stanza, the forty-sixth thus makes an honest issue of the more nearly anthropomorphic, if still mythological, forms toward which the Garden has been moving, evolving, ascending. Yet it would be a mistake, I think, to overemphasize this issue, making an everyday, worldly context primary rather than momentarily pres-ent—fully realizing the world in the Garden rather than glimpsing it on the horizon, a horizon which, while still within the poem, remains primarily beyond the Garden in the landscape of quest. The basic issue here pertains to the nature of *containment* as merely suppression or as inclusion and constructive acknowledgment, as completion and generative surmounting, and it involves suppositions about reading and ways of reading not simply in general but in particular passages. To a very great extent such reading is what the whole *Faerie Queene* is about. Reading this poem is very much like reading the world, and our ways of reading it are variously implicated in ethics—sexual, psychological, and otherwise. To add that one person's ethics is an-other's politics would neither satisfy nor really suffice here. Instead, I prefer to recognize and to maintain at least a valid conceptual differ-ence between ethics and politics, while also affirming the productive and provocative instability of their relation.

Stanza 47 shifts away from the anthropomorphic issue by insisting on Adonis's existence primarily as a principle, rather than as a charac-ter. Now he is seen as "the Father of all formes," who, though "subiect to mortalitie, / Yet is eterne in mutabilitie, / And by succes-sion made perpetuall." Between these lines and the preceding stanza, however, come other lines indicating that Adonis "may not / For euer dye, and euer buried bee / In balefull night, where all thinges are forgot." While recognizing the obvious reading that Adonis can-not die forever, Berger suggests the possibility that the sexually ex-hausted lad may want to, and I suppose one might also read the poet's phrase "may not" as indicating some doubt about the whole proposition of perpetuity through succession: "And sooth it seemes they say," even after all that has been said, and done, to this point (114).

But at this juncture, what interests me more is the way the poem shifts from one point of view to another, using ambiguity, or dou-bleness, to do so. The shift in this instance is from a point of view at the end of stanza 46 that is becoming prematurely and unproductively personal and gendered to one more generalized and species-oriented. As a shift hinging on ambiguity, it is similar to that in the cyclical

first stage of the Garden from the seminary of recycling forms to the
eternity of matter, and it typifies progression in the Garden canto.
In this first stage, the shift occurs in the word "stocke" of stanza 36,
which refers equally to the preceding seed-forms and to the following
material substances: "Daily they grow, and daily forth are sent / Into
the world, it to replenish more, / Yet is the stocke not lessened, nor
spent." With the double reference of "stocke" to form and to (material) substance, our perspective flips from one side of a single cosmic
coin to the other—the view from on high to that from below, from
an eternity of forms to one of matter.[24] Similarly, in the stanzas moving from Venus's possession of Adonis to his resulting perpetuity,
our perspective shifts from one angle of reading to another and coin-
cidentally once again from one more formally individuated to one
more generalized and organic. The point, I think, is precisely the
shift, or better, the hinge that, instead of embracing one view or the
other, includes *and by succession* relates them. With an imaginative
capaciousness almost incredible and seemingly inexhaustible, it thus
contains them, while refusing containment by either one of them.[25]

★

With the gendering at the end of stanza 46 modified—neutralized,
enlarged, and productively enriched—by stanza 47, stanza 48, which
includes the encaved boar, can open with a (re)affirmation of the joy
shared by Venus and Adonis: "There now he liueth in eternall blis, /
Ioying his goddesse, and of her enioyd." As Hamilton and Berger
explain between them, the second of these lines is susceptible of
readings that make either or both Venus and Adonis the recipient of
joy in significantly differing yet balanced verbal phrases.[26] Once again,
I would think conjunction, inclusion, and even mutuality the point
rather than the personalized male anxiety that Berger's Actaeonic
essay on the Garden continues to privilege. The Spenserian stanza
proceeds, referring to Adonis's situation:

> Ne feareth he henceforth that foe of his,
> Which with his cruell tuske him deadly cloyd;
> For that wilde Bore, the which him once annoyd,
> She firmely hath emprisoned for ay,
> That her sweet loue his malice mote auoyd,
> In a strong rocky Caue, which is they say,
> Hewen vnderneath that Mount, that none him losen may.
>
> (III.vi.48)

Circling, not to say recycling, back to the ambisexuality of the pubic
Mount, the hateful, wild Boar of winter, passion, chaos, and death
within and beneath this Mount is also a bisexual figure in Spenser's
artistic and thematic regeneration of the old generative myths. The
boar's situation is a culminating emblem of containment in every
sense of this fertile word. On the one hand, the gender of the Boar
is pronominally masculine, and he is imprisoned beneath the pubic
Mount, an obvious reference to the cave vaginal. Most traditional
myths also enforce his maleness. Yet, on the other hand, Venus is
his notably "firm" captor, once again giving her a dominant role,
and a growing consensus of readers assents to Lauren Silberman's
discovering in the figure of the boar himself the *vagina dentata*, or
"an icon of fearsome venereal power" (48). The ambisexed, toothed
cave is, of course, also erotically suggestive.[27]

Although the *vagina dentata* is an obscure myth, I suspect we would
find it more often if we chose to look for it: Bosch's paintings (not
to mention Edward Gorey's drawings) come to mind. Shakespeare's
virtual tusking of Venus in his epyllion about her frustrated seduction
of Adonis relevantly gives added pause—"Had I been tooth'd like"
the boar, Venus confesses, "With kissing him, I should have kill'd
him first"—and thereby the epyllion suggests that both these Elizabethan poets might have encountered reference to the *vagina dentata*,
unless they imagined it independently.[28] At the end of the central
stanzas treating the Mount, as at their beginning, the totality and
complexity of the depiction of Venus and Adonis is therefore emphatically ambisexual.[29] To be true to the succession of generations
in every sense of this phrase imaginable and thus to Spenser's mythic
Garden, it not only may but also *should* be, in the full sense of Sidney's
ethical imperative.[30]

Momentarily in stanza 48, even the word "cloyd" in itself may
suggest the deadly (or deathly) boar's containment. As Berger observes, *cloy* can mean "glut," as well as the contextually more obvious
"penetrate," and it therefore recalls the wanton boy's "expense of
spirit ['semen, vitality']" to the possible point of exhaustion and
disgust (114). "Life is sweet," as we say, but as the poet of the Faerie
quest knew well, excess sweetness, whether in the honied words of
Despair or the honied tones of Melibee, can be "deadly cloy[ing]"
(vi.48). Yet I wonder whether Berger underplays another, less as-
suredly negative coloration even of *cloy*, when glossed as "satiate,"
which is glossed in turn as "satisfy (an appetite or a desire) fully," a
sense whose potential lies within yet beyond and rises above passion's
wild and hateful excesses.[31] Satisfaction is fullness, enoughness (*satis*),

and, conceivably, contentment (from *continere*: "to hold, keep together," and thus "contain"), rather than glutting, as intimated in
Shakespeare's *Antony and Cleopatra*, where Antony's appetite is sharp-
ened with "cloyless sauce" that never satiates, and Enobarbus, describing Cleopatra's "infinite variety," at once contrasts *and*
rhetorically aligns "cloy" with "satisfies" to the extent that a double
take is needed to separate them: "Other women cloy / The appetites
they feed, but she makes hungry / Where most she satisfies" (II.i.25,
ii.235–37).[32] Who knows when enough is too much or, in Antony's
problematical words, how "love[, or eros,] . . . can be reckoned"
(I.i.15)? While not wanting to reduce the savage boar to a house pet
or to discount the deadliness of his cloying, I would notice even
here some blunting of a sharp edge, some trace *and* glimmer of the
nearness of cloying to satisfaction. Although otherwise inflected,
since in the everyday world outside a mythic *aevum*, Shakespeare's
sonnet 129, invoked earlier in my paragraph by the phrase "expense
of spirit," affords another telling comparison at its end, where "none
knows well / To shun the heaven that leads men to this hell."[33] Even
in the more worldly, relatively more negative ending of Shakespeare's
sonnet, the syntactical ambiguity of the phrase "knows well," like
the syntactically analogous phrase "does well," glances at the "bliss,"
the "joy," and the "dream" of an erotic heaven: none does well (or
knows well) to shun the possibility of what *could* be.[34] In Spenser's
aevum, taken whole, the balance is different: we glimpse the world
even while recurrently and emphatically perceiving a totality that
goes beyond it.

There remains one line of those I have cited from stanza 48 that
seems to me to capture our final impression of the couple, or mythic
principle of coupling. Venus has forever encaved the boar, "That her
sweet loue his malice mote auoyd." While there may be further
ambiguities to be considered in the stanza in question, the one that
interests me most concerns the phrase "sweet loue" in the line just
cited. "Sweet loue" (again, "sweet") refers either to the object of
Venus's love, Adonis, or to the nature of her relation to him. By
these readings, he *is* actually there. By yet another reading, however,
if in herself she is Love (and the *if* is real), the whole idea of relation,
along with Adonis, would be swallowed back into her self-enclosure
and thus, in effect, either into Uranus's and Saturn's urge to suppress
and consume or into her own self-mirroring. This would be a denial
of her alienation from her origin in dis-semination, and a denial of
her consequent otherness—a cancellation at once of her difference
from destructive male gods and of the difference, the real otherness,
of the wanton Adonis from her. The very succession of the central

stanzas on the Mount, with their shifts in perspective and significant form, seems to me to work against such a reading, effectually having already carried us beyond its likelihood. Successive, dynamic totality, not competition; ambisexuality, not visual, humanoid hermaphroditism; the mythic *aevum*, not the everyday world—herein lie the true character and thrust of Spenser's amazing, fictive, earthly Garden.

Indiana University

NOTES

1. The past to which I refer is *The Growth of a Personal Voice: "Piers Plowman" and "The Faerie Queene"* (New Haven: Yale University Press, 1976), 98–113.

2. No Spenserian approaches the Garden of Adonis without having incurred a huge debt to the rich critical tradition on it. I gratefully acknowledge mine over many decades, particularly to John Erskine Hankins, *Source and Meaning in Spenser's Allegory: A Study of "The Faerie Queene"* (Oxford: Clarendon, 1971), 228–86; James Nohrnberg, *The Analogy of "The Faerie Queene"* (Princeton: Princeton University Press, 1976), 490–569; Harry Berger, Jr., "Spenser's Garden of Adonis: Force and Form in the Renaissance Imagination" (1961), rprt. in *Revisionary Play: Studies in the Spenserian Dynamics* (Berkeley: University of California Press, 1988), 131–53; and "Actaeon at the Hinder Gate: The Stag Party in Spenser's Garden of Adonis," in *Desire in the Renaissance: Psychoanalysis and Literature*, ed. Valeria Finucci and Regina Schwarz (Princeton: Princeton University Press, 1994), 90–119; Jon A. Quitslund, *Spenser's Supreme Fiction: Platonic Natural Philosophy and "The Faerie Queene"* (Toronto: University of Toronto Press, 2001), esp. 184–266; Kenneth Gross, *Spenserian Poetics: Idolatry, Iconoclasm, and Magic* (Ithaca: Cornell University Press, 1985), 181–209; Humphrey Tonkin, "Spenser's Garden of Adonis and Britomart's Quest," *PMLA* 88 (1973): 408–17; Maureen Quilligan, *Milton's Spenser: The Politics of Reading* (Ithaca: Cornell University Press, 1983), 190–97; Donald Cheney, *Spenser's Image of Nature: Wild Man and Shepherd in "The Faerie Queene"* (New Haven: Yale University Press, 1966), 117–45; Alastair Fowler, *Spenser and the Numbers of Time* (London: Routledge and Kegan Paul, 1964), 132–44; Thomas P. Roche, Jr., *The Kindly Flame: A Study of the Third and Fourth Books of Spenser's Kindly Flame* (Princeton: Princeton University Press, 1964), 117–28; Stevie Davies, *The Feminine Reclaimed: The Idea of Woman in Spenser, Shakespeare, and Milton* (Lexington: University Press of Kentucky, 1986), 77–93; Theresa M. Krier, "Mother's Sorrow, Mother's Joy: Mourning Birth in Spenser's Garden of Adonis," in *Grief and Gender, 700–1700*, ed. Jennifer C. Vaught, with Lynne Dickson Bruckner (New York: Palgrave Macmillan, 2003), 133–47; David Lee Miller, *The Poem's Two Bodies: The Poetics of the 1590 "Faerie Queene"* (Princeton: Princeton University Press, 1988), esp. 261–81; Lauren Silberman, *Transforming Desire: Erotic Knowledge in Books III and IV of "The Faerie Queene"* (Berkeley: University of California Press, 1995), 35–48.

3. Visually represented mounts, as Leah Marcus has remarked to me, are often peaked, pointed, or sharply protuberant in Tudor times, although they could also be given a more gently rounded contour.

4. *Webster's New World Dictionary*, 3rd ed. (1988; rpt. New York: Macmillan, 1997); *The American Heritage College Dictionary*, 3rd ed. (1993; rprt. Boston: Houghton Mifflin, 1997). The definition I offer is a compressed composite.

5. On the myrtle, see Fowler, 137; cf. Hankins, 240.

6. Hankins, 246, cf. 255. For the reference to *Colin Clouts Come Home Againe,* see The Yale Edition of the Shorter Poems of Edmund Spenser, ed. William A. Oram et al. (New Haven: Yale University Press, 1989), 527–62, here 801–02; further reference to the shorter poems is to this edition. Cf. *The Faerie Queene*, IV.x.41. Unless otherwise noted, reference to *The Faerie Queene* is to the edition of A. C. Hamilton et al., 2nd ed. (Harlow: Pearson Education, 2001).

7. *Theogyny*, in *Hesiod and Theognis*, trans. Dorothea Wender (Harmondsworth: Penguin, 1973), 27–29.

8. "Loves Growth," in *The Elegies and the Songs and Sonnets* of John Donne, ed. Helen Gardner (Oxford: Clarendon, 1965), 76–77; "The Flower," in *The English Poems of George Herbert,* ed. Helen Wilcox (Cambridge: Cambridge University Press, 2007), 567–69. See also the association by François Rabelais of codpieces (and their contents) with sap, moisture, verdancy, flowers, fruit, delight: *Gargantua and Pantagruel* (London: Penguin, 1955), I.8 (55). Rabelais was a physician as well as a monk.

9. My essay "Britomart's Armor in Spenser's *Faerie Queene*: Reopening Cultural Matters of Gender and Figuration" is forthcoming in *English Literary Renaissance*.

10. Thomas Laqueur's one-sex, unimorphic, structural, and fundamentally Galenic model of sexuality could be seen as an inspiration for Spenser, as it were, and, at some level, I consider it so: *Making Sex: Body and Gender from the Greeks to Freud* (Cambridge, MA: Harvard University Press, 1990). But Laqueur's persuasive model, we should recognize, is composite and interpretative. For example, while concluding that "a two-sex and a one-sex model had always been available," he invests strongly in the one-sex model for early periods, neutralizing the two-sex view, specifically Aristotle's, by reading it both interpretatively and holistically (viii, 28–43, 114; cf. 124). It does not take much awareness of the variety of reading and other interpretative practices in the Renaissance or of the availability of reliable texts (not to mention the reliability of human memory) to have reservations about philosophic holism. Spenser did not have the benefit of Laqueur's brilliant composite, which, in interpreting Spenser, cannot be imposed without benefit of the careful words of Spenser's own text. Spenser's mythic model is more complex, inclusive, and layered than Galen's, and it belongs to a realm of writing other than science, although it is also deeply touched and intellectually provoked by the science available to him. Another important touchstone for me in the context of sex and gender is Valerie Traub's thoughtful, precise introduction in *Desire and Anxiety: Circulation of Sexuality in Shakespearean Drama* (London: Routledge, 1992), 1–22. Cf. Grant Williams, "Early Moden Blazons and the Rhetoric of Wonder," in *Luce Irigaray and Premodern Culture: Thresholds of History*, ed. Theresa Krier and Elizabeth D. Harvey (New York: Routledge, 2004), 126–37: "early modern culture's dependence on Galenic homology necessitated the exaggeration of anatomical distinctions" in order to exclude women from dominant social and discursive positions (126).

11.   Thanks to Jerry Findley and Mary Ellen Lamb for asking questions that led me to clarify this paragraph.

12.   Hankins, Nohrnberg, and Quitslund provide the most extensive review of sources and analogues. Both Hankins and Nohrnberg find these enormously eclectic; Quitslund more narrowly privileges Neoplatonic sources. A recent and relevant discussion of matter and specifically of vitalism is Philippa Berry's in her introduction to *Shakespeare's Feminine Endings: Disfiguring Death in the Tragedies* (London: Routledge, 1999), 12–20, esp. 13–14.

13.   See Roche, 118–19.

14.   In a paper delivered to a conference of the International Spenser Society in Toronto in 2006, David Wilson-Okamura relevantly noted that "sweet" is a traditional descriptor for poetry written in the middle style. In his view, Spenser is characteristically a poet of the middle voice.

15.   Sir Philip Sidney, *An Apology for Poetry*, ed. Geoffrey Shepherd (1965; rprt. Manchester: Manchester University Press, 1973), 101, lines 14–24.

16.   For a broadly based discussion of punning that includes philosophical and psycholinguistic reference, see my essay "Donne's (Im)possible Punning," *John Donne Journal* 23 (2004): 59–68. My words here, as at the end of the essay on Donne, reflect those of Wolfgang Iser, *The Fictive and the Imaginary: Charting Literary Anthropology* (Baltimore: Johns Hopkins University Press, 1993), xiv–xv. Referring to the simultaneity of a pun, I have in mind both its existence as text and as read text but primarily and definitively as text. Responding to my present argument, Lauren Silberman has asked whether a pun might be successive, and I certainly accept this possibility in reading: some puns in some readings might occur sequentially or even belatedly; moreover, one reader's simultaneity might be experienced by another reader as succession.

17.   On the stages of the Garden, see Cheney, 129–31; Silberman, 45.

18.   Hamilton, ed., 347n33.7; *OED*, s.v. "Or," def. C.b.; cf. B.b.

19.   While Berger, "Actaeon," tries not to give rein to these anxieties, the thrust of his argument is to do so. Evidently endorsing Hamilton's reading, he concludes "that the garden and the world must be the same" (107). This "dissolution of boundaries" is important to his carefully crafted and productive argument. But gendered egos preeminently belong to this world, rather than to the *aevum*: cf. Gross, 195–98; Silberman, 40; Quitslund, 217–18. Gross's explanation and qualification of the use of the term *aevum* are alike pertinent (195–96), but the concept of a liminal *aevum* suspended between binary terms, realms, realities, or the like remains useful only as long as we remember that Spenser rarely leaves an inherited concept as he finds it. In Nohrnberg's observing the "*symbolic* reversibility of the garden-world into a world-garden," his word "symbolic" also maintains a significant distinction (530; my emphasis). The concept of the *aevum* within commentary on the Garden of Adonis traces back to Frank Kermode's *The Sense of an Ending: Studies in the Theory of Fiction* (New York: Oxford University Press, 1967), 74. Of course the concept has longer, more complicated roots as well.

20.   Sidney, 123, lines 38–39.

21.   For the quotation, see *Colin Clouts Come Home Again*, 800. Notably, in the myth leading to Venus's birth, Gaea (Earth), mother and wife of Uranus, arms

Cronus (later Chronos: "Time"), or Saturn, with the scythe. The Roman Saturnus was a god of sowing. Berger's spin on the mythic birth of Venus ("Actaeon," 112–13) differs considerably from mine. His resists the irreparable alienation of the sperm and the consequent otherness of Venus.

22.   *Wan* is "a prefix, expressing privation or negation," i.e., "want" (*OED*, s.v. *Wan*). The other element in wanton is Old English *towen/togen*, "to discipline, train (*OED*, s.v. *Wanton, a.* and *sb.*). See also *MED*, s.v. *Wantoun*, adj: "unregulated," "recalcitrant," "rebellious," "willful," "lascivious," "lustful."

23.   See my "*Venus and Adonis*: Shakespeare, Spenser, and the Forms of Desire," in *Grief and Gender*, 149–60. Modern editors generally agree that Shakespeare's epyllion was written in 1592–93.

24.   Surprisingly, Hamilton, ed., takes "stocke" exclusively to mean "matter," evidently connecting "For" in line 6 with line 3 alone, whereas it readily connects with line 2 as well (347n36.3–9). In the same note, he also assumes an exclusively material meaning of the word "substances" in line 9, but *substance* is a highly controverted term with multiple possible meanings in this period, more than one of which is relevant here: on *substance*, see my *Translating Investments: Metaphor and the Dynamic of Cultural Change* (New York: Fordham University Press, 2005), 49–51. Hankins, 259–60, and Tonkin, 411, similarly recognize the ambiguity, or doubled reference, of "stocke." Not without relation, Christopher Hill notes Spenser's and his friend Lodowick Bryskett's deep interest in the mortalist controversy (i.e., death of the soul, along with the body): *Milton and the English Revolution* (London: Faber and Faber, 1977), 74; cf. *The Faerie Queene*, VII.vii.19: "Ne doe their bodies only flit and fly: / But eeke their minds (which they immortall call)."

25.   Cf. Miller, 272; Fowler, 136; Gross, 196; Silberman, 47–48. References could be multiplied.

26.   Hamilton, ed., 350n48.2; Berger, "Actaeon," 114 and 119n39.

27.   Cf. Quitslund's observation that Cupid's wanton play with Adonis in Spenser's Garden is homoerotic, keeping "Venus's consort ready for her" (208).

28.   *Venus and Adonis*, in *The Riverside Shakespeare*, ed. G. Blakemore Evans et al., 2nd ed. (Boston: Houghton Mifflin, 1997), pp. 1797–1813, here verses 1117–18; cf. verses 1105–16: unless otherwise noted, reference to Shakespeare is to this edition. In a discussion I led at Vanderbilt University, I found reassuring Lynn Enterline's quickly connecting the *vagina dentata* in the Garden's cave with Shakespeare's virtual tusking of Venus. In Spenser's Book IV.vii.5, the bisexual figure of Lust is tusked, as is the figure of Hate in IV.x.33. William Oram observes that Spenser's figure of Lust combines male and female genital imagery: "Elizabethan Fact and Spenserian Fiction," *Spenser Studies* 4 (1983): 33–47, here 42.

29.   Cf. Davies's observation that "Venus and Adonis in the act of coition make up an androgyne within the feminine gender" (89). Together, they more fully and frankly represent bisexuality in my view. Spenser's androgynes belong to the landscape of quest. Davies goes on to characterize Adonis as "transformed matter" (89).

30.   Sidney's "right poet" considers "what may be and should be": 102, lines 21–37.

31.   I actually quote a modern definition of *satiate* from *The American Heritage College Dictionary*, s.v. *Satiate*, 1, but its historicized equivalents can be found less succinctly in *OED*, s.v., *Satiate v.* 1, cf. *Satiate ppl.* and *ppl. a.*

32.   John Wilders, ed., glosses "cloyless" in the first of these quotations as sauce "that never cloys (or satiates)": *Antony and Cleopatra* (London: Routledge, 1995), 126n25. Likewise, David Bevington, ed., *Antony and Cleopatra*, updated ed. (Cambridge: Cambridge University Press, 2005). Reviewing the *OED's* definitions of *cloy*, I notice another Shakespearean example that is at least ambiguous: Richard II asks, "who can . . . cloy the hungry edge of appetite / By bare imagination of a feast?" (I.iii.294–97). In addition to *OED* examples, the alignment of *cloy* with *satiate* and *satisfy* is marked in *Cymbeline*, I.vi.47–48: "The cloyed will— /That satiate yet unsatisfied desire. . . ."

33.   On *aevum*, see note 19, above.

34.   Reverse the order of Shakespeare's phrase, making it "well knows," and the syntactical ambiguity is gone. For anyone aware of Renaissance editions and printings of *Piers Plowman*, the focal term, name, and virtual character Do-well (Dowel) bears on the syntactical pun *does well/ knows well*. Memory of Langland supports the early modern currency of the phrase, or saying, *do[es]-well*. Cf. Sidney's syntactical paralleling: "with the end of well-doing and not of well-knowing only (104, lines 29–30).

BRAD TUGGLE

Memory, Aesthetics, and Ethical Thinking in the House of Busirane

This essay investigates how Edmund Spenser borrows the architecture of the Old Testament Temple to build what Mary Carruthers describes as a ductus, or shaped experience, for readers of the House of Busirane episode of *The Faerie Queene*. A key figure in the historiography and uses of the Temple is Bernard of Clairvaux, who supported and helped found the Knights Templar. I suggest that Bernard might also be a key figure in Spenser's thinking about what I call the ethical programs of his poem, and I give evidence of the plausibility of this for a Protestant thinker. Considering the episode as a poem for readers to use, I argue that the episode is built to allow readers to think and remember in ways that are simultaneously unique and common.

I. INTRODUCTION

*E*ARLY MODERN ENGLISH studies have long fluctuated between Catholic and Protestant emphases. In the 1960s, the whiggish reformation narrative of A. G. Dickens was tempered somewhat by the literary work on Catholic modes of poetry by Louis Martz. But the increasingly historicist scholarship of the 80s and 90s focused heavily on early modern permutations of Protestantism. A complex issue like iconoclasm, for example, was ceded to those critics who, like John King, chose to treat it in Protestant contexts, leaving aside the strong tradition within Catholic writings (patristic, monastic, recusant) of defending the soul against undue attention to idolatrous objects. Currently, though scholars like John Wall have argued that Establishment Church of England theology and praxis are central to early modern historiography and literary studies, the late 1990s and now the first decade of our present century have seen overall emphases yet once

more shift toward the Catholic. Scholars such as Eamon Duffy, Frances Dolan, Stephen Greenblatt, and Arthur Marotti have continued
to investigate the unavoidable Romanist margins of the early modern
period in England. [1]

The binary opposition of Catholic and Protestant is itself often
misleading. Many practicing Catholics identified as Church of England members out of legal propriety, while many honestly Protestant
politicians, writers, and preachers clung to older Catholic traditions
in their laws, poems, and exegeses. We are now perhaps more than
ever prepared to understand the ways in which early modern English
men and women were "neither integral Tridentines nor fully Protestant or Calvinist."[2] Instead, it appears that most men and women
merely suffered the ruptures of the Reformation. Michael Questier
writes, "A decision to become a Catholic or Protestant in England
[was] always partly a matter of politics and partly a matter of religion,
and . . . try as they might, people could not consciously adhere to
the Roman or the English Church without having an eye constantly
to both sorts of motive."[3]

While politics and religion are two very important motives in
these matters, I think another warrants emphasis, one we might call
the motive of established intellectual tradition. In the late sixteenth
century, a writer's religious or political identity does not always determine her literary and cultural sources. Eamon Duffy has enhanced
our understanding of the way that traditionally Catholic religious
practices asserted influence long after the official break with Rome;
yet to be fully examined, however, is the lingering and perhaps inex-
tinguishable influence of the Latin and Greek fathers on the ethical
and aesthetic thinking of late sixteenth-century England.[4] The inertia
of religious canons can be very strong. Writers and sermonizers of
the sixteenth century could not suddenly abandon their Romanist
heritage since it was what and whom they and their forbears had
read and for the most part still revered. Augustine, Jerome, Anselm,
and even Bernard of Clairvaux: these and others formed an important
core of a tradition that would never be eradicated from English memory. Thus Nicholas Ridley, in a "disputation" at Oxford, claims his
argument against the real presence is in agreement not only with
Paul, but also with Cyprian, Augustine, Athanasius, Hilary, Cyril,
Basil, Ambrose,and Jerome; and William Perkins openly hopes that
he "shall sufficiently perswade an indifferent iudge, that these things
haue not beene lately hatched at home, which wee deliuer in our
Congregations and Schooles, but that we haue also deriued and
fetched them from the Fathers themselues."[5] And though the fathers
of late antiquity such as Augustine are never anything but central to

Protestant thinking, I argue that even less prominent medieval Catholic writers continue to dwell in the memories of English Protestants.

There has been a minority in Renaissance studies paying attention to such memories. Kenneth Gross, for example, writes that he is not comfortable "with the work of recent critics who have tried to make English Renaissance literature into a predominately Protestant or Calvinist phenomenon."[6] In Spenser studies, Darryl Gless, Anne Lake Prescott, and Carol Kaske have kept reminding early modern scholars not to forget the important heritage of residual Catholic practices.[7] For these critics and others, a deep indebtedness to Catholic thought lies behind the officially-sanctioned Protestantism of the age in England. In the present essay, I want to show how Spenser might have employed medieval Romanist traditions in *The Faerie Queene* by arguing that the disposition of architectural space in the House of Busirane is shaped by two surprising influences: the practice of architectural memory in medieval monasticism and the aesthetic theories of Bernard of Clairvaux.

II. Moving and Ductus

Partly as a response to the diatribes against their craft, but also as an inheritance of classical and medieval ideas, Elizabethan poets conceived of poetry in general as an ethical instrument. Sidney, replying to Gosson's *School of Abuse* in his *Defence of Poesy*, borrows the Horatian prescription that poetry must "teach and delight," but also adds an idea at least as old as Cicero: the poem must also *move* the reader. "[M]oving is of a higher degree than teaching," he writes. "For as Aristotle saith, it is not *gnosis* but *praxis* must be the fruit. [. . .] But to be moved to do that which we know, or to be moved with desire to know: *hoc opus, hic labor est*."[8] This moving quality is how poetry bridges the gap between gnosis and praxis, knowledge and action, says Sidney. Valuable ethical education (e.g., that "to make many Cyruses," or "to take that goodness in hand,"[9]) can be accomplished by means of poetry, says Sidney, through moving a reader to praxis. I would argue a primary sense of Sidney's *move* is "to urge or incite (a person) *to* an action."[10] Sidney views this movement as a path to be followed. The poet is monarch of all sciences because he "giveth so sweet a prospect into the way, as will entice any man to enter it. Nay, he doth, as if your journey should lie through a fair vineyard, at the first give you a cluster of grapes, that full of that taste, you may long to pass further."[11] As Sidney's essay states, this moving that poetry can perform by means of its "heart-ravishing knowledge"[12] is more powerful than the logic of philosophy or the examples of history alone. And it is in this movement toward ethical action that poetry's real value lies.

The work of Mary Carruthers on the emotive and memorial significance of sacred architecture in medieval monasticism suggests one powerful way of understanding how poetry moves its readers. In *The Craft of Thought*, she introduces the ancient rhetorical concept of *ductus*, that is, the way we are led through a composition, be it poetic or architectural: "The *ductus* is what we sometimes now call the 'flow' of a composition. *Ductus* is an aspect of rhetorical 'disposition,' but it is [also] the movement within and through a work's various parts. Indeed, *ductus* insists upon movement, the con*duct* of a thinking mind on its *way* through a composition."[13] Carruthers describes the tradition of using pictures, statues, and buildings—in both textual and built forms—as tools of the craft of thought in reading and composing. She has called the virtual and material art that embodies these rhetorical programs "machine[s] for thinking."[14]

In the writings of Cicero, rhetorical patterns are explicitly directed toward proof of one side of a question or the other. Even in the case of *disputatio in utramque partem*, the goal of the rhetor is persuasion to an intellectual position; that position is the final cause of the rhetoric. In medieval monasticism the final cause of such rhetoric is often conversion, conviction, or concentration. In the humanist age, though, poets began to see poems as machines that, yes, move readers in certain ways and to certain points, but that crucially leave undetermined the final causes of such movement. Renaissance poets instead expect poems to be used as instruments for the exercise of thought and ethical development, even with all the attendant possibilities of misuse. Carruthers's presentations of rhetorical *ductus* and of the readerly use of texts as machines for thinking have not yet influenced studies of early modern texts. But I think it may be time to consider how her version of the history and uses of rhetoric might change our understanding of Renaissance poetry and ethics.

Ethics in the classical world was heavily virtue-based, whether the virtues of Aristotle's *Nicomachean Ethics* or the *ataraxia* of the Stoics. In the Middle Ages, virtue is by and large still the end of ethics, but the virtues are Christianized. In the Renaissance, I would argue, virtue-based ethics is beginning to be rethought, and one important site of this philosophical work is literary fiction. Spenser structures *The Faerie Queene* as legends about virtues, but the critiques of those very virtues within the books themselves (for example, the strong rewriting of chastity as married love) suggests that Spenser and his contemporaries are powerfully revising their understanding of the efficacy of virtue-based ethics. Pyrocles in Sidney's *The Countess of Pembroke's Arcadia* exclaims, "[I]f we love virtue, in whom shall we love it but in a virtuous creature—without your meaning be, I should love this word "Virtue" where I see it written in a book!"[15] His complaint about the uselessness of an abstract virtue is similar to the complaint that Spenser's legends imply. So, instead of creating structures that simply induce virtues, some Renaissance poets are rather more interested in finding a "taxis" that induces praxis.[16] They do not want poems merely to instill virtue; they want poems to move readers to virtuous action. Such a shift toward a praxis-inducing poetics inevitably forced Renaissance poets to reconceive the mechanical disposition of their poems, and to reconfigure the poems' relations to ethics. Fortunatianus (4th c. C.E.), Bernard of Clairvaux (1090–1153), Philip Sidney (1554–86), and Edmund Spenser (1552–99) might have very different products in mind when they imagine the results of the practice of "ethike"—but they are all part of a tradition of presenting texts, images, and artifacts as instruments in the process of "moving" souls to virtuous action. In this essay, I explore what it might mean to consider Spenser's House of Busirane as such a machine for thinking and moving—both in its uses of the site of the Temple of Solomon and in its verbal consideration of the ethical instrumentality of poetry.

III. A TEMPLAR DUCTUS

Spenser's poem thinks about literature's moving quality in part, I argue, by appropriating the medieval tradition of architectural ductus. Frances Yates deftly described how Renaissance thinkers borrowed the memorial techniques of the pseudo-Ciceronian *Rhetorica ad Herennium* that encouraged the practice of architectural mnemonic devices. But her foundational work presents the *Rhetorica ad Herrenium* as the central text of the practice that Carruthers calls locational memory, the mnemonic use of space.[17] Whereas the Ciceronian model uses remembered buildings simply to place the images of what one wishes to remember, many medieval memory experts, as Carruthers has shown, use locational memory to invent and compose their own mental buildings.[18] Like other medieval practices, the orthopraxis of thinking in buildings continued into the early modern period, even as its aims changed. In Spenser's case, such medieval memorial practices, I want to argue, underlie some of his most impressive imaginary edifices. A central example in Spenser's work is his taking up the traditional memorial space par excellence, the Temple of Solomon, in his construction of the episode in which Britomart walks through the House of Busirane.

"The most interesting and fruitful of all the inventional tropes developed from the Bible from the point of view of literary invention," Carruthers writes, "is the temple-city on a hill which Ezekiel sees in a vision . . . a version of the actual temple of Solomon described in I Kings chapter 6."[19] According to Hebraic tradition, the pre-exilic Temple of Solomon was destroyed by Nebuchadnezzar's Babylonians in 586 BCE, the Second Temple by Titus's Romans in 70 CE. The Temple is from that time no more than a memory; but the Temple is now no *less* than a memory. As Alfred Edersheim writes in his examination of Second Temple Judaism at the time of Christ, "In every age, the memory of Jerusalem has stirred the deepest feelings. Jews, Christians, and Mohammedans turn to it with reverent affection."[20] This is the resonance that the Church of Jesus Christ of Latter-day Saints attempts to capture when it borrows the inscriptions and designs of Solomon's Temple for its LDS temples. Peter and Linda Murray note that many Christian churches have also been based on the Old Testament Temple.[21] These "ancient memories" of the Temple Complex, as Edersheim calls them, have remained a remarkable repository of cultural memory, powerful as both presence and loss. Jon D. Levenson writes, "A central paradox of Jewish spirituality lies in the fact that so much of it centers upon an institution that was destroyed almost two millenia ago, the Jerusalem Temple."[22] Indeed, the loss of the Temple is problematic in practical ways: some commandments in the Mishnah apply only when the Temple is standing. In those cases, it is as if the loss of the Temple directly means loss of a tradition; an absence that perhaps weakens the force of law. But of course, absence only strengthens the motives of memory. Memory is strong where presence of the object is denied, much as the sense of touch is strong in a person who has been deprived of sight. In the Middle Ages, memories of the tabernacle and temple famously became meditation machines for, among others, Richard of St.-Victor, Abbott Suger, and Bernard of Clairvaux.[23] Spenser, I believe, also draws upon these memories to form a recognizable ductus for readers of his poem who are aware of the meditational resonance of the Temple "which that wise King of *Iurie* framed, / With endlesse cost, to be th'Almighties see" (IV.x.30).[24]

The physical obstacle to Britomart and Scudamour's entrance to Busirane's House is a fiery barrier before the gate:

> But in the Porch, that did them sore amate,
> A flaming fire, ymixt with smouldry smoke,
> And stinking Sulphure, that with griesly hate
> And dreadfull horror did all entraunce choke,
> Enforced them their forward footing to reuoke.
>
> (III.xi.21)

Editors of the poem, including Roche and Hamilton, rightly note the literary sources of the fire in medieval and Renaissance romance and epic.[25] But I would argue that Spenser combines these literary sources with the woodcuts of the Temple of Solomon in the Geneva Bible, a visual source Spenser would have known well.[26] Incorporating this biblical source into an understanding of the House of Busirane makes possible an investigation of its program for readers, as I will show.

In figure 1, "The Temple Vncovered" (151ᵛ), a fire sits before the entry to the porch (G). In figure 2, "The Temple Covered" (152ʳ), the flames in the first picture are revealed as originating from the altar of burnt offering (D), not from the floor as they appear to do in the first illustration. This three-dimensional fact is obscured in the two-dimensional representation of the first woodcut, which inadvertently suggests a fiery barrier. The distortion is repeated in other early modern visualizations of the Temple.[27] In these depictions, "a flaming fire, ymixt with smouldry smoke" appears to present a distinct and symbolic barrier between the commoners in the foreground and the Temple in the background.

Figure 1 also makes clear the tripartite division of the Temple: the porch (G–H), "the holy place" (Q), and "the holiest of all" (R, i.e., *sanctum sanctorum* or "the holy of holies"). The House of Busirane has a corresponding tripartite structure: the room of tapestry, the room of gold relief, and the inner room where Amoret is held hostage. The tripartite division of the Old Testament Temple, each room more sacred than the last, ending in the *sanctum sanctorum*, provides a negative pattern for Busirane's house, where each room is more profane than the last, so that the third room of Busirane's house represents what I would call the *profanum profanorum* or "worst of the impious places."

The verses from 1 Kings 6 that the Geneva Bible woodcuts accompany describe the walls of the Temple, specifically the enormous

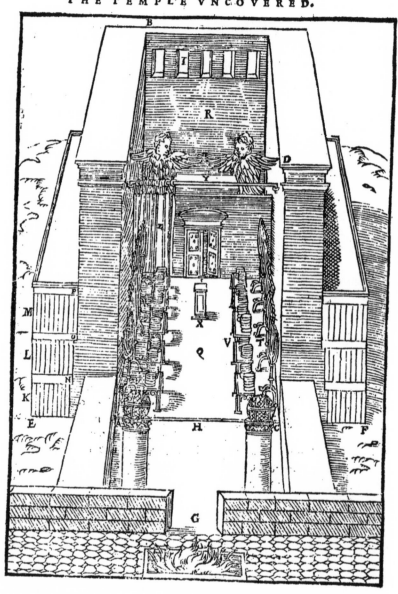

Fig. 1. "The Temple Vncovered," *The Geneva Bible*, 151v. By Permission of the Huntington Library.

I. Kings.

THE TEMPLE COVERED.

Fig. 2. "The Temple Covered," *The Geneva Bible*, 152r. By Permission of the Huntington Library.

amount of gilt work they support. Verses 20–22 repeatedly emphasize this. Verse 20 says, "[H]e couered it [i.e., the holy of holies] with pure golde." Verse 21 elaborates: "So Salomon couered the house within with pure golde: and he shut the place of the oracle with chaines of golde, and couered it with golde." Verse 22 concurs: "And he ouerlaied the house with golde." Verses 29–32 continue the precious metallic overload by describing the figurative work on the walls and doors, also covered with gold. This shows up in Spenser's poem first as the gold thread lurking in the tapestries of the first room, and then in the gilded altar of Cupid. In the second room Britomart finds "with pure gold it all was ouerlayd" (III.xi.51), in language directly echoing that of the Geneva Bible (verse 22 above).

Finally, there is at least one more resemblance between the two imagined spaces: the placement of a censing altar in the Geneva woodcut (fig. 1, "X") provides a source for the altar of Cupid in the House of Busirane's first room.

> And at the vpper ende of that faire rowme,
> There was an Altar built of pretious stone,
> Of passing valew, and of great renowme,
> On which there stood an Image all alone,
> Of massy gold, which with his owne light shone.
>
> (III.xi.47)

What this visual analysis of the Geneva Bible woodcuts provides, then, is a set of strong resemblances between Spenser's House of Busirane and an image of the Temple that would have been familiar to him and, more importantly for my argument, his readers.

Such parallels with the Temple in liturgical spaces such as cathedrals, synagogues, and monasteries throughout Byzantine and Gothic architecture are commonplace and need little explanation. And Carruthers has shown how biblical architecture was the *ne plus ultra* of monastic memory practices.[28] But if one wishes (as I do) to make the argument that Spenser uses such a structure for a decidedly non-Judaic, non-Christian space in the Renaissance, one needs to look for evidence of more unexpected borrowings. In fact, the idea of reconstructing Solomon's Temple for secular use would not have been extraordinary. For example, Tudor estates were constructed along the idea of an outer and inner court leading ultimately to the privy chamber, where the monarch or lord of the manor admitted important or intimate visitors, lending the feel of a trinal procession to many of the great English houses built and used in this period.[29] Such borrowings suggest that the ideological import of a spatial archetype is in some cases less important than the varying uses that can be made of it.

Even more to the point, at the very time *The Faerie Queene* was being composed, a distinctly Solomonesque country house was being designed and erected in Nottinghamshire. Mark Girouard thoroughly explores this example of what he thinks may be a direct attempt to rebuild the Temple of Solomon as a country estate. He reproduces pictures and plans of Wollaton Hall, created between 1580 and 1588 by Francis Willoughby (patron) and Robert Smythson (architect). The house intrigues Girouard for the same reason it has baffled most architectural historians and critics—its mysterious and awkward central prospect room, around which the rest of the house is built. Rising like a central watchtower, Girouard says, "the general effect is of a combination of church and castle," a combination which might also describe Busirane's odd house.[30] Even Girouard's evocation of the patron, Willoughby, sounds a little bit like Busirane: "There, up in the clouds in his great desolate prospect room, he could think he was the superman or even God himself."[31] Girouard locates possible parallels for the tower in other English houses such as Mount Edgcumbe. Girouard also explains that Sir Francis Willoughby was an eccentric, wealthy intellectual with a large collection of books, who also considered himself something of a theologian, writing theological treatises. Girouard shows that it is very likely that Willoughby would have used, if not owned, one of the many editions of Anton Koberger's Latin Bible, which included the *Postilla Super Totam Bibliam* of Nicolaus de Lyra. In de Lyra's commentaries, illustrations of the Temple and Temple Complex accompany the last chapters of Ezekiel. Girouard helpfully juxtaposes Koberger's engraving, based on Nicholas of Lyra's, with Robert Smythson's plan for Wollaton (figs. 3 and 4) to show the likely borrowing.[32]

Girouard notes that the grandeur of temple design made it an appealing model for the aristocracy. He writes:

It was therefore appropriate that a king's palace should follow the model of the house of God; for this reason, according to a contemporary witness, Herrera used the Temple as a prototype for the Escorial, and John Webb almost certainly used Villalpando's reconstruction of the Holy of Holies as the basis of his design for Charles II's bedchamber at Greenwich Palace. To extend imitation to the house of a great landowner and local magnate was only to move one step further down the chain.[33]

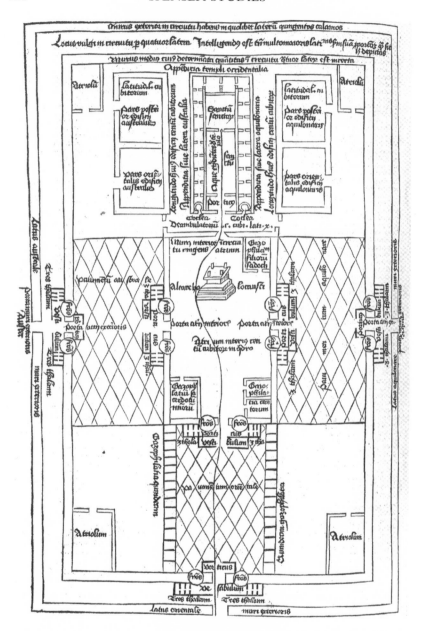

Fig. 3. "The temple layout, as engraved by Anton Koberger in 1481, after the reconstruction by Nikolaus de Lyra," Girouard 1992, p. 190. By permission of the British Library.

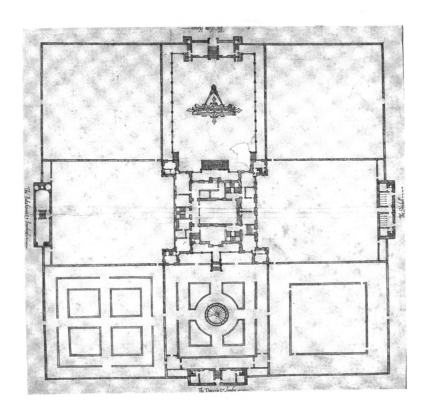

Fig. 4. "Robert Smythson's plan of Wollaton," Girouard 1992, p. 190. By permission of Yale University Press.

Spenser's use of temple design therefore has a precedent in the architecture of the era. But what might this mean for interpretation of the House of Busirane episode?

To begin with, I think it suggests that interpretation is not as important as use. The patterns of the Temple provide a *ductus* for the memorial work of its readers, a gymnasium for the exercise of the mind, and a workbook for ethical thought. Perhaps the most telling indicator of this is the description of the artwork in the House of Busirane as "the goodly ordinaunce of this rich Place" (III.xi.53). Hamilton glosses ordinaunce as "warlike equipment," a gloss faithful to interpretations of the episode as an obstacle course for Britomart.[34] But this meaning of *ordinaunce* is not the most likely one. While *OED*'s "*ordnance, n.*" gives Hamilton this definition, the far larger entry for *ordinance, n.* is perhaps more relevant to Spenser's poem. In the latter entry, ordinance is defined as an orderly progression like that of religious ceremony, or a planned, orderly, systematic arrangement, such as the "goodly order" of Fansy's "paynted plumes" (III.xii.9) amidst the maskers "enranged orderly" (III.xii.5).[35] This orderliness has long been remarked,[36] most singularly by Alastair Fowler in his numerological studies. But his discoveries of numerical patterns were published almost a half century ago, when Spenser studies were still focused on psychological questions such as, "Is Busyrane Amoret's emotional state, or its objective cause?"[37] and "why is Amoret tortured by Busyrane?"[38] Such questions unfortunately occlude the possibility that the ordinance of the house of Busirane is itself a dispositional order, based largely on the Temple of Solomon, that underlies the poet's composition and supports the memory work, or thinking, of the reader.

IV. BERNARDIAN AESTHETICS

Interpretation of the House of Busirane episode has most usually focused on the ramifications of psychological and anti-Petrarchan "sexual ideology."[39] But some recent essays have started to think about the house in other ways. Judith Anderson's idea of a house of rhetoric[40] and Genevieve Guenther's argument for "instrumental aesthetics"[41] both seek to redress an imbalance that has privileged the psychology of Britomart and Amoret over the astonishingly clever ecphrastic treatment of the house. The poem itself, though, cautions against treatments of Britomart as a character in a number of ways.

Britomart completely drops out of the poem for over 21 stanzas during the poet's long ecphrasis of tapestry in the first room of Busirane's house. In stanza 27, "the Championesse now decked has / The vtmost rowme;" in stanza 49, "That wondrous sight [i.e., Cupid's altar] faire Britomart amazd;" in between, there is not even a hint of the heroine. Even at the one point where the extended ecphrasis makes reference to witnessing the tapestry, it is an objective, impersonal construction: "Wondrous delight it was, there to behould" (III.xi.34). At the end of the room's description, when the poem has Britomart amazed (III.xi.49, above), the amazement is precipitated by the altar of Cupid, so that no reaction on Britomart's part to the tapestries is ever given. So what are the 19 stanzas devoted to the tapestries doing in the poem? In short, some very odd things.

The brief impersonal construction in stanza 34 is followed in stanzas 36–37 by an even stranger second-person address—to Phoebus! No doubt the apostrophe is conventional, but placed amidst a large ecphrasis that proceeds very differently (in the third person), the stanzas have a wonderfully energetic quality. Suddenly, Phoebus is not a set of threads in a tapestry but a person being addressed. The poem heightens the effect by repeating Phoebus's second person pronoun 14 times in as many lines and in three different cases ("thou" 4 times, "thy" 5 times, and "thee" 5 times). Spenser brilliantly follows this assault with a pronoun that is easily passed over: *ye*. After the address to Phoebus ends with the transformation of Hyacinct and Coronis into flowers, the poet comments: "For griefe whereof, ye mote haue liuely seene / The God himselfe rending his golden heare" (III.xi.37). If one catches the passing two-letter pronoun for what it is, the effect is jolting. Here, I submit, we find the real audience for the description of the tapestries; not Britomart as is usually assumed, but any reader of the poem, an interpretation that should cause critics to reassess the work the ecphrasis performs.

Of all the books of Spenser's encyclopedic poem, Book III is most concerned with art. The heroine Britomart and her lover Arthegall are linked by art (BritomARThegall). The proem calls attention to the art of the "life-resembling pencil" (III.proem.2). And artistic objects are strewn throughout the book: the architecture, tapestries, and music of Castle Joyeous; the natural art of the Gardin of Adonis; and the false Florimell artfully constructed by a witch. But it is in the last two cantos that Spenser's thinking about art culminates. There Britomart encounters an artistic cornucopia of architecture, tapestry, statuary, bas-relief, and theater; a rag-tag but impressive collection of art reminiscent of the ducal palace at Urbino (c. 1444) described by Castiglione and built by Federico of Montefeltro, who "furnished it not only with what is customary, such as silver vases, wall hangings of the richest cloth of gold, silk, and other like things, but for ornament he added countless ancient statues of marble and bronze, rare paintings, and musical instruments of every sort."[42] Though preceeding the advent of the modern-day museum, Britomart's worries about the art marks her as what today would be recognized as a budding museum curator: "Straunge thing it seem'd, that none was to possesse / So rich purveyance, ne them keepe with carefulnesse" (III.xi.53). The House of Busirane cantos also abound in stanzaic rhymes that hint at this important theme: art, smart, hart, dart, pervart, desart, part, dispart (e.g., III.xi.1, 30, 36, 44; III.xii.16, 21, 28, 31, 38). And there are artful puns as well: the opening stanza of the episode says of Fowle Gealosy, "Of all the passions in the mind thou vilest art" (III.xi.1), the copula art punningly foreshadowing Busirane's "vilest art" which is referred to later as the "straunge characters of his art" (III.xii.31).

The elaborate artwork inside the House of Busirane and the correspondingly elaborate description by Spenser have received much commentary in the history of Spenser scholarship. Beginning with Warton's notes, critics have taken up various stances toward the ecphrases detailing the tapestries, gold-relief, and altar of the house. Most approaches have ended by making essentially negative claims about the artwork.[43] Depicting as it does sinister forms of eros, the art inside the house is often coupled with the house itself, so that the vanishing of the idolatrous castle is taken as more proof of the worthlessness of the art inside it, a view that I think needs to be reconsidered.

Because the Temple was one of the chief places of monastic memory, it might be helpful to consider Spenser's poem with reference to medieval thinking about art. Specifically, I want to explore the poem's musings on aesthetics and ethics through a reading of this scene in the light of what I have found to be a possible material source for Spenser's thinking on the use of art: the vexed Protestant inheritance of the writings of Bernard of Clairvaux and the aesthetic traditions of Cistercianism.

One important fact leads me to the writings of Bernard: he was one of the early sponsors of the Knights Templar, also called the Knights of the Temple of Solomon. Spenser makes reference to the order in Prothalamion as the narrator passes the Inner Temple: "There whylome wont the Templar Knights to byde, / Till they decayd through pride" (134–36). Red Crosse Knight's insignia, as has always been known, links him to St. George. But a red cross on a white background was also the dress of the Knights Templar. It would seem possible then that, beyond the legend of St. George, the Red Crosse Knight's symbolic outfit is a nod to the Knights Templar. The parallel of Arthegall's judicial debut with Solomon's (V.i.26–28) further makes plausible the connection of Busirane's house (where Arthegall's lover, Britomart, makes her heroic debut) with the Temple of Solomon. All these hints suggest that the Knights Templar provide one of the vital foundations of Spenser's memory work in *The Faerie Queene*. This military religious order, now much fabled, was created to protect pilgrims to the Holy Land after the capture of Jerusalem in the First Crusade. They called themselves "Templar" after the old Temple compound in Jerusalem where they made their headquarters. Up to this time, the site had been under Muslim contol. The only religious buildings on the hill were al-Aqsa mosque and the Dome of the Rock (covering the rock from which Muhammed began his journey heavenward). After the Christians took over the site, they ignored the Muslim significance of the buildings, calling them instead the Temple of Solomon and the Temple of the Lord, respectively, a powerful example of inventive memory. Bernard, who was the chief preacher of the Second Crusade, was very glad to help prop up the newly distinguished military order. He not only wrote *De Laude Novae Militiae [In Praise of the New Knighthood]*; he also helped write the seventy-two rules of the order.[44]

As Benedicta Ward, William Paulsell, and others have shown, Bernard perhaps more than any other patristic writer, has often been viewed as a proto-Protestant.[45] John Wyclif cites Bernard often in his tract against papal power.[46] Chaucer's humble Parson invokes Bernard frequently.[47] And all the major spokespersons for the sixteenth-century English church were also steeped in Bernard: Cranmer, Whitgift, Grindal, Hooker, Becon, and Jewell. Lancelot Andrewes, Spenser's fellow student at Pembroke, also liked to quote Bernard.[48] As Gregory Schweers notes, even the recusant poet Robert Southwell called on Bernard in his writings as a ploy to garner support from the Protestant regime. When being sent to the Tower, Southwell requested two books: the Bible and the works of Bernard.[49] John Panke, in a treatise published in 1618, regards both Bernard and Gregory the Great as proto-Protestant voices.[50] Cistercianism, always associated with its early abbot Bernard, thrived in England up to the dissolution. In Lancashire, possible ancestral home of Spenser, there were two monasteries, Whalley and Sawley—both Cistercian. The order was so robust that it had a college in Oxford: the pre-dissolution incarnation of St. John's College was Bernard's College, a place for Cistercian monks to study.[51]

There were around a dozen continental editions of Bernard's works in the sixteenth century, including a 1547 Paris edition now held by Spenser's Pembroke College (though, as my conversations with the current librarian have indicated, probably not acquired until 1599). A biographical note in Bateman's augmented version of Bartholomew's encyclopedic *De Proprietatibus Rerum* gives an overview of the Bernardian canon for late sixteenth-century English readers:

> *Bernard,* was borne in *Burgondy,* in the Castle of *Fountaynes,* of noble lygnage, he became a Muncke in the Monestarie of *Clareuallencis,* gaue himselfe to studie, and wrote diuers Bookes, as *De Consideratione, ad Eugenium Papam, De Cantica canticorum, De amore Dei, Librum meditacionum,* and manye other Homelies, Epistles and Sermons. He was about *Anno. 1112.* and lyued to the yeares of *63.* After the *Legenda,* de- / ceased *Anno. 1156.*[52]

That some of these writings provide an intertext for sixteenth-century English literature is an idea that has been put forward in the past. Work by Anne Lake Prescott and Susie Sutch on the relationship between Bateman's *The trauayled pylgrime* (1569) and its continental predecessors has shown that Bernard's allegorical treatment of the Prodigal Son in *Parabola I, De pugna spirituali* is the source of the characters and plot of these later stories.[53] Also, Noam Flinker's work on Canticles in the seventeenth century, though it does not mention the abbot of Clairvaux, inevitably implicates Bernard's allegorical exegesis of the work. And George Scheper and Stanley Stewart, writing on the same subject, do name Bernard.[54]

Though Bernard was the most powerful Catholic abbot of the twelfth century, counting as personal friends two popes, he was also reform-minded. In the theoretical and practical debates between the black monks of Cluny and the white monks of Citeaux, Bernard wrote an impassioned defense of his view denouncing what he saw as Cluniac indulgence in art and Epicureanism: "I shall say nothing," he writes, "about the soaring heights and extravagant lengths and unnecessary widths of the churches, nothing about their expensive decorations and novel images, which catch the attention of those who go in to pray, and dry up their devotion."[55] Bernard theorized that any attention to narrative or pictorial representations obstructed one's contemplation of God:

> What excuse can there be for these ridiculous monstrosities in the cloisters where the monks do their reading, extraordinary

things at once beautiful and ugly? Here we find filthy monkeys and fierce lions, fearful centaurs, harpies, and striped tigers, soldiers at war, hunters blowing their horns. Here is one head with many bodies, there is one body with many heads. Over there is a beast with a serpent for its tail, a fish with an animal's head, and a creature that is horse in front and goat behind, and a second beast with horns and the rear of a horse. All round there is such an amazing variety of shapes that one could easily prefer to take one's reading from the walls instead of from a book. One could spend the whole day gazing fascinated at these things, one by one, instead of meditating on the law of God.[56]

In polemically stark contrast, Bernard affirmed the ascetic principles of the Cistercian way of life and instituted the theories of meditation and contemplation that led Cistercians to adopt the austere, non-narrative, non-pictorial architectural decoration they are known for. It is this Bernardian proto-iconoclasm that I believe becomes important to sixteenth-century theories (and acts) of iconoclasm.

The Cistercian commitment to an ascetic aesthetics was in practice always full of tensions. Bertrand Russell comments, wryly as usual, that "Fountains Abbey, in Yorkshire [which is one of the most majestic medieval ruins in all of Britain] is Cistercian—a remarkable work," he writes, "for men who thought all beauty of the Devil."[57] And Kilian Hufgard opens his investigation of the aesthetics of Bernard by calling attention to a similar paradox: "Ascetic or aesthete?" he asks. "Is it possible to reconcile these apparently paradoxical roles within a single personality?"[58] A similar question might be asked of Spenser. But if the last twenty or thirty years of Spenserian scholarship have taught us anything, it is that contradiction is an inherent feature of Spenser's work. The nature of *The Faerie Queene*'s thinking about art and ethics is no different.

Bernard's rationale for an ascetic aesthetics is that experienced Cistercian monks do not need images because they are experts at meditation, that is, at creating mental images. And almost all of his sermons, letters, and treatises are addressed to clerics and monks, a fact we should bear in mind when trying to ascertain his ethical and aesthetic views. In fact, it seems that Bernard saves space for the fact that novices and lay folk *need* images to set their minds to work on holy conversation. Mary Carruthers, reading the story of the monk Isaac and the hermit Sarapion in John Cassian's *Conference* (from which she quotes), concludes, "Those who pray most purely will not only 'reject all representations of the divine and all that is of human shape' but will banish from their minds even the memory of words or actions, whatever mental form they may take. *But these young monks are beginners, not yet among the* purissimi."[59] The eventual banishment of such images is then, for Cassian, a further step in ethical growth. Bernard is acutely aware of these developmental stages as he opens his *Sermons on the Song of Songs*:

> The instructions that I address to you, my brothers, will differ from those I should deliver to people in the world, at least the manner will be different. The preacher who desires to follow St Paul's method of teaching will give them milk to drink rather than solid food, and will serve a more nourishing diet to those who are spiritually enlightened.[60]

In this passage, Bernard describes the Pauline development from limited and accommodated perspective to the strong wisdom that only comes through practice. Spenser contemplates a related question for a largely lay audience: how is the transition made from the images of art to one's own action? For the truly chaste, almost all earthly images are profane distractions from and distortions of God's kingdom, which for Bernard is contemplative, but for Spenser and his contemporaries is active. Nevertheless, Renaissance poets posit that these profane images can lead beyond themselves, making their role in the active life a positive one. Ethical agents leave these images behind because they have been moved (by these very images) to action. It seems that Spenser tries a radical experiment in allowing the images of art themselves to function as signposts to their own hibernation, as it were. For the images are not set aside forever. One can return to them periodically for the emotional empowerment they induce. The House of Busirane episode is a perfect example of this experiment—an experiment that allows the novice a set of images as a kind of elementary ethical workbook, while also expecting him or her to come to the realization that such images must be left behind. Spenser is an unexpected precursor of Wittgenstein in this regard, the vanishing of the House of Busirane foreshadowing the paradox of the penultimate statement of the *Tractatus Logico-philosophicus*: "My propositions serve as elucidations in the following way: he who understands me eventually recognizes them as nonsensical, when he has used them—as steps—to climb up beyond them. (He must, so to speak, throw away the ladder after he has climbed up it)."[61] Spenser's poem thinks about itself in much the same way that Wittgenstein's prose does: by anticipating, even encouraging its being put aside. And like Wittgenstein, Spenser sets up the work that must be left behind as containing the steps of a ductus. Like proto-Gothic imagery, both the House of Busirane and Wittgenstein's *Tractatus* should be understood as elementary workbooks to be left behind once the novice has become more adept, akin to what Stanley Fish long ago called "self-consuming artifacts."[62] The poem's paradoxical ductus through art to the end of art shows a poet thinking deeply about a key concern of his age: the desire for an ethical aesthetics.

V. ONE DUCTUS DESCRIBED

Carruthers writes, "A locational memory system is any scheme that establishes a set of ordered, clearly articulated, and readily recoverable background locations into which memory "images" are consciously placed."[63] In the present essay, I am mainly concerned to make Spenser's locational memory system in the House of Busirane a plausible concept. But some idea of the actuality of this system, or ductus, is warranted here. Through the ekphrases of tapestry and masque, I argue, Spenser sets up a ductus that leads readers to think about ethical interaction. Specifically, the objects in the episode are placed and described in ways that problematize the relation of self to other through a problematization of the relation of fictional entity and actual entity. One way to use the ductus the episode provides, then, is as an intellectual excercise[64] about the philosophical problems of fiction (which will become clearer as I proceed) as they relate to interpersonal ethics.

The tapestries in the House of Busirane begin with a series of acts: Ram, Bull, golden showre, snowy Swan—the acts of Jove. By acts, I here mean something close to a routine, like a comedian's "act." But I also mean something like actions, the things that one does. What Jove does in these stanzas is to modulate Paul and become all things to all women.[65] The tapestries as described never show Jove, the person behind all the masks. For some reason, though, readers do not notice this. It is as if readers *expect* only masks, only acts. It is as if readers do not expect to know Jove, only to inspect his surfaces. Even when Semele requests to see Jove "in his souerayne maiestee, / Armd with his thunderbolts and lightning fire" (33), she requests merely another mask. The thunderbolts and lightning are merely props in Jove's most popular act. So where is Jove? The poem almost conjures the real presence of the god when Alcmena enjoys his love "in likenes more entire." The phrase introduces the possibility that Jove will be more like himself in this vignette. But it is only a fleeting possibility that context betrays. The Ovidian subtext has Jove in likeness of Alcmena's husband.[66] In this context Spenser's "more entire" means more entirely *human*, or more entirely fulfilling Alcmena's desire. But *not* more like Jove *ipse*; the phrase "God himselfe" is used to refer to Apollo (37) and Neptune (41), but not to Jove. Jove's masks, "the hard beginne" (III.iii.21) of Spenser's ductus, starts an intellectual trajectory by sowing the seeds of suspicion in the minds of readers as to the ability to discern a person behind any of the many masks he or she wears.

Harry Berger, in the magisterial study *Fictions of the Pose*, situates the self-portraits of Rembrandt within Renaissance conventions of dress and class, and within an intellectual query about the difference between selves and acts.[67] For Berger, portraits are always pictures not of persons, but of acts, specifically acts of posing-for-a-portrait. If this is the case, Berger's theory of the pose is similar to a reader's recognition of Jove's "acts." The spiral of thought leads one finally to conclude that there is no thing other than acts. As Berger and Spenser are both well aware, these acts are not limited to the theater: our lives are a series of acts.

To confuse a performance with a self is an intellectual mistake akin to idolatry. Idolatry is a religious mistake whereby one mistakes an image of God for the "God himselfe," consequently substituting worship of the image for worship of the essential God. In the epistemological sphere, taking a performace for a person is obviously misguided. For example, to mistake Adam in *As You Like It* for Shakespeare, who legendarily played Adam, is wrong. Adam is an act, not a person.

The masque of Cupid in the second room of the House of Busirane marks a crucial transition in the episode's ductus. The theatrical presentation of highly iconic "persons" eases, we might say, Britomart toward her encounter with the flesh-and-blood magician and his captive. Spenser's choice of the masque form is carefully chosen here. The masque was always an art form of thresholds and transformations and transitions. Used in the Elizabethan court as a way of "presenting" aristocratic behavior *in bono* and *in malo*, the masque took on the feel of giving real persons a highly artificial tone. Favorite disguises included allegorical figures such as Time, Government, and Chastity. It is, of course, this allegorical nature of the art form that makes the form so appealing to Spenser. For many of Spenser's major characters are closely akin to maskers. Despair, Care, Mutability, even Calidore are all allegorical representations of moods and moralities that, because of this quality, lose some of the verisimilitude we have been programmed as readers of novels to expect. But it is exactly this threshold between icon and human that Spenser wishes us to recognize in the masque scene.

Within the pageant of passions that constitutes the masque of Cupid, Amoret's appearance in the middle of the progression signals a final development of concern with persons. The fleshy reality of her wounds and skin shocks and haunts Britomart and her readers, situated as it is among a cast of fantastic characters. At first glance, she partakes of the symbolic ontology of the masquers with "Deathes owne ymage figurd in her face" (xii.19). But her humanity is ultimately insuppressible: "Yet in that horror shewd a seemely grace" (19) Unlike Hope, Amoret is "without adorne of gold or siluer bright, / Wherewith the Craftesman wonts it beautify" (20). Amoret, then, presents Britomart with a mirror-image that is painfully real. Like Britomart, Amoret has a wide wound from a deadly dart that mixes red blood and white skin. And paralleling Britomart's original love-sickness, Amoret's "vitall powres gan to fade" (21).

The vibrancy of Amoret's portrayal, however, does more than present a truly living mirror for Britomart. Amoret's vividness, I would argue, causes the reader to interrogate Britomart's own status as fictional character.[68] For both Britomart and Amoret are ultimately products of a mage-figure, the poet Spenser. This leads Susanne Wofford to treat the tension between figure and character as a gendered problem (i.e., as a struggle of women to break free from the figuration given them by male poets). Coupled with her assertion that "Britomart stands in the same place as the reader,"[69] Wofford's argument rightly decenters not only notions of literary character but also notions of personhood itself. It is as if Spenser invites readers to confront both the ontological status of his own creations and the figuration of real persons, his readers. Because Spenser's literary characters are mere "signs on a white field," as Joyce would write in *Ulysses*,[70] the move to see in them figurations of ourselves should provide pause. This pause for thinking is, I believe what Spenser's poem sets up. In the House of Busirane we witness the poet simultaneously at his most unsure and most daring, confronting his creations on their own terms. Like Busirane, "figuring straunge characters of his art" (III.xii.31), Spenser comes to know the futility of trusting such figured persons.

The maskers in the House of Busirane are necessarily strangely unreal characters. We are told that Ease, the presenter, was "a graue personage" (xii.3), and the poem later describes the maskers as "persons" (xii.25). The terminology seems carefully chosen and used in a certain way here. For the very terminology of *persons* and *personages* hints at the sort of transitional stage the poem presents in this scene. The central meanings of the terms for this scene seem to be the meanings deriving from symbolic and theatrical registers. For *personage*, *OED* begins with the following definition, a sense now obsolete but common in Spenser's day: "A representation or figure of a person; an image or effigy; a statue or portrait." The definition plays up the second-level ontology of such a figure as re-presentation. Interestingly, but not very helpfully, the definition uses *person* to define *personage*. The meaning of *person* here is certainly "real life human being." But even the word *person* carries with it hints of artificiality and iconicity, being derived from the Latin, *persona*, "a mask used by a player, a character or personage acted (*dramatis persona*), one who plays or performs any part, a character, relation, or capacity in which one acts, a being having legal rights, a juridical person; in late use, a human being in general; also in Christian use (Tertullian *c* 200) a 'person' of the Trinity."[71] Elizabeth Fowler explores what she calls "social persons," socially constructed modes of existence (i.e., habitus).[72] It is the constructed side of personhood that Spenser emphasizes in his masque.

The iconic nature of the maskers' existence is emphasized by the repeated structure of their descriptions, including allegorical name, clothes description, movement description, and accompanying objects, usually held in the hands and always heavily symbolic. Thus Fansy wears "paynted plumes" (8), his movement is "vaine and light" (8), and he carries a "windy fan" (8). Desire's "garment was disguysed very vayne," and he holds sparks between his hands (8). Doubt had a "discolour'd cote," and "nycely trode" with "feeble steps" with the help of a cane of "broken reed" (10)

The ontology of (fictional) personhood is then something that the reader of the House of Busirane episode becomes intimately engaged with, a fact that might cause us to revise Maureen Quilligan's insistence on "how unmodern Elizabethan senses of personhood are."[73] From our question relating to the ontology of the maskers, we inevitably move to question the ontology of Britomart, Scudamour, Busirane, and Amoret. By highlighting the symbolic nature of the maskers, the poem also highlights the artificiality of the major characters. We are reminded that all characters are merely black signs on a white page. As Quilligan suggests, "Britomart's character, far from realistic, is a remarkable amalgam of traditional literary figures and historical negotiations."[74] This causes us, as readers, to question the validity of Britomart as a model for us as readers, for she herself is always already a product of that very reading act. But instead of this undermining Spenser's educational project, it actually performs that project exceedingly well. The ductus that the episode sets up is fundamentally one about objects of concern, primarily fictional, artistic objects. Britomart reading the mask helps the reader to see his own relation to the fiction he is reading. The entire story of Britomart in Book III consists in the gradually changing ontological status of the objects of her concern. From the mirage of Artegall in Merlin's mirror to the physicality of Amoret's human body, the poem presents readers with a series of object encounters designed to precipitate ethical education: this is one ductus the poem as thinking machine makes possible.

V. CONCLUSIONS

The stance toward art that the House of Busirane episode implies is more balanced, even more paradoxical, than any straightforwardly iconoclastic reading allows for. Spenser takes pains to show that the destruction of the art is a problem first of all for Britomart, who spends a whole day gazing at the gold of the second room: "All that day she outwore in wandering, / And gazing on that Chamber's ornament" (III.xii.29). Here, Spenser invokes a common Renaissance pun linking "wondering" to moral "wandering." But the moral that such a pun implies is undercut by the "dismay" Britomart feels after the art has disappeared (III.xii.42). In this dismay, there is a suggestion that Britomart grieves the loss of the art that she had earlier felt needed preserving (III.xi.53). Spenser's "instrumental aesthetics"[75] also supposes that the destruction of the house plays some part in the meditational practice of its readers. This entails perhaps a rethinking of the role of idolatry and iconoclasm in the poem and in the world Spenser knew. Linda Gregerson has argued that epic poets like Spenser and Milton had to work in specific ways to differentiate their poems from the idolatrous, so as to justify their existence.[76] I am arguing instead that Spenser's poem might be making an argument for the efficacy of an idol properly used, even if in the end it must be disenchanted.

The Western doctor most often considered alongside Spenser is, of course, Augustine.[77] I by no means want to suggest that Bernard was as influential as the Bishop of Hippo; rather, it strikes me that each of them would have been interesting for some of the same reasons. Most importantly, Bernard and Augustine are probably the two Western doctors of the church who exhibit styles most heavily indebted to classical rhetoric. Indeed, Bernard is often referred to as the "Doctor Mellifluus."[78] This stylistic affinity suggests one powerful reason why sixteenth-century writers such as Spenser would have found Bernard and Augustine appealing. For Spenser and his contemporaries were performing similar balancing acts: trying to find justification for their use of conventionally pagan rhetoric.

What we might call Edmund Spenser's ethical aesthetics is, like most everything else in his poetry, riddled with contradiction and paradox. *The Faerie Queene* contains no statement of belief or rigid argument regarding the role that art plays in one's moral development. But the poem evinces a poet closely attentive to the dynamic interplay of literature and ethics. Gordon Teskey has argued that "Spenser is not primarily a narrative poet but a poet whose main concern is to think."[79] If Teskey is right, then Spenser's thinking about aesthetics and ethics, I suggest, is acute in the House of Busirane episode at the end of Book III, where the technique of ductus produces a Bernardian meditation on the way that art and architecture nurtures the ethical thinking of its readers.

Early in *The Craft of Thought* Carruthers makes a foray into recent art history to discuss the cultural success of the Vietnam War Memorial, where, she argues, visitors find common ground upon which to build their own inventions, no matter whether they supported or protested the war. It is in this function that the memorial's memory exists.[80] That the House of Busirane has remained such a contested site of interpretation is evidence for its powerful memorial qualities. Drawing on the resonance of templar architecture, the last two cantos of Book III offer a meditational ductus that is as unpredictable as it is instrumental. This suggests that for Spenser doctrinal context is less important than memorial utility. Considered as a place for readers to use, rather than as a poem to be interpreted, the House of Busirane episode will no doubt continue to allow readers to think and remember in ways that are simultaneously unique and common.

Spring Hill College

NOTES

1.   A. G. Dickens, *The English Reformation* (New York: Schocken Books, 1964; 2nd rev. ed. University Park: Pennsylvania State University Press, 1991); Louis

Martz, *The Poetry of Meditation: A Study in English Religious Literature of the Seventeenth Century*, Yale Studies in English 125 (New Haven: Yale University Press, 1954; rev. ed. New Haven: Yale University Press, 1962); John N. King, *English Reformation Literature: The Tudor Origins of the Protestant Tradition* (Princeton: Princeton University Press, 1982); John N. Wall, *Transformations of the Word: Spenser, Herbert, Vaughan* (Athens: University of Georgia Press, 1988); Eamon Duffy, *The Stripping of the Altars: Traditional Religion in England, 1400–1580* (New Haven: Yale University Press, 1992); Frances E. Dolan, *Whores of Babylon: Catholicism, Gender, and Seventeenth-Century Print Culture* (Ithaca: Cornell University Press, 1999); Stephen Greenblatt, *Will in the World: How Shakespeare Became Shakespeare* (New York: Norton, 2004); Arthur F. Marotti, *Religious Ideology and Cultural Fantasy: Catholic and Anti-Catholic Discourses in Early Modern England* (Notre Dame: University of Notre Dame Press, 2005).

2.   D. M. Palliser, "Popular Reactions to the Reformation during the Years of Uncertainty 1530–70," in *Church and Society in England: Henry VIII to James I*, ed. Felicity Heal and Rosemary O'Day (Hamden: Archon Books, 1977), 36.

3.   Michael C. Questier, *Conversion, Politics, and Religion in England, 1580–1625* (Cambridge: Cambridge University Press, 1996), 2.

4.   Duffy, *The Stripping of the Altars*.

5.   Nicholas Ridley, *Works*, ed. Henry Christmas (Cambridge: Cambridge University Press, 1843), 201–02; William Perkins, *A C[hristian] and [plain]e treatise of the manner and order of predestination and of the largenes of Gods grace*, trans. Francis Cacot and Thomas Tuke (1606), n.p.

6.   Kenneth Gross, *Spenserian Poetics: Idolatry, Iconoclasm, and Magic* (Ithaca: Cornell University Press, 1985), 20.

7.   Darryl J. Gless, *Interpretation and Theology in Spenser* (Cambridge: Cambridge University Press, 1994); Carol V. Kaske, "The Eucharistic Cup: Romanist, Establishment and Communitarian," *Reformation* 6 (2002), 125–32; "The Audiences of *The Faerie Queene*: Iconoclasm and Related Issues in Books I, V, and VI," *Literature and History* 3.2 (1994): 15–35; *Spenser and Biblical Poetics* (Ithaca: Cornell University Press, 1999). On navigating between Protestant and Catholic influences, Anne Lake Prescott, "Complicating the Allegory: Spenser and Religion in Recent Scholarship," *Renaissance and Reformation* 25.4 (2001): 9–23, is especially useful.

8.   Philip Sidney, *The Major Works*, ed. Katherine Duncan-Jones (Oxford: Oxford University Press, 2002), 212–50 (226).

9.   Sidney, *The Major Works*, 217, 218.

10.   *OED*, "move," *v.* 31a.

11.   Sidney, *The Major Works*, 226.

12.   Sidney, *The Major Works*, 214.

13.   Mary Carruthers, *The Craft of Thought: Meditation, Rhetoric, and the Making of Images, 400–1200* (Cambridge: Cambridge University Press, 1998), 77.

14.   Carruthers, *The Craft of Thought*, 276. Elsewhere in *The Craft of Thought*, Carruthers uses the terms "*machina memorialis*," "*machina mentis*," and "meditation machines," 7, 92, 230. The concept of rhetorical devices meant to be used dynamically in the thinking of their users pervades her book.

15.   Philip Sidney, *The Countess of Pembroke's Arcadia*, ed. Maurice Evans (New York: Penguin, 1977), 136.

16. On "taxis" as "order or arrangement of words," see *OED*, "taxis," 4. On the idea of praxis-inducing rhetoric, see Kathy Eden, *Hermeneutics and the Rhetorical Tradition: Chapters in the Ancient Legacy and Its Humanist Reception* (New Haven: Yale University Press, 1997), 46.

17. Frances A. Yates, *The Art of Memory* (Chicago: University of Chicago Press, 1966); Mary Carruthers, "The Poet as Master Builder: Composition and Locational Memory in the Middle Ages," *New Literary History* 24 (1993): 881–904; Carruthers, *The Craft of Thought*, 10–16.

18. Carruthers, *The Craft of Thought*, 16–21.

19. Carruthers, "The Poet," 897–98.

20. Dr. [Alfred] Edersheim, *The Temple: Its Ministry and Services as They Were at the Time of Jesus Christ* (New York: Hodder and Stoughton, [1908]), 23.

21. Peter and Linda Murray, "Temple of Jerusalem," *The Oxford Companion to Christian Art and Architecture* (Oxford: Oxford University Press, 1996), 517.

22. Jon D. Levenson, "The Jerusalem Temple in Devotional and Visionary Experience," *Jewish Spirituality [I]: From the Bible through the Middle Ages*, ed. Arthur Green (London: Routledge and Kegan Paul, 1986), 32.

23. Carruthers, *The Craft of Thought*, passim.

24. All quotations from Edmund Spenser, *The Faerie Queene*, refer to the edition edited by A. C. Hamilton (New York: Longman, 2001). On the temple in *The Faerie Queene* Angus Fletcher writes, "[T]he Bower of Bliss and the House of Busirane are demonic parodies of temples of pleasure and love" (*The Prophetic Moment: An Essay on Spenser* [Chicago: University of Chicago Press, 1971], 35). Though Fletcher is concerned with more general notions of temples as artfully conceived sacred ground and never mentions Solomon or the O.T. temple, his work might be seen as a first step toward the more specific analogue I find for the House of Busirane. He writes, "Spenser depends heavily on two cardinal images for his prophetic structure: the temple and the labyrinth. . . . The image of the temple is probably the dominant recurring archetype in *The Faerie Queene*. Major visions in each of the six books are presented as temples: the House of Holiness, the Castle of Alma, the Garden of Adonis, the Temple of Venus, the Temple of Isis, the sacred round-dance on the top of Mount Acidale. Even the Mutabilitie cantos display this 'symbolism of the center,' as the trial convenes at the pastoral *templum* of Diana, Arlo Hill" (11, 12).

25. *The Faerie Queene*, ed. Thomas P. Roche, Jr. (London: Penguin, 1978), 1161n21–25; *The Faerie Queene*, ed. A. C. Hamilton, 385n7–25.

26. *The Geneva Bible: A facsimile of the 1560 edition* (Madison: University of Wisconsin Press, 1969). All biblical illustrations and quotations are taken from this edition.

27. See, for example, the title page to an early-eighteenth-century *Mishnah* reproduced in *The New Encyclopedia of Judaism*, ed. Geoffrey Wigoder (New York: New York University Press, 2002), 540.

28. Mary Carruthers, *The Book of Memory: A Study of Memory in Medieval Culture* (Cambridge: Cambridge University Press, 1990), passim.

29. Susan Frye, *Elizabeth I: The Competition for Representation* (Oxford: Oxford University Press, 1993) specifically compares the House of Busirane with Hampton Court: "Busirane's three rooms open sequentially, like Elizabeth's presence chambers

at Hampton Court, described in 1598 as 'adorned with tapestry of gold, silver, and velvet, in some of which were woven history pieces' " (124). The golden-threaded tapestry is an older epic motif, though: "Gold thread shone / in the wall-hangings, woven scenes / that attracted and held the eye's attention" (*Beowulf: A New Verse Translation*, trans. Seamus Heaney [New York: Farrar, Straus, and Giroux, 2000], lines 993–95).

30.   Mark Girouard, *Town and Country* (New Haven: Yale University Press, 1992), 188.

31.   Mark Girouard, *Robert Smythson and the Elizabethan Country House* (New Haven: Yale University Press, 1983), 108.

32.   Both the Koberger/Lyra illustration and the plan of Wollaton are reproduced from Girouard, *Town and Country*, 190. For a facsimile of the Lyra Bible, see Nikolaus de Lyra, *Postilla Super Totam Bibliam* [Strassburg, 1492], facs. ed. 2 vols. (Frankfurt: Minerva, 1971).

33.   Girouard, *Town and Country*, 195–96.

34.   *The Faerie Queene*, ed. A. C. Hamilton, 397.

35.   *OED*, "ordinance," *n.* 4–5, 12a-b.

36.   James W. Broaddus, in *Spenser's Allegory of Love: Social Vision in Books III, IV, and V of* The Faerie Queene (London: Associated University Presses, 1995), states that "the key to [his] reading [of the episode] is progression, not within Britomart as she moves through the House but the progression of the rooms themselves" (91). Alastair Fowler's numerological reading of the episode can be found in Alastair Fowler, *Triumphal Forms: Structural Patterns in Elizabethan Poetry* (Cambridge: Cambridge University Press, 1970).

37.   Alastair Fowler, *Triumphal Forms*, 50.

38.   Paul J. Alpers, *The Poetry of* The Faerie Queene (Princeton: Princeton University Press, 1967), 14.

39.   Lauren Silberman, *Transforming Desire: Erotic Knowledge in Books III and IV of* The Faerie Queene (Berkeley: Univeristy of California Press, 1995), 2. Thomas P. Roche, Jr. ("The Challenge to Chastity: Britomart at the House of Busyrane," *PMLA* 76 (1961): 340–44) concentrates on "Amoret's mind," "Amoret's mental attitude," and "Renaissance love psychology" (341). Though the reading of the episode remains substantially the same, Roche softens its impetus somewhat when it is reprinted in *The Kindly Flame: A Study of the Third and Fourth Books of Spenser's* Faerie Queene (Princeton: Princeton University Press, 1964). There he calls the episode "extremely problematical" and, in a footnote, seems to warn against "reading the allegory as psychological realism" (73). The House of Busirane has received much commentary, mostly psychological character criticism, from Harry Berger, Jr. through the years: "The masculine mind wounded first by desire and then by jealousy and envy: this is the center of the emotional and psychological experience visualized by Spenser as Busirane's house and depicted in the concluding two cantos of Book III of *The Faerie Queene*" ("Busirane and the War Between the Sexes: An Interpretation of *The Faerie Queene* III.xi-xii," *English Literary Renaissance* 1 (1971): 99–121; 99). Spenser's " 'world picture' exists primarily as a function of the changing psychic development of the major characters" (*Revisionary Play: Studies in the Spenserian Dynamics* [Berkeley: University of California Press, 1988], 23). The many anti-Petrarchan readings of the episode include the brilliant work of Lauren Silberman,

who, again, reads the House of Busirane episode as an expression of "Spenser's critique of Petrarchan poetics" ("Singing Unsung Heroines: Androgynous Discourse in Book 3 of *The Faerie Queene*," in *Rewriting the Renaissance: The Discourses of Sexual Difference in Early Modern Europe*, ed. Margaret W. Ferguson, Maureen Quilligan, and Nancy J. Vickers (Chicago: University of Chicago Press, 1986), 259–71; 263).

40.   Judith H. Anderson, *Translating Investments: Metaphor and the Dynamic of Cultural Change in Tudor-Stuart England* (New York: Fordham University Press, 2005). Anderson argues that "the first two rooms in the House of Busirane consist of rhetorical 'places' or topoi familiar both to Spenser's heroine Britomart and to his contemporary readers" (112).

41.   Genevieve Guenther, "Spenser's Magic, or Instrumental Aesthetics in the 1590 *Faerie Queene*," *ELR* 36 (2006): 194–226. Thomas Roche writes, "The description of these tapestries is one of Spenser's greatest poetic achievements; his mastery of the stanza never once falters" ("Challenge," 343).

42.   Baldesar Castiglione, *The Book of the Courtier*, trans. Charles S. Singleton (Garden City: Anchor, 1959), 13.

43.   For example, Page Dubois, *History, Rhetorical Description and the Epic: From Homer to Spenser* (Cambridge: D. S. Brewer, 1982).

44.   See Bernard of Clairvaux, *In Praise of the New Knighthood: A Treatise on the Knights Templar and the Holy Places of Jerusalem*, Cistercian Fathers Series 19b (Kalamazoo: Cistercian Publications, 2000). For a more thorough history of the Templars, see Malcolm Barber, *The New Knighthood: A History of the Order of the Temple* (Cambridge: Cambridge University Press, 1994).

45.   See Benedicta Ward, "Bernard and the Anglican Divines: Reflections on Mark Frank's Sermon for the Circumcision," in *Bernard of Clairvaux: Studies Presented to Dom Jean Leclercq*, Cistercian Studies 23 (Washington, DC: Cistercian Publications-Consortium Press, 1973), 187–95; and William O. Paulsell, "The Use of Bernard of Clairvaux in Reformation Preaching," in *Erudition at God's Service: Studies in Medieval Cistercian History XI*, ed. John R. Sommerfeldt, Cistercian Studies 98 (Kalamazoo: Cistercian Publications, 1987), 327–37.

46.   Johannis Wyclif, *Tractatus De Potestate Papae*, ed. Johann Loserth (London: Wyclif Society, 1907; New York: Johnson Reprint Corporation, 1966).

47.   Geoffrey Chaucer, *The Canterbury Tales*, ed. Larry Benson (Boston: Houghton Mifflin, 2000).

48.   See "Bernard (St), abbot of Clairvaux" in Henry Gough's index to the Parker Society publications.

49.   See Gregory Schweers, O. Cist., "Bernard of Clairvaux's Influence on English Recusant Letters: The Case of Robert Southwell, S. J.," *American Benedictine Review* 41.2 (June 1990): 157–66; 159.

50.   John Panke, *Collecteana Out of St. Gregory the Great, and Bernard the devout, against the Papists who adhere to the doctrine of the present church of Rome, in the most fundamentall points betweene them and vs* (Oxford: John Lichfield and James Short, 1618; *STC* 19169).

51.   See Clare Hopkins, *Trinity: 450 Years of an Oxford College Community* (Oxford: Oxford University Press, 2005), 9; and J. I. Catto and Ralph Evans, eds., *The History of the University of Oxford*, vol. 2, *Late Medieval Oxford* (Oxford: Clarendon, 1992), passim.

52. Stephen Bat[e]man, *Batman vppon Bartholome his booke De proprietatibus rerum, newly corrected, enlarged and amended: with such additions as are requisite, vnto euery seuerall booke: taken foorth of the most approued authors, the like heretofore not translated in English. Profitable for all estates, as well for the benefite of the mind as the bodie* (London, 1582), ¶iir/v.

53. Anne Lake Prescott, "Spenser's Chivalric Restoration: From Bateman's Travayled Pylgrime to the Redcrosse Knight," *Studies in Philology* 86 (1989): 166–97; Susie Speakman Sutch and Anne Lake Prescott, "Translation as Transformation: Olivier de la Marche's *Le Chevalier délibéré* and Its Hapsburg and Elizabethan Permutations," *Comparative Literature Studies* 25 (1988): 281–317.

54. Noam Flinker, "Canticles and the Juxtaposition of Holy and Sexual in Seventeenth-Century England," in *Biblical Patterns in Modern Literature*, ed. David H. Hirsch and Nehama Aschkenasy (Chico, CA: Scholars, 1984), 61–71; Flinker, "Milton and the Ranters on Canticles," in *A Fine Tuning: Studies of the Religious Poetry of Herbert and Milton*, ed. Mary A. Maleski and Russell A. Peck (Binghamton: Medieval & Renaissance Texts & Studies, 1989), 273–90; Flinker, "Ranter Sexual Politics: Canticles in the England of 1650," in *Identity and Ethos: A Festschrift for Sol Liptzin on Occasion of His 85th Birthday*, ed. Mark H. Gelber (New York: Peter Lang, 1986), 325–41; George L. Scheper, "Reformation Attitudes toward Allegory and the Song of Songs," *PMLA* 89 (1974): 551–62; Stanley Stewart, *The Enclosed Garden* (Madison: University of Wisconcin Press, 1966).

55. Bernard of Clairvaux, "An Apologia to Abbot William," trans. Michael Casey, in *The Works of Bernard of Clairvaux*, vol. 1, Cistercian Fathers Series, no. 1 (Spencer, MA: Cistercian Publications, 1970), 33–69; 63–64.

56. Bernard of Clairvaux, "An Apologia," 66.

57. Bertrand Russell, *A History of Western Philosophy* (New York: Simon and Schuster, 1972), 411.

58. M. Kilian Hufgard, *Saint Bernard of Clairvaux: A Theory of Art Formulated from His Writings and Illustrated in Twelfth-Century Works of Art*, Medieval Studies 2 (Lewiston, NY: Edwin Mellen Press, 1989), 1.

59. Carruthers, *Craft*, 71, my emphasis.

60. Bernard of Clairvaux, *Sermons on the Song of Songs 1*, trans. Kilian Walsh, Cistercian Fathers Series Number 4 (Kalamazoo, MI: Cistercian Publications, 1971), 1.

61. Ludwig Wittgenstein, *Tractatus Logico-Philosophicus*, trans. D. F. Pears and B. F. McGuinness (London: Routledge, 2001), 74. Here the medieval figuration of ascent-through-contemplation as a ladder gets further troped. Cf. Carruthers, *Book of Memory*, 27.

62. Stanley Fish, *Self-Consuming Artifacts: The Experience of Seventeenth-Century Literature* (Berkeley: University of California Press, 1972).

63. Mary Carruthers, "The Poet as Master Builder: Composition and Locational Memory in the Middle Ages," *New Literary History* 24 (1993): 881–904; 881–82.

64. Lauren Silberman writes, "Each book [of *The Faerie Queene*] has something of the character of a thought experiment" (*Transforming* 3).

65. 1 Corinthians 9:22.

66. Ovid, *Metamorphoses: Books I-VIII*, Loeb Classical Library 42, 3rd ed. (Cambridge: Harvard University Press, 1977), 6:112.

67. Harry Berger, Jr., *Fictions of the Pose: Rembrandt against the Italian Renaissance* (Stanford: Stanford University Press, 2000).

68. Silberman, *Transforming Desire*, writes that "the real poetic point of the masque lies in how the language comes to life the moment Amoret enters. The appearance of a flesh-and-blood woman among the walking allegories gives a genuine shock" (64). Like me, James Broaddus, in *Spenser's Allegory*, sugggests that the characters in the House of Busirane be "approached as fictional personages," though I look at them in the framework of the philosophical problem of fictional ontology and he treats them as they are "created within the framework of Renaissance psychology" (90).

69. Susanne Lindgren Wofford, "Gendering Allegory: Spenser's Bold Reader and the Emergence of Character in *The Faerie Queene* III," *Criticism* 30 (1988): 1–21; 12. A fashionable assertion. Roche, "Challenge," writes that "Britomart's response to the mask and to Busyrane is that of the intelligent moral reader, who can detect the difference between true and false love" (343). Wofford, in "Gendering," writes that "Here Britomart stands in the same place as the reader" (12). Wofford, in *The Choice of Achilles: The Ideology of Figure in the Epic* (Stanford: Stanford University Press, 1992), notes "the insistent puns on 'read,' which make Britomart a figure of the unknowing reader" (308). Silberman, *Transforming Desire*, writes that "Britomart's encounter with Busirane presents a reasonably clear-cut model of the relationship of reader to poet" (61). But, for Silberman as for me, the model is more unstable than a "clear-cut model": "The introduction of Amoret's subjective resistance to the magic visions conjured up by Busirane complicates this model. Amoret's dual role as a character in Spenser's *Faerie Queene* and as an unwilling participant in Busirane's Masque of Cupid provides a fictive model of the link between a conscious subject and an object of representation. The episode represents a living person reduced to the status of a fictive object while from a slightly different perspective, the content of the fictive masque apparently comes to life and resists its author's intentions. Spenser's initial model of subjective participation in the object of reading has become an unstable exchange between subject and object as Amoret wavers from one position to the other. Throughout the House of Busirane, we see the interaction of reader and text as a vigirous and highly charged exchange" (61). The work of Silberman, Mary Ellen Lamb, and other recent critics has broadened our sense of Britomart as a specifically female reader, but the trope of Britomart as reader (which, it must be admitted, the poem encourages) is still, it seems, pervasive in criticism of the episode.

70. James Joyce, *Ulysses: A Critical and Synoptic Edition*, 3 vols., ed. Hans Walter Gabler (New York: Garland, 1984), "Proteus," line 415.

71. *OED*, "person."

72. Elizabeth Fowler, *Literary Character: The Human Figure in Early English Writing* (Ithaca: Cornell University Press, 2003).

73. Maureen Quilligan, *Incest and Agency in Elizabeth's England* (Philadelphia: University of Pennsylvania Press, 2005), 261n1.

74. Quilligan, *Incest*, 134.

75. Guenther, "Spenser's Magic."

76. Linda Gregerson, *The Reformation of the Subject: Spenser, Milton, and the English Protestant Epic* (Cambridge: Cambridge University Press, 1995).

77.   See, for example, James Schiavone, "Spenser's Augustine," *Spenser Studies* 20 (2005): 277–81.

78.   See for example "Doctor Mellifluus: Encyclical of Pope Pius XII on St. Bernard of Clairvaux, The Last of The Fathers May 24, 1953," *Papal Encyclicals Online*, 2 January 2008 <http://www.papalencyclicals.net/Pius12/P12DOCTO.HTM>.

79.   Gordon Teskey, "Mutabilitie, Genealogy, and the Authority of Forms," *Representations* 41 (Winter 1993): 104–22; 108.

80.   Carruthers, *Craft*, 35–40. "[T]he Vietnam memorial is a communally, ethically useful tool for fashioning certain kinds of memories" (38).

SEAN HENRY

How doth the little Crocodile improve his shining Tale: Contextualizing the Crocodile of *Prosopopoia: Or Mother Hubberds Tale*

By including a crocodile in the list of animals recruited as mercenaries by the Ape and the Fox in *Mother Hubberds Tale,* Spenser invokes a complicated discourse concerned with the natural history and symbolism of crocodiles in the early modern period. This essay ranges over *The Faerie Queene,* the sonnets of *Visions of the Worlds Vanitie,* the works of Pliny the Elder and his Renaissance followers, an anti-League text, and a painting commemorating the defeat of the Spanish Armada, to seek to set this one crocodile in context and to show how Spenser employs natural history for pointed allegorical ends.

S PENSER INCLUDES A BRIEF, puzzling list of animals late in *Mother Hubberds Tale.* The Ape, having performed as ingenious an act of taxidermic legerdemain as ever recorded in verse (namely, making off with a lion's skin without waking the creature), disputes with the Fox over which of them should claim the usurped rule of the animal kingdom. In the end, the Ape takes upon himself the Lion's "royal ornaments" of skin, sceptre, and crown; the Fox, as the disguised Ape's chief minister, then perfects the disguise through a show of two of the Lion's chief responsibilities as monarch—the granting of largesse, and the dispensation of justice—while the Ape discreetly maintains a dignified distance from the unwitting animal subjects (998).[1] The first of the enormities wrought by the Ape and the Fox once they have seized the animal throne involves the hiring of mercenary "forreine beasts" (1119) as a kind of Praetorian Guard to protect their new power:

The Ape thus seized of the Regall throne,
Eftsones by counsell of the Foxe alone,
Gan to prouide for all things in assurance,
That so his rule might lenger haue endurance.
First to his Gate he pointed a strong gard,
That none might enter but with issue hard:
Then for the safegard of his personage,
He did appoint a warlike equipage
Of forreine beasts not in the forest bred,
But part by land, and part by water fed;
For tyrannie is with strange ayde supported.
Then vnto him all monstrous beasts resorted
Bred of two kindes, as Griffons, Minotaures,
Crocodiles, Dragons, Beauers, and Centaures:
With those himselfe he strengthned mightelie,
That feare he neede no force of enemie.
Then gan he rule and tyrannize at will.

                                        (1111–27)

Notice the legalistic "pointed" and "appoint" used by Mother Hubberd to describe the Ape's decrees: until their power is secure, the
Ape and the Fox must be seen to legislate by correct procedure.
Mercenaries free the duo from fear of force or law, but Mother
Hubberd implies that this kind of purchased loyalty is the only means
the pair has to ensure that they could continue to have "all things
in assurance." The Ape and the Fox obviously do not want to find
themselves in the same tight spot as that other usurper Claudius,
vainly calling for his Switzers when faced with trouble at home.
The Ape's warrant for "a warlike equipage / Of forreine beasts" is
promulgated and "then vnto him all monstrous beasts resorted."
    With these particular hirelings, however, Spenser emphasizes that
the fear they engender derives not only from the rapacious behavior
usually ascribed to mercenaries, but also from their foreign origins;
they were "not in the forest bred, / But part by land, and part by
water fed" (1119–20), and are "all monstrous beasts . . . bred of two
kindes" (1122–23). Setting aside any possible topical satirical meaning
to these animals[2] for the moment, I want to address the significance
of Spenser's choice to include a crocodile among the members of the
usurpers' guard. The revulsion the reader is expected to feel at the
Ape's act of hiring foreign mercenaries is amplified, I argue, by the
way Spenser translates the animals' foreign origins into terms of natural history—terms in keeping with the zoomorphic world Mother

Hubberd describes in her tale—and by the whole charged discourse coming from early modern natural history and elsewhere concerned with crocodiles that was available when *Complaints* appeared off William Ponsonby's press in 1591. When Spenser gets mentioned in association with crocodiles, it is almost always in the context of Book V of *The Faerie Queene* and the symbolism of the crocodile at the feet of the statue of Isis at V.vii.6ff. The crocodile of *Mother Hubberds Tale* remains neglected. In this essay, I seek to set this one mercenary crocodile into its Renaissance context, Spenserian or otherwise, in order to suggest why a crocodile might answer the Ape's call to arms.

Early modern natural historians, working in a discipline that rapidly developed through the sixteenth century but still employing traditions derived from antiquity, emphasized three basic attributes in the crocodile.[3] Spenser alludes to one of these attributes in Mother Hubberd's statement that each of the animals hired by the Ape is of "two kindes"—that is, inhabiting two different elements (and not just the forest, which is taken as the norm for the tale), or being themselves hybrids of two different creatures. So, crocodiles and beavers live between land and water; griffins and dragons live in the air and on the earth; and minotaurs and centaurs blur the lines between the human and the animal. Early modern natural historians and poets particularly emphasize this dual nature of the crocodile; they also emphasize the special association between Egypt and the crocodile, and the crocodile's reputation for deceit, symbolized by its famous false tears. Two widely repeated anecdotes about the enemies of the crocodile are also central to the Renaissance natural history of the creature, closely related to these three attributes. I shall approach the significance of the crocodile's three attributes for Spenser in an appropriately serpentine route through these two anecdotes: the first through a pair of allusions to crocodiles—one in an anti-League text, and one in a painting—that are nearly contemporary to *Mother Hubberds Tale*, and the second through the two other crocodiles swimming through *Complaints*.

In *The birth, purpose, and mortall vvound of the Romish holie League* (1589), the author (one I. L.) describes the Spanish Armada as a fleet of "huge and mightie shippes, readie to ioyne with the bloodie *Guise*, and also to vnite them to the Prince of *Parma*, that in a moment they might swallow vp little *England*, as the rauenous Crocodile dooth the smallest fish in the seauen mouthd Riuer *Nilus*." The simile takes the three basic attributes of the crocodile for granted. Like the crocodile, the forces arrayed against England are amphibious—though they never get to bask on English shores—and necessarily deceitful, employing such allies as "that caitiffe Cardinall, and English Arch-traitor," William Allen, to force their cause.[4] For the Egyptian connection, although "seauen mouthd" is a usual epithet for the Nile, the term irresistibly recalls the seven-headed beast of the Book of Revelation and the seven-hilled city of Rome. The Nile, as James Nohrnberg remarks, is often employed as a symbolic double for the Tiber, and I. L. does not stray far from the familiar and bitter anti-catholic interpretations of the Church of Rome as "that purple Whore sitting on the Beast with seauen heads, or rather (as the Angell interpreteth in the Reuelation) on the Citie with seauen hills."[5] The Apocalypse and its attendant diabolic beast were thought by many to be coming upon a decaying world in the fateful year 1588. Prophetic works such as John Securis's *A Newe Almanacke and Prognostication* (1569) and Thomas Rogers's translation of Sheltco à Geveren's *Of the End of this Worlde, and Second Coming of Christ* (1577), building upon the prophecies made by Regiomontanus almost a century earlier, confidently announced that the Day of Judgment would come in 1588, but as Frank Ardolino observes, the victory over the Armada "gave England assurance that it was the divinely favored nation in the struggle with Babylon/Spain and the Antichrist."[6] In this pattern of thought, the crocodile easily stands as a type of the Beast of the Apocalypse, itself the summation of the serpent of Eden and to whom the dragon gave his power and throne—"that is, the deuil," as the Geneva commentary states.[7]

A remarkable example of the pervasiveness of this association in English minds among the Armada, crocodiles, serpents, and other allied draconic beasts is found in a church painting commemorating the English victory against the Armada (see fig. 1). The painting was executed on a piece of ship's board, and was either painted or presented by one Robert Stephenson, likely in about 1610 (to judge from the reference to Great Britain rather than to England in the inscription). The painting portrays the Armada in its famous crescent formation as a dragon encircling a fleet of English fire ships, just at the moment the creature is attempting to swallow them.[8] England, France, Ireland, and Scotland are shown in the four corners; Spanish ships are shown being lost on the Irish coast, while a figure carrying a prominent flag of St. George and supported by a troop of soldiers, complete with a drummer, observes the allegory from the English shore. The inscription below the image reads:

Spaines proud Armado with great strength & power
Great Britains state came gapeing to devour
This Dragon's guts like Pharoas scattered hoast
Lay splitt and drown'd upon the Irish coast,

Fig. 1. Robert Stephenson (?), *Armada painting*. Private Collection. Image copyright © 2003 by C. B. Newham. Used with permission.

For of eight score save too ships sent from Spaine
But twenty five scarce sound return'd again.
Non nobis Domine

St. George has again defeated his dragon. The fire ships represent the "hoatt welcome" that Gabriel Harvey boasts was given to "the terrible Spanishe Armada to the coast of Inglande that came in glory, and went in dishonour."[9] I. L.'s crocodile and the painting's dragon both court indigestion in seeking to "swallow vp little *England*"—a metonymic England represented by the fire ships, too hot indeed to swallow as events proved.

What might be less obvious is how both these crocodilian images depend upon the first of my two anecdotes drawn from natural history concerning the crocodile's enemies. Both the painting and I. L.'s image stress the hungry, gaping mouth of the creature, ready to swallow up England like a little fish, and herein lies the key to the crocodile image. Pliny the Elder offers the influential anecdote in his *Historia Naturalis*:

> Hunc saturum cibo piscium et semper esculento ore in litore somno datum parva avis, quae trochilos ibi vocatur, rex avium in Italia, invitat ad hiandum pabuli sui gratia, os primum eius adsultim repurgans, mox dentes et intus fauces quoque ad hanc scabendi dulcedinem quam maxime hiantes, in qua voluptate somno pressum conspicatus ichneumon per easdem fauces ut telum aliquod inmissus erodit alvom.

> [This creature when sated with a meal of fish and sunk in sleep on the shore with its mouth always full of food, is tempted by a small bird (called there the trochilus, but in Italy the king-bird) to open its mouth wide to enable the bird to feed; and first it hops in and cleans out the mouth, and then the teeth and inner throat also, which yawns as wide as possible for the pleasure of this scratching; and the ichneumon watches for it to be overcome by sleep in the middle of this gratification and darts like a javelin through the throat so opened and gnaws out the belly.][10]

Solinus, a third-century follower of Pliny, unwittingly introduced a long-standing confusion over the identity of the gnawing enemy of the crocodile: in an attempt to be more specific about the name of the creature, he applied "enhydrus" to this particular ichneumon—a term derived from the Greek ενυδριφ, "otter," but also, alas, "water snake." Thereafter, in Laurence A. Breiner's words, Everything else shimmers . . . the crocodile is dependable, but neither the motivation nor the nature of the small creature is fixed. Hostile or friendly, he may be mammal, reptile, fish, or bird. He may be identified as ichneumon, enhydros, hydrus, trochilos, even Hydra."[11] The linguistic confusion over the crocodile also led to the creation of the cockatrice sometime in the early thirteenth century, though it is unclear whether the beast sprang from confusion over terms for the crocodile or over those for the creature that gnaws out the crocodile from within; as the *OED* confesses, "The sense-history of this word is exceedingly curious," and too involved to be explored here at any length.[12] In English, "cockatrice" became equated with the creature known in Latin as *basiliscus* and *regulus*—the enmity between the cockatrice and the weasel becoming analogous to that between the crocodile and the weasel-like ichneumon.[13] I shall return to the connection between the crocodile and the cockatrice.

As for the story of the crocodile and its little gnawing foe, not surprisingly, the tale was widely interpreted in the bestiary traditions as representing the Incarnation and the Descent into Hell—and, by extension, the Harrowing of Hell. George C. Druce identifies the hell mouth of many manuscript illustrations and ecclesiastic sculptures in England as a crocodile's mouth; this tradition would bear Spenserian fruit, as shall be seen.[14] The story appears with slight variations in John Maplet's 1567 *A Greene Forest*, Stephen Batman's 1582 *Batman uppon Bartholome*, and Edward Topsell's 1608 *The Historie of Serpents*.[15] Ignoring Pliny, for example, Batman cuts out the middleman, and has the bird, rather than an ichneumon, attack the crocodile from within. Once inside,

this bird claweth him first with clawes softly, and maketh him haue a manner lyking in clawing, and falleth anone asleepe, and when this bird *Cuschillos* knoweth and perceiueth that this Beast sleepeth, anone hee descendeth into his wombe, and foorthwith sticketh him as it wer with a dart, and biteth him full grieuouslye and full sore.

(Ppp5r)

Maplet agrees with Batman concerning the bird, stating that once the bird has lulled the crocodile to sleep, it "goeth further to his heart, and pecketh at it with hir bill, and at the last gnaweth it out, and so feedeth hir selfe full and escapeth away." Maplet preserves the ichneumon under another name (and species) as a separate foe of the crocodile, adding to the bird story that "The like thing is read of *Enidros* the Serpent, which creepeth in the grasse of *Nilus* who being eaten downe quicke of the *Crocodile*, gnaweth his heart out in sunder within, and so killeth him" (L6v). Topsell reverts to Pliny's pattern of the trochilus and ichneumon having distinct functions, but adds the detail that "when all is clensed, the ingatefull Crocodile endeuoureth suddainely to shut his chappes together vppon the Bird, and to deuoure his friend" (N2r-v). The trochilus, however, possesses sharp thorns on its head, with which it persuades the crocodile to open its mouth again.

Spenser uses this trope of the trochilus and the crocodile in Sonnet 3 of *Visions of the Worlds Vanitie*. The speaker sets the scene:

Beside the fruitfull shore of muddie *Nile*,
Upon a sunnie banke outstretched lay
In monstrous length, a mightie Crocodile,
That cram'd with guiltless blood, and greedie pray
Of wretched people travailing that way,
Thought all things lesse than his disdainfull pride.
I saw a little Bird, cal'd *Tedula*,
The least of thousands which on earth abide,
That forst this hideous beast to open wide
The greisly gates of his devouring hell,
And let him feede, as Nature doth provide,
Upon his jawes, that with blacke venime swell.
Why then should greatest things the least disdaine,
Sith that so small so mightie can constraine?

Here, Spenser invokes the allegorizing traditions of the bestiaries, describing the crocodile's mouth as "the greisly gates of his devouring hell," but does not offer a clue to his readers about how far to take the emblem, beyond the somewhat pat final couplet. The "guiltless blood" does have a Christological resonance, however. A notable late addition to the various noms de guerre for the creature that goes into the crocodile would, of course, be Spenser's "Tedula." Thomas

P. Harrison, Jr., suggests that Spenser saw a connection between the habits of the trochilus (the more usual name for the crocodile-bird) and the jackdaw, *monedula*, and blended them to create the portmanteau "tedula," utterly of his own coining.[16] Spenser's poem lacks the inevitable conclusion to this little riverside scene, the destruction of the crocodile from within by the bird or some other small creature, but any alert reader familiar with the traditions of natural history from which Spenser draws his emblem would know just how much farther the small can (and will?) constrain the mighty. Tedula and crocodile have exchanged places, and now the crocodile is the one in grave peril.

A crocodile also lurks in Sonnet 5 of *Visions of the Worlds Vanitie*. Here, the speaker sees "the fish (if fish I may it cleepe)" Leviathan, who lords over the sea like a bully in a playground, "making his sport, that manie makes to weep" (58–63). A "sword-fish small" then attacks the beast "in his throat him pricking softly under," forcing Leviathan "his wide Abysse . . . forth to spewe," like Error, another spewing monster (64–66). The Geneva commentary identifies Leviathan as a whale (see Job 40:20), and, as W. L. Renwick observes, "The combats of the swordfish and the whale are, curiously enough, authentic."[17] But Spenser may have another combat in mind—that between the crocodile and the dolphin, the second of my two anecdotes about the crocodile's enemies. Pliny gives the classic version of the tale (8.38.91), which the bestiaries take up, and which Batman and Topsell repeat. Pliny reports that the crocodile is too great a plague for Nature to allow it to have only one enemy, the ichneumon, and so (according to Topsell) "Fishes also in their kinde are enemies to Crocodiles, the first place whereof belongeth to the most noble Dolphin," taking fish in the broadest sense to include sea mammals. Two kinds of dolphin are "professed enemies" to the crocodile: one native to the Nile, and one coming into the river from the sea, both armed with "sharp thorny prickles or finnes, as sharp as any speares poynt." The dolphin will "allure and draw out the Crocodile from his denne or lodging place, into the depth of the Riuer, and there fight with him hand to hand," and just as the dolphin "knoweth his owne armour and defence . . . so doth it knowe the weakest parts of his aduersary, and where his aduantage of wounding lyeth," and therefore aims its attacks at the soft underbelly of the crocodile. "The belly of the Crocodile is weake, hauing but a thinne skin, and penetrable with small force," Topsell assures his readers,

wherefore when the Dolphin hath the Crocodile in the midst of the deepe waters, like one afrayd of the fight, vnderneath him he goeth, & with his sharp finnes or prickles on his backe, giueth his weake and tender belly mortall wounds, whereby his vitall spirits, with his guts & entralls, are quickly euacuated.

(N3r)

Spenser gives his Leviathan the same thin skin as the crocodile in the convoluted "in his throat him pricking softly under"—for if the creature had a harder hide beneath, then surely it would not react as it does to being pricked there. Other sixteenth-century poets were aware of the enmity between crocodiles and dolphins; Maurice Scève, for example, puns upon the trope in his elegiac eclogue on the death of François the Dauphin, *Arion. Eclogue sur le trespas du feu Monsieur le Daulphin* (1536), where for once, the crocodile has gotten the best of the dolphin/Dauphin.[18]

I think it very likely that Spenser means to invoke this detail of early modern natural history in Sonnet 5, particularly given the close biblical association between Leviathan, Egypt, and crocodiles. In the book of Ezekiel, God instructs the prophet concerning the coming punishment of Pharaoh and proposes a fate not unlike the conclusion of the conflict between the crocodile and the dolphin:

Thus saith the Lord God, Beholde, I *come* agai[n]st thee, Pha- roah King of Egypt, ye great drago[n], that lieth in the middes of his riuers, [which] hathe said, The riuer is mine, & I haue made it for my self. But I wil put hokes in thy chawes, & I wil cause [the] fish of thy riuers to sticke vnto thy scales, & I wil drawe thee out of the middes of thy riuers, & all the fish of thy riuers shal sticke vnto thy scales. And I wil leaue thee in [the] wildernes, *bothe* thee & all the fish of thy riuers: [you] shalt fall vpon the open field: [you] shalt not be broght together, nor gathered: *for* I haue giuen thee for meat to [the] beastes of the field, and to the foules of the heauen.

(Ezek. 29:3–5)

Like the crocodile Topsell describes, this great dragon ends up pierced by fish, doubtless with his "guts & entralls" similarly "euacuated." One can also only assume that should the tedula of Sonnet 3 do as the trochilus or ichneumon does, then this particular crocodile will also end up as bird food like Pharaoh. The prophetic image depends entirely upon the metonymous links between the crocodile and

Egypt, and between Egypt and the Nile; indeed, as the Geneva commentary remarks, "He compareth Pharaoh to a dragon [which] hideth him self in the riuer Nilus." In Job, God speaks of Leviathan in similar terms, asking "Canst thou draw out Liuiathan with an hooke, and with a line which thou shalt cast downe vnto his tongue? Canst thou cast an hooke into his nose? canst thou perce his iawes with an angle?" (Job 40:20–21). Leviathan shares the same end as the river dragon of Ezekiel, right down to being served up as meat in the wilderness. As the psalmist sings to God, "Thou smotest the heades of Leuiathan in peeces: and gauest him to be meate for the people in the wildernesse" (Ps. 74:14).[19] The Geneva commentary on the line defines Leviathan as "a great mo[n]stre of the sea, or whale, meani[n]g Pharaoh." Whale or not, Leviathan is linked to Egypt and the Nile as a representation of Pharaoh, and what emerges from this series of biblical images is some sort of evil water monster, sometimes river-based, sometimes ocean-borne, that is going to get its comeuppance at the hands of God.

Spenser's Sonnet 5 represents this confusion of images in miniature. Through his tentative identification of Leviathan in Sonnet 5 as a "fish (if fish I may it cleepe)," Spenser suggests the blurring between species (whale—or "fish"—and crocodile) that he found in the Bible. Even his tentativeness seems to echo that of the Geneva gloss of Psalm 74: "a great mo[n]stre of the sea, or whale, meani[n]g Pharaoh." The sporting beast is monster, whale, Pharaoh, crocodile—or all at once.[20] Spenser introduces a crocodile in Sonnet 3, and in Sonnet 5 expects his readers to recall the creature under the guise of Leviathan and all of his Egyptian associations, as well as the enmity between dolphins and crocodiles found in Pliny and his followers. Spenser links the Egyptian imagery of Sonnets 3 and 5 through the intervening sonnet, concerning an eagle running afoul of "the simple Scarabee," the scarab or dung-beetle, another creature closely (though admittedly not exclusively) associated with Egypt.

As Richard Schell comments, Sonnet 3 and Sonnet 5 carry overtones recalling the Egyptian tyrant (linked, I would add, by Sonnet 4 and by the allusion in Sonnet 5 to the battles between crocodiles and dolphins), which in biblical symbolism is a type for all tyrants, whether those of Egypt, Babylon, or Rome.[21] With the allegorical Armada painting and I. L.'s "rauenous Crocodile" trying to "swallow vp little *England*" in *The birth, purpose, and mortall vvound of the Romish holie League,* the biblical symbolism of the tyrannical crocodile gains another layer of meaning through the Anglo-Spanish conflicts of the 1580s and 1590s. A new (and New World) Leviathan makes his sport, making many weep in the process; the monster dares to try to swallow up little England, only to find itself bursting asunder, its "guts like Pharoas scattered hoast / Lay splitt and drown'd upon the Irish coast," as the inscription on the Armada painting interprets Ezekiel 29. England plays the role of the trochilus, ichneumon, and dolphin to the Spanish crocodile in this construction. I do not think it too much to claim that whenever written, in 1591 the sonnets of *Visions of the Worlds Vanitie* are "Armada poems" thanks to the ways in which Spenser employs his crocodile imagery. Sonnets 3 and 5 have a far more triumphant tone to them than any of the other poems in the group. In the other poems, with the exception of the dragon of Sonnet 6, the greater protagonists generally have positive or relatively neutral associations: a bull, an eagle, a cedar, an elephant, a ship, a lion, and the grandeur that was Rome. In contrast, the smaller antagonists of Sonnets 3 and 5 attack creatures heavily loaded with negative associations. In other words, in Sonnets 3 and 5, "the good guys" win, and whatever lesson about the vanity of the world that might be derived from them is a lesson most pointedly for the presumptuous mighty.

The enmity between the crocodile and the dolphin, and between the crocodile and the tedula, trochilus, or ichneumon always depends upon the three basic attributes of the crocodile, as I have suggested, and it is these three traits (being Egyptian, amphibious, and deceitful) that come most readily to early modern authors when describing the crocodile. Topsell, for example, in his account of the animal's distribution, notes they are "especially [of] Egypt, for the Crocodiles of Nilus are Amphibii, & liue in both elements: they are not only in the riuer Nilus, but also in all the pooles neere adioyning" (M4v). For Josuah Sylvester, in his translation of Du Bartas, the crocodile is

Nile's fell Rover . . .
Who runs, and rowes, warring by Land and Water
'Gainst men and Fishes subject to his slaughter.[22]

Sylvester sees this ease in water and on land as an especially fearsome attribute of the creature, allowing it to wage a kind of total war on those beings that inhabit either element. Something of Sylvester's discomfort with this trait can be seen in Topsell's statement that "the Crocodiles of Nilus are Amphibii." In "amphibii," we have, of course, the root of our modern zoological meaning—animals living between water and land—and the *OED* gives the earliest use of this meaning with the cluster of words derived from "amphibian" as

1609, from Jonson's *Epicoene*.[23] But the dictionary also records early seventeenth-century uses of the word to mean "having two modes of existence" and, figuratively, "of [a] doubtful nature."[24] Milton would also emphasize this ambiguity of proper environment or state in *Paradise Lost*, when the archangel Raphael refers to "the river horse and scaly crocodile" (7.474)[25] as "ambiguous between sea and land" (7.473), punning upon the taxonomic and figurative meanings of the crocodile's amphibiousness.

Spenser takes the association between Egypt and crocodiles for granted in *The Faerie Queene*, as well as the crocodile's amphibiousness and falsehood. For the moment, I want to ignore the Temple of Isis in Book V and concentrate on the 1590 *Faerie Queene*, already published when *Mother Hubberds Tale* appeared. Only one crocodile directly appears in the first three books of the poem (and the only one outside of the Temple of Isis, in fact). In Book I, Spenser combines all three of the crocodile's special attributes in a simile linking the weeping Duessa to a crocodile. In this simile, a hapless traveller

> By muddy shore of broad seuen-mouthed Nile,
> Vnweeting of the perillous wandring wayes,
> Doth meet a cruell craftie Crocodile,
> Which in false griefe hyding his harmefull guile,
> Doth weepe full sore, and sheddeth tender teares:
> The foolish man, that pitties all this while
> His mournefull plight, is swallowd vp vnwares,
> Forgetfull of his owne, that mindes anothers cares.
> So wept *Duessa* vntill euentyde.
>
> (I.v.18.2–I.v.19.1)[26]

Like the crocodile, Duessa is a hybrid being, bred in her case of more than two kinds (human, fox, eagle, and bear) and trading under different names (Duessa, Fidessa). Moreover, like the crocodile, she glides between different realms—between the human and the bestial, and between the mortal realm of the poem and certain infernal regions. In the simile, "the muddy shore" marks the liminal zone between earth and water inhabited by the crocodile—the ambiguous realm between two elements Spenser here associates with danger and duplicity, made emblematic in the crocodile's tears. In his essay attacking self-centeredness, "Of Wisdome for a Mans selfe," Bacon remarks with irony that "it is the *Wisdome of Crocodiles*, that shed teares, when they would deuoure."[27] Topsell glosses this proverbial attribute:

The common prouerbe also, *Crocodili lachrimæ*, the crocodiles teares, iustifieth the treacherous nature of this beast, for there are not many bruite beasts that can weepe, but such is the nature of the Crocodile, that to get a man within his danger, he will sob, sigh, & weepe, as though he were in extremitie, but suddenly he destroyeth him.

(N2r)

Like Bacon, Topsell sees crocodile tears as an emblem of deception—that practiced upon others as well as self-deceit. For Topsell, crocodile tears "noteth the wretched nature of hypocriticall harts, which before-hand will with fayned teares endeuour to do mischiefe, or els," Topsell continues, offering his coup de grâce, "after they haue done it[,] be outwardly sorry, as *Iudas* was for betraying of Christ, before he went and hanged himselfe" (N2r). Whatever ambiguity Topsell records of the crocodile's preferred environment, he has no doubt about the character of the beast: the crocodile is "fearfull, ravening, malitious, and trecherous in getting of his prey, the subtiltie of whose spirit, is by some attributed to the thinnesse of his blood" (M6r).

In this statement, Topsell ascribes the character of the crocodile to its bodily nature in an act of elemental psychology; in other words, crocodiles are treacherous because they are just made that way. In Duessa's simile, the extent to which the general association between deceptiveness and the crocodile depends upon Duessa's nature (rather than whatever choices she makes) is unclear in the text, but suggests a further and thoroughly misogynist aspect to Renaissance crocodile lore. Does the comparison rely upon Duessa's being a woman, as well as upon her guile? Other early modern authors seem to suggest so. Alphus, a typical woman-hating shepherd in Mantuan's fourth eclogue, claims that women are (in Turbervile's translation) "as ruthfull . . . as *Crocodile*, / or beast *Hyena* hight," and complains that "the viler mischiefe they pretende" comes when

> They deawe their cheekes [with] trickling teares,
> and vse their sweetest call:
> Then they conspire thy cruell death
> (fell Monsters) most of all.
> O Shephierd shun the Womans looke
> and flie hir fleering face:

For harling nets and hurtfull ginnes
are pight in beauties place.

$$(4.535–46)^{28}$$

The other slur, "hyena," adds a smack of irony to the nature of the beast that the witch sets after Florimel in *The Faerie Queene*, which the narrator states "likest . . . to an *Hyena* was, / That feeds on wemens flesh, as others feede on gras" (III.vii.22.8–9). In annotating the witch's beast, A. C. Hamilton points to the Geneva gloss on Ecclesiasticus 13:19 that defines the hyena as "a wilde beast [that] counterfaiteth the voyce of men, and so entiseth the[m] out of their houses and deuoureth them," just as the crocodile lures the hapless traveller closer with tears.

To John Florio, women

are like Cocodrills,
They weepe to winne, and wonne they cause to dye,
Follow men flying and men following flye.[29]

Drayton also invokes the crocodile during a lover's tirade in *Ideas Mirrour* (1594) that deserves quoting in full:

Three sorts of serpents doe resemble thee;
That dangerous eye-killing Cockatrice,
Th'inchanting Syren, which doth so entice,
The weeping Crocodile; these vile pernicious three.
The Basiliske his nature takes from thee,
Who for my life in secret wait do'st lye,
And to my heart send'st poyson from thine eye:
Thus do I feele the paine, the cause yet cannot see.
Faire-mayd no more, but Mayr-maid be thy name,
Who with thy sweet aluring harmony
Hast playd the thiefe, and stolne my hart from me,
And, like a Tyrant, mak'st my griefe thy game.
The Crocodile, who when thou has me slaine,
Lament'st my death with teares of thy disdaine.[30]

Each of the "three sorts of serpents" the speaker uses as points of comparison with Idea's perceived cruelty is assumed to be, by nature, vile and pernicious. Each is also associated with the traits the speaker laments in Idea: the killing glance, the voice drawing the lover to destruction, and the hypocritical tears. Drayton includes a zoological doublet in the crocodile and basilisk or cockatrice, and thereby indirectly evokes a reproachful slang term of the period for prostitutes, "cockatrices."[31] I presume the term refers to the deceit of the crocodile, the hellish gaping mouth of the beast ("hell" has many such gendered overtones), and the perils of the basilisk, which can kill with both its glance and its diseased breath. Moreover, Idea is not unlike Duessa in being "faire-mayd no more, but Mayr-maid" or siren: a hybrid creature transgressing boundaries of being, notably thought by Drayton to be a serpent along with the crocodile and basilisk (Batman admits that some call sirens serpents).[32] The tag also reveals Idea's sexual history, at least in the vitriolic mind of the speaker: like "cockatrice," "mermaid" ("Mayr-maid") was sixteenth—and seventeenth-century slang for a prostitute.[33] The word also carries a weak secondary pun, suggested by Drayton's parallel structure of "faire-mayd" and "Mayr-maid," where the reader expects a descriptive term attached to the second "maid," as with the first. In this pun, Idea is maid no more, but "marred maid," which thoroughly dismays the would-be lover. The unspoken finale of the crocodile trope, the beast weeping while it eats its human victim, offers a disturbing cannibalistic postscript to the poem, and suggests a further bitter hybrid name for Idea: harpy. For Mantuan, Florio, and Drayton in these poems, the characteristic point of similarity between women and crocodiles is hypocrisy. Of course, such misogyny has nothing to do with the real animal but is instead a symptom of early modern natural history's practice of remaking of animals in a human image—not anthropomorphized, but instead placed within a recognizably human system of values. The habits, conduct, and nature of the crocodile are interpreted according to human cultural and social constructs—here, a tradition of misogynist rhetoric about hypocrisy and love.[34] Spenser's crocodile tears simile is one of two references to the Nile in Book I of *The Faerie Queene*. The first, and perhaps most famous, occurs when Redcrosse Knight chokes Error in the first canto:

Therewith she spewd out of her filthy maw
A floud of poyson horrible and blacke,
Full of great lumpes of flesh and gobbets raw,
Which stunck so vildly, that it forst him slacke
His grasping hold, and from her turne him backe:

Her vomit full of bookes and papers was,
With loathly frogs and toades, which eyes did lacke,
And creeping sought way in the weedy gras:
Her filthy parbreake all the place defiled has.
As when old father Nilus gins to swell
With timely pride aboue the Aegyptian vale,
His fattie waues do fertile slime outwell,
And ouerflow each plaine and lowly dale:
But when his later spring gins to auale,
Huge heapes of mudd he leaues, wherein there breed
Ten thousand kindes of creatures, partly male
And partly female of his fruitfull seed;
Such vgly monstrous shapes elswhere may no man reed.

(I.i.20–21)

How are we to take this simile? Spenser is unequivocal about the horror of Error's vomit; as the tenor of the simile, the "floud of poyson horrible" threatens to overwhelm the vehicle. What may be called an unusual but natural process for early modern natural history, the abiogenesis or spontaneous generation engendered by the flooding of the Nile, becomes a grotesque spectacle, and the fruits of that spontaneous generation "ugly monstrous shapes" are worth being the point of comparison with Error's "filthy parbreake." Spenser follows tradition by singling out the Nile as a place particularly prone to abiogenesis.[35] Moreoever, in observing that the "Ten thousand kindes of creatures" engendered by the Nile in that two-fold element mud are "partly male / And partly female," Spenser seems to suggest not just that some of the creatures are female and some are male, but also that "such vgly monstrous shapes" are themselves hybrid animals of both sexes.

In spite of the reports of crocodiles (or, more accurately, alligators) in the New World brought back to England, the crocodile was pre-eminently a creature of the Nile.[36] Topsell describes how the Egyptians know when the flooding of the Nile is about to take place, for crocodiles through some special knowledge lay their eggs beyond the reach of the flood just before it happens. For all the pains shown on the part of the natural historians, however, we see that the lines between the natural habits of the crocodile and the supposed genera-tive habits of the Nile blur. As that poor dolt Lepidus remarks to Antony in *Antony and Cleopatra*, "Your serpent of Egypt is bred now of your mud by the operation of your sun; so is your crocodile."[37]

I suppose this blurring happens because of the close association between crocodiles and their most famous native river, as well as the
association between crocodilian procreation and the Nile's flood. The
egg-laying crocodiles are, of course, females of the species, but
Spenser may consciously or not be suggesting a kind of procreative
union between the creatures and the Nile, now explicitly made pater-
nal as "old Father *Nilus*" in *The Faerie Queene* who (in loaded sexual
imagery) "gins to swell / With timely pride," making ready once
again to "outwell" and to "ouerflow" with his "fertile slime"
(I.i.21.1–4). Such is the fertility of the river that at the Marriage of
Thames and Medway, it is introduced simply as "The fertile Nile,
which creatures new doth frame" (IV.xi.20.3). Gordon Braden remarks on the hermaphroditic quality of this passage, which I believe
Spenser mirrors in Error's epicene offspring, and later in the strangely
dual-gendered crocodile of the Temple of Isis.[38]

Whatever the case, Spenser in the Error episode interweaves associations of crocodiles, deceit, the Nile, and abiogenesis to create a
sense of potentially diabolical strangeness. He points to the similarity
between the Nile's flood and Error's vomit, and as I have suggested,
crocodiles and the Nile are almost synonymous. Error herself is serpentine and deceitful as a crocodile (all serpents are suspect in a post-
Edenic world). The crocodile is an unspoken presence in the canto.
As Error vomits forth monsters, so it seems her offspring pour forth
from her womb, transforming the snake-like and by extension, river-
shaped, Error into the Nile herself, ambiguously caught between the
characteristics of female crocodile and the river Spenser calls male.
Like any simile, the one Spenser uses concerning the flooding of the
Nile to illustrate the act of Error vomiting suggests a similitude that
allows tenor and vehicle to be reversed. The flood of the Nile is like
a monster pouring forth—a comparison with which Ezekiel seems
perfectly familiar. As Northrop Frye interprets Ezekiel's prophecy on
Leviathan, "As the Nile is the source of the life of Egypt, [so] the
catching of the leviathan will be followed by the fertilizing of the
desert he is thrown into."[39] Life comes out of death; life overflows
death, as death is shattered and made fruitful.

Spenser's flood has much to it. Error's vomit is a rich and complicated brew, full of epicenes, biblical allusions (e.g., Rev. 16:13), and
the fruits of the polemical presses. The wordiness of the substance,
"full of bookes and papers," all held together by an inky black poison,
befits the sophistry that Error represents, but also hints at another
type of crocodile: one of rhetorical trickery. Thomas Cooper cites
"Ambiguitates crocodilinæ" in his *Thesaurus linguae Romanae et Britannicae* (1565), defining it as "Sophistical arguments" and referring

the reader to Quintilian. Quintilian refers in passing to the crocodile's syllogism or fallacy in his *Institutio oratoria*, and much later it is one of the dialectical subtleties Erasmus has Folly state she will not use in *Moriae encomium* to argue her role in the pursuit of pleasure. The syllogism is a bloodthirsty paradox: a crocodile promises a mother to return her child if she correctly guesses what he will do with it. If she says he will return the child, he will eat it to prove her wrong; if she says he will not return the child, the mother will be wrong unless the crocodile eats her child. Thomas Wilson includes the croc-odile's syllogism among those he calls "trappyng Argumentes, because few that answere vnto them, can auoide daunger"—in other words, precisely the sort of argument with which Redcrosse finds himself wrestling when wrapped in Error's endless train.[40]

Finally, when Redcrosse beheads Error, the monster becomes a parodic version of the self-sacrificing pelican:

> Her scattred brood, soone as their Parent deare
> They saw so rudely falling to the ground,
> Groning full deadly, all with troublous feare,
> Gathred themselues about her body round,
> Weening their wonted entrance to haue found
> At her wide mouth: but being there withstood
> They flocked all about her bleeding wound,
> And sucked vp their dying mothers blood,
> Making her death their life, and eke her hurt their good.
>
> (I.i.25)

But Error's offspring clearly have not read Book II, and intemperately devour their mother until "Their bellies swolne . . . with fulnesse burst, / And bowels gushing forth," more or less exploding through the excess of their meal (I.i.26.5–6). In his annotation to these lines, A. C. Hamilton sees Error's offspring as a type for Judas, who also "brast a sondre in the middes, and all his bowels gushed out" (Acts 1:18). I am tempted to draw a connection between Error's offspring as a type of Judas and Topsell's remarks about the Judas-like behavior of those with "hypocriticall harts" weeping crocodile tears (N2r), but instead, I will turn to John Maplet's comments on the crocodile in *A Greene Forest*. According to Maplet, the crocodile "is a most glotonous serpent, and a verie rauener, who when he is farced full, lyeth all long by the Banckes side belching and panting as though he woulde burst" (L6v). Through Error's offspring, Spenser enacts the end results of this gassy and colicky crocodilian excess, even without the aid of his tedula.

This, then, is the nature of the "strange ayde" (1121) with which the tyranny of the Ape is in part supported in *Mother Hubberds Tale*: an ambiguous, amphibious creature with a thoroughly bad reputation in the discourse of early modern natural history, appearing elsewhere in the same *Complaints* collection with such charged political and apocalyptic overtones. But even in this ambiguity there is ambiguity, so to speak. In ignoring the crocodile in the Temple of Isis, I have largely ignored anything positive in the crocodile's hybrid nature, and can only cite Jane Aptekar's learned exploration of the iconography of the Isis crocodile as a counterweight. The hybrid Egyptian crocodile clearly is another one of those elements Spenser employs with both good and bad associations—a concept repeated *in bono et in malo*, as Carol V. Kaske suggests of certain repeated images in *The Faerie Queene*. To paraphrase a parallel observation by A. Bartlett Giamatti, each version of the crocodile's monstrosity sums up and enriches the previous one, and so the justice crocodile tamed by Isis and fathering a lion with her carries with it the memory of old Father Nilus and Error, of a Leviathan spread out to feed the land, and even of the apocalyptic vision of broken Spanish ships, which unfolds again a canto later in the careening crash of the Souldan's chariot.[41] These "halfway beasts," as Grace Tiffany calls them,[42] can be symbols of erotic union, as in the hermaphrodite image at the end of the 1590 Book III, or in Iago's much more crude "beast with two backs"—or, indeed, the union between Isis and Osiris in Book V. Even the Nile's mud, "wherein there breed / Ten thousand kindes of creatures" (I.i.21.6–7) is the same "*Ægyptian* slime" (II.ix.21.5) from which that architectural body the Castle of Alma is built; it is "an energized substance, an active reality that supplies us with all that we have—indeed, is what we are made of," as Gordon Braden observes.[43] Frye calls the Leviathan crocodile "the element of chaos within creation: that is . . . creation as we see it now, the world of time and space that extends away from us indefinitely, the limitless expanse that is the most secure and impregnable of all prisons" (190), namely the flesh made up from that Egyptian slime and the decay to which it is subject, from which there is but one escape, as the bestiary crocodile taught and all of Spenser's spewing and spilling beings seem to suggest. But in concentrating here upon how this particular rapacious crocodile of *Mother Hubberds Tale* "neatly spreads his claws, /

And welcomes little fishes in," I fear that any final improvement of the creature must be another tale—and one, as Spenser would have it, only found in Sabaoth's sight.[44]

The University of Western Ontario

NOTES

I delivered an earlier version of this paper at Kalamazoo in 2007, and I am grateful for the comments and suggestions of those who heard it then, and for the suggestions made by William A. Oram, Anne Lake Prescott, Kaya Fraser, Judith Owens, Lana Simpson, and the anonymous reviewer at *Spenser Studies* who read an intervening draft.

1.   All quotations from Spenser's shorter poems are hereafter given parenthetically by line number and are drawn from *The Yale Edition of the Shorter Poems of Edmund Spenser*, ed. William A. Oram et al. (New Haven: Yale University Press, 1989).

2.   The fable invites many topical interpretations. For example, the mercenaries might refer to recent events in France at the time of *MHT*'s publication in 1591—in particular the use by the Guise faction and the Holy League of Spanish troops to attempt to sort out the French succession after the assassination of Henri III in August 1589. The sleeping lion of the tale would then stand for Henri of Navarre, Spenser's Burbon, whom Anne Lake Prescott demonstrates had a reputation in English propaganda texts for being able to deal handily with threatening monsters like crocodiles. The ambiguity of the mercenary beasts might also be a comment on the court of the late Henri III and the king's reputed sexual preferences. If we are to take Spenser at his word that the poem was composed earlier, then possible connection between the amphibious mercenaries and France may strengthen the case for reading the fable as a comment on the negotiations for match between Elizabeth and the then duke of Anjou, the future Henri III, starting in the late autumn of 1570 but coming to a dramatic conclusion in January 1571, when Anjou declared he had no desire to marry the English queen; the French ambassador and negotiator was Paul de Foix—an easily anglicized pun. The poem may refer to the other more famous attempt at a "French match" for Elizabeth, that with the duke of Alençon, which began shortly after Anjou's rejection of the courtship. This interpretation is supported by such familiar evidence as the name of the chief French envoy, Simier, nicknamed by Elizabeth "the monkey," and the identification of Lord Burghley as the fox. If the poem refers to Scottish politics, as Thomas Herron suggests, then reading the amphibians as a comment on sexual taste could just as easily apply to the court of James VI; see *Spenser Studies* 19 (2004): 245–52. For the French interpretations, see Anne Lake Prescott, "Foreign Policy in Fairyland: Henry IV and Spenser's Burbon," *Spenser Studies* 14 (2000): 189–214; Mack P. Holt, *The French Wars of Religion, 1562–1629*, 2nd ed. (Cambridge: Cambridge University

Press, 2005); as well as Holt, *The Duke of Anjou and the Politique Struggle during the Wars of Religion* (Cambridge: Cambridge University Press, 1986).

3. For a recent and convincing account of the invention and rise of natural history during the late fifteenth and sixteenth centuries, see Brian Ogilvie's *The Science of Describing: Natural History in Renaissance Europe* (Chicago: University of Chicago Press, 2006), esp. 87–138. The cultural connotations of the crocodile in western culture are the subject of a recent doctoral thesis by James M. Reitter, "Modern Dragons: The Crocodilian and the Western Mind" (Ph.D. diss., University of Louisiana at Lafayette, 2006); however, perhaps because of the broad scope of his project, Reitter gives but short shrift to the early modern crocodile.

4. *The birth, purpose, and mortall vvound of the Romish holie League: Describing in a mappe the enuie of Sathans shauelings, and the follie of their wisedome, through the Almighties prouidence* (London, 1589; *STC* 15106), A3r, in Early English Books Online, <http://eebo.chadwyck.com> (accessed 22 October 2007).

5. James Nohrnberg, *The Analogy of* The Faerie Queene (Princeton: Princeton University Press, 1976), 204; *The birth, purpose, and mortall vvound of the Romish holie League*, A2r.

6. Frank Ardolino, *Apocalypse and Armada in Kyd's Spanish Tragedy* (Kirksville, MO: Sixteenth Century Essays and Studies, 1995), 125. Ardolino's work offers an excellent overview of the influence of the *annus mirabilis* in a broad sweep of English authors. See also in particular Richard Mallette, *Spenser and the Discourse of Reformation England* (Lincoln: University of Nebraska Press, 1997), 143–68, for more on the Armada year, as well as Kenneth Borris, *Spenser's Poetics of Prophecy in* The Faerie Queene *V* (Victoria, BC: English Literary Studies, 1991); and Florence Sandler, "*The Faerie Queene*: An Elizabethan Apocalypse," in *The Apocalypse in English Renaissance Thought and Literature*, ed. C. A. Patrides and Joseph Wittreich (Ithaca: Cornell University Press, 1984), 148–74, for more on Spenser's apocalyptic thought in general.

7. Commentary on Rev. 13:2 in *The Geneva Bible: A Facsimile of the 1560 Edition* (Madison: University of Wisconsin Press, 1969). Hereafter, all biblical quotations are cited parenthetically.

8. For an informative illustrated discussion of the crescent-shaped formation of the Armada, see Colin Martin and Geoffrey Parker, *The Spanish Armada*, 2nd ed. (Manchester: Manchester University Press, 1999), 15ff. Robert Stephenson's identity was the subject of a brief flutter of correspondence just before the First World War in *Notes and Queries* 11.9 (1914): 470; 515–16. The correspondents assume that Stephenson presented the painting to his parish church as a thanksgiving offering, having reportedly lead eighty men into the field against the expected Spanish invasion in 1588. The painting appeared as part of the exhibition at the National Maritime Museum in Greenwich organized to mark the four-hundredth anniversary of the Armada; see *Armada 1588–1988: The Official Catalogue*, ed. M.J. Rodríguez-Salgado and the staff of the National Maritime Museum (London: Penguin, 1988), 16.30.

9. Gabriel Harvey, *Pierces Supererogation or A new prayse of the old asse*, in *The Works of Gabriel Harvey*, ed. Alexander B. Grosart (London, 1884), 2:96–97.

10. Pliny the Elder, *Natural History*, ed. and trans. H. Rackham (London: William Heinemann, 1949), 8.37.90; hereafter cited parenthetically.

11. Laurence A. Breiner, "The Career of the Cockatrice," *Isis* 70 (1979): 33.

12. *OED*, "cockatrice," etymology.

13. See Breiner 30–36 for a detailed account of the mingled linguistic destinies of the crocodile and the cockatrice.

14. George C. Druce, "The Symbolism of the Crocodile in the Middle Ages," *The Archaeological Journal* 66 (1909): 311–38. For an example of the crocodile in the allegorizing bestiary tradition, see *Bestiary: Being an English Version of the Bodleian Library, Oxford MS Bodley 764*, ed. and trans. Richard Barber (London: The Folio Society, 1992), 61–63.

15. John Maplet, *A Greene Forest* (London, 1567; facs. rpt., Amsterdam: Theatrum Orbis Terrarum, 1979); Stephen Batman, *Batman uppon Bartholome* (London, 1582), in Early English Books Online, <http://eebo.chadwyck.com> (accessed 11 July 2005); Edward Topsell, *The Historie of Serpents* (London, 1608; facs. rpt., Amsterdam: Theatrum Orbis Terrarum, 1973). All citations from these texts are given parenthetically.

16. Thomas P. Harrison, "Two of Spenser's Birds: Nightraven and Tedula," *Modern Language Review* 44 (1949): 232–35. As an incidental note, the word *tedula* does not appear in the *OED*—which is more a measure of the word's limited currency rather than necessarily marking an oversight on the part of the editors.

17. Qtd., *The Works of Edmund Spenser: A Variorum Edition*, ed. Edwin Greenlaw et al. (Baltimore: Johns Hopkins University Press, 1932–57), 8:407.

18. Scève's poem was first published in the collection *Recueil de vers latins et vulgaires, de plusieurs Poëtes françoys, composés sur le trespas de feu Monsieur le Dauphin* (Lyon, 1536); see *Arion. Eclogue sur le trespas du feu Monsieur le Daulphin*, in *Œuvres complètes de Maurice Scève*, ed. Pascal Quignard (Paris: Mercure de France, 1974), 353–60.

19. *The Psalter or Psalmes of Dauid after the translation of the great Bible, pointed as it shall be soong in churches* (London, 1580), in Early English Books Online, <http://eebo.chadwyck.com> (accessed 29 September 2007).

20. The fact that Leviathan has a tongue but the crocodile of early modern natural history derived from Pliny most notably does not should not be a difficulty, since the creatures represent parallel strands of animal lore that did not influence one another until late antiquity.

21. Richard Schell, "Introduction to *Visions of the Worlds Vanitie*," in *The Yale Edition of the Shorter Poems of Edmund Spenser*, 431.

22. *The Divine Weeks and Works of Guillaume de Saluste, Sieur Du Bartas*, ed. Susan Snyder, trans. Josuah Sylvester (Oxford: Oxford University Press, 1979), 1:1.6.166–68.

23. See *OED*, "amphibious," *a*.1, which cites as its earliest example of usage an exchange between La Foole and Dauphine on the amphibiously-named Captain Otter in Jonson's *Epicoene* (1.4.24–26):

> La Foole: Captain Otter, sir; he is a kind of gamester, but he has had command both by sea and land.
> Dauphine: O, then he is *animal amphibium*?

Otter, as a name, also carries with it the story of the ichneumon, ἐνυδριῳ.

24. *OED*, amphibian, *a*.1. The word appears to lose its doubtful overtones through the seventeenth century. For example, Marvell refers to the salmon-fishers of "Upon Appleton House" as "rational amphibii" (774) without any sense of ambiguity surrounding their characters.

25. Milton, *Paradise Lost*, ed. Alastair Fowler, 2nd ed. (Harlow: Longman, 1998).

26. All quotations from *The Faerie Queene* come from the 2nd edition by A. C. Hamilton (Harlow: Longman, 2001), and are cited parenthetically in the text.

27. Francis Bacon, "Of Wisdome for a Mans Selfe," *Essays* (Oxford: Oxford University Press, 1955), 98.

28. Mantuan, *The Eglogs of the Poet B. Mantuan Carmelitan*, trans. George Turbervile (London, 1567; facs. rprt., New York: Scholars' Facsimiles and Reprints, 1937).

29. See John Florio, *Florios Second Frvtes* (1591; facs. rprt., Amsterdam: Theatrum Orbis Terrarum, 1969), Z4r.

30. See Michael Drayton, "Amour 30," *Ideas Mirrour*, in *The Works of Michael Drayton*, ed. J. William Hebel (Oxford: Basil Blackwell, 1961), 1:113.

31. *OED*, "cockatrice," 3.

32. Batman, Ttt2r. For another examination of sirens, crocodiles, and cockatrices as a group, see Katherine Duncan-Jones, " 'Syren Teares': Enchantment or Infection in Shakespeare's Sonnet 119," *Review of English Studies* 48 (1997): 56–60.

33. *OED*, "mermaid," 3a.

34. "Crocodile tears" remain a byword for deceitfulness. But for the record, and in the crocodile's defence, although the creatures do weep, they do so only under the most guileless of circumstances. Clifford B. Moore, observing crocodilians in the Forest Park Museum of Springfield, Massachusetts during the early 1950s, re-marks that "crocodile tears" are a purely involuntary reaction in struggling to swallow over-sized morsels of food: in spite of having a formidable collection of teeth, crocodilians "can do little in the way of tearing their food into smaller portions," and in straining to swallow "an especially oversized fish or frog," the creatures Moore observed would shed tears whilst choking down their prey (228). The same tears have been known to fall on human cheeks, hypocritical or otherwise. See Clifford B. Moore, "The Grinning Crocodile and His Folklore," *Scientific Monthly* 78 (1954): 225–31. Moreover, the lachrymal ducts and salivary glands in the crocodile are situated so closely together that the action of the one involves the secretion of the other, even when tackling more manageable portions of food. Among humans, such weeping in parallel with salivation occurs most often as a result of nerve damage through facial paralysis. The Russian neurologist F. A. Bogorad published the first full description of the phenomenon in 1928, and the condition is variously known as Bogorad's syndrome, the gusto-lachrymal reflex, and crocodile tears (Bogorad's own term for it). Bogorad's paper first appeared in Russian in *Vrachebnoe delo* 11 (1928): 1328–30. The most readily accessible English language version of the paper is that introduced and translated by Austin Seckersen, "The Symptom of Crocodile Tears," *Journal of the History of Medicine and Allied Sciences* 34 (1979): 74–79.

35. In fact, every mention of the Nile by name in both the 1590 and 1596 versions of *The Faerie Queene* relates to abiogenesis, apart from that in Duessa's crocodile simile.

36. These New World reports are noteworthy, not necessarily for their strictly zoological value but for what they show of how far Old World crocodile lore became calqued onto alligators; natural history is clearly portable knowledge. Sir John Hawkins, for example, describes the "Crocodils of sundry bignesses" he saw in the Caribbean:

> His nature is ever when hee would have his prey, to cry and sobbe like a Christian body, to provoke them to come to him, and then hee snatcheth at them, and thereupon came this proverbe that is applied unto women when they weep, *Lacrymae Crocodili*. (33)

See Hawkins's account of his second voyage in *The Principal Navigations, Voyages, Traffiques, and Discoveries of the English Nation*, ed. Richard Hakluyt (London: J. M. Dent, 1907), 7:6–53. Another interesting report comes from Ulrich Schmidl (or Schmidel), a German conquistador who spent twenty years in South America in the service of Charles V. He comments upon what is known about the creature he calls a crocodile in his 1567 memoirs (here in Joël Lefebvre's French translation of Schmidl's German):

> On dit aussi qu'on le trouve dans les sources, où il nait spontanément, et que le seul moyen de le tuer est de lui présenter un miroir pour qu'il s'y voie et qu'alors l'horreur de sa propre image le fait mourir sur-le-champ. Mais tout ce qu'on dit de ce poisson n'est que fable et néant. Car si cela était vrai, je serais mort cent fois, car j'en ai pris et mangé plus de trois mille. (qtd., Lefebvre 104)

> It is also said that it is found in springs, where it is born spontaneously, and that the only method of killing it is to show it a mirror so that it sees itself, and the horror of its own image kills it on the spot. But everything said of this fish is but empty fable; for if it were true, I would have died a hundred times, since I have caught and eaten more than three thousand of them.

Schmidl's remarks show the application of Old World knowledge and assumptions about animals to New World fauna. His remarks demonstrate the continued confusion between the crocodile and the cockatrice, and the familiar ghost of the Nile's generative powers haunting waters far from Egypt. Both Schmidl and Hawkins also show the tendency for animal lore to be grouped together: confronted with a crocodile-like creature on the other side of the Atlantic, early modern Europeans presume the beast has all the same attributes as its more familiar cousin, including the nature of its environment. If the alligator looks like a crocodile, then the river it lives in must also be like the Nile, so close is the association between animal and habitat. Schmidl's work reached a wider European readership when it was published in 1599 in a Latin translation, *Vera historia admirandae nauigationis, quam Huldericus Schmidel, 1534–1554 in Americam iuxta Brasiliam & Rio della Plata, confecit*. H. M. Adams notes that there are five copies of this edition among the Cambridge college and university libraries, though none of the 1567 German edition (2.192). The Hakluyt Society published an English translation of Schmidl's work in *The Conquest of the River Plate (1535–1555)*, ed. and trans. Luis L. Dominguez (London: Hakluyt Society, 1891). Dominguez's translation is unsatisfactory, however, probably because it is a translation itself of his Spanish version of the text. But at times, it is positively strange: for the passage on abiogenesis in the crocodile, Dominguez renders it "Further it is said that if such a fish is found in a well, there is no other means to kill it than to show it a mirror . . . " (43). For this reason, I quote the version provided in Joël Lefebvre, "Un Allemand dans la ruée vers l'or: le journal de voyage d'Ulrich Schmidel en Amérique du Sud (1534–1554)," in *Voyager à la Renaissance*, ed. Jean Ceard and Jean-Claude Margolin (Paris: Maisonneuve et Larose, 1987), 99–114. For a succinct discussion of the relations between Schmidl's 1567 printed German text, the manuscript of his memoirs, and the translation history of the book, see Marion Lois Huffines, "The Original Manuscript of Ulrich Schmidl: German Conquistador and Chronicler," *The Americas* 34 (1977): 202–06.

37.   Shakespeare, *Antony and Cleopatra*, ed. Barbara A. Mowat and Paul Werstine (New York: Washington Square Press, 2005), 2.7.29–31. In the exchange between Antony and Lepidus about crocodiles, Antony offers a better description of the animal than he is usually given credit:

> Lepidus: What colour is it of?
> Antony: Of it own colour too.
> Lepidus: 'Tis a strange serpent.
> Antony: 'Tis so, and the tears of it are wet. (2.7.54–56)

Antony's response, "Of it own colour too," comes across as dismissive of the drunken Lepidus, but is nevertheless accurate according to received early modern philological wisdom derived from Isidore of Seville about the origin of the word "crocodile." Maplet states that "the *Crocodile* is called yelow Snake for that he is in colour most Saffron like" (L6r). Topsell agrees that "the name *Crocodilus* commeth of *Croceus color,* the colour of Saffron, because such is the colour of the Crocodile," and adds that "this seemeth to be more reasonable" than other etymological explanations because he himself had seen "a Crocodile in England brought out of Egypt dead, and killed vvith a Musket, the colour whereof was like to Saffron growing vpon the stalkes in fieldes" (M4v). A rare moment of field work for Topsell, but one suggesting the accuracy of Antony's answer—inasmuch as "crocodile" carries its own color in its etymology, as the dismissive tone perhaps suggests Lepidus should already know.

38.   Gordon Braden, "riverrun: An Epic Catalogue in *The Faerie Queene*," *Literary Renaissance* 5 (1975): 25–48.

39.   Northrop Frye, *The Great Code: The Bible and Literature* (Toronto: Academic Press Canada, 1982), 189.

40.   Thomas Cooper, *Thesaurus linguae Romanae et Britannicae* (London, 1565; facs. rprt., Menston, Yorks: Scolar Press, 1969), Gg2v; Quintilian, *The Orator's Education*, ed. and trans. Donald A. Russell (Cambridge, MA: Harvard University Press, 2001), 1.10.5; Erasmus, *Moriae encomium*, trans. Betty Radice, in *Literary and Educational Writings 5*, ed. A. H. T. Levi (Toronto: University of Toronto Press, 1986), 96, vol.

27 of *Collected Works of Erasmus*, ed. Peter G. Bietenholz et al. (Toronto: University of Toronto Press, 1969–); Thomas Wilson, *The rule of reason, conteinyng the arte of logique, set forth in Englishe* (London, 1551; facs. rpt., Amsterdam: Theatrum Orbis Terrarum, 1970), V6v.

41.   See Jane Aptekar, *Icons of Justice: Iconography and Thematic Imagery in Book V of* The Faerie Queene (New York: Columbia University Press, 1969), 87–107; Carol V. Kaske, *Spenser and Biblical Poetics* (Ithaca: Cornell University Press, 1999); A. Bartlett Giamatti, *Play of Double Senses: Spenser's* Faerie Queene (Engelwood Cliffs: Prentice-Hall, 1975), 69.

42.   Grace Tiffany, *Erotic Beasts and Social Monsters: Shakespeare, Jonson, and Comic Androgeny* (Newark: University of Delaware Press, 1995), 76.

43.   Braden, 42.

44.   My title and final quotation are, of course, drawn from Lewis Carroll, *Alice's Adventures in Wonderland* (New York: Random House, 1946), 18.

RACHEL E. HILE

Louis du Guernier's Illustrations for the John Hughes Edition of *The Works of Mr. Edmund Spenser* (1715)

In 1715, Jacob Tonson published in duodecimo the first illustrated edition of the works of Edmund Spenser, edited by John Hughes and illustrated by Louis du Guernier. The du Guernier illustrations were undoubtedly an important part of the eighteenth-century reader's experience of Spenser, yet Spenserians have had little to say about them. This article begins with a discussion of du Guernier's life and work, offering some explanations for why his work has been so often disparaged as well as a defense of his importance as an illustrator at the time he made the Spenser illustrations. An analysis of John Hughes's ideas about the affinities between painting and allegory leads to a consideration of how these ideas affected du Guernier's attention to allegory in illustrating Spenser's works. The article closes by examining several of du Guernier's Spenser illustrations, focusing attention on both du Guernier's allegorical illustrations and the ways in which his illustrations of particular episodes show the influence of Hughes's criticism of Spenser's poetry.

*I*N 1715, JACOB TONSON published in duodecimo the first illustrated edition of the works of Edmund Spenser, edited by John Hughes and illustrated by Louis du Guernier.[1] Critical work on eighteenth-century illustrations of Spenser has largely ignored du Guernier and has tended instead to focus on William Kent's sequence of thirty-two illustrations of *The Faerie Queene* (posthumously published in octavo in 1751).[2] The rare critical references to du Guernier's work are generally lukewarm at best: Edward Hodnett claims that du Guernier did not have "any more than an elementary grasp of the dramatic action [of a Shakespeare play] or the ability to present even that in other than elementary terms"; Laurel Bradley dismisses the 1715 Spenser illustrations as "hav[ing] little aesthetic merit"; and Iolo Williams damns du Guernier's illustrations of John Gay's *Shepherd's Week* as "stilted little designs."[3] Perhaps because of judgments such as these, Spenserians have had little to say about du Guernier's efforts.

Yet du Guernier's images were probably a more important part of the eighteenth-century reader's experience of Spenser than the Kent illustrations. For one thing, the Hughes edition was more widely available throughout the eighteenth century than the one by Birch that included Kent's illustrations. The Hughes-du Guernier Spenser was published three times in the eighteenth century: the six-volume *The Works of Mr. Edmund Spenser* in 1715, a second edition of the *Works* in 1750, and a two-volume edition of *The Faerie Queene* alone in 1758.[4] Furthermore, the cheaper price of the midcentury Hughes-du Guernier editions, compared to rivals such as Birch's illustrated Spenser, would have ensured that du Guernier's illustrations remained before the public eye for much of the eighteenth century.[5]

In addition to the impact that the work's availability would have had on its influence, the Hughes edition presents itself quite self-consciously as an important book. Robert B. Hamm, Jr., in a study of Nicholas Rowe's *The Works of Mr. William Shakespear* (Tonson, 1709), analyzes the ways in which Tonson worked to make his series of English-language "vernacular classics" as prestigious as the illustrated classics he was already known for publishing.[6] Like Rowe's *Shakespear,* the 1715 Spenser also shows Tonson's characteristic ways of making these small-format books convey the appearance of quality: care in selecting an editor, extensive editorial additions (the 1715 Spenser edition includes Hughes's *The Life of Mr. Edmund Spenser, An Essay on Allegorical Poetry, Remarks on the Fairy Queen,* and *Remarks on the Shepherd's Calendar, &c.*), and lavish (for the time) numbers of illustrations. Tonson's reputation as a publisher and Hughes's renown as poet and editor suggest as well the importance and reputation of the illustrator; and indeed, having all the illustrations designed, engraved, and signed by the same artist does suggest the collaborators' sense of du Guernier's skill as an illustrator.[7] Finally, the edition aims at comprehensiveness, including even the non-Spenserian *Britain's Ida,* which Hughes includes, as he notes in his *Remarks on the Shepherd's Calendar, &c.,* only because it had appeared in early collections of Spenser's poetry. The illustrations maintain the focus on comprehensiveness, with nineteen engravings covering the range of Spenser's body of work.

In this article, I begin with a fuller discussion of Louis du Guernier's life and work than has been provided to date, offering some explanations for why his work has been so often disparaged as well as a defense of his importance as an illustrator at the time he made the Spenser illustrations. I then discuss John Hughes's ideas about the affinities between painting and allegory and consider how these ideas affected du Guernier's attention to allegory in illustrating Spenser's works. These ideas contributed as well to Hughes's creation of what Richard C. Frushell describes as the "Moral Spenser" of the eighteenth century.[8] I close by examining several of du Guernier's images, focusing on his allegorical ones and the ways in which his illustrations of particular episodes show the influence of Hughes's criticism.

LOUIS DU GUERNIER: ''THE FOREMOST OF ENGRAVERS''

How can we reconcile George Vertue's description of Louis du Guernier as "the foremost of engravers" with the generally low opinion critics of the past century have had of his work?[9] I believe that this disparagement stems from who he was—French; what he was—an illustrator, not an "artist"; and when he worked—the early eighteenth century, when the obsession with neoclassicism influenced everything from literary criticism to architecture to book illustration. These facts, all of which contrast with the Englishness, artistic pretensions, and picturesque/Gothic illustrative style of William Kent, provide an explanation for the greater critical attention paid to Kent.

Previous generations' comments on English book illustration in the eighteenth century betray a certain defensiveness about the pre-eminence early in the century of French and Flemish illustrators. Iolo Williams, in an anecdotal study (published in 1936) of the proportions of English-born to foreign-born illustrators represented in books published in the first three quarters of the eighteenth century, found that the proportion of English illustrators rose from under 25 percent in the first quarter-century to almost 90 percent in the third quarter-century.[10] For Williams, one of whose criteria for excellence in English book illustration is "interpretation of the English spirit," the change is by definition a change for the better.[11] T. S. R. Boase, commenting in 1947, implies the same criterion in his assessment of foreign artists' (including du Guernier's) illustrations of Shakespeare: "it is . . . hardly surprising that these foreign artists failed to catch some of the essential and very English quality of Shakespeare. . . . Here was a field where the native genius could have done better."[12] This same distrust of the ability of foreign-born artists to illustrate

English books appears in an eighteenth-century context in Horace
Walpole's comment that although du Guernier arrived from Paris
"with very moderate talents," "he was reckoned to improve much
here by drawing in the academy."[13] Here, du Guernier manages to
mitigate his suspicious foreign provenance (and foreign artistic influence—his father and grandfather were both Parisian miniature
painters) by assiduous practice in the English academy.[14]

Walpole's biographical sketch of du Guernier, which summarizes
information from the notebooks that the engraver and antiquary
George Vertue compiled in the decades before his death in 1756,
appears in *A Catalogue of Engravers, Who Have Been Born or Resided
in England* (1765) and emphasizes his work as an illustrator and engraver, not as an artist:

LEWIS DU GUERNIER 1708: Studied under Chatillon at
Paris, and came to England in 1708, but with very moderate
talents, though he was reckoned to improve much here by
drawing in the academy, which was then frequented, though
established only by private contributions among the artists. Du
Guernier was chosen director of it, and continued so to his
death, which was occasioned by the small-pox Sept. 19, 1716,
when he was but 39 years old. His chief business was engraving
frontispieces for plays, and such small histories. His share in the
plates of the duke of Marlborough's battles has been mentioned.
At the instance of lord Hallifax he did a large print of Lot and
his two daughters from Michael Angelo di Caravaggio, and two
ample heads of the duke and duchess of Queensberry.[15]

In contrast, Walpole discusses William Kent in his *Anecdotes of Painting
in England; with Some Account of the Principal Artists* (1765–71). Although Walpole's criticisms of Kent's illustrations of *The Faerie
Queene* are well known, at least Walpole views Kent as one of the
"principal artists" of England, not just an engraver.[16]

A final reason for the low critical esteem for du Guernier relates
to the change in pictorial stylistic preferences over the course of the
eighteenth century, a change in taste that has had far-reaching influence on how critics have viewed art and illustrations over the past
two centuries. Whereas du Guernier's work, created in the early
eighteenth century, looks backward to classical art and architecture

for inspiration, Kent's midcentury work, by drawing on seventeenth-century Italian landscape artists, looks ahead to the increasing popularity in England of picturesque and Gothic art.[17] An enduring critical preference for this latter artistic style has certainly shaped critical responses to du Guernier's work.

Instead of faulting du Guernier for not being William Kent—or Henry Fuseli, for that matter—it makes sense to consider briefly some of the achievements that can help to explain why Tonson chose him to work with Hughes on the illustrations for *The Works of Mr. Edmund Spenser*. Walpole mentions du Guernier's role as director of the academy, and Vertue's comment on du Guernier's reputation as "the best of engravers" also suggests the high esteem in which other engravers held him. Additionally, the way that publishers presented his work suggests du Guernier's good reputation: whereas many illustrations in early-eighteenth-century books are unsigned (including the illustrations for Tonson's 1709 *The Works of Mr. William Shakespear*), du Guernier did several series of signed illustrations for important authors. He designed the illustrations for Pope's *Rape of the Lock* (Lintott, 1714) and designed and engraved the illustrations for John Gay's *The Shepherd's Week* (Tonson, 1714). Following his work on the Spenser edition, du Guernier did eleven plates for *The Works of Mr. Ben. Jonson* (Tonson, 1716).

Another significant sign of Tonson's appreciation of Louis du Guernier's talents is his decision to have him redesign some of the plates for the 1714 edition of *The Works of Mr. William Shakespear*. Presumably because of increases in paper costs, Tonson made the decision to publish the second edition in duodecimo instead of octavo, which meant that all the illustrative plates had to be reengraved.[18] But instead of simply hiring engravers to re-engrave the same designs, in sixteen cases (fourteen canonical Shakespeare plays and two noncanonical works), Tonson had du Guernier redesign the plate. The publication history thus allows us to compare du Guernier's 1714 illustrations of Shakespeare with the nearly contemporary 1709 illustrations of the same plays—to compare apples to apples, so to speak. Both John H. Astington and Bernice W. Kliman agree that du Guernier's revision of the *Macbeth* plate represents a significant aesthetic improvement over the 1709 illustration.[19] In her comparison of the 1709 and 1714 illustrations of *Hamlet,* Kliman comments that du Guernier's new work, in general, "enhanced the second volume"; she goes on to argue that the image for *Hamlet* represents a complex interpretation of the sexual subtext of the closet scene.[20]

JOHN HUGHES'S INFLUENCE ON DU GUERNIER'S
ILLUSTRATIONS OF SPENSER

Modern scholars have praised John Hughes's gifts as a critic, in particular because Hughes changed the tenor of critical debate on *The
Faerie Queene* by commenting that to hold it to the standards of
ancient epic poetry was an injustice to a poem that was not designed
by those rules.[21] Hughes betrays the preferences of his age by commenting on the lack of unity in the work but then goes on to argue
against viewing this lack as a defect. He writes:

> The want of Unity in the Story makes it difficult for the Reader
> to carry it in his Mind, and distracts too much his attention to
> the several Parts of it; and indeed the whole Frame of it wou'd
> appear monstrous, if it were to be examin'd by the Rules of
> Epick Poetry, as they have been drawn from the Practice of
> *Homer* and *Virgil*. But as it is plain the Author never design'd
> it by those Rules, I think it ought rather to be consider'd as a
> Poem of a particular kind, describing in a Series of Allegorical
> Adventures or Episodes the most noted Virtues and Vices: to
> compare it therefore with the Models of Antiquity, wou'd be
> like drawing a Parallel between the *Roman* and the *Gothick* Ar-
> chitecture.[22]

The essay by Hughes that opens the edition thus advocates a more
tolerant approach to the poem than we might expect, given his era's
preference for the neoclassical prescriptions of unity.

In Hughes's work we can see two ways of approaching the poem,
one emphasizing the pictorial qualities of Spenser's description and
the other focusing on the poetry's salutary moral meanings. Many
scholars have noted that later eighteenth-century critics and writers
interpreted Spenser as a "painterly" poet, with Alexander Pope
speaking of *The Faerie Queene* as a "gallery of pictures" and Joseph
Warton asserting that "the pencil of Spenser is as powerful as that of
Rubens, his brother allegorist."[23] This view predominated by the
beginning of the nineteenth century in the responses of the Romantic
poets to Spenser, but even in the early eighteenth century, a consideration of Spenser's pictorialism had been an important part of Hughes's
response, though with a sense that his painterly qualities served his

moral, allegorical purposes.[24] Thus, we find Hughes, in a letter accompanying a gift of the *Works* to Sir Godfrey Kneller, complimenting both Kneller and Spenser by citing Rubens:

> Knowing how great an admirer you are of Rubens, and of his genius for allegorical painting, I could not avoid thinking of you when I undertook to publish Spenser, who had the same genius with Rubens, and is the most painter-like poet, and the finest designer of the virtues and vices of any writer extant.[25]

Hughes here avoids bifurcating these two approaches to Spenser's poetry and appears to see being "the most painter-like poet" as quite compatible with being "the finest designer of the virtues and vices of any writer extant." This view reflects the ideas he puts forth in his edition of Spenser. In *An Essay on Allegorical Poetry, &c.,* he argues that "The Resemblance which has been so often observ'd in general between Poetry and Painting, is yet more particular in Allegory; which . . . is a kind of Picture in Poetry."[26] In his *Remarks on the Fairy Queen,* he continues to use the metaphor of painting to describe Spenser's method: "the Strength of the Painting is superior to the Design" of the work; additionally, Hughes describes Spenser's "Painter-like Genius" and comments on the "Strength of Painting" that appears in the description of the underworld in Book I.[27]

Whereas Kent and later pictorial interpreters of Spenser focus almost entirely on illustrating particular episodes in Spenser's poetry, a majority of the du Guernier illustrations instead attempt an allegory or summary of an entire work.[28] Here, although du Guernier was certainly constrained by the Tonson house style that dictated one illustration per work, he also shows the influence of Hughes's belief in the compatibility of detailed visual representations and allegorical purposes. In a discussion of Spenser's poetic method in the Bower of Bliss scene, Hughes argues that "the Ornaments of Description, which Spenser has transplanted out of the Italian Poem, are more proper in his Work, which was design'd to be wholly Allegorical, than in an Epick Poem, which is superior in its Nature to such lavish Embellishments."[29] Extrapolating from this poetic analysis to illustration, we can surmise that, far from imagining allegorical illustration as sterile and intellectualized, Hughes would expect it to have even more attention to visual detail than, for example, an illustration of an epic. As I shall discuss later, in some instances, du Guernier bases his illustrations quite closely on Hughes's critical descriptions of notable "beauties" in Spenser's work. Hughes's broader influence on du Guernier appears, however, in the emphasis on allegorical illustrations, an emphasis we do not see, for example, in the same artist's illustrations of Shakespeare, each of which depicts a particular scene in the play.

The du Guernier Series of Spenser Illustrations: Allegory Vs. Episode

The decision to create a single frontispiece for each book of *The Faerie Queene* and for each of the other poems included was certainly made by Jacob Tonson, in accord with his house style. Though motivated primarily by economic considerations, this serves to constrain du Guernier's approach, forcing him to represent an entire poetic work in one image. His response to the problem, and the ways in which it shows Hughes's critical influence, reveal the hierarchy of values governing this particular project. When du Guernier could create only one image to illustrate a whole poem, he was overwhelmingly likely to choose an allegorical or summary representation. However, he had more scope in creating illustrations for *The Faerie Queene,* because he was allowed one image per book in addition to a frontispiece representing the entire work. His decision to illustrate particular scenes in the images for Books I through VI and the Mutabilitie Cantos suggests an interest in illustrating particular episodes of the poem, but this interest is clearly subordinated to the emphasis on allegorical and summary representations that governs the entire illustration series.

The illustration with the biggest task—in terms of visually representing the longest work—is the frontispiece for *The Faerie Queene* as a whole. Laurel Bradley mistakenly reads this image as a representation of Book I only, which leads her to blame du Guernier for "not read[ing] the six books thoroughly."[30] Thomas Herron's reading of the illustration as an allegorical representation of the entire poem is more persuasive: the Muse holds a portrait of Elizabeth/Gloriana, to which the laurel-crowned Poet points. Each of the surrounding figures iconographically represents an entire book of the poem: Book I holds a cross; to her left, Book II makes a modest gesture, suggesting temperance. To Book I's right, Book VI bows courteously; and to her right, Book V holds the scales and sword of justice. In the foreground, Book IV pats a dog, symbol of friendship and fidelity; and

Book III holds a vestal lamp to signify chastity.[31] It is quite a trick to condense the entire *Faerie Queene* into one image, requiring allegories of allegories in one highly abstract and demanding illustration. But this interpretation does not include the Mutabilitie Cantos, nor does it explain the presence of five figures crawling up the stairs from below—who are they? My guess involves imagining the image as picturing a stage: these figures from Book I wait in the wings for the summary characters to vacate before their own action can start. The bearded figure looks like one of the satyrs who worship Una; bare-breasted Una certainly looks a damsel in distress; the man removing a mask may represent Archimago's duplicity; and the blindfolded man would then be Redcrosse, separated from Una by the masked man. As for the woeful face behind the satyr and next to Una: the dwarf?

Other allegorical illustrations, because they summarize less, are more easily interpretable; like the frontispiece for *The Faerie Queene,* though, they provide intellectual pleasure for the viewer, who must make sense of the iconography to understand the allegory. The illustration accompanying *Fowre Hymnes* represents each hymn in a series of receding monuments: the young man in the foreground has the look of a lover; the naked figures on the second monument suggest earthly beauty; the third, with a sculpture of an angel, implies heavenly beauty; and the fourth, which becomes an altar with sacrificial smoke rising skyward, represents heavenly love. The illustration for *The Teares of the Muses* requires more specific knowledge by a viewer who wishes to understand the allegorical image representing the entire poem. The laurel-crowned Poet is easy enough to identify (note his resemblance to the Poet in the frontispiece to *The Faerie Queene*), but viewers can identify the Muses only by recognizing the objects that represent their fields of influence. The puzzling inclusion of ten female figures, rather than nine, seems designed to invite further reflection from the viewer. The proximity of Pegasus to the woman in the foreground pouring water reveals that the extra figure identifies the setting of the poem: the woman allegorically represents the well of Hippocrene, the fountain on Mount Helicon sacred to the Muses that was formed when Pegasus's foot struck the mountain. The water the woman pours from the vase is presumably "the true, the blushful Hippocrene" that Keats was to request for poetic inspiration a century later. The water takes on added allegorical significance in a poem about the Muses' tears, and in this context it seems tantalizingly significant that she pours those inspiring waters *away* from the Poet.

These details indicate some care in creating the allegorical illustrations of the *Works,* suggesting collaboration between Hughes and du Guernier, but we can argue for clear evidence of Hughes's influence only when the illustrations allude specifically to the critic's work in the text. For example, Hughes notes that in *Colin Clouts Come Home Againe,* Spenser is "less a Shepherd than at first" and "that in the Pastoral Kind it is not so simple and unmix'd, and consequently not so perfect as the Eclogues."[32] Du Guernier's illustration follows this critical assessment by making some of the main figures decidedly courtly in posture and costume, especially in contrast to the rusticity of the foregrounded figures in his illustration of *The Shepheardes Calender.*

In the illustrations that depict a particular moment or episode, we see again evidence of the influence of Hughes. Whereas some images, such as those for Books I and V, privilege closure over conflict, the illustrations that most show Hughes's influence represent suspense and anticipation. For example, the image accompanying Book II does an excellent job of conveying how Spenser makes the Bower of Bliss seductive, even at the expense of the titular virtue of temperance. In his *Remarks on the Fairy Queen,* Hughes praises the use Spenser makes of his Italian models in this canto, going even beyond the Italians in his lush use of detail and description. Hughes notes that "the *Italian* Genius for Luxury appears very much in the Descriptions of the Garden, the Fountain, and the Nymphs," and du Guernier's illustration captures this quality of excess.[33] In the illustration, the Bower of Bliss takes up almost the entire picture. Guyon and the Palmer appear only as tiny figures in the background, heading toward the Bower to destroy it. This image, summarizing as it does the whole book with a picture of the Italianate, romantic Bower of Bliss, neatly alludes to the problem that the most attractive location in this book is precisely the one that must be destroyed.

Despite its attractiveness, however, du Guernier leaves no doubt as to the moral corruption that characterizes the Bower, and here we see allegorical illustration used to support the reader's moral understanding of the poem. Between Guyon and Acrasia, two naked couples embrace lasciviously. The two female figures in the background are presumably C. S. Lewis's "Cissy" and "Flossy" gamboling in the fountain. The nearer pair, one female and the other of indeterminate gender, gaze at one another. The musicians and singer in the foreground providing music for all this debauchery call to mind Spenser's outrage in Book II against the misuse of art, as well as his more specific invective—in *The Teares of the Muses, Mother Hubberds Tale, Colin Clouts Come Home Againe,* and elsewhere—against misusing poetry. In the midst of all this, Verdant lies in Acrasia's lap under one of the canopies that du Guernier loved to engrave. His forgotten armor hangs on a tree, his erect spear standing in sharp contrast to his own flaccid pose. The illustration provides a beautiful image, but one designed to make the discerning reader welcome those tiny figures approaching to destroy this haven for intemperance.

The illustration for the Mutabilitie Cantos also shows du Guernier's engagement with Hughes's interpretation of the text. Hughes reserves some of his strongest praise for these cantos, arguing that they constitute "the most sublime and best invented Allegory in the whole Work."[34] Hughes's appreciation here is at least as much moral as aesthetic (as Spenser no doubt intended), and he calls attention to the moment that du Guernier illustrates as the image for these cantos:

> All Creatures are represented looking up in the Face of Nature, in expectation of the Sentence. The Conclusion is great, and contains a noble Moral; That tho all things are vary'd and shift their Forms, they do not perish, but return to their first Beings; and that *Mutability* only shall be at last entirely destroy'd, and the time shall come in which *Change shall be no more.*[35]

Du Guernier's illustration of this moment captures the eager anticipation of the crowd gathered to hear Dame Nature's verdict. The surprise of Nature's mysterious veiled face—the sight of blank space against the heavily detailed engraving—draws the viewer's eye, and the postures and gestures of the assembled figures convey the feeling of suspense Spenser describes: "all creatures, looking in her face, / Expecting th'end of this so doubtfull case, / Did hang in long suspence what would ensew" (*FQ* VII.vii.57.4–6).[36]

Similar in its focus on suspense is the illustration for Book IV. Hughes describes the scene that du Guernier illustrates as "one of the most shining Passages in this Legend": the very moment before Cambina touches the combatants with her wand.[37] The headless body in the foreground reminds viewers of the violence that has already passed, and the wand in Cambina's right hand and cup in her left hand point to the immediate future of peace and amity. Showing a single episode that represents an entire book, this image succeeds in suggesting the complex interplay of discord and concord presented by Book IV.

Space does not permit a careful analysis of each of du Guernier's nineteen illustrations of Spenser. I have aimed instead, through careful attention to the allegorical method in a few illustrations, at suggesting the richness of the interplay here among image, text, and criticism. Louis du Guernier's Spenser is not the picturesque Spenser created by Kent, nor the Gothic Spenser of Fuseli. However, his pictorial interpretations of the poems, informed by Hughes's views on allegory and on particularly "shining" moments in the poetry, provide more visual and intellectual interest than previous critical comments have suggested. As the first series illustrating almost the entire corpus of Spenser's works, du Guernier's work merits attention both for what it tells us about early-eighteenth-century response to Spenser and for initiating a long history of interpretations of that poet by visual artists.

Indiana University—Purdue University Fort Wayne

NOTES

1.   An earlier version of this paper was presented in a Spenser at Kalamazoo session at the 40th International Congress on Medieval Studies, Kalamazoo, MI, 5–8 May 2005. I appreciate the careful readings of an earlier draft by Joseph Loewenstein and Richard Hardin as well as useful comments from Thomas Herron and Anne Sussman.

2.   See, for example, Laurel Bradley, "Eighteenth-Century Paintings and Illustrations of Spenser's *Faerie Queene*: A Study in Taste," *Marsyas* 20 (1979–80): 31–51; Andrew Hadfield, "William Kent's Illustrations of *The Faerie Queene*," *Spenser Studies* 14 (2000): 1–82; and John Dixon Hunt, "William Kent's Work as Illustrator," Joachim Moller, ed. *Imagination on a Long Rein: English Literature Illustrated* (Marburg: Jonas, 1988), 56–65.

3.   Edward Hodnett, *Five Centuries of English Book Illustration* (Aldershot, England: Scolar Press, 1988), 76; Bradley, 32; Iolo A. Williams, "English Book-Illustrations, 1700–1775," *The Library* 17 (4th series, 1936): 1–21.

4.   See Jewel Wurtsbaugh, "The 1758 Editions of *The Faerie Queene*," *Modern Language Notes* 48 (1933): 228–29; and Jewel Wurtsbaugh, *Two Centuries of Spenserian Scholarship* (Baltimore: Johns Hopkins University Press, 1936).

5.   On the price of the eighteenth-century Hughes editions, Heffner argues that a second, cheaper printing of the 1715 Hughes edition on smaller paper followed a surprisingly strong interest in the first printing, which was done on large paper for subscribers; Ray Heffner, "The Printing of John Hughes' Edition of Spenser, 1715," *Modern Language Notes* 50 (1935): 151–53. John Barnard, in an analysis of Tonson's printing of the large- and small-paper copies of Dryden's *Virgil,* suggests a more self-interested motive for the two paper sizes: with the edition of Virgil, Tonson had to share profits on the large-paper copies with Dryden, who was in charge of engaging subscribers for the edition; but the profits for the small-paper copies were his to keep; John Barnard, "The Large- and Small-Paper Copies of Dryden's *The Works of Virgil* (1697): Jacob Tonson's Investment and Profits and the Example of *Paradise Lost* (1688)," *Papers of the Bibliographical Society of America* 92 (1998): 259–71. There were also large- and small-paper printings of Tonson's 1709 edition of the works of Shakespeare (see Robert B. Hamm, Jr., "Rowe's *Shakespeare* (1709) and

the Tonson House Style," *College Literature* 31 [2004]: 179–205, at 192), so this may have been part of Tonson's usual printing strategy. Regarding the 1758 edition of the Hughes-du Guernier *Faerie Queene,* Jewel Wurtsbaugh posits that Tonson's issuing the book responded to market desire for a cheaper edition of Spenser than the other editions that came to market that year (the reprint of the Hughes *Faerie Queene* sold for ten shillings, whereas the Upton and Church editions of that year sold for a guinea [twenty-one shillings] each); Wurtsbaugh, *Two Centuries,* 73.

6.   Hamm; see esp. pp. 182–84 and 187–88 for discussion of the ways that Tonson worked "to develop a particular style that would materially unite the respective editions of a series" (184) for both classical and vernacular series. Thus, part of the prestige of the Spenser edition came from its status as part of a series of "vernacular classics" that was initiated in 1707 with *The Works of Mr. Abraham Cowley.*

7.   The perception of Hughes's prestige and suitability for the job of editing Spenser is suggested by the editor of *The Correspondence of John Hughes . . . and Several of His Friends* (Dublin: Thomas Ewing, 1773): "Spenser and Hughes seem to be allied by genius. Both great poets, both remarkable for their strict morals, both public-spirited men, both well received by the great, and yet neither of them much indebted to fortune. It was happy for the memory of Spenser, that the revival and illustration of his writings were committed to a person of such candour and capacity" (69–70).

8.   Richard C. Frushell, *Edmund Spenser in the Early Eighteenth Century: Education, Imitation, and the Making of a Literary Model* (Pittsburgh: Duquesne University Press, 1999), 106.

9.   George Vertue, quoted in Hanns Hammelmann (edited and completed by T. S. R. Boase), *Book Illustrators in Eighteenth-Century England* (New Haven: Yale University Press, 1975): 47–48, at 47.

10.   Williams, 4–6.

11.   Williams, 16.

12.   T. S. R. Boase, "Illustrations of Shakespeare's Plays in the Seventeenth and Eighteenth Centuries," *Journal of the Warburg and Courtauld Institutes* 10 (1947): 83–108, at 88.

13.   Horace Walpole, *A Catalogue of Engravers, Who Have Been Born or Resided in England; Digested by Mr. Horace Walpole from the MSS. of Mr. George Vertue* (Twickenham, 1765), 123.

14.   On du Guernier's background, see Laurence Guilmard Geddes, "du Guernier," *Grove Art Online* (2000).

15.   Walpole, *A Catalogue of Engravers,* 123. Hammelmann notes that if du Guernier did indeed die in 1716 (and the only record of his death date is the Vertue information), then his illustrations continued to appear for some time after his death; Hammelmann, 47. Hodnett posits a death date of approximately 1735; Hodnett, 75.

16.   See Hadfield, 5–6, for a quotation from Walpole finding faults with Kent's work on *The Faerie Queene.*

17.   See Bradley, 33.

18.   See Hamm, 185–86, 193.

19.   John H. Astington, "*Macbeth* and the Rowe Illustrations," *Shakespeare Quarterly* 49 (1998): 83–86, at 86; Bernice W. Kliman, "Rowe 1709 *Macbeth* Illustration Again," *Shakespeare Newsletter* 48.3 (1998): 59–60, at 59.

20.   Bernice W. Kliman, "The Bed in *Hamlet*'s Closet Scene," *The Shakespeare Newsletter* 43.1 (1993): 8–9.

21.   See, for example, David Hill Radcliffe, *Edmund Spenser: A Reception History* (Columbia, SC: Camden House, 1996), 45; Frushell, 105–12.

22.   John Hughes, *Remarks on The Fairy Queen*, in *The Works of Mr. Edmund Spenser. With a Glossary Explaining the Old and Obscure Words. Publish'd by Mr. Hughes* (London: J. Tonson, 1715), lviii–xcvi, at lx.

23.   On Spenser as a "painterly" poet, see, for example, Bradley, 33; Hadfield, 3, 9. The Pope quote is from Joseph Spence, *Anecdotes . . . from the Conversation of Mr. Pope* (1820), quoted in Rudolf Gottfried, "The Pictorial Element in Spenser's Poetry," *ELH* 19 (1952): 203–13; and the Warton quote is Joseph Warton, *An Essay on the Genius and Writings of Pope* (1756), quoted in Hadfield, 9.

24.   See Gottfried, 203–04, for a survey of the many Romantic and Victorian critics who compared Spenser with Rubens.

25.   *The Correspondence of John Hughes,* 69–70.

26.   John Hughes, *An Essay on Allegorical Poetry, &c.*, in *The Works of Mr. Edmund Spenser. With a Glossary Explaining the Old and Obscure Words. Publish'd by Mr. Hughes* (London: J. Tonson, 1715), xix–xli, at xxii.

27.   Hughes, *Remarks on the Fairy Queen,* lxiii, lxvii, and lxxi, respectively.

28.   The list of titles of eighteenth- and nineteenth-century artworks on Spenserian subjects exhibited at the Royal Academy between 1769 and 1900, in Bradley, 48–51, aptly conveys a sense of how much later artists focused on representing specific scenes, rather than attempting to convey an overall, allegorical impression of the work. Of eighty-seven titles of artworks, only two (W. Ford's 1847 sculpture *Spenser's Faerie Queene, Under the Legend of Constancie* and William Riviere's 1827 *The Legend of Sir Guyon*) suggest even the possibility of an allegorical interpretation.

29.   Hughes, *An Essay on Allegorical Poetry,* xxix.

30.   Bradley, 32. On the unlikelihood of seventeenth- and eighteenth-century French illustrators actually reading the works they illustrated, see Raymond Picard, "Racine and Chauveau," *Journal of the Warburg and Courtauld Institutes* 14 (1951): 259–74, at 273.

31.   Thomas Herron, personal conversation, 8 May 2005.

32.   John Hughes, *Remarks on The Shepherd's Calendar, &c,* in *The Works of Mr. Edmund Spenser. With a Glossary Explaining the Old and Obscure Words. Publish'd by Mr. Hughes* (London: J. Tonson, 1715), xcvii–cxiii, at xcix.

33.   Hughes, *Remarks on The Fairy Queen,* lxxxiii.

34.   Hughes, *Remarks on The Fairy Queen,* xci.

35.   Hughes, *Remarks on The Fairy Queen,* xciii.

36.   Edmund Spenser, *The Faerie Queene,* ed. A. C. Hamilton, text ed. Hiroshi Yamashita and Toshiyuki Suzuki (Harlow: Pearson Education, 2001).

37.   Hughes, *Remarks on The Fairy Queen,* lxxxvii.

Fig. 1. Frontispiece to entire *Faerie Queen*. Harry Ransom Humanities Research Center, The University of Texas at Austin.

End of the life. Vol. 1.　　　　　　*Lud. Du Guernier in et Sculp.* 7

Fig. 2. *Life of Spenser.* Harry Ransom Humanities Research Center,
The University of Texas at Austin.

Vol. 1. p. 21.   *Lud. Du Guernier inv. et Sculp.* 2

Fig. 3. *Faerie Queen*, Book I. Harry Ransom Humanities Research Center, The University of Texas at Austin.

Frontespice Vol. 2.   Lud. Du Guernier inv. et Sculp. 5

Fig. 4. *Faerie Queen*, Book II. Harry Ransom Humanities Research
Center, The University of Texas at Austin.

Fig. 5. *Faerie Queen*, Book III. Harry Ransom Humanities Research Center, The University of Texas at Austin.

Fig. 6. *Faerie Queen*, Book IV. Harry Ransom Humanities Research Center, The University of Texas at Austin.

Vol. 3. p. 705.   Lud Du Guernier inv. et Sculp. 1

Fig. 7. *Faerie Queen*, Book V. Harry Ransom Humanities Research Center, The University of Texas at Austin.

Fig. 8. *Faerie Queen*, Book VI. Harry Ransom Humanities Research Center, The University of Texas at Austin.

Vol. 4: p: 1009.   Lud. Du Guernier inv. et sculp.

Fig. 9. *Faerie Queen*, Mutabilitie Cantos. Harry Ransom Humanities Research Center, The University of Texas at Austin.

Fig. 10. *Shepheardes Calender.* Harry Ransom Humanities Research Center, The University of Texas at Austin.

Vol. 4: p: 1121   Lud. Du Guernier inv. et Sculp. 8

Fig. 11. *Colin Clouts Come Home Againe.* Harry Ransom Humanities Research Center, The University of Texas at Austin.

Fig. 12. *Mother Hubberds Tale*. Harry Ransom Humanities Research Center, The University of Texas at Austin.

Fig. 13. *Amoretti.* Harry Ransom Humanities Research Center, The University of Texas at Austin.

Fig. 14. *Prothalamion*. Harry Ransom Humanities Research Center, The University of Texas at Austin.

Fig. 15. *Fowre Hymnes*. Harry Ransom Humanities Research Center, The University of Texas at Austin.

Fig. 16. *Teares of the Muses*. Harry Ransom Humanities Research Center, The University of Texas at Austin.

Fig. 17. *Apostrophel*. Harry Ransom Humanities Research Center, The University of Texas at Austin.

Fig. 18. *The Ruines of Time*. Harry Ransom Humanities Research Center, The University of Texas at Austin.

Fig. 19. *Britains Ida*. Harry Ransom Humanities Research Center, The University of Texas at Austin.

DAVID SCOTT WILSON-OKAMURA

Errors about Ovid and Romance

What is the difference between epic and romance? Spenser did not use either term and contemporaries who did gave varying accounts. Since the late 1970s, epic has been associated with Virgil and closure, romance with Ovid and digression. Today the conventional wisdom is that Ovid was an anti-Virgil; that he furnished Spenser with a model for honorable exile; and that he licensed a style of narrative, romance, in which endings are deferred indefinitely. The evidence for this view needs to be reexamined. Is our reading of Ovid sentimental? Was Ireland, for Spenser, a place of exile or, as Jean Brink has argued, preferment? What did commentators say about Ovid's conclusion? Finally, is it true that romance, as a genre, is more open-ended than epic? What was the practice of romance authors, and how was it theorized by literary critics?

*I*N THE RENAISSANCE, COMPLICATED STORIES about love and chivalry were popular with readers of every class, all nations, and both sexes.[1] As fiction, their only serious rival was saints' lives—and those were not supposed to be fiction. We know, then, that romance was important. Do we know, though, what romance was? The answer, like the thing, is complicated, because when a genre succeeds, it propagates itself through variation; and in the case of romance, variety is one of the genre's main features. It is possible, as Helen Cooper has done, to describe the patterns of romance, to catalogue its memes and motives. But actually to sit down in the siege perilous and declare its essence, *hoc opus, hic labor est.*

Spenserians sometimes imagine their author choosing or hesitating between epic and romance, but Spenser does not actually use either term. When, in the *Letter to Ralegh*, Spenser mentions his predecessors, he does not distinguish between Virgil and Ariosto, except to say that Virgil is "antique": they are both "Poets historicall" and

215

they both follow the same method, of combining all the knightly virtues into one character. A contemporary of Spenser, George Puttenham (1529–90/91), says that the chronicler John Hardying (1378–1465) was "a Poet Epick or Historicall," as if *epic poet* and *historical poet* were synonyms.[2] In his discussion of the various genres, there is no mention of epic per se, but there is a long chapter on "Poesie historicall," which, next to divine poetry, is the "most honorable and worthy" genre of them all. This is also the section where Puttenham talks about romance, a term that Spenser does not use at all. For Puttenham, romance is a subspecies of historical poetry, which he calls the "historicall ditty." A ditty is a lyric and therefore has a different meter: unlike the "very histories," which have long lines of uniform length, the "*Romance* or historicall ditty" has an alternating meter of long lines and short. This metrical difference is the only one that Puttenham mentions.[3]

In Italy, the difference between *epopeia* and *romanzo* is a subject of controversy. The theorists of romance, Cinzio and Pigna, argue that romance is a new genre, distinct from epic, which did not exist in Aristotle's time and has its own rules. Tasso denies this. Romance, he argues, is not a separate genre at all and the rules of Aristotle still apply. But Tasso does allow for changes in taste. Thus, while he does not condone or employ the term *romance*, he does distinguish between two kinds of epic, ancient and modern. For Tasso, the modern epic differs from the ancient in several important ways: its divine machinery is Christian; it has more variety (because modern audiences are easily bored); it has more love stories; and its style is more lyrical.[4]

These are some ways that romance was defined in the Age of Spenser. Of course, there have been other ways since then. For example, it used to be argued (a hundred years ago) that epic is a more democratic genre than romance, because its hero "is the man who is best at the things with which everyone is familiar. . . . There is a community of prosaic interests."[5] Thus, in Homer we find a princess who does her own laundry and a king who brags about mowing hay. This would never happen in a romance because, as Auerbach says, "Strata other than that at the top of the feudal system simply do not appear. The economic bases of society are not even mentioned."[6]

This theory, of what makes romance different from epic, is now so ancient and obscure as to seem almost new and plausible. But it is mentioned here, not to "revive old factions," but to suggest that our current theory, which is only about thirty years old, is not in fact inevitable; nor, if history is any guide, likely to be permanent.

Since the late 1970s, epic and romance have been conceptualized as polarities: hierarchy vs. community, war vs. love, masculine vs. feminine, duty vs. desire, history vs. fiction, unity vs. variety, linear extension vs. cyclical dilation, closure vs. digression, Virgil vs. Ovid. As originally formulated, these categories were suggestive rather than schematic.[7] But categories, when successful, have a way of getting calcified; what, for one generation of scholars, was a useful rule of thumb, becomes for the next generation an established fact, an iron-clad law, of literary history, which everybody knows, and which therefore no one questions.

There is nothing sinister, or even unscholarly, in any of this. Scholarship, to be progressive, must be cumulative. But errors can accumulate, as well as understanding. It is true, for example, that love was one of romance's main themes. But so was war: as Paul Grendler has shown, books of romance were known in Italy as "books of battle" (*libri di battaglie*) and their title pages were usually decorated with "a picture of Charlemagne with his knights or a battle scene or a single knight. Small woodcuts of knights and/or battles dotted the text. Even though Italian chivalric romances always included significant love stories, women almost never appeared on the title page illustrations and seldom in the very small illustrations throughout the book."[8] This did not stop women from reading the books, but it should stop us, as scholars, from saying that epic is about war and romance is about love, or when a romance veers in the direction of war, that it does so under the influence of epic—as if epic were some baleful planet, luring a hitherto-innocent moon into cruel and tortuous epicycles. Romances *were* books of battle. They were books of love, too, but there is no evidence that love was considered more essential than war, or that war was felt to be a foreign element.

If we are careful, the most we can probably say is that an epic without love would still be an epic; but that a romance without love would no longer be a romance. There is a distinction here, though it may not be the generic one that we expect. Tasso, for example, acknowledged that love was less important in Virgil than it was in, say, Ariosto. But for Tasso, this was a difference between ancient and modern, not a difference in genres; and the difference was one of degree not kind, because ancient writers wrote love stories too.[9] Tasso, of course, was only one voice and later in this essay I will summarize the views of two critics from the 1550s who argued that, sometimes, a difference in degree amounts to a difference in kind. But that does not affect Grendler's point about books of battle, that in poems heroical Mars and Venus are not rivals, presiding over competing genres, but lovers. They may take turns being active, as in

Botticelli's painting, where Mars sleeps and Venus holds our gaze. But Mars will wake up eventually, and the story when he takes over from Venus will not be more of an epic or less of a romance; it will be a song, in Spenser's phrase, moralized by fierce wars no less than faithful loves.

Most binaries break down somewhere; most rules admit of exceptions, and are still valid most of the time. But there are some rules, such as "Do not use contractions" or "Do not end a sentence with a preposition," which don't deserve to be rules, because they were never valid to begin with; meaning, they do not accurately describe the practice of authors we admire, whose writings the rules are supposed to explain. Something similar, in my view, has happened with the categories of epic and romance. Spenser, as we have said, did not use either term and contemporaries who did gave varying accounts. We could hypothesize, of course, that Spenser read the same books we do, and that being a smart reader he would naturally arrive at the same generalizations. But that is guessing, not scholarship.

In this essay, I am going to review three additional pieces of conventional wisdom about epic and romance, beyond the war vs. love polarity that Grendler has already exploded, which began as insights, and have since hardened into paradigms. Two of these concern Ovid, as the classical prototype of a romance author. The first piece of conventional wisdom is that Ovid was an anti-Virgil and that he furnished Spenser with a model for honorable exile. The second, that Ovid licensed a type of narrative in which endings are deferred indefinitely. The third piece, which I call the myth of infinity, is that romance as a genre avoids closure on principle; this view, I shall argue, is consistent neither with the history of the genre, as practiced in the Middle Ages and Renaissance, or with the theory of the genre, as it was elaborated by defenders of Ariosto.

Assumptions About Ovid

For many years now, the *Metamorphoses* has been introduced to undergraduates as an anti-*Aeneid*. This explains so much about the two poems that it seems almost self-evident, once someone has pointed it out. But so far as I am aware, no one in the Renaissance did point it out. Commentators in the Renaissance did call attention to places where Ovid was alluding to Virgil, but they did not make the (to us) self-evident generalization, that Ovid was composing a sustained parody or even response. I say "they did not," although it is possible, even probable, that someone did say this somewhere, on some crowded page of some forgotten commentary, unpublished lecture, or unedited letter. But it was not something that everybody learned in school and then repeated to each other, solemnly, at cocktail parties, without fear of contradiction. Ovid in the Renaissance was not the opposite of Virgil.

Was he ever? There is a danger today, at least among non-classicists, of sentimentalizing Ovid and making Virgil into a heavy-handed bogeyman. Several years ago, I received a conference abstract in which Virgil was characterized as "strident." Virgil strident? Not even in translation. Sexually, Ovid is less of a prude than Virgil, and he does have more women characters. But the fate of women is bad in both: in Virgil, madness; in Ovid, rape. One can argue about which is better, but the outcome is grim either way.[10]

Politically, Virgil was probably more conservative than Ovid; certainly that was his image in the Renaissance.[11] But for abject, servile cringing, there is nothing in Virgil to match some of the things in Ovid's *Tristia* (A.D. 9–12) or his *Epistulae ex Ponto* (A.D. 13–16). We call these his exile poems even though, technically, Ovid's punishment was relegation, not exile: he lost his freedom, but not his property or his citizenship. The point is an important one, because relegation was something that one could return from, without a revolution, and resume one's former life. This was what Ovid hoped for, and it gives rise in these, his last works, to a mixture of tones and approaches: some of the poems are tender, others are caustic; some complain of the emperor, and others court his favor. Companionless on the Black Sea, Ovid was desperate to be recalled back to the city and there seems to have been no device of fawning or flattery which Ovid was not willing at least to simulate.[12]

Why Ovid was relegated is still unknown, although there have been many theories: for example, that Ovid was part of a secret resistance movement, or that he witnessed something that was embarrassing to the regime.[13] But the most popular explanation, among Elizabethan writers, was that Ovid got sent away on a morals charge, for writing that handbook of seduction, *Ars amatoria*, and for corrupting Rome's youth—maybe even Julia, the emperor's granddaughter.[14] It requires an effort now to keep this in mind, because for us, exile is a political category with heroic overtones. In the Renaissance, this was not the default position. Poets, being poets, might be expected to sympathize with Ovid, and historically many of them have.[15] But identification was not automatic either: Dante, for example, borrowed from Ovid even more freely than from Virgil, and yet the (to us) obvious-seeming parallel, between Ovid's exile from Rome and Dante's exile from Florence, was not one he developed.[16] Pardon, where it was offered, was not always complete either. Ovid was a seducer of young women, a villainous abominable misleader of young men, and if banishment was too severe a punishment, censorship was not. Thus Thomas Lodge, in his *Defense of Poetry, Musick and Stage Plays* (c. 1580): "I like not of an angrye Augustus which wyll banish Ouid for enuy, I loue a wise Senator, which in wisedome wyll correct him and with aduise burne his follyes."[17]

That did not happen. Instead, Ovid's follies became part of the curriculum. But while the *Metamorphoses*, the *Fasti*, and the *Tristia* were all standard in Renaissance schoolrooms, their influence is tricky to judge. Many poets would have learned their mythology from Ovid, but does someone who borrows a story from Ovid also borrow his attitude? Again, I think the answer must be "Not automatically." Stories from Ovid (or that were transmitted through Ovid) color almost every genre of writing in the Renaissance, from poetry to theology; and in Spenser's case, the borrowing is so extensive as to persuade some critics that Gloriana's would-be Virgil was really Naso-in-embryo, a free-speaking, prince-defying rebel-in-exile.[18] And, indeed, there are striking parallels. Like Ovid, Spenser did become annoyed at his sovereign, did publish a poem that lost him his royal patronage (almost),[19] and did characterize Ireland, where he spent most of his career, as "saluage soyl" (dedicatory sonnet 7), an echo perhaps of Ovid's *barbara terra* (*Tristia* 3.1.18). In *Colin Clouts Come Home Againe* (1595) there is also a sea voyage (lines 196–289) with echoes from Ovid's *Tristia*; the passage has been called a "close *imitatio* [of Ovid's storm descriptions] . . . firmly establishing in the reader's mind the connection with Ovid's exile poetry."[20]

But the Irish Sea, as Spenser describes it, is crowded with allusions, and not all of the fish that swim in it come from the Black Sea. For example, when Colin likens waves to mountains (198), is he echoing the *montes . . . aquarum* in Ovid's *Tristia* (1.2.19), or is he remembering Ovid's source, the *aquae mons* in Virgil's famous storm scene at the beginning of the *Aeneid* (1.105)?[21] Again, when the ship pulls away from land, "And nought but sea and heauen to vs appeare" (227), should we be reminded of Ovid going into exile, "Quodcunque aspicio nihil est nisi pontus & aer" (*Tristia* 1.2.23; "Wherever I look there is nothing but sea and sky") or should we think here of Aeneas embarking for Italy, "nec iam amplius vllæ / Apparent terræ, cœlum vndique, & vndique pontus" (*Aen.* 3.192–93; "and now land appears no longer, but sky everywhere, and everywhere sea")?[22] The point here is not to dismiss the Ovidian parallels, but to be cautious in finding patterns.

Colin, when he sails to London, is not going into exile, but visiting Spenser's birthplace; logically, that is the opposite of exile, and yet the habit once formed, of picturing Spenser as an exile, is hard to break. For example, a 1640 translation of Ovid's *Fasti* contains a preface which, it has recently been suggested, "implicitly associates Spenser . . . with the exiled Ovid."[23] But the text of that preface must be studied carefully. Spenser is listed, with Ovid and two other poets, as one of those authors who "Have lost their heads out of their Prince's sight." This could be through exile or disfavor, but in this case it is neither. Says Apollo, god of poetry, "Thus *Maro*, *Lucane*, by [fate's] spiteful hand / At unawares were banish'd from my light, / And that arch-Poet of the *Faerie* lond, / With diverse more." Why is Spenser paired with Virgil and Lucan? Not because they lost royal favor: that would explain Lucan but not Virgil. What associates them, rather, is untimely death: all three died suddenly, "unawares," and all three were writing epic poems, which they did not live to complete or (in Virgil's case) revise. This is what removes Spenser from the "Prince's sight": not exile (which Virgil and Lucan never had to endure) but death that interrupted his work.

Scholars have been writing about Spenser's exile for so long now (since at least 1910) that we assume there must have been one.[24] And yet, as Jean Brink has shown, Spenser's appointment to Lord Grey was probably "a preferment rather than a punishment." While not lucrative in itself, it enabled Spenser to join the landowning class and "assured his new or renewed access to a larger circle of courtiers, including Sir Edward Denny, Sir Walter Ralegh, Sir Humphrey Gilbert, and Fulke Greville, all of whom had received or would later receive knighthoods or titles as soldiers or councilors."[25] Maybe exile is relative, but that is *not* what happened to Ovid: he did not go to Tomis and marry a new wife (as Spenser did in Ireland), he did not become a man of property, and he did not make influential friends; while it might be argued that Tomis was good for Ovid's character (there is something more personal, less haughty, in the poems that he wrote there), it did not improve his fortunes. Admittedly, Tomis was not devoid of diversions, and Ovid took an anthropological interest in local customs, which is not unlike Spenser's in the *View*. But the island of Tomis never replaced the city of Rome as Ovid's true home, the way Ireland has replaced London in *Colin Clouts Come Home Againe*.

We can speculate about the psychology (of what happens when we revisit the scenes of our youth and notice for the first time how small, even shabby, they really were), but certain facts (of chronology) are clear. Early on, Spenser had an opportunity of leaving Ireland—of ending his exile, if that was how he saw it—but chose to stay on instead. As secretary to Lord Grey, Spenser copied out scores of letters, including some in which Grey prayed, urgently, to be re-called.[26] But when, after only two years in office, Grey obtained the wished–for release and returned to England, Spenser did not go with him. What might have seemed, when he first arrived there, a place of exile had become, in a relatively short space of time, a land of opportunity. That will be, to some of us, a familiar pattern; but it was not the Ovidian one.

This is not to minimize the influence of Ovid's text, which is indisputable. But the application of that text was not automatic. Quoting Ovid, even his exile poems, was not tantamount to rejecting Virgil, or claiming exile status. As we shall see in the next section, the interpretation of Ovid was not automatic either.

OVID'S ENDING

There is a notion, widely held since the late 1970s, that epics are end-stopped and seek closure, whereas romances are open-ended and merely tolerate closure as a concession to classical decorum. This notion is based, partially, on a reading of Ovid's *Metamorphoses* which seems obvious to us, but was not widely held in the Renaissance.

Actually, the *Metamorphoses* comes to a very tidy end with the translation of divine favor from Greece to Rome (*Met.* 15.622–744), the deification of Julius Caesar (745–850), and the extension (during Augustus's reign) of Roman power over the whole known world (850–70). What could be more conclusive, unless perhaps it were Ovid's boast at the very end, that his fame will endure "through all generations" (*perque omnia sæcula*), as long as Rome's empire?

Obviously, Ovid was being ironical: the whole poem is about change and, if that were not obvious enough, the philosopher Pythagoras has just delivered a long sermon on the text "Nothing in the whole world stays the same" (15.177). Surely, then, Rome's empire will not be permanent either.

And yet, what seems obvious to us was not always self-evident in the Renaissance. That Rome's empire had turned out not to be permanent *was* obvious to everyone. But commentators on Ovid did not take the next, to us obvious, step of saying that Ovid was really mocking Augustus when he seemed to be praising him. The most influential of the early commentators was probably Raffaele Regio (c. 1440–1520). Regio has a lot to say about the ending, but he does not say anything about irony. He interprets the whole passage literally and with a straight face—though he is more than capable, in other places, of finding out hidden meanings.[27] Among those who used Regio's commentary was Arthur Golding (1535/6–1606), the translator of Ovid who inspired several of our favorite passages in Shakespeare. Another English translator, George Sandys (1578–1644), did manage to tease some irony out of the ending, but not the kind we expect. Here is how Sandys characterizes Ovid's ending: Julius Caesar

> ioyes to see him selfe from heauen excelled by *Augustus*; in whose transcendent praises, & prayers for his safety, our Poet concludes this admirable Poem, now arriuing at the end of his first intention. Nor [was this poem] ouervalued in his propheticall rapture, it hauing so long outlasted the *Roman* empire, and his fame outstretched the bounds of their Conquests.[28]

The irony, such as it is, is that Ovid outlived his empire. This does not negate, however, Ovid's praise of Augustus, which Sandys calls "transcendent." And it does not detract, either, from the finality of Ovid's conclusion, because Ovid has achieved now "the end of his first intention." What is that intention? Apparently, it is the project announced in the poem's famous opening lines:

> Of bodies chang'd to other shapes I sing.
> Assist, you Gods (from you these changes spring)
> And, from the Worlds first fabrick to these times,
> Deduce my never-discontinued Rymes.

Sandys explains, in a marginal gloss, that the phrase "to these times" (*ad mea . . . tempora*) means "the raigne of *Augustus*."[29] Why does Sandys make a point of something so basic? Because it defines the *terminus ad quem* of Ovid's narrative: when the story gets to Augustus, the poem will be over and Ovid will have completed his task, "his first intention."[30]

But wait: doesn't the phrase "never-discontinued Rymes" (*perpetuum . . . carmen*) imply that maybe the poem will go on forever? Sandys has no note here, so we turn back to Regio, whose commentary he relied on. According to Regio, the adjective *perpetuum* should be glossed as *continuum* 'connected, uninterrupted', "because there is no kind of transformation that Ovid omits to describe and because the stories are connected to one another neatly and with a tight fit (*concinne apteque*)."[31] That *perpetuus* can also mean "everlasting,"[32] in the sense of never stopping, either was rejected by Regio as irrelevant in this context or did not occur to him.

As why should it? In point of fact, Ovid's poem has an ending. Though the story of bodies changing seems as if it might go on forever, it does not.

THE MYTH OF INFINITY

It is the same with most books that have been classified as romance. What scholars today call "Greek romance" or the "ancient novel" is invariably a love story and, with one exception, all of the stories "end by reestablishing the initial situation. At the beginning the protagonists fall in love; in the center we have a series of adventures and trials; and at the end the couple is reunited and (if they were not in the first part) they are married."[33] The exception is Heliodorus's *Ethiopica*, which wraps up with the loving couple being crowned as priest and priestess of the sun and moon, with nuptials to follow when they get home. If that's not a happy ending, what is?

In medieval romance, happy endings are standard though not mandatory: as Helen Cooper observes, "a surprising number—numerically a minority, but including some of the most famous—opt for bleak fate over benevolent Providence."[34] But closure and providence are still the norm: both in England, as Andrew King has noted,[35] and (we might add) on the Continent. In the most famous and influential of all medieval cycles, King Arthur is killed in battle by his incestuously-begotten son Mordred, Guinevere joins a convent, and Lancelot, her former lover, expires piously in the odor of sanctity. This is the story as it was told in France c. 1230. Later versions would fill in more of the backstory or elaborate certain themes (the grail, in particular);[36] there was also persistent disagreement over whether Arthur had really died, or might still be healed of his wounds and return. But the endpoint of the story was fixed. Malory's version, which he compiled from various sources, English and French, still concludes, two hundred years later, with the same two events: Guinevere becomes a nun and Lancelot becomes a saint. *Plus non ultra*. The related story of Perceval and the grail also went on for very a long time, and took many generations to complete, but eventually it too comes to an end when, in what is called the Third Continuation, Perceval is crowned as the Grail King.[37]

Romances in the Renaissance are conclusive, too. Luigi Pulci's *Morgante* (1478, rev. 1483) ends with the poet bringing his ship into harbor and contemplating new projects: since he has just finished with Charlemagne, perhaps he will write a new epic about Charlemagne's son; or perhaps he will change genres altogether and write Alcaean pastorals. Like Chaucer, at the end of *Troilus and Criseyde* (c. 1385), Pulci ends his poem with a prayer to Mary. *Tirant lo blanc* (1490), begun by Joanot Martorell and finished by Martí Joan De Galba, has a sad ending—Tirant dies before he can marry the Byzantine princess he has been courting—but it is an ending all the same. Boiardo's romance, *Orlando innamorato* (1483; rev. 1494), was interrupted by the poet's death, but it still has a discernible endpoint, the battle of Paris.[38]

Of the many attempts that were made to complete Boiardo's story, the most successful by far was Ariosto's *Orlando furioso* (1516, rev. 1521, 1532). So much has been written about the *Furioso*'s refusal of closure, its endless digressions and deferrals,[39] that scholars who had not actually read Ariosto might be surprised to learn that this seemingly interminable story does, in fact, terminate. As in Pulci, the poet sails his ship into the harbor and waves to his friends who are waiting for him on the quay; the founders of the Este dynasty, long separated by distance, misunderstanding, and misfortune, are united in what we are assured will be a brief but fruitful marriage; and, in the very last verses, the villain of the story dies, Turnus-style, in single-combat and his soul goes to hell. It is a finish that would satisfy even the most severe classicist.

There is, one might say, no reason it should end there. And, in a sense, it didn't. No one reads them anymore, but there were scores of sequels to *Orlando furioso*, featuring various characters from the *Orlando* "franchise." Stories about Ruggiero's brother-in-law—*Rinaldo furioso* (1526), *Rinaldo appassianato* (1528), *Innamoramento di Rinaldo* (1533)—were particularly well liked, but there was also a *Madness of Marfisa* (*Marfisa bizzarra,* 1545), a *Marfisa in Love* (*Amor di Marfisa,* 1562), even a *Rodomonte in Love* (*Rodomonte innamorato,* 1558).[40] Another romance that spawned sequels was *Amadís de Gaule*. As first published in 1508 by Garci Rodriguez de Montalvo, the story of Amadís had four books and seemed, in the fourth book, as if it were going to end neatly, with the hero getting married to his childhood sweetheart, Oriana. But then the story dribbled on for several more chapters: Amadís's new father-in-law had got himself enchanted, and would need to be rescued. This spoiled the ending, and prepared the way for a sequel. Indeed, there were many sequels, in several different languages.[41] The French version was the longest and extended, by century's end, to no fewer than twenty-four books. There would have been twenty-six books, but two of the Spanish books were rejected from the French version: one, by Páez de Ribera, because nobody liked it (it was reprinted only one time); another, by Juan Díaz, because Amadís dies in it.

But what do the sequels really tell us? It is tempting, at this stage, to puff out our chests and intone something solemn and universal, that epic is the genre of climax, romance of crisis; that it is in the nature of romance to admit of sequels; or, even more grandly, to define romance as the genre in which endings are never final. This would be a good definition, if it helped us to distinguish romance from epic, which it does not. The last verse of the *Iliad* was as final as anything in fiction: "Thus was their burial of Hector, breaker of horses." And yet it did not prevent Homer (or someone else) from writing a sequel, *The Odyssey*.[42] The *Aeneid* seems final, but it produced sequels as well.[43]

Continuability, the aptitude for sequels, is not a sufficient definition of romance, because epics can also have sequels; this is implied in the term *epic cycle*.

A better theory, proposed by Colin Burrow, is that romance is a mode or tendency within epic itself.[44] In the *Odyssey*, for example, there is a desire, apparently shared by hero and storyteller alike, to sample or flirt with various sexual partners before coming back to Penelope. There is also an impulse, again evident in both poet and protagonist, to delay and extend first the hero's homecoming, then his reckoning with the suitors, and even when that is accomplished, the longed-for reunion with Penelope.

The romance urge to extend the narrative, explore other options, and postpone the ending was part of the epic tradition, long before the term *romance* was even invented. And yet, as we have seen, most epics—and most romances—do come to an end sometime. No ending, not even Virgil's, is so final that a sequel cannot set things going again. This has nothing to do with epic or romance: it is a property, rather, of sequels themselves: "to open up," as David Quint says, "the endings of the works they follow."[45]

And yet there are some endings that do seem forced and it is these forced endings that, for some critics, distinguish the true epic from its romance imitators. That the *Aeneid* would end—and, in a general way, how it would end—was discernible on page one: "so much labor there was to dig the foundation for (*condere*) the Roman nation"

(*Aen.* 1.33). As many modern readers have pointed out (though not, to my knowledge, any Renaissance ones), this image of digging is echoed at the end of the *Aeneid*, when Aeneas buries (*condit*) his sword in Turnus's chest (12.950). But how Ariosto's poem will end, or even that it will end, is not obvious at all, until it is halfway over. For the last half is different, both in substance and in style. In substance, the characters are settling down, either by getting married or by getting killed. In style, the narrative is becoming less layered and more linear; the fugue is slowing down now, and there are fewer plot-lines to follow.[46]

Many readers do not enjoy the second half of *Orlando furioso* as much as the first, and when those readers are also scholars, they have sometimes blamed Virgil for the falling off, because he seems to divert Ariosto from his own natural and best way, so that instead of writing more episodes of free-wheeling romance, he panics halfway through and clamps down, hard, on the narrative, converting it into a pseudo-epic. "The mistake, which is radical and disastrous, is to graft on to an open-structured poem a close-structured ending."[47] Tasso seems closer to Virgil in spirit, but he too has been seen as forcing himself to write a poem that is correct and orthodox, when his heart was elsewhere: in boundless variety, unstructured desire.[48]

There is nothing wrong with liking some parts of Ariosto and Tasso better than others. We should be cautious, though, about calling those parts "romance." For romance, closure is constitutive. This cannot be explained as the influence or contamination of epic, since the great majority of romance narratives have no epic pretensions whatsoever, and yet still they end. If it is true that romances want to defer their endings for a long time, it is also true that they want to end some time: not because they aspire to become epics, but because that is what romances do.

THEORY OF THE ROMANCE ENDING

The main theorists of romance in the sixteenth century were Giovambattista Giraldi Cinzio (1504–1573) and his pupil Giovanni Battista Pigna (1530–1575). Their treatises, Cinzio's *Discorso intorno al comporre dei romanzi* and Pigna's *I romanzi*, were both published in 1554. Immediately both authors accused each other of plagiarism, and indeed there was much overlap. Both authors agreed that romance is a modern genre distinct from epic; that it was unknown to Aristotle;

and therefore that not all of Aristotle's rules apply to it. In particular, whereas an epic should have one main action, a romance should have multiple actions.

Multiple, but not infinite: for the author of a romance must not, says Cinzio, try to tell every story, even about the main hero. The example he gives is Ovid's *Metamorphoses*, "which, cutting free of Aristotle's rules for art, begins with admirable mastery at the beginning of the world and handles, through an amazing chain of events, a great variety of materials. Yet he accomplished this in fewer books than Homer did in his *Iliad* or *Odyssey*, though the first poem contains only one action, and so does the second."[49] Ovid here is the acknowledged father of romance, but not of narrative sprawl. Among classical poets, he is the model for multiple plots, but he is also compact.

Multiple storylines are a type of variety, which was a paramount value in Renaissance aesthetics.[50] But variety is not the same as infinity. For length, Cinzio says there is a lawful point, *giusto termine*, which the well-constructed romance will not exceed.[51] He does not say how to locate that point, but his pupil, Pigna, gives us a test. How many plots, asks Pigna, should a romance have? "There are enough," he answers, "when all of the dangers have taken place that confer honor, and all of the great deeds that we look for in a complete knight (*perfetto cauagliere*). And this is how we avoid going into infinity (*il gire in infinito*)." Pigna goes on to explain that a poem is like an object moving through space. In Aristotle's physics, an object moves because it lacks something, but when its attributes are complete, *cessa il moto* "motion ceases."[52] A romance should end in the same way, when the elements of a perfect knight have all been assembled.

Did Spenser read Pigna? Not necessarily, but Spenser's plan, as described in the *Letter to Ralegh*, was consistent with Pigna's formula. According to the Letter, the "generall end" of Spenser's epic was "to fashion a gentleman or noble person in vertuous and gentle discipline." To this end each book was supposed to exemplify a virtue: private virtues in the first half, public virtues in the second. Spenser does not say what all of the virtues are, but their number is finite: twelve books for twelve private virtues. For several decades now, scholars have objected to this plan, arguing that it does not really describe what Spenser wrote; that a book of twelve (or, worse yet, twenty-four) books on this scale would be too long; that Spenser, when he reached Book VI, was tired of writing for the public; or that Spenser was skeptical of endings on principle. None of these objections will be answered here, except to say that there was nothing in the history of romance before Spenser to stand in the way of a very long poem, and nothing in the theory of romance to discourage such a poem from ending, once its attributes were complete: the virtues, in this case, of a gentleman or noble person.

Romances were expected to end, but our terminology has drifted away from that. Today when we use the word *romance*, we have in mind a story that is all crisis and no climax; or in which, if there is a climax, it is a concession, a parasite. This is another anachronism. The term *romanzo* was indeed a period term, and its various meanings have been well mapped.[53] "Never-ending story" was never one of them, until recently.

THE RECEPTION OF ROMANCE

We have listed examples and we have looked at theory; it remains to say a few words about reception. In 1545, Ariosto's illegitimate son published some fragments of a new poem about Orlando, which he titled simply *Cinque canti*. Ariosto had been dead for twelve years, and the five cantos were found among his papers. What were they: the beginnings of a sequel, or something else? The question is still not settled.[54] It was already being asked, though, in the Renaissance. According to Sir John Harington, in his "Life of Ariosto," the *Cinque canti* are probably spurious, because the style is wrong for Ariosto and because

> it is not likely, that a man of his iudgement hauing made so absolute a *peece* of worke, as his *Furioso* is, and hauing brought euery matter to a good and well pleasing conclusion, would, as it were, mar all agayne, and set them all by the eares and bring *Rogero* into the Whales bellie, and *Astolfo* with him for companie, that a little before were Conquerors of the world, & vnmatchable for courage & learnynge. . . .[55]

In other words, Ariosto was too much of an artist to undo all of his loose ends again, just when he had got them all tied up. Harington, it should be said, did not know Ariosto personally or have access to any of his papers. His testimony is still valuable, though, for what it tells us about reader expectations. Harington had just finished translating all of *Orlando furioso*, so he had a pretty good idea of what a romance should sound like. And to Harington's ear, *Orlando* sounds "absolute," in the old sense of "self-sufficient." Critics today still refer to this quality, when they talk about the poem's heterocosm, the autonomy of its art-world. For Harington, though, the poem is complete because it is closed, because it is has a "good and well pleasing conclusion."

East Carolina University

Notes

A shorter version of this paper was delivered at the Renaissance Society of America conference in Miami, Florida on 22 March 2007. I am grateful to Carol V. Kaske, who invited me to be on her panel, and to the anonymous readers of *Spenser Studies*, who offered encouragement as well as correction and who saved me from several errors, both of fact and tact.

1.   See Marina Beer, *Romanzi di cavalleria: il* Furioso *e il romanzo italiano del primo Cinquecento* (Rome: Bulzoni, 1987), part 2 and appendix 2; Paul F. Grendler, "Chivalric Romances in the Italian Renaissance," *Studies in Medieval and Renaissance History* n.s. 10 (1988): 57–102; Michael Murrin, "The Audience of *The Faerie Queene*," *Explorations in Renaissance Culture* 23 (1997): 1–21; Helen Hackett, *Women and Romance Fiction in the English Renaissance* (Cambridge: Cambridge University Press, 2000), ch. 1; Michael L. Hays, *Shakespearean Tragedy as Chivalric Romance* (Cambridge: Brewer, 2003), ch. 2; and Helen Cooper, "Appendix: Medieval Romance in English after 1500," in *The English Romance in Time: Transforming Motifs from Geoffrey of Monmouth to the Death of Shakespeare* (Oxford: Oxford University Press, 2004), 409–29.

2.   George Puttenham, *The Arte of English Poesie* (1589) 1.31, ed. Gladys Doidge Willcock and Alice Walker (Cambridge: Cambridge University Press, 1936), 62.

3.   Puttenham, *Arte* 1.19 (ed. Willcock and Walker, 39–42).

4.   Tasso, *Discorsi del poema eroico* (1594), book 2 (love and religion, in *Prose*, ed. Ettore Mazzali [Milan: Ricciardi, 1959], 545–52), book 3 (variety, 577–91), and book 4 (style, 657–58). Cinzio and Pigna are discussed below.

5.   W. Ker, *Epic and Romance: Essays on Medieval Literature* (1896, rev. 1908; rprt. London: Macmillan, 1931), 7.

6.   Erich Auerbach, *Mimesis: The Representation of Reality in Western Literature* (1946), trans. Willard R. Trask (Princeton: Princeton University Press, 1953), 121.

7.   See, in particular, Patricia Parker, *Inescapable Romance: Studies in the Poetics of a Mode* (Princeton: Princeton University Press, 1979), on error in Ariosto and *dilatio* in Spenser; and David Quint, "The Figure of Atlante: Ariosto and Boiardo's Poem," *MLN* 94 (1979): 77–91, on "endless fiction" in Boiardo.

8.   Paul F. Grendler, "Form and Function in Italian Renaissance Popular Books," *Renaissance Quarterly* 46 (1993): 451–85, at 474, 475. According to an etymology that was popular in the Renaissance, "*Romanzi* was the name given in French to

the early chronicles. The term came next to be applied to the accounts of wars contained in those chronicles, and thence to fictitious stories of war and battle" (Walter L. Bullock, "A Cinquecento Meaning of the Word *Romanzo*," *PMLA* 46 [1931]: 441–49, at 445). See also John J. O'Connor, *Amadis de Gaule and Its Influence on Elizabethan Literature* (New Brunswick: Rutgers University Press, 1970), ch. 2, "*Amadis* as a Book of War."

9. Tasso, *Discorsi del poema eroico*, book 2 (*Prose*, 545–52).

10. Critics who take Virgil's side are rare, but see Theresa M. Krier, *Gazing on Secret Sights: Spenser, Classical Imitation, and the Decorums of Vision* (Ithaca: Cornell University Press, 1990), ch. 1.

11. See M. L. Donnelly, "The Life of Vergil and the Aspirations of the 'New Poet,' " *Spenser Studies* 17 (2003): 1–35.

12. See Kenneth Scott, "Emperor Worship in Ovid," *Transactions of the American Philological Association* 61 (1930): 43–69.

13. For a review of facts and hypotheses, see John C. Thibault, *The Mystery of Ovid's Exile* (Berkeley: University of California Press, 1964).

14. For references to and explanations of Ovid's exile, see Clyde Barnes Cooper, *Some Elizabethan Opinions of the Poetry and Character of Ovid* (Menasha, WI: Banta, 1914), 27–31. Thomas Lodge's remarks, which have come to light more recently, are considered below.

15. See Kurt Smolak, "Der verbannte Dichter: Identifizierungen mit Ovid in Mittelalter und Neuzeit," *Wiener Studien* N.F. 14 (1980): 158–91; and Theodore Ziolkowski, *Ovid and the Moderns* (Ithaca: Cornell University Press, 2005), 99–145.

16. Robert Wilson, "Exile and Relegation in Dante and Ovid," *Annali d'Italianistica* 20 (2002): 55–72.

17. *The Complete Works of Thomas Lodge*, 4 vols. (New York: Russell & Russell, 1963), 1:21. Qtd. in Heather James, "Ovid and the Question of Politics in Early Modern England," *ELH* 70 (2003): 343–73, at 372n56.

18. E.g., Richard McCabe, "Edmund Spenser: Poet of Exile," *Proceedings of the British Academy* 80 (1993): 73–103; Andrew Hadfield, "The Permanent Exile of Edmund Spenser," in *Literature, Politics and National Identity: Reformation to Renaissance* (Cambridge: Cambridge University Press, 1994), 170–201; John Breen, "Edmund Spenser's Exile and the Politics and Poetics of Pastoral," *Cahiers élisabéthains* 53 (1998): 27–41; and idem, "*The Faerie Queene*, Book I and the Theme of Protestant Exile," *Irish University Review* 26 (1996): 226–36; Raphael Lyne, *Ovid's Changing Worlds: English Metamorphoses, 1567–1632* (Oxford: Oxford University Press, 2001), ch. 2; and Syrithe Pugh, *Spenser and Ovid* (Aldershot: Ashgate, 2005).

19. See Richard Peterson, "Laurel Crown and Ape's Tail: New Light on Spenser's Career from Sir Thomas Tresham," *Spenser Studies* 12 (1998): 1–36.

20. Pugh, *Spenser and Ovid*, 180.

21. Ovid is quoted from *Publii Ovidii Nasonis sulmonensis poetae clarissimi opera* (Venice: Lazaro de Saviliano, 1492), sig. x ii^r; Virgil from *Virgilii Maronis opera* (Venice: Giunta, 1544), fol. 161^r.

22. Ovid, sig. x ii^r; Virgil, fol. 244^v.

23. Colin Burrow, " 'That arch-Poet of the *Fairie* lond': A New Spenser Allusion," *Notes and Queries* 245 (2000): 37.

24.   Edwin A. Greenlaw, "Spenser and the Earl of Leicester," *PMLA* 25 (1910): 535–61.

25.   Jean R. Brink, " 'All his minde on honour fixed': The Preferment of Edmund Spenser," in *Spenser's Life and the Subject of Biography*, ed. Judith H. Anderson, Donald Cheney, and David A. Richardson (Amherst: University of Massachusetts Press, 1996), 45–64, at 63.

26.   See Christopher Burlinson and Andrew Zurcher, " 'Secretary to the Lord Grey Lord Deputie here': Edmund Spenser's Irish Papers," *The Library* 6 (2005): 30–75, at 43.

27.   See *Ovidii Nasonis metamorphosis cum integris ac emendatissimis Raphaelis Regii enarrationibus* (Venice: Augustino Barbadico, 1497), sig. u vii^v.

28.   George Sandys, *Ouids Metamorphosis Englished, Mythologiz'd, and Represented in Figures* (London: John Lichfield, 1632; *STC* 18966), 531.

29.   Sandys, *Ouids Metamorphosis*, 1.

30.   Cf. Dante's correspondent Giovanni del Virgilio: "The immediate objective [of Ovid's poem] is the identification of natural, spiritual, and magical metamorphosis, so that when the idea of metamorphosis had been established, Ovid could prove that it was possible for Julius Caesar to have been turned into a god." Trans. A. J. Minnis and A. B. Scott, *Medieval Literary Theory and Criticism c. 1100–c. 1375: The Commentary Tradition*, rev. ed. (Oxford: Clarendon, 1991), 364.

31.   Regio on *Met.* 1.4 (ed. cit., sig. ai^v).

32.   Thomas Cooper, *Thesaurus Linguæ Romanæ & Britannicæ* (London: [Henry Denham], 1578; *STC* 5688), sig. Bbbbbij^r, shows how *perpetuus* could be understood: "Perpetuall: euerlasting: continuall: whole: not in portions, or deuided."

33.   Massimo Fusillo, "How Novels End: Some Patterns of Closure in Ancient Narrative," in *Classical Closure: Reading the End in Greek and Latin Literature*, ed. Deborah H. Roberts, Francis M. Dunn, and Don Fowler (Princeton: Princeton University Press, 1997), 209–27, at 214–15.

34.   Cooper, *English Romance*, 361.

35.   Andrew King, The Faerie Queene *and Middle English Romance: The Matter of Just Memory* (Oxford: Clarendon, 2000), 22–23.

36.   See Fanni Bogdanow, *The Romance of the Grail: A Study of the Structure and Genesis of a Thirteenth-Century Arthurian Romance* (Manchester: Manchester University Press, 1966).

37.   See D. D. R. Owen, "The Development of the Perceval Story," *Romania* 80 (1959): 473–92.

38.   See Jo Ann Cavallo, "Denying Closure: Ariosto's Rewriting of the *Orlando Innamorato*," in *Fortune and Romance: Boiardo in America*, ed. Jo Ann Cavallo and Charles Ross (Tempe, AZ: Medieval & Renaissance Texts & Studies, 1998), 97–134.

39.   The following are representative: D. S. Carne-Ross, "The One and the Many: A Reading of the *Orlando Furioso*," part 1, *Arion* 5 (1966): 195–234, and part 2, *Arion* n.s. 3 (1976): 146–219; Parker, *Inescapable Romance*, ch. 1; David Quint, "The Figure of Atalante: Ariosto and Boiardo's Poem," *MLN* 94 (1979): 77–91; Daniel Javitch, "*Cantus Interruptus* in the *Orlando Furioso*," *MLN* 95 (1980): 66–80; idem, "Narrative Discontinuity in the *Orlando Furioso* and Its Sixteenth Century Critics," *MLN* 103 (1988): 50–74; Sergio Zatti, *Il Furioso fra epos e romanzo* (Lucca: Fazzi,

1990); Hans Ulrich Gumbrecht, "Cosmological Time and the Impossibility of Closure: A Structural Element in Spanish Golden Age Narratives," in *Cultural Authority in Golden Age Spain*, ed. Marina S. Brownlee and Hans Ulrich Gumbrecht (Baltimore: Johns Hopkins University Press, 1995), 304–21; Cavallo, "Denying Closure."

40.   See Beer, *Romanzi di cavalleria*, part 2, ch. 1.

41.   See Henry Thomas, *Spanish and Portuguese Romances of Chivalry* (Cambridge: Cambridge University Press, 1920), ch. 2, and O'Connor, Amadis de Gaule *and Its Influence.*

42.   Some scholars hold that the *Odyssey* was written first; whatever the merits of this view, no one adhered to it in the Renaissance.

43.   See Hans Kern, *Supplemente zur* Äneis *aus dem 15 und 17 Jahrhunderdt* (Nuremberg: Stich, 1896), and Paul Gerhard Schmidt, "Neulatinische Supplemente zur *Aeneis*. Mit einer Edition der *Exsequiae Turni* von Jan van Foreest," in *Acta conventus neo-latini lovaniensis*, ed. Jozeph Ijsewijn and Eckhard Kessler (Louvain: Leuven University Press, 1973), 517–55. The most famous sequel to Virgil was *Das Aeneissupplement des Maffeo Vegio*, ed. Bernd Schneider (Weinheim: Acta Humaniora, 1985).

44.   See *Epic Romance from Homer to Milton* (Oxford: Clarendon, 1993), chs. 1–4. All epics, Burrow argues, aspire to the seriousness and self-discipline of Homer's *Iliad*. But in every epic that has been written since then, including Homer's own *Odyssey*, there is an element of playfulness which threatens to turn the poem into a romance and which eventually has to be suppressed: in Homer, by going home to Penelope; in Virgil, by leaving Dido and killing Turnus; in Ariosto, by the marriage of Angelica and the "ruthless execution of Rodomonte" (68); in Tasso, by chopping down the enchanted forest. Cf. John Watkins, *The Specter of Dido: Spenser and Virgilian Epic* (New Haven: Yale University Press, 1995), 1–8, on the repudiation of enchantresses in Spenser.

45.   David Quint, introduction, *Cinque Canti*, trans. Alexander Sheers and David Quint (Berkeley: University of California Press, 1996), 4.

46.   C. Brand, "L'entrelacement nell' 'Orlando Furioso,' " *Giornale storico della letteratura italiana* 154 (1977): 509–32, at 527–32.

47.   Carne-Ross, "The One and the Many," part II, 205. Cf. Javitch, "The Grafting of Virgilian Epic in *Orlando furioso*," in *Renaissance Transactions: Ariosto and Tasso*, ed. Valeria Finucci (Durham: Duke University Press, 1999), 56–76; what Carne-Ross decries as bastardy, Javitch defends as hybridity.

48.   See Burrow, *Epic Romance*, ch. 4; Quint, *Epic and Empire: Politics and Generic Form from Virgil to Milton* (Princeton: Princeton University Press, 1993), ch. 5; and Sergio Zatti, *L'uniforme cristiano e il multiforme pagano: Saggio sulla* Gerusalemme liberata (Milan: Saggiatore, 1983).

49.   G. B. Giraldi Cinzio, *Scritti critici*, ed. Camillo Guerrieri Crocetti (Milan: Marzorati, 1973), 56.

50.   See, most recently, *La varietas à la Renaissance*, ed. Dominique de Courcelles (Paris: Champion, 2001).

51.   Cinzio, *Scritti critici*, 56.

52.   Qtd. in Bernard Weinberg, *A History of Literary Criticism in the Italian Renaissance*, 2 vols. (Chicago: University of Chicago Press, 1961), 1:446n52.

53.   See Bullock, "Cinquecento Meaning."

54.   The sequel theory, long out of favor, has been revived recently; see Beer, *Romanzi di cavalleria*, 143–49.

55.   *Orlando Furioso in English Heroical Verse, by Iohn Harington* (London: Richard Field, 1591; *STC* 746), 416.

BAS JONGENELEN AND BEN PARSONS

The Sonnets of *Het Bosken*
by Jan Van der Noot

Jan Van der Noot (c.1540–c.1601) is a central figure in Dutch
literature, widely regarded as the first true Renaissance poet in
the Netherlands. He was the earliest Dutch poet to imitate
Ronsard, Baïf, and Petrarch, and the first to use the sonnet-
form. Van der Noot also has vital links with sixteenth-century
England and English literature. While living in London
(1567–72), he produced the source-text for Spenser and Roest's
Theatre of Voluptuous Worldlings. Yet despite this contribution,
he is frequently overlooked by English-speaking critics. Even
when he does receive consideration, he is seldom viewed as a
poet in his own right. As an attempt to redress this, we offer
here fresh translations from Van der Noot's work, lightly annotated throughout, concentrating on the sonnets that are the
lynchpin of his reputation.

LIFE AND WORK

*I*F JAN VAN DER NOOT IS known at all outside Holland, it is as
a stagehand in the service of more renowned authors. For English
readers especially, he is a figure working in the wings, supporting
other writers but eclipsed by them. His limited fame rests on a single
work, *Het Theatre oft Toon-Neel*, the source of the English *Theatre for
Voluptuous Wordlings*. This later work is, of course, not only notable
for being the first emblem book in English, but also for containing
the earliest published work of Spenser, who translated the verse sections of Van der Noot's original.[1]

In the literary history of the Netherlands, however, Van der Noot
occupies a place of central importance. He is a regarded as a towering

figure of the *Gouden Eeuw*, the first true *renaissancedichter* of Dutch
poetry. For modern critics he is the first writer to introduce the key
ideas of the Pléiade into Dutch. Even in his lifetime Van der Noot's
standing as a poet was honored: his fellow Antwerpians Gerard Goos-
sens and Lucas d'Heere both salute his "excellence." Subsequent
centuries have not dimmed his reputation. G. Kalff's assessment is
still widely echoed: "Van der Noot had clearly seen the future for
the arts of poetry and music."[2]

Many of the key details of Van der Noot's life are sketchy. His
dates of birth and death are equally uncertain: the former is generally
fixed at 1539 or 1540, while the latter can only be placed between
1595 and 1601. He is known to have been a *schepen* or alderman at
Antwerp in 1562–63, and again in 1565–66. At some point in the
1560s he was converted to Calvinism, becoming a member of the
so-called *Antwerpse Consistorie*. The circumstances underlying this are
not known, but it is unlikely that he joined the *Consistorie* while still
an alderman. In *Het Theatre*, Van der Noot claims to have persecuted
"the true Word" of Protestantism during his service as a magistrate.
One thing is beyond doubt: Van der Noot was an enthusiastic advo-
cate of his new faith, proving an ardent champion of the Reformers'
cause. He played a central role in the uprising of 1567, in which a
Calvinist faction attempted to depose the Margrave of Antwerp, and
install Van der Noot in his place.

The coup, however, was a complete fiasco, failing entirely in its
objectives. Van der Noot's involvement in this *geuzenoproer* soon
forced him to flee the Netherlands. In March 1567 he reached London, where he would remain for half a decade. He apparently took
lodgings at Botolph Ward, between London Bridge and Billingsgate:
a 1568 mayoral census names one "John van de Note" as a resident
of this area.[3] While living in London, he seems to have inhabited the
fringes of a vibrant, itinerant intellectual community. According to
J. A. Van Dorsten, he was in the orbit of such figures as Jacob Acontius and Michel de Castelnau.[4] He also had firm connections with
the English intelligentsia. One of his kinsmen was Emmanuel van
Meteren, author of the *Nederlantsche Historien*, and an associate of
Richard Mulcaster.[5]

In terms of literary output, Van der Noot's exile was certainly
productive. *Het Theatre* appeared in 1568. This sequence of twenty-
one visionary epigrams, accompanied by prose commentaries and a
virulent disquisition on the papacy, is a bold statement of Van der
Noot's Calvinism. As Witstein's careful dissection has shown, *Het
Theatre* is the work of an author familiar with many currents of Protestant thought. While Van der Noot's main sources are Du Bellay

and Petrarch, he grafts on to this stem material from John Bale and the Swiss Reformer Heinrich Bullinger.[6] The work was printed by John Day, "the great Elizabethan master printer" responsible for Foxe's *Actes and Monuments* and Golding's *Metamorphoses*, inter alia.[7] Day also published Van der Noot's French translation of *Het Theatre*, which appeared shortly after the Dutch original. This version of the text provided the base for the English *Theatre for Voluptuous World-lings*, printed by Henry Bynneman in 1569.

The year 1570/1 saw the publication of *Het Bosken*, the volume from which our selection is taken. While the oldest surviving edition of this work does not quote its place or date of publication, it is most likely the work of Bynneman. This is the conclusion of F. S. Ferguson, who compares "the ornaments and the initial" of *Het Bosken* with Bynneman's other works. Smit reconfirms these findings in his edition of the text.[8] The book's title means "the copse," or "the little forest," and is designed to convey the miscellaneous character of the work. The volume certainly encompasses a wide variety of poetic forms: its contents range from psalms to elegies, epithalamia to Pindaric odes, and from *rondelen* to sonnets. This formal diversity implies that the book was an anthology of earlier work, possibly assembled from texts printed in Antwerp but now no longer extant. Despite its variety, the dual influences of Petrarch and the Pléiade permeate *Het Bosken*, lending it a unifying core.

There is some indication that Van der Noot was held in high regard while he lived at London. In 1569, William How published *The Governance and Preservation of Them That Fear the Plague*, by one "John Vandernote." This is probably the work of a quack-doctor from Flanders who had died sixteen years earlier: but the mere fact that How chose to publish the work of a "Vandernote" soon after Day and Bynneman's editions suggests some demand for Van der Noot's work, which How was keen to exploit.[9] Van der Noot was also introduced at court during his exile, possibly by the diplomat Adolf van Meetkercke. In the English version of *Het Theatre*, Van der Noot recalls hearing Elizabeth speak to a party of "Embassadours" in "their owne naturall language, with a singular dexteritie and princely maiestie."[10]

By 1572 Van der Noot had left London for Cologne. Here he revisited his most successful work, and produced a German translation of *Het Theatre*, the *Theatrum das ist Schawplatz*. This version of the text differs considerably from its predecessors, in that the antipapal passages have been carefully excised. These modifications may well indicate that Van der Noot had already returned to Catholicism by

the early 1570s. He had certainly abandoned Calvinism by the sum-
mer of 1578, when he was readmitted to Antwerp as a Catholic.
Once again, what motivated this reconversion is unknown. In 1579
Van der Noot published *Het cort begryp der XII boecken Olympiados*, a
long and densely allegorical dream-vision. The following decade
seems to have been one of prolonged hardship for Van der Noot.
Between 1581 and 1592, appeals to the aldermanic council for financial support provide the last verifiable references to him.

THE TRANSLATION

Our translation—which is, to our knowledge, the first attempted
in English—has endeavored to remain as faithful as possible to the
meaning of original poems. Because of this, some formal aspects of
the texts may not be clear from our rendering. For example, Van der
Noot frequently experimented with meter and line-length, writing
in pentameter and alexandrines with equal ease. He also used highly
varied rhyme-schemes to produce different emphases and effects: the
sestets of his sonnets employ the full range of possible rhymes. Since
our priority has been the accurate re-creation of Van der Noot's
sense and syntax, it has not been possible to preserve these features.
Hopefully the inclusion of the original Dutch text will enable the
reader to identify these characteristics for themselves.

Nor does our work pretend to give a full translation of *Het Bosken*.
It concentrates solely on the Dutch sonnets collected in that volume.
We have selected these poems in the belief that they provide the best
possible introduction to Van der Noot. Indeed, it is with this form
of poetry that Van der Noot's name is most firmly associated in the
Netherlands. In many key respects the sonnets are representative of
his work as a whole. First, they reveal the engagement with new
Renaissance forms that is the cornerstone of Van der Noot's reputation. As our notes attest, a number of these works are derived from
Petrarch, Ronsard, or Baïf.[11] The fondness for oxymoron and antithesis, the manipulation of blazon conventions, the preference for loose
rhythm over strict meter: all of these features betray the influence of
Petrarch and the Pléiade. But the sonnets also demonstrate Van der
Noot's equal commitment to older Dutch forms. He is not a slavish
imitator of the French and Italian writers: he evidently believed that
drawing modern forms into Dutch should not involve abandoning
older traditions. Often this desire generates a peculiar hybrid of Renaissance and medieval conventions. Sonnet IV, for example, is in

fact a *rondeel*, a traditional Dutch lyrical form related to the French *rondeaux* and English roundelay. While pressed into sonnet-form, the piece retains the marked repetition that is characteristic of *rondelen*. The overall effect is a curious compromise between the older and newer conventions.

The sonnets also showcase the stylistic variety of Van der Noot's work. Although mostly concerned with conventional love conceits, a wide variety of tones are on display here. The poems move from the light satire of Sonnet I to the fervent piety of Sonnet XVIII, from the elegiac timbre of Sonnet VI to the more conversational tone of Sonnet XV. Lastly, Van der Noot's sonnets are the part of his canon most likely to appeal to English readers. The strong elements of Petrachanism in these poems connects them with several works in English, as Van der Noot feeds in the same cultural waters as Spenser, Wyatt, Sidney, even Chaucer. At the very least these pieces offer an interesting counterpoint to some of the best-known pieces of the English Renaissance, from the *Amoretti* to the "Canticus Troili."

Our translation is based on *Het Bosken en Het Theatre*, ed. W. A. P. Smit (Amsterdam and Antwerp: W.B., 1953; rprt. Utrecht: H. E. S. Publishers, 1979). This is available online at http://www.dbnl.org/tekst/noot001bosk01_01/index.htm. Editorial apparatus has been used sparingly. Rather than imposing a full reading on the poems, our notes merely suggest Van der Noot's likely sources, and indicate where the original text is corrupt.

Fontys University of Professional Education, Tilburg and *University of Sheffield.*

Sonet I: *Venus spreect tot Cupido om sommighe oorsaken.*

Het is wel waer dat ghy verscheyden laghen
Hem hebt gheleyt, en u netten ghespreyt,
Maer ghy en hebt alst al wel is gheseyt,
Niet eerst ghemerct wat vrouwen hem behagen:
5   Weer een rycke of een edele van maghen,
Oft een die heur gheerne dickmael vermeyt
T alder feesten, oft die de digniteyt
Soekende is doer costelycke baghen:
Weer een seeghe, wyse ende ghestichte,
10   Oft een wilt dier, oft woeste Venus nichte:

Oft een die is seer deuchdelyck van leven.
Dees' ionghe man is van goeder nature,
En yeghelyck soect gheerne syn parture,
Dus moet ghy hem een syns ghelycke gheven.

Sonnet I: *Venus to Cupid on the Nature of Things*

It is true that you have launched many attacks
Against him, and you have cast your nets,
But you did not—to speak plainly—
First discover what kind of female he prefers.
5 Is it a wealthy or a noble maiden,
Or one that likes to indulge herself
At every festival, or is it one who pursues
Honor in expensive adornments:
Is it one that is chaste, wise, and pious,
10 Or a wild beast, or a kinswoman of Venus:
Or is it one who is virtuous in her living.
This young man is of good character,
And everyone seeks out his mirror-image,
Thus you must bring him one like himself.

Sonet II

Een hiende reyn sach ick wit van colure
In een groen bosch lustich in een valleye,
(Wandelen gaen int soetste vanden Meye)
Gheleghen fraey by een rivire pure,
5 Neffens een bosch seer doncker van verdure:
Des morghens vroech deur der sonnen beleye
Sach ick soo soet en fierkens het ghereye
Heurs schoons ghesichts, dat ic van dier ure
Heur volghen moet latende alle saken.
10 Niemant en roer my, sach ic staen gheschreven,
Om heuren hals met fyne Diamanten
Int gout gheset. Ick wil gaey slaen en waken
Nam ick voor my, want yemant straf van leven
Mocht dese leet aen doen in vremde canten.

Sonnet II[12]

A spotless hind I saw, white of color
In luscious green woodland in a valley
(While wandering in the sweetest time of May)
Lying gracefully by a river pure,
5   Beside a forest that was dark with foliage:
As morning was being crafted by the hands of the sun
I saw, so sweet and fair in its bearing,
Her beautiful face, and I from that hour
Feel compelled to follow her, forsaking all else.
10   "No man may touch me," I saw inscribed,
About her neck with fine diamonds
Set in gold. I will be ready and alert
I vowed to myself, for some brutish man
May do her harm in alien lands.

Sonet III

Heur ooghen syn als twee schoon Esmerauden,
Blinckende claer gheensins om te verlichten
Fraeykens gheset voor alle mans ghesichten,
In tweé peerlen de schoonste die bedauden
5   Aurora oyt alssy d'Oosten verlauden:
Schoonder dan gout syn die my dick bevichten,
Heur wynbraukens ende heur suyver vlichten,
Soo schoon gheveruft dat sy my dick benauden:
Dan out yvoir syn witter heur schoon tanden,
10   Neerstich bewaert met twee coralen randen.
Dees' veruwen al, heur soo suyver vertoonen
In heur aensicht, wel weerdich om te croonen,
Dat sy my ghants van herten en van sinne
Verandert nou hebben deur heur reyn minne.

Sonnet III

Her eyes are like two beautiful emeralds
Glistening clear, polished to perfection
Neatly embedded for every man's esteem,
In two pearls of great beauty, which bedewed them
5   As Aurora when she warms the east:
Finer than gold are those rivals for my heart,

Her eyebrows and her plaited hair,
So fair-colored that I can barely breathe:
Whiter than ivory are her fair teeth,
10   Delicately sheathed in two arcs of coral.
These colors all, she so purely displays
In her face, most deserving of a crown,
That is why she has changed my heart and senses
Twisting me inside out with her pure love.

Sonet IV

Waer wilt ghi loopen lief, waer wilt ghi toch al loopen?
Ghy vliet van my scoon lief eer ghy weet wat ick meyne.
Hoe wilt ghi my altyts deen pyn op dander hoopen?
Myn liefde is schoon lief gestadich goet en reyne.
5   Waerom vliet ghy van my? waer wilt ghi toch al loopen?
Myn liefde touwaerts is gestadich goet en reyne,
Dies en wilt my niet meer d'een pyn op dander hoopen
Maer blyft staen lief, vertoeft en verstaet wat ick meyne.
U schoonheyt suyver maecht en u goede manieren,
10   U wijsheyt, u verstant en u deucht goedertieren,
U oochskens scoon en claer, en u reyn eerbaer wesen
U suyver blondich haer, u wynbraukens by desen,
Behaghen my soo wel, dat ick tot alle tyen,
By u wel wilde syn twaer in vreucht oft in lyen.

Sonnet IV[13]

Where do you wish to go, my love, where do you plan to go?
You flee from me, sweet love, before you know my mind.
Why do you always pile one pain upon another?
My love is, sweet love, steadfast, good and pure.
5   Why do you flee from me? where do you plan to go?
My love for you is steadfast, good and pure,
So, do not pile one pain upon another
But wait, my love, stay and take heed of my mind.
Your beauty, pure maiden, and your good habits,
10   Your wisdom, your wit and your fine virtues,
Your eyes comely and clear, and your pure noble ways
Your flawless blonde hair, your twinned eyebrows,
Please me so greatly, that until the end of time
I long to be with you in joy or in anguish.

Sonet V

Ick sach myn Nimphe int suetste van den Iare
In eenen beemt gheleghen aende sye
Van heuren hof, alleene als de vrye:
Neffens een gracht, waer af het water clare
5   Gheboort met lisch, cruyt en bloemen eenpare,
Lustigher scheen dan alle schilderye,
Noyt man en sach schoonder tappisserye,
Soo schoon was tvelt ghebloeyt veer ende nare:
Ghelyck Flora sadt sy daer op de bloemen,
10   Om heur schoonheyt machmense Venus noemen,
Om heur verstant Minerva wys van sinne,
Diana oock om heur reyn eerlyck wesen,
Boven Iuno is sy weert t'syn ghepresen:
Tsynts desen tyt queelt myn siele om heur minne.

Sonnet V[14]

I saw my Nymph at the sweetest time of year
In a pasture that lay alongside
Her courtyard, alone and free:
Next to a canal, in which clear water
5   Carried irises, plants, and flowers in great number;
Lovelier it seemed than any painting;
No man ever saw a finer tapestry,
So finely the field blossomed far and near:
Like Flora she sat there upon the flowers;
10   For her beauty one may name her Venus,
For her wits Minerva, wise in senses,
Diana too for her flawless, honorable ways;
Above Juno is she in meriting praise:
Since that time my soul has pined for her love.

Sonet VI

Soo haest als myn ooghen heur schoon figure
Hebben ghesien soo suyver ende reyne,
Merckende veel gratien (niet ghemeyne)
In dese maghet eerbaer, goet ende pure,
5   Werde ick ghetreft recht op die selve ure,
Van Cupido, en na der minnen treyne,

Werde ick dienaer van dit maechdeken cleyne:
Wiens liefde my dickwerven het sure
Doen prueven heeft met suchten ende beven:
10   En wederom is my deur heur ghegheven
Blyschap' en vreucht, maer altyts onghedurich:
Hope gheeft troost, maer duchten doet my pyne,
Ick hop' nochtans noch eens vertroost te syne,
Maer vast vinde ick my nu dicwerven treurich.

Sonnet VI

As soon as my eyes her beautiful figure
Had seen, so glorious and innocent,
Noting many graces (none of them common)
In this worthy maiden, good and pure,
5   I was struck in that same instant,
By Cupid; in love's usual manner,
I became dedicated to this fine maiden:
Her love frequently the bitter
Makes me taste, with sighing and quivering:
10   On the other hand she also causes me
Blissfulness and glee, but only briefly:
Hope gives solace, but pain makes me fear;
I hope that consolation may come,
But for now I find myself utterly saddened.

Sonet VII

Isser iemant onder des hemels ronde
Die gheproeft heeft Cupidos tyrannie,
Dat ben ick wel, die met herten onblye
Ghequetst ben met een dootelycke wonde
5   Die hy my ghaf door d'ooghe van de blonde,
Stellende heur soo in de heerschappye
Over myn hert en sinnen t'allen tye,
Beruerende myn siele tot den gronde.
Nacht ende dach en doen ick niet dan claghen,
10   Suchten, kermen, ende myn herte cnaghen,
Biddende hem dat hy myn leven eynde.
Maer laes hy neempt in myn smerte behaghen,
Want hoe ick hem roepe en smeeke by vlaghen,
Hy en vertroost my niet waer ick my weynde.

Sonnet VII[15]

If any man under the circle of heaven
Has experienced the tyranny of Cupid,
It is I, who with a miserable heart
Has been made to suffer a deadly wound
5   Which he dealt me with the eyes of a blonde,
Installing her firmly in the office
Of my heart and senses for all time,
Piercing my soul to its foundation.
Night and day I do nothing but complain,
10   Sighing, groaning, and gnawing at my heart,
Begging that he might end my life.
But alas he delights in my agony,
As I shout out and implore him to stop,
He gives me no relief wherever I go.

Sonet VIII

En ist de liefde niet, wat ist dan dat my quelt?
En ist de liefde ooc, wat mach de liefde wesen?
Is sy soet ende goet, hoe valt sy hert in desen?
Is sy quaet, hoe is dan soo suete heur ghewelt?
5   Brande ic met mynen danc, hoe ben ic dan ontstelt?
Ist teghen mynen danc, sal tsuchten my genesen?
Vreucht van pynen vol, pyne vol vreucht geresen
Droefheyt vol ioleyts! o blyschappe verfelt!
Levende doot hoe moecht ghy teghen mynen danck
10   Dus vele over my? maer ben ick willens cranck,
My claghende tonrecht, de liefde ick tonrecht blame.
Liefde goet ende quaet, my leet en aenghename,
Gheluck en ongheluck, suer en soet ick ghevule:
Ic suke vryicheyt, en om slaven ick wule.

Sonnet VIII[16]

And if it is not love, what is it that torments me?
And if it is love as well, what might love be?
If it is sweet and good, why is it so harsh now?
Is it is angry, then why is its assault so sweet?
5   If I burn by choice, why am I so unsettled?
If it is against my choosing, shall sighing make me well?

Joy with pains filled, pain filled with joy rising,
Sadness filled with pleasure! o savage bliss!
Living dead, how can you against my will
10   Rule over me? but if I am willingly infected,
Pitying myself falsely, then love I falsely chide.
Love good and faulty, my delight and odium,
Pleasure and displeasure, bitter and sweet I feel:
I seek freedom, but I choose to be enslaved.

Sonet IX

Noyt en is u minlyck wesen gheweken
Wt myn verstant, maer sie altyts present
U wesen soet, u schoonheyt excellent,
U aenschyn claer, ende de soete treken
5   Uwer oochskens die machtich syn te breken
De strafficheyt van een hert dat ghewent
Tot quade is, en in wreetheyt verblent,
Doende t'selfde virighe tranen leken.
U suyver haer (sweer ick u op myn trouwe)
10   Dunct my gemengt syn met draykens van gouwe.
U wynbraukens syn boochskens van Hebenen:
Den mont corael, de borstkens van albaste,
De tanden van yvoir als de ghepaste,
Ermkens massyf, en wel ghemaecte schenen.

Sonnet IX

Never has your lovely being faded
From my understanding, but it is always present
Your sweet being, your excellent beauty,
Your face clear, and the sweet devices
5   Of your eyes that are mighty enough to break
The harshness of a heart that is bent
To evil, and by wrathfulness blinded
Causing it to pour forth fiery tears.
Your hair (I swear upon my honor)
10   To my mind seems woven with gold thread.
Your eyebrows are longbows of ebony:
The mouth coral, the breasts of alabaster,
The teeth of ivory as is most fitting,
The arms shapely, with well-crafted shin-bones.

Sonet X

Wil iemant sien in een seer ionghe ieucht
Alle schoonheyt, alle suyverheyt reene,
Ootmoedicheyt, en hoefsheyt niet ghemeene,
Alle eerbaerheyt, wysheyt, verstant en deucht?
5   Wil iemant sien (compt te wyl ghyt sien meucht)
Twee ooghen claer, en een godheyt niet cleene?
De glorie oock van onsen tyt alleene?
Come besien die my 't herte verheucht:
Hoe Cupido byt en lacht sal hy leeren,
10   Hoe hy gheneest, en hoe hy ooc doorwont,
Dan sal hy heur siende segghen terstont
Gheluckich is, die een vat soo vol eeren,
Wysheyt, verstant en deucht, aenschouwen mach,
Maer salich hy, die heur noch trouwen mach.

Sonnet X[17]

Does any man wish to see a youthful creature
All beauty, all spotless purity,
Cordiality, and grace not widely found,
All delicacy, wisdom, wit and nobility?
5   Does any man wish to see (come while you still can)
Two clear eyes, and a divinity of no trifling kind?
The glory found in our age alone?
Come and see the one who cheers my heart:
You shall learn how Cupid bites as he laughs,
10   How he soothes, but how he stabs as well;
Then shall he say at once on seeing her:
Lucky is he, who such a trove full of honor,
Wisdom, wit and nobility, might witness,
But blessed is he, who might also wed her.

Sonet XI

Soo langhe mynen gheest dees leden sal doen ruren
(Sweere ic u suete lief) en sal nemmermeer vrouwe
Dan ghy, over myn ieucht (in des werelts landouwe)
Heerschappye hebben, want myn liefde sal duren
5   Ghestadichlyck altyts, wat leet ick moet besuren.
U alleene (schoon lief) sal ick blyven ghetrouwe,

Want veel liever wil ick u dienaer syn in trouwe,
Dan eens anders dienaer wat vreucht my mocht ghebeuren.
U schoonheyt is soo hooch in mynen gheest verheven,
10   En u liefde is soo vast in myn herte gheschreven,
Dat noch den langen tyt, noch Atropos geruchten
Niet keeren en sullen, ick en sal 't allen daghen
In myn herte geprint ende gheschildert draghen,
U ooghen, uwen mont, u lachen, u versuchten.

Sonnet XI[18]

As long as my spirit still stirs these limbs
(I swear my sweet love) nevermore will a woman
Other than you, over my youth (in all the world's lands)
Hold authority, for my love will endure
5   Throughout all time, whatever hardship I must bear.
To you alone (fair love) shall I remain true,
For I would rather be your sworn servant,
Than servant to another no matter what mirth I gain.
Your beauty is so elevated in my mind
10   And your love is so firmly on my heart inscribed
That not the expanse of time, nor the threats of Atropos
May ruin or soil it, that which I keep all my days
In my heart printed and stained with inks,
Your eyes, your mouth, your smiles, your sighs.

Sonet XII

U suet ghesichte en u seer eerlyck wesen
Reyn suyver maecht, so suyver van aenschyne,
Doen lancx soo meer vermeerderen myn pyne:
Nochtans worden van my altyts ghepresen
5   U aenschyn claer, u bruyn oochskens by desen,
U blondich haer waer deure ick ten fyne,
Hopende ben volcomen medecyne,
En soo deur u noch te worden ghenesen.
Versmaeyt ghy my, myn leven sal haest eynden,
10   Deur pyne swaer in droefheyt onghemeten,
Maer seght my lief en sou u dit niet deeren,
Dat ghy alsoo myn schaduwe soudt seynden
Naer Lethes vloet om te blyven verghelten?
God (hope ic) sal die wreetheyt van u weeren.

Sonnet XII

Your sweet face and your most honorable being
True pure maiden, so bright of appearance,
While I suffer the more my pain will grow:
Yet nonetheless I will always praise
5   Your fair appearance, your brown eyes as well,
Your blonde hair which I adore for its fineness;
I hope you are the welcome medicine
And thus will cure me with your being.
If you deny me, my life will soon end
10   Due to this grave pain of measureless woe,
But I ask you my love, would it not grieve you
To know that you will also send my shade
To the Lethe and to outright oblivion?
God (I hope) shall keep this cruelty from you.

Sonet XIII

Had ic tverstant so grof, so plomp en onbesneden
Als vele die int velt spitten, graven en spayen,
Oft waer ick als sy syn die als weerhanen drayen,
Soo en sou u schoonheyt, noch u verchierde leden,
5   Weerde suyver maecht my niet houden tonvreden
Noch ic en sou altyts niet staen t'uwer genaeyen,
Maer sou nu hier nu daer vast myn ghenuchten maeyen,
Die ick ghisteren sach sou syn vergeten heden:
Boven dese acht ic my nochtans gheluckich t'syne,
10   En boven alle goet acht ick myn bitter pyne
Die ic om u reyn lief lyde nachten en daghen:
Want sonder liefde lief sou ick sonder ghenuchten
Leven gelyck sy doen (al moet ic nu dick suchten)
Die na eere noch deucht, noch reyn liefde en vraghen.

Sonnet XIII[19]

Had I understanding so gross, so rude and unrefined
Like the folk in the fields that root, grub and dig
Or if I resembled those who spin like weathercocks,
Neither your immense beauty, nor your comely limbs,
5   Worthy bright virgin, might keep me in confusion
Nor would I be always so fixed to your bidding,

But here and there I would swiftly seek pleasures,
Those I found yesterday would be forgotten today:
Above such men however I rate myself lucky,
10   And above all goodness I rate my bitter pain
Which I bear for you, sweet love, night and day:
For without love, my love, I would be without joys
Living as they do (although I must now sigh heavily)
Who do not pursue honor, or pure love and virtue.

Sonet XIV

Suet ghepeys, o sware fantasyen!
Groote vreucht! die my comt deur t'gedencken
Van u minlyck wesen het welck my schenken
Can een eerlyck ende salich verblyen.
5   Droefheyt bly', ô ghenuchelyck lyen!
Ghesontheyt, ô daghelycx vercrenken!
Scherp verbot, ô lieffelyck weerwenken!
Suren peys, ô aldersoetste stryen!
T is my al vreucht, al goet ende bequame:
10   T is my al lief, wilcome en aenghename,
Wat ick deur u liefde (reyn lief) ontfanghe:
Tsy suer oft suet, alst u wel mach behaghen:
Maer nochtans is al myn vlieghen en iaghen,
Naer uwen troost, en naer u ick verlanghe.

Sonnet XIV[20]

Sweet misery, o somber daydream!
Great gladness comes to me with the thought
Of your lovely being, which grants to me
An honorable and a blithesome joy.
5   Doleful bliss, o joyful suffering!
Robust health, o daily decline!
Sharp restraint, o lovely regret!
Bitter peace, o sweetest conflict!
To me all is mirth, all is good and pleasing:
10   Everything is love to me, welcome and true,
That I derive from your love (fair love):
Whether bitter or sweet, as it may please you:
Yet still all my haste and urgency are,
Ever in your service, as for you I yearn.

Sonet XV

Ghy en syt my niet wreedt, niet hert, noch ongenadich,
Maer vriendelick sydy, beleeft en goedertieren:
Seer minlyck en seer goet, soet en seech van manieren:
Ghy en syt oock gheensins wilt, straf noch onghestadich:
5   Ghy en syt my ooc niet verachtich noch versmadich
En ic en sueck' ooc niet dan u deucht te verchieren
Waerom doet my dan nu u liefde dus crayeren?
Segget my toch scoon lief, en weest my toch beradich:
U eere en u deucht, en u manierlyck wesen,
10   Gaen als den noorden wint d'oneerbaarheyt veriaghen.
En ic heb ooc altyts in dorperheyt mishaghen:
Ontbeyt lief ic verstaet, ic sueck' de deucht gepresen
En die en is toch hier beneden niet te vinden,
So veele als in u dees' doet my touweerts winden.

Sonnet XV

You are not cruel, not hard, not unmerciful,
But are cordial, courteous and tender-hearted:
Most charming and good, sweet and shy in manners:
You are not wild at all, nor coarse and fickle:
5   You do not dislike me and do not despise me
And I wish for nothing but to honor your grace
Then why does my love for you make me cry out?
Tell me this beautiful love, and give me relief:
Your dignity and virtue, your well-mannered ways
10   Carry away vice like the northern wind.
And I have always loathed all roughness:
Wait my love, I know now. I seek cherished virtue
And that which may not be found in this world,
So that which is in you makes me turn to you.

Sonet XVI

Hoe sou ick van u (lief) scheydende connen spreken
Dat druckich woort Adieu, oft God moet u bewaren
Ghemerct my het gepeys alleene can beswaren?
Voorwaer tsceyden van u doet myn tranen als beken
5   Seer overvloedelyck over myn wanghen leken:
Nu god beware u lief alst dus met u moet varen,

Myn leven, mynen troost, alder liefste der charen:
Adieu ghy die myn pyn cunt meerderen of breken
Adieu reyn suete lief: vaert wel schoone meestersse,
10   Die my dic suchten doet, en weerom meucht verheughen,
Ghy die ic dienen sal altyts na myn vermeugen.
Bewaren moet u God, myn vreucht en bitter persse,
Die my dic branden doet en ooc dicmael doet vrisen
Leeft met my soo ghy wilt, ken sal gheen ander kiesen.

Sonnet XVI[21]

How at your departure (my love) might I speak
That dire word Adieu, or may God keep you
When the thoughts alone cause me sadness?
For your departure makes my tears run
5   Flowing like brooks down my cheeks:
God keep you, my sweet, if this must pass,
My life, my solace, my loveliest companion:
Adieu to you, who can increase or break my pain.
Adieu, pure sweet love: farewell, bonny mistress
10   Who makes me sigh gravely, and cheers me again,
I will always serve you as well as I can.
God must keep you, my joy and bitter torment,
Who makes me burn and also causes me to freeze
Live with me if you wish, I will never choose another.

Sonet XVII: *Tot sijn muse*

Veel herder dan in stael, in coper of pourphier,
Heb ick dit werck volbrocht so dat de loop der Iaeren,
Den reghen noch den wint, noch ooc Mulsibersscharen,
Dat selfde nymmermeer en sullen schenden fier:
5   Als mynen lesten dach my sal doen slapen schier,
Dan en sal *Vander Noot* niet al gaen inde baren:
Want synen boeck sal dan synen naem bet verclaren
Dan Marmer of Pourphier, al en ist maer pampier,
Den welcken over all ieuchdich tot allen tyen
10   Sal vliegen (wiet benyt) om dat ick my geveucht
Hebbe tot d'eerlyck werc dat den musen geneucht.
Musa wel aen, vliecht op en bootschapt met verblyen
Inden hemel, dat ick al ree heb' overwonnen,
Deur ulie ionste goet, deur dwerck met u begonnen.

Sonnet XVII: To His Muse[22]

Much harder than steel, copper or porphyry,
I have brought forth this work, so that the years,
The rain and the wind, and Mulciber's kindred,
May never inflict fierce damage upon it:
5   When my last day puts me forever to sleep
Van der Noot will not be entirely borne to his grave:
For his book will assert his name more boldly
Than marble or porphyry, though it be mere paper,
Bearing it up ever-youthful through all ages,
10   Who will look on in envy, because I set myself to this,
This honorable work that delights the muses.
Come Muse, soar upwards and joyously proclaim
To the heavens, that I have already triumphed
By your blessing, through the work I began with you.

Sonet XVIII

Op u betrou ick God, weest toch myn toeverlaet,
Ghy hebt over my macht, onnut syn myn goey wercken:
Maer ick suecke belust den voorspoet uwer kercken
Want op d'afgods dienaers sal comen alle quaet.
5   De Heere is den gront daer myn rent' vast op staet,
D'best eerfdeel (siet) es my toe comen tot versterken,
Gheloeft sy god die my onderwyst en doet mercken,
Ick roep hem, hy verhoort en troost my hoe dat gaet.
Siet hierom is myn hert verheucht, myn tonge lacht,
10   Wel wetende dat ghy myn lichaem inder eerden
Gheenen eewigen slaep en sult laten aenveerden,
Maer sult my inden wech des levens deur u cracht
Leyden, daer ic sal sien u aensicht met verblyen,
Want de oprechte vreucht is by u t'allen tyen.

Sonnet XVIII[23]

Preserve me, O God; in thee do I put my trust,
Thou hast dominion over me, fruitless are my works
Unless I seek with glad heart the glory of thy Church,
Confounded shall be all that serve graven images.
5   The Lord is the ground that maintaineth my lot,
The goodly inheritance which strengthens mine heart.

I will bless the Lord, who hath given me counsel,
I call upon him, he gives ear, and attends unto me,
Therefore my heart is glad, and my glory rejoiceth,
10   For I know that when my flesh cleaveth unto the dust
Thou wilt not leave my soul to sleep in endless sleep.
In thy righteousness thou wilt show the path of life
And lead me to look on thy face with bliss,
For in thy presence is the fullness of true joy.

NOTES

1.   See Jan Van der Noodt, *A Theatre for Voluptuous Worldlings*, trans. Theodor Roest and Edmund Spenser, ed. L. S. Friedland (New York: Scholars' Facsimiles and Reprints, 1936).

2.   G. Kalff, *Geschiedenis der Nederlandsche letterkunde* (Groningen: J. B. Wolters, 1907), 183.

3.   Karel Bostoen, "Van Der Noot's Apocalyptic Visions: Do You 'See' What You Read?," *Anglo-Dutch Relations in the Field of the Emblem*, ed. Bart Westerweel (Leiden: Brill, 1997), 49. See also Laura Hunt Yungblut, *Strangers Settled Here Amongst Us: Policies, Perceptions and the Presence of Aliens in Elizabethan England* (London: Routledge, 1996), 18

4.   J. A. Van Dorsten, *The Radical Arts: First Decade of an Elizabethan Renaissance*, Publications of the Sir Thomas Browne Institute 4 (New York: Oxford University Press, 1970).

5.   Richard Rambuss, "Spenser's Life And Career," in *The Cambridge Companion to Spenser*, ed. Andrew Hadfield (Cambridge: Cambridge University Press, 2001), 17.

6.   S. F. Witstein, *De Verzencommentaar in Het Theatre van Jan Van der Noot*, Utrechtse Publikaties voor Algemene Literatuurwetenschap 8 (Utrecht: Utrecht University Press, 1965).

7.   John N. King, "The Light of Printing: William Tyndale, John Foxe, John Day, and Early Modern Print Culture," *Reniassance Quarterly* 54 (2001): 53.

8.   W. A. P. Smit, "Inleiding," in Jan Van der Noot, *Het Bosken en Het Theatre*, 19.

9.   See Ben Parsons and Bas Jongenelen, "Jan Van der Noot: A Mistaken Attribution in the Short-Title Catalogue?," *Notes and Queries* 53 (2006): 427.

10.   Van der Noodt, *A Theatre for Voluptuous Worldlings*, f.Aiiij.

11.   For further information, see Van der Noot, *Het Bosken en Het Theatre*, 79–130.

12.   A free translation of Petrarch, Sonnet CLVII, "Una candida cerva sopra l'herba." 10: "No man may touch me" (see John 20:17).

13.   Although not a direct translation, this piece resembles Ronsard, "Dittes, maistresse, hé que vous ay-ie fait" (*Continuation des Amours*, 11).

14.   Compare Ronsard, "Ie vy ma Nymphe entre cent damoiselles" (*Amours* I, 114).

15.   Here, the octave is reminiscent of Baïf, "O Brinon, si quelcun a senty la rigueur" (*Amour de Francine* I, 107), while the sextet recalls Ronsard, "Dame, depuis que la premiere fleche" (*Amours* I, 47).

16.   Owing to textual corruption, Smit has reconstructed this sonnet in his edition. Compare Baïf, "Si ce n"est pas Amour, que sent donques mon coeur?"—itself a translation of Petrarch, Sonnet CII, "S"amor non è . . ." (Baïf, *Amour de Francine* I, 22).

17.   See Ronsard, "Qui voudra, voir dedans vne ieunesse" (*Amours* I, 63).

18.   Reconstructed by Smit.

19.   Reconstructed by Smit. The opening quatrain appears to be based on Ronsard, "Petit barbet, que tu es bienheureux" (*Amours* I, 78).

20.   Reconstructed by Smit. This sonnet bears certain similarities to Petrarch, "O passi sparsi, ò pensier uaghi, et pronti," separately translated by Clement Marot, Louise Labé, and Baïf. Van der Noot probably knew Baïf's version alone (*Amour de Francine* II, 44).

21.   See Ronsard's madrigal "Comment au departir adieu pourroy-ie dire" (*Amours* II, 48).

22.   Compare Ronsard, "A Sa Muse" (*Odes* V, 36), itself adapted from Horace (*Carmina* III, 30).

23.   This sonnet directly alludes to several psalms, and contains echoes of numerous others. Compare especially Psalms 16, 13, and 97. Van der Noot produced many verse translations from the Psalms in his lifetime: see Van der Noot, *Het Bosken en Het Theatre*, 131–81.

On the Margins of *The Faerie Queene*

These paired but independent essays report on the marginalia in several copies of Spenser's *Faerie Queene*. The first, by Tianhu Hao, describes the annotations in a copy of the 1609 edition held by Columbia University's Rare Book and Manuscript Library, annotations that illustrate the degree to which early modern readers could actively participate in the texts they read. The second, by Anne Lake Prescott, describes notes or markings in two badly damaged copies of the 1596 *Faerie Queene*, both in the possession of the essay's author, that likewise show such participation. One of the volumes was later owned by one John Sheridan, probably an Irish barrister of that same name living in England and a member of the Middle Temple, who in 1771 wrote his ecstatic appreciation of the poet in a hitherto unpublished Spenserian stanza.

TIANHU HAO

An Early Modern Male Reader of *The Faerie Queene*

THE COLUMBIA UNIVERSITY RARE Book and Manuscript Library holds a 1609 copy of *The Faerie Queene* (London: H. Lownes; *STC* 23083) with written marginalia.[1] This book was once owned by Professor Jefferson Butler Fletcher (1865–1946), a Renaissance scholar and translator of Dante's *The Divine Comedy* (1931). On its flyleaf is written: "Jefferson B. Fletcher Esq. 1898 with the best wishes of his friend and pupil H. O. Eaton." Fletcher served as an English instructor at Harvard University from 1890 to 1902. Later, from 1904 to 1939, he was Professor of Comparative Literature at Columbia University. Presumably during that period one of his students presented the book to him.[2] The marginalia are not by Fletcher. On the last page of the book there are various barely legible scribbles. The legible words include "his book" (twice). Although I cannot recognize the signature of the earlier owner, I am fairly certain, on paleographical grounds, that behind the marginalia is an early modern male reader of *The Faerie Queene*.[3]

This male reader is engaged in various reading activities. He puts an asterisk beside a line, underlines words, phrases, or lines, explains an unfamiliar word, clarifies the references or allusions, and occasionally makes a commentary. He especially has difficulties with the word *wonne*, which he annotates thrice (II.vii.49.2, II.xii.11.4, II.xii.69.8). He answers the poet's rhetorical question "Who knows not Arlohill" with "In Ireland" (VII.vi.36.6), showing his geographical knowledge. He clarifies the syntax by annotating "that" ("For there is nothing lost, that may be found, if sought") as "but" (V.ii.39.9).[4] The only full-sentence comment made by this reader occurs at II.xii.22.9: "mighty & great men puffe vp wth proud disdaine." The phrase "puffe vp wth proud disdaine" is drawn from a previous line: "And the great sea puft vp with proud disdaine" (II.xii.21.7). Spenser depicts a natural scene, whereas the reader makes a social commentary, his imaginative mind working in free association. This example indicates that this reader responds to the poem personally: he writes his own social experience while reading an allegorical romance. The roles of reader and writer fuse into one another.

The reader's twenty-five marginalia in the first two cantos of Book I, and thirty-eight more in the twelve cantos of Book II, demonstrate that he is a careful reader who understands how to interpret an allegory. Paying particular attention to such lines as "Fierce warres and faithfull loues shall moralize my song" (I.0.1.9) and "And learne from pleasures poyson to abstaine: / Ill by ensample good doth often gayne" (II.ii.45.4–5), he seems to be a conscious moralist. He consistently interprets the characters in the allegory in terms of the virtues and vices they represent. For instance, Una is truth, the dragon is Error, Archimago is hypocrisy, Sir Guyon is temperance, and so forth. In particular, the reader describes Archimago in different terms: *hermite, hipocrisie, magitian, enchaunter*. While aware of Archimago's deceitfulness, he seems to be fascinated by his multiple identities. In addition, he annotates Sans foy as faithles (I.ii.12.8), Sans loy as Lawles (II.ii.18.1), and Medina as modesty, moderatōn (II.ii.14.4). His linguistic competence allows him to grasp the allegorical characters correctly. Sometimes he does make mistakes, however. At the beginning of Book II, he repeatedly mistakes Sir Guyon as "holynes" or "redcros k^t."—as if lingering in Book I—and then corrects his errors. The reader has a literary capability as well, for he explains "Two goodly Beacons" as "2. eyes" (II.ix.46.3) and "dyde in white and red" as "youthfull" (II.xii.12.5). In a word, the marginalia prove the reader to be a careful and capable one who is sensitive to the allegorical form.

This reader, moreover, copies eight pages of *The Faerie Queene* (I.iii.20–I.v.8, 13–20) and inserts them into the book to replace the missing pages. These written pages illustrate several things, most importantly the coexistence of manuscript and print, the early modern reading practice and what I elsewhere call "space economy."[5] The abbreviated words we observe include the following: y^e, w^{ch}, y^t, S^t, wth, Therewth, wthstand, wthout, &, Champiō, whō, y^m (i.e., them, I.iv.43.9). These abbreviations occur largely because of the limitation of space, for each page is divided into two columns, making the poetic lines rather crowded. Space economy often functions in the manuscript version, but it also appears in this printed book. In the line "For trũpets stern to change mine oatê reeds" (I.0.1.4), for example, the compositor shortens the words trumpets and oaten to fit them into the space.

The ways in which this reader deals with the original text indicate that he is no slavish copier but rather a spontaneous editor, an active reader and writer at the same time. Except for possible slips of the quill or eye (at I.iv.13.6, *where* becomes *were*; I.iv.38.5 confuses *And* and *An*; with I.iv.12.2, an *a* is missed), which are unintentional, the reader-writer-editor makes free and frequent changes of the text he is supposed to copy. The copied text departs from the original in many respects, including spelling (such as with *their-there*; and he sometimes changes spelling for the sake of eye rhyme: I.iii.25: *haire/ teare/feare-heare/teare/feare*); tense (the line I.iii.30.5 shifts *had forgot* to *has forgot*); diction (I.iv.43.4 changes *aveng'd* to *reuenged*); and word order (I.iv.15.5, *her well they knew-they well her knew*; sometimes the change in word order destroys the rhyme: I.iv.29.6, *in foote and hand* becomes *in hand & foot*). The reader is particularly concerned with metrical regularity, for he replaces the final *e* in words like *discouered* (I.iii.21.1) and *crownes* (I.iii.31.9) with an apostrophe so as to omit one syllable, or he inserts the final *e* into words like *weened* (I.iii.21.9), *amazed* (I.iii.22.7), *returned* (I.iii.24.2) so as to add one syllable. The fact that he changes the final *e* into an apostrophe in words *ruled* (I.iv.12.7) and *perceiued* (I.v.2.6) is telling enough. Sometimes he emends the original text, almost automatically, as in the case of *fesh* turned into *fresh* (I.iv.17.3). Envy is the fifth in the line of seven deadly sins, so the spontaneous editor corrects *first* to *fifth* (I.iv.32.9). The accumulation of the above evidence inclines me to conclude that the fluidity of texts is a rule in early modern reading practice, for the reader actively participates in the process of writing. Authorial intention is not as respected as it is in modern times; rather, readerly intention is on a par with authorial intention. Authorial intention is never seen as pure, but is mediated by such agents as the reader and the publisher in the process of its realization and materialization. Early modern reading practice is characterized by the fluidity of the text, the subjectivity of the reader, and the multiplicity of authorial intention.[6]

The University of Peking

NOTES

1. Special Collections B823Sp3 Q5 1609. Columbia University Rare Book and Manuscript Library in New York. *STC* 23083.

2. On Fletcher's career, see *Who Was Who in America* (Chicago: A. N. Marquis, 1950), vol. 2 (1943–1950).

3. Although women seem to have been the primary audience for early modern romances, men were also the readers of romances. See, for example, Robert Brounrigg's commendatory poem to *The Cyprian Academy* (Wing B890): "Each gallant here may have his fill / Each Lady please her eye / Such are thy streames of eloquence / Such is thy poesie" (sig. A1). For a useful discussion of women readers of romances, see Helen Hackett, *Women and Romance Fiction in the English Renaissance* (Cambridge: Cambridge, 2000), ch. 1 ("The readership of Renaissance romance"), 14–19.

4. This word is in pencil, while all the other marginalia are in ink.

5. Tianhu Hao, *"Hesperides, or the Muses' Garden*: Commonplace Reading and Writing in Early Modern England" (Ph.D. diss. Columbia University, 2006), 54–62.

6. For a similar discussion of early modern reading practice in connection with the commonplace book, see Hao, 100–14.

ANNE LAKE PRESCOTT

Two Copies of the 1596 *Faerie Queene*: Annotations and an Unpublished Poem on Spenser

*T*HIS ESSAY DESCRIBES TWO badly damaged or partial copies of the 1596 *Faerie Queene* that I recently acquired. Both have annotations, if usually minimal ones, and one has a never before published poem in Spenser's honor.

I start with the complete but much repaired volume I of what had been a two-volume set; it has a handsome but later binding and has been carefully mended. Could it be the "imperfect" 1596 put up for sale by William Collins in 1786? That would have cost the buyer ten shillings sixpence, had there been a buyer that year—the set was still for sale, at the same price, in Collins's catalogue for 1791.[1] In any case, the first page of my volume has a little crowd of names, only some of which are readily legible. The most interesting is the inscription "Shelley," in what seems a fairly late hand, but it is crossed out and there is, alas, no "P.B." or "Mary W." attached to it. There is also a date, partially crossed out, underneath a line of writing that has been entirely crossed out saying that somebody died on 9 January 1817 (or possibly 1827), at the age of two; why the erasures and crossings out? To affirm a transfer of ownership? Another name, an owner's I assume, is "T. Tayler." Not Jeremy, alas. There's also a "Will" but the following name is, alas, not "Shakespeare." And then, on the verso of signature A2, is the name "Walter Ralegh" with the date 1591. The "Ralegh" has been partially erased but remains legible. Did some forger develop a conscience? The book has other peculiarities. The title page of the volume clearly identifies itself as the 1596 edition, but one owner seems to have repaired a damaged volume by replacing presumably lost or torn pages with some cropped ones from a 1590 copy. The result is that we now leave Amoret and Scudamore in their ecstatic clinch, their romance unescaped, and then turn to some dedicatory poems and the *Letter to Ralegh*. The

jump from 1590 to 1596 is clear enough on page 15, as is the reverse
jump at the end, and a number of pages in the middle are evidently
from 1590 as well. As a modern note on the flyleaf puts it, this is a
"mixed volume." Since I do not have the second volume I do not
know how we are to get from the happy hermaphrodite of 1590 to
the companionship of Britomart and Amoret at the start of Book IV.

There are, as I have said, annotations, and although few have
historical interest as incisive cultural commentary (not even as amus-
ingly foolish incomprehension), they have several points of interest.
They are in several hands and, to my admittedly inexpert eye, seem
relatively early. The ink is usually very faint and quite reddened.

The first point of interest is the frequency with which some reader
has taken care to make Spenser more overtly sententious by converting a number of lines into "gnomes" or *sententiae* through the
addition of quotation marks in the left margin. Recent criticism, and
I believe rightly, has tended to make Spenser seem *less* sententious,
or at least it has suggested that his treatment of the virtues—and of
his queen—is as much interrogatory and explorative as it is didactic
or demonstrative. It is easy to see, though, that for whoever added
the quotation marks Spenser was indeed a sage and serious teacher
whose narrator's statements can be converted into nuggets of wise
discourse that one might cross-stitch in a sampler, embroider on a
pillow, record in a commonplace book, or commit to memory. There
is a dissertation to be done on passages in this and many other volumes that the reader, although not the printer, pricks out for moral
or psychological emphasis. A *Garden of Gnomes*, one might entitle
such a study. In this volume, for example, the already sometimes
sententious narrator is made to sound more often like Polonius by
having his reflections signposted: "Forgetful of his owne, that mindes
anothers cares" (I.v) is selected for this stress, for example, as are "To
make one great by others losse, is bad excheat" (I.v) and "The fish
that once was caught, new bait will hardly bite" (II.i), among many
others. The hexameter, of course, adds to the Polonian—or William
Cecilian—quality, but pentameters, too, can have such finality, giving the impression of saying "don't argue" or "no irony intended."
Marks single out "For greater love, the greater is the losse" (I.vii), a
statement that was always true and is now, thanks to its little inky
indications, a truism, and flagged as such.

Whoever put in such marks, however, was not just thinking *morally*
but *rhetorically*, for he (or that not impossible she) gives the same
traditional marker to, of all things, some lines by Despair. And why
not? Despair is one of our literature's great rhetoricians, as darkly
gifted in the art of persuasion as, say, Shakespeare's Mark Anthony

manipulating those viewing Caesar's body or Milton's Satan at the ear of Eve, and thereby demonstrating for alert readers the dangers of a smooth tongue. And so Despair's poisonously sweet lines, "Is not short paine well borne, that brings long ease, / And layes the soule to sleepe in quiet grave? / Sleepe after soyle, port after stormie seas, / Ease after warre, death after life does greatly please," here become—well, what? Wisdom? In another mouth they might almost pass for such, despite their gesture at a quasi-unorthodox mortalism. Whoever put in the marks next to these particular lines was not, or not at this point, trying to separate the sententiously wise from the persuasively evil so much as noticing the intensities, the levels, the modes of language.

The same reader (if one may judge from the ink) has also, like so many who write in book margins, attempted a sort of retrieval system by adding not comments but notes on what the author is up to at a given moment. When Spenser describes Idleness, the annotator writes that this is a description of Idleness. This might seem to be an exercise in redundancy, unless one recalls that of course the volume has no index and that if one—not least if one were a tutor or student—wanted to find that bit with Idleness it might help to have the word in the margin. What might have been a brief index is thus scattered, unalphabetically, throughout the margins, the items to be retrieved when needed. Perhaps here, too, the issue is not just moral ("You lazy boy, listen to what the famous Spenser says about Idleness) but rhetorical ("Let me find it for you; yes, here it is; here's how you describe the sins to make them come alive before your eyes; we call in *enargia*, children"). That such notes come in two different inks and, from what I can tell, different hands (one in darker ink and different penmanship says, for example, "description of Dyspayrs situation") simply shows what we already knew—such annotation was common practice.

One note in the now blacker ink corrects Spenser's slip in III.ii confusing Guyon with Redcrosse (there's an argument to be made, perhaps, on how this is not a slip at all, any more than are the slippery pronouns at the start of Book II), but even more interesting are two notes that identify Spenser's sources in Ariosto. The hand does not look very late to my uninformed eye—no later than 1800, probably—but it certainly belonged to someone who had spotted and thought it worth noting connections between the two singers of knights' and ladies' gentle deeds. Next to Spenser's description of the anti-magical bugle with which Arthur's squire assaults Orgoglio's castle (I.vii.3) we read "Astolfos horne in ari[osto]." And when in stanza 7 of Book III canto I Britomart's magic spear lays Guyon low

on the grassy green, a marginal annotation cites a parallel "in orlando." Source studies, perhaps for pedagogical reasons, have begun
to intrude into what seems the older annotator's world of moral
compression and rhetorical arts.

The other volume, largely because it is lacking its first thirty-five
pages or so (the bookseller sent me some loose pages by Spenser, but
they are not the missing ones and seem to come from some other
volume entirely), has little or no indication of ownership. The volume has received physical attention from its owners over the years;
for example, one leaf missing from Book I has been replaced by a
handwritten one that even includes the catchword. Despite such signs
of care the volume is in bad shape, but it still has, together with
what look to me like the original boards stiffened by some vellum
with a few sheets of old letters, an ancient faded blue velvet cover
(or what feels like velvet to the touch), prettily embroidered with
flowers and the initials "E. T." Who might that be? I have had a
number of fruitless fantasies about E. T.'s identity. Not Elizabeth
Tyrwhit, who was dead. Not Elizabeth Tudor, of course; she would
be "E. R." Elizabeth Throckmorton? Edward Tilney? Not unexpectedly, several friends have made suggestions involving a certain Steven
Spielberg movie, but there is no evidence that this most famous
E. T., despite his long alien fingers, was interested in embroidery.

The volume has a few probably post-1700 annotations of the retrieval sort: notes such as "Dispair pictured," give little indication of
a response, although a global search of extant copies of Spenser might
turn up interesting statistics on which passages tend to be thus flagged
for later use. Fidelia and Speranza are identified as Fidelity and Hope,
Humilita as Humility, and Zele as Zeal. Are such notes by a master
hoping to help his pupil? Or by the pupil hoping to remember his
master's explanation? Sometimes, as with the identification of z-e-l-e
as z-e-a-l, we may be seeing problems with an older spelling, particularly now that English orthography had settled down. Thus Spenser's
"Hierusalem" is identified as "Jerusalem the city of God," and indeed
most modern editors would also want to gloss the older name; similarly, Spenser's "Ewghen" is glossed as "Yew," which again makes
sense if one wishes to help students or to recall what one has learned
from one's master. Here too, though, is the older interest in rhetoric:
when Spenser addresses his Muse, the margin notes "The Poets Invocation." And information is recorded as well, so that "that great
Champion of the antique world" is identified as "Hercules," the
"eyas hauke" as the "Goshawke," the woodcut of a knight fighting
a dragon is labeled "George of England," and next to "Acontius"
(sig. T1) is written the whole story of that figure.[2] What is the point

of such annotations? To make the book easier to follow for the child one is tutoring, or for one's wife? As preparation for a new edition? Just for the owner's amusement? The glosses are few enough to make either possibility seem unlikely, but perhaps the owner (or borrower) had planned more.

The volume is even more intriguing, though, for what is written at the end of Book II in large bold script: "Jn Sheridan his Book" and, as though that claim to ownership were not enough, on the first page of Book IV is written again "John Sheridan his Book," this time with the date "1771." I think, although I cannot claim to be an expert paleographer, that the hand that wrote this is the same that penned the helpful information next to an allusion to Tobacco: "In the Authors time Tobacco was first brought to England by Sir Walter Raleigh."

On the facing page is a poem "by J. Sheridan," presumably the "John Sheridan" who signed his name. In form, which makes the compliment to the book's author even more clever, it is a Spenserian stanza. It reads (and reads better if "Elizabeth is given two syllables):

Immortal poet that with stile Sublime
Points out the way to Chastity and Love
Thy allegories drest in Antient Rhyme
Dictates the Sphere where all our Acts should move
In friendly Converse as the Blest above
Thrice happy Land. & Ever happy Queen
Albion or England . and Eliza's name
here Methaphorically May be seen
Elizabeth the Worlds Glory. & old Englands fame.

By Jn Sheridan

Below this, in a different hand, is written "Queen Elizabeth born 7th Sept 1535 Died March 24. 1632." That information apparently seemed problematic to another reader (or teacher), for someone has added, in pencil and in what may or may not be the same hand, a little "3" under the "5" in "1535" and a "1602" under the "1632." Modern readers might object that the supposedly corrected date of Elizabeth's death, "1602," is still wrong, but according to the older, Julian, calendar Elizabeth died on 24 March, hours before Lady Day and the official new year. Were the penned pieces of misinformation and their penciled corrections made before the calendar reform of 1752, after which Elizabeth began to have died in 1603, so to speak, and hence perhaps before Sheridan wrote his little paean to Spenser? True, old calendars die hard, and maybe the notes were made by somebody who didn't hold with, or could not get used to, the new-fangled, foreign, and papist Gregorian system.

So far I have been able to determine, this poem appears nowhere else. Its opening line is not on the Web, nor is some earlier version of it in Steven May's first-line index of verse in books from 1559 through 1603, nor in the collection of Spenser allusions collected by Ray Heffner and others.[3] David Radcliffe, an authority on Spenser's reception, has not seen it published or quoted.[4] For Dr. Radcliffe the lines sound as though they were by a young man, and I am inclined to agree, if only because such rapture is likely to seem naïve to a parental generation. The most plausible candidate I can find, though, is John Sheridan of the Middle Temple. According to the archivist of the Middle Temple, a "John Sheridan, eldest son of John Sheridan, of Dublin, gentleman, deceased, was admitted to the Middle Temple on 13th June 1776, and was Called to the Bar here on 29th June 1781. His brother James Sheridan . . . was admitted on 18th June 1779 and was Called to the Bar here on 12th November 1784."[5] This Sheridan, then, like a number of other Sheridans from the great playwright to the gentleman lawyer John Sheridan who figures in lists of books subscribers and to the John Sheridans identified as drapers or vintners in legal documents, had a Dublin connection, which lends further interest to the several annotations in the volume's sparse marginalia that identify Irish place names.[6]

Several years after being called to the bar, the likely author of this poem published his long *Present Practice of the Court of King's Bench* (London: W. Flexney and J. Walker, 1784); he died in 1787, if he is the same "John Sheridan, Esq; barrister at law" whose death on 24 June 1787 is noted in that year's *Gentleman's Magazine*.[7] There was a Dublin edition of his book in 1792, if nothing else a reminder of the many Sheridans' usual Irish connections. And he is, I would imagine, the same John Sheridan, barrister, whom *The Gentleman's Magazine* describes as having organized a forum to help fashion, as Spenser might say, a gentleman or noble person in the virtuous and gentle discipline of public speaking. *The Gentleman's Magazine*'s long obituary for the Scottish-born London journalist James Perry, who died 4 December 1821, mentions that in 1780–82 there had been "numerous Debating Societies in every part of the metropolis," attended by those who would one day make their mark politically, "and it is not perhaps generally known, that the Lyceum was fitted up and received that title, expressly for a superior school of oratory, by John Sheridan, esq. a barrister, with the view of enabling such young gentlemen as were destined for the Senate and the Bar to practice public speaking before a genteel auditory." It cost five shillings to get in, but although William Pitt himself dropped by, "the enterprise fell to the ground."[8]

For the John Sheridan who owned this volume, whether or not in truth the middle-aged Middle Temple barrister, the "stile" in which (or with which, if the word still connoted for the classically educated an writing implement) Spenser writes is "sublime," a word with increasing glamour in 1771. In Sheridan's day, however, not everyone was impressed by Spenser's "stile," sublime or not, and whatever the shifts in taste then getting under way or the new annotated editions of his work and a rush of parodies and imitations. "His style," writes Dr. Johnson in *The Rambler*, was "vicious," "darkened with old words and peculiarities of phrase."[9] Even earlier, after all, there had been strictures, whether Ben Jonson's notorious comment in his *Timber* (quoted by Johnson in the same *Rambler* essay) that in "affecting the ancients" Spenser "writ no language" or humbler criticisms like that of the Norfolk farmer whose manuscript denigrations Steven May has described in *Spenser Studies*.[10] And yet, if Sheridan does not, like Samuel Daniel in 1592, dismiss Spenser's "aged accents" and "untimely words" (*Delia*, sonnet 46), he does indeed imagine the poet's allegories "drest in Antient Rhyme."[11] He does not seem to think that Spenser merely "affected" the ancients, though—his poem's costume is either genuinely ancient or the allegories' creator is genuinely reviving an antique manner (one can read the line either way). If Spenser's accents are agèd, in 1771, moreover, for a growing number of English readers such antiquity was increasing its power and charm—like ruins, hermits, and, in about one more generation, ancient mariners. It is true that at least one perhaps understandably anonymous Englishman thought that Spenser might be better in blank verse ("No more my Muse her shepherd's weeds shall wear, / But change her oaten-pipe for trumpets loud, / And sing of noble deeds which long have slept: / Fierce wars and faithful loves shall grace my song"). True also that the author of those lines can note that but a few years earlier a reviewer of an earlier edition (1774) had praised his efforts as changing Spenser's "uncouth phrases and obsolete stile" into something more "intelligible," so that "what the Fairy Queen loses of the grotesque in this transmutation is amply compensated by the facility with which it will now be understood."[12] Needless to say, the question of modernizing Spenser remains a matter for discussion. Sheridan shows no such distaste for the "grotesque."

Does John Sheridan, then, admire Spenser for being a modern who revives the ancients? His encomium does not quite fit all of the expected categories, for what the antique rhyme dresses is allegory, by 1771 a suspect mode to the likes of, say, Lord Kames ("However agreeable long allegories may at first be by their novelty, they never afford any lasting pleasure: witness the Faery-Queen, which with great power of expression, variety of images, and melody of versification, is scarce ever read a second time") and one that in this case exploits themes or tropes contemptible to the likes of, say, David Hume ("the affectations, and conceits, and fopperies of chivalry, which appear ridiculous as soon as they lose the recommendation of the mode").[13] Those who scorned him, suggests David Radcliffe, from whose book I take these passages, sometimes did so as a way of registering distaste for the structures and constrictions of established religion and traditional morality. To do so, of course, entails making both allegory and Spenser more conventional, stable, and conservative than they need be. For Sheridan himself, what Spenser "points" us to is the "way"—an appropriately spatial metaphor for Spenser—toward chastity and love. Is Sheridan focusing on Book III (and maybe IV), or does he see love everywhere in Spenser, sustaining the other virtues? True, by 1771 "chastity" had lost some of its Spenserian and Miltonic moral depth and come closer to our own meaning of "obeying the (perhaps repressive) rules relating to sex." It is pleasing nonetheless that what Spenser here points to ends in love and not mere good behavior.

Sheridan, then, finds Spenser an "Immortal poet" not only for his "stile Sublime" but for his guidance. By going where he points we move to another "sphere." The sphere is not necessarily spatially high, like the crystal ones of Spenser's own day, for those who follow the poem's "way" are only "as the Blest above" and not yet joining the "Blest" themselves. Still, they are *compared* to the "Blest," and are like them in "friendly Converse." The poem, then, is relevantly situated after the legend of Chastity (and Love) and before that of Friendship, friendship that here reflects Heaven's own amity.

The poem now turns to Elizabeth, associating her with England but also with Albion, which in the previous century on occasion had been punningly associated with the entire United Kingdom ("Al-bi-on" means "all be one").[14] Here is the same nostalgia for her "happy" time that many came to feel after a few years under the Stuarts. Is Sheridan depressed by George III? Does he associate Eliza's "old" England, as some now did, with knights and paladins, with a lost golden time of chivalry and beauty, of magic casements and fairylands as yet not quite forlorn, of a time before commerce gave

Mammon his victory and a few dark satanic mills were already being built? If so, he was more romantic about the period than Spenser himself had been, but in this he was not alone. The poem concludes by reading *The Faerie Queene* as mirroring Elizabeth. The syntax and punctuation of the last several lines are confusing. Sheridan seems to think that Elizabeth's "name" is somehow indicated metaphorically—he probably means allegorically—by the poem. Not Elizabeth, apparently, but her name. This is fair enough, if we read that name as some in her own day had done ("God's rest or peace"—Eli Sabbath), but Sheridan seems to think, also fair enough, that the name in turn means glory—not the fame sought by Gloriana's knights, but Glory itself. Or does he mean that we can perceive, in the allegory under the ancient rhymes, Elizabeth, the glory of the world, and the fame of old England? What Sheridan means by "glory" is unclear, but Spenser himself did not and perhaps could not spell it out.

John Sheridan's Spenser is not the early twenty-first century Spenser, but we too could use more "friendly Converse." It is pleasant to imagine Sheridan, barrister or not, reading an old volume with a cover almost certainly embroidered by an Elizabethan or Jacobean woman named E. T. or the wife or daughter of an E. T., and feeling moved by its ancient rhymes to think about love and friendship, although also feeling moved by pride to write elsewhere, and twice, that this is *his* book.

Barnard College, Columbia University

Notes

1.   William Collins, *A catalogue (for 1786) of several libraries and parcels of books lately purchased* (London, 1786), 32; Collins, *A catalogue of books, books of prints, volumes of scarce tracts* . . . (London, 1791), 102. The 1596 edition figures frequently in booksellers' catalogues from 1700 to 1800, presumably some of them the same copies.

2.   Other such identifications include II.ix's "fennes of Allan" as "the bogge of Allen in Ireland." On page 569 Semelee is "Mother of Bacchus" and Alcmena as "Mother of Alcides." Page 571 Hippodames is "In Homer." Page 572 Pegasus is "The Poets winged horse." Page 573 Dan Cupid is "God Cupid." Volume 2, page 44 "the Shenan" is glossed as "River Shannon in Ireland." Page 329 "Monster" is "This was that monster Spynx [sic] whom Œdipus King of Thebes made Kill itself."

3.   Steven May and William Ringler, Jr., *Elizabethan Poetry: A Bibliography and First-line Index of English Verse, 1559–1603*, 3 vols. (London: Thoemmes Continuum, 2004); William Wells, ed., with Ray Heffner, Dorothy E. Mason, and Frederick M. Padelford, *Spenser Allusions in the Sixteenth and Seventeenth Centuries*, Studies in Philology 68.5 and 69.5 (1971, 1972).

4.   In an e-mail responding to my query. I thank Dr. Radcliffe for his kindness in reading an earlier draft of this essay and for his thoughtful comments and speculations. The tone and style of Sheridan's poem strike him, he writes, as the work of a young man, and I am inclined to agree, but the John Sheridan who seems, so far, the best but hardly certain candidate for the owner of this volume, would have been around forty in 1771.

5.   I quote the helpful e-mail that Mrs. LesleyWhitelaw, archivist of The Honourable Society of the Middle Temple library was kind enough to send me after I sent an inquiry. I thank her, and also Prof. Gordon Turnbull at Yale, who, out of kindness and curiosity, did a preliminary "nominal identification" and directed me to some relevant websites and sources for further investigation.

6.   These other, socially lesser, John Sheridans turn up in a global search of Eighteenth Century Collections Online, appearing several times in Irish books on statutes. Some Irish John Sheridans more likely to be connected with the man who wrote on Spenser also appear, most of them in lists of subscribers and doubtless most of them the same person. One counselor at law, perhaps the father of the Middle Temple Barrister, subscribed in 1731 to a Dublin edition of Horace's Epistles and to a book of maxims and so forth in 1737.

7.   *The Gentleman's Magazine* (London: John Nichols for David Henry, 1787): 2:640, in a list of "considerable Persons" who died that year. Sheridan's death is noted but there is no comment or narrative, as there is for the even more "considerable" among the deceased.

8.   *The Gentleman's Magazine* 91 (London: John Nichols for John Harris, 1821): 2:566. The title page credits the volume to "Sylvanus Urban, Gent."

9.   This and other strictures are quoted by Edward Payson Morton's old but valuable essay, "The Spenserian Stanza in the Eighteenth Century, *Modern Philology* 10 (1913): 365–91.

10.   Ben Jonson, *Timber: or Discoveries*, in *The Complete Poems*, ed. George Parfitt (New York: Penguin Classics, 1996), 428, adding that he would have Spenser read "for his matter"; Steven May, "Henry Gurney, A Norfolk Farmer, Reads Spenser and Others," *Spenser Studies* 20 (2005): 183–223.

11.   Daniel almost certainly did not, however, mean to be very denigrating; in his sonnet he is performing the traditional *recusatio* by a love poet who feels, perhaps a little uneasily, that he should be working on his epic. There are many ways to do this, from Ovid's complaint in *Amores* I.i that Cupid has stolen the syllable necessary for dactylic hexameter to Ronsard's hopeful suggestion that he would get on faster with the *Franciade* if better patronized. Daniel, whatever his admiration for Spenser, relegates his "stile" to the past.

12.   *Spenser's Fairy Queen Attempted in Blank Verse, with Notes Critical and Explanatory* (London: T. and J. Egerton, 1783); the same writer had published his blank verse version of I.i in 1774.

13.   David Radcliffe, *Edmund Spenser: A Reception History* (Columbia, SC: Camden House, 1996), 75

14.   Alexander Craig begs: "Let us . . . Al-bi-on" with "one King, one law" (*Poeticall essayes*, 1604), sig. C2v. In his *A Garden of Grave and Godlie Flowres* (Edinburgh, 1609), Alexander Gardyne makes the same Stuart-loyal pun: under James, he says, "Al-bi-on" (sig. B1v).

Fig. 1. The once blue cover, embroidered with flowers and bearing the initials E. T., of a badly damaged 1596 *Faerie Queene* in the possession of the author.

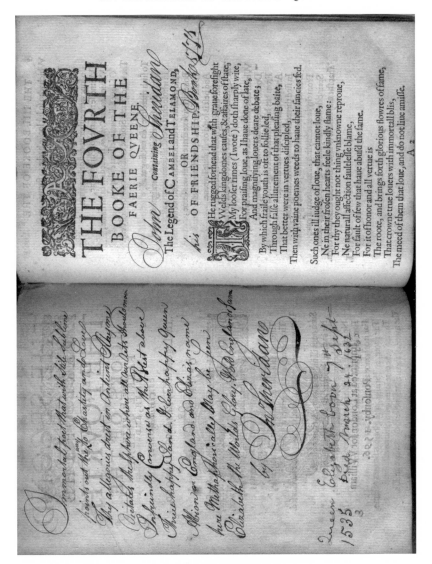

Fig. 2. A poem from the 1770s in praise of Spenser by John Sheridan, probably the Irish barrister of that name living in London, in a now badly damaged copy of *The Faerie Queene* in the possession of the author.

GLEANINGS

DAVID SCOTT WILSON-OKAMURA

When Did Spenser Read Tasso?

*W*HEN DID EDMUND SPENSER (1554–99) read Torquato Tasso (1544–95)? Specifically, when did he read Tasso's second epic, *Gerusalemme liberata* (1581)?[1] Was it in England, where he read Ariosto and Marot, and where he wrote *The Shepheardes Calender* (1579)? Or was it in Ireland, where Spenser spent almost his whole adult life and composed most of *The Faerie Queene* (1590, 1596)?

The dates, on Spenser's side, are assembled by Willy Maley in *A Spenser Chronology* (1994). On 15 July 1580, Arthur Grey (1536–93) was appointed lord deputy of Ireland. We do not know when he hired Edmund Spenser to be his secretary, but presumably it was before he departed England, on or about 10 August. If Spenser accompanied his master, he would have arrived at Dublin on 12 August. By the end of the month, we assume that Spenser was in Ireland, because he copied a letter for Grey dated 29 August.

This was almost a full year before the first authorized edition of *Gerusalemme liberata*, which was published in Ferrara on 24 June 1581.[2] Before this, however, there was an unauthorized edition, titled *Il Gofredo*, published in Venice on 7 August 1580. Spenser, if he was quick and lucky, could conceivably have acquired a copy of this earlier printing before he jumped on the boat for Ireland, but the odds are against it. The book would have had to travel very fast from Venice to London, to wherever Spenser was staying until he left for Ireland, and Spenser would have had to be on the lookout for new reading material, at the same time he was getting his affairs in order to leave the country (and probably short of cash).

In fact, we can say with some certainty that Spenser did *not* have the 1580 edition; or if he did, he used another one for writing *The Faerie Queene*. The Venice edition was based on uncorrected manuscripts, the text of which differs substantially from the authorized edition. By collating these two texts with passages where Spenser is imitating Tasso, it can be shown which text he was working from.

Spenser's longest and most famous imitation of Tasso is the Bower of Bliss episode (*FQ* II.xii), which is modeled on Armida's Palace

277

(*Gerusalemme liberata* cantos 15 and 16). At some points, Spenser's adaptation of Tasso is so close as to approach translation. An example is the Song of the Rose. Here is the Song in Spenser's English:

74

The whiles [Acrasia sighed] some one did chaunt this louely lay;
 Ah see, who so fayre thing doest faine to see,
 In springing flowre the image of thy day;
 Ah see the Virgin Rose, how sweetly shee
 Doth first peepe foorth with bashfull modestee,
 That fairer seemes, the lesse ye see her may;
 Lo see soone after, how more bold and free
 Her bared bosome she doth broad display;
Lo see soone after, how she fades, and falls away.

75

So passeth, in the passing of a day,
 Of mortall life the leafe, the bud, the flowre,
 Ne more doth florish after first decay,
 That earst was sought to deck both bed and bowre,
 Of many a Lady', and many a Paramowre:
 Gather therefore the Rose, whilest yet is prime,
 For soone comes age, that will her pride deflowre:
 Gather the Rose of loue, whilest yet is time,
Whilest louing thou mayst loued be with equall crime.

76

He ceast, and then gan all the quire of birdes
Their diuerse notes t'attune vnto his lay,
As in approuaunce of his pleasing wordes.

Now here is Spenser's Italian source, in a text based on the authorized edition of 1581:

14

Deh mira, egli cantò, spuntar la rosa
Dal verde suo modesta e verginella,
Che mezzo aperta ancóra, e mezzo ascosa,
Quanto si mostra men, tanto è piú bella.
Ecco poi nudo il sen già baldanzosa
Dispiega: ecco poi langue, e non par quella,
Quella non par, che desïata avanti
Fu da mille donzelle e mille amanti.

15

Cosí trapassa al trapassar d' un giorno
De la vita mortale il fiore e 'l verde;
Né, perché faccia in dietro april ritorno,
Si rinfiora ella mai, né si rinverde.
Cogliam la rosa in su 'l mattino adorno
Di questo dí, che tosto il seren perde;
Cogliam d' amor la rosa; amiamo or quando
Esser si puole rïamato amando.

16

Tacque; e concorde de gli augelli il coro,
Quasi approvando, il canto indi ripiglia.[3]

How do we know which version Spenser was using? In 74.7, Spenser's rose bares its bosom "more bold and free"; this comes from Tasso's 1581 text *già baldanzosa* 'bold indeed', not the 1580 text, which has *men vergognosa* 'less demure' (14.5).[4] In 75.1, the flower of Spenser's rose "passeth, in the passing of a day"; Spenser got this from the 1581 text, *trapassa al trapassar* 'passes in the passing', not from 1580, which has *dilegua al dileguar* 'vanishes in the vanishing' (15.1). In 75.3, Spenser's rose "Ne more doth florish after first decay," where "florish" translates *rinfiora* 'reflower' (1581), not *rinforza* 'recharge' (1581). Likewise in stanza 76, Spenser's birds attune their lay to the singer's song "As in approuaunce" (line 3) because his text of Tasso says *Quasi approvando* (16.2 in 1581); had he been following the 1580 text, he would have read *Quasi accordando* and written, "As in accordance."

From this collation we can derive the following terminus a quo: Spenser worked from an authorized printing of Tasso's text, which was not possible before 24 June 1581. Therefore he probably read Tasso after that date.

For *terminus ad quem*, a reasonable date is 1 December 1589, when *The Faerie Queene* was entered in the Stationers' Register. So when did Spenser read Tasso? Apparently, while he was in Ireland. There was a brief window at the end of this period, after Spenser returned to England and before he registered his poem, when Spenser might have purchased Tasso's book from an English bookseller. (He was in Ralegh's company at the time.) But that window was very brief indeed: only six weeks at the outside. Conceivably, there might have been time in this six weeks to read Tasso's epic (or at least the first sixteen books of it), and then write the Bower of Bliss. But that seems unlikely. For one thing, the Italian was difficult, even for a native speaker.[5] Moreover, it was not just the last canto of Book II that Spenser would have needed to rewrite: according to an early German survey, Spenser borrows from or alludes to the *Liberata* at least thirteen times in the 1590 *Faerie Queene*, not counting his many borrowings in the Bower of Bliss episode, with echoes detectable in twelve different cantos.[6] The number of these echoes and their diffusion suggest that Spenser had been living with Tasso's poem— and writing with Tasso's voice in his head—over a span not of six weeks but of several years.

It seems then that Spenser read Tasso the same place he wrote *The Faerie Queene*: in Ireland. This matters because it shows what kind of reader Spenser was. As a young man, he was known as liking foreign books; Gabriel Harvey, in one of his letters, calls Spenser "my yunge Italianate Seignior and French Monsieur."[7] But that was at Cambridge. After college, many people—thoughtful people, even—don't have the energy. They are starting careers, starting families, and if they are feeling "cultural" they rent a movie with subtitles. But Spenser, it seems, made an effort to keep up, not only with local bards and London poets, but also with new works from the Continent—including at least one epic, *Jerusalem Delivered*.

It cannot have been easy. Ireland, when Spenser lived there, was perceived by English residents as a place "where there is no great choice of books to be had"; there was some book trade with Bristol, but that was mainly in textbooks.[8] And yet, somehow, Spenser did manage to find a copy of Tasso's new poem. A likely source was his friend and benefactor, the amateur physician Lodowick Bryskett (c.1546–1609x12). Spenser worked under Bryskett for almost twenty years as deputy clerk of the Council of Munster. The son of Italian immigrants, Bryskett traveled with Sidney on his Grand Tour, took service with Sidney's father while he was Ireland's lord deputy, was seen by his neighbors in Ireland to receive "continuall advertisements from Florence,"[9] and based both of his elegies for Sidney on poems by Tasso's father, Bernardo (1493–1569).[10]

Whether in Bryskett's house or elsewhere, Spenser did find *Jerusalem*, and the finding shows Spenser to have been a certain kind of reader, on the lookout for new books. The notion of literature which he formed at Cambridge was an evolving one, outward-looking and international, and he carried it with him into adult life. This is rarer, one fears, than teachers like to think. Too easily the circle of reading, which was broad in youth, narrows into a spiral, of those books which are congenial or merely comfortable. Even creative minds are not immune. J. R. R. Tolkien, for all his learning and inventiveness, seems hardly to have read any current fiction except what his fellow Inklings pressed on him. Evidently Spenser was different and resembled more the creator of Narnia, who read widely into his fifties and reviewed new fiction for the *TLS*.

East Caroline University

NOTES

1.   Tasso's first epic, *Rinaldo* (1562), was also known to Spenser; see Harold S. Blanchard, "Imitations from Tasso in *The Faerie Queene*," *Studies in Philology* 22 (1925): 198–221.

2.   For the *Liberata*'s publication history, see Angelo Solerti, "Bibliografia delle stampe," in his critical edition, *Gerusalemme liberata*, 3 vols. (Florence: Barbèra, 1895–96), 1:131–39.

3.   Here and below, Tasso's text and variants are cited from Solerti's ed., vol. 3.

4.   Where possible, English translations of Italian words are from John Florio, *A Worlde of Wordes, or Most Copious, and Exact Dictionarie in Italian and English* (London: Arnold Hatfield for Edw. Blount, 1598; *STC* 11098).

5.   In 1585 Lionardi Salviati complains, "when we hear [Tasso's words and figures of speech] recited by somebody, rarely do we understand them, and we have to take the book in our hands and read them by ourselves; for they are such that the sound and the voice are not sufficient, but in order to understand them we have to see the writing; and sometimes even this is not enough." Bernard Weinberg, *A History of Literary Criticism in the Italian Renaissance*, 2 vols. (Chicago: University of Chicago Press, 1961), 1:1008.

6.   E. Koeppel, "Die Englischen Tasso-Übersetzungen des 16. Jahrhunderts. II. La Gerusalemme Liberata," *Anglia* 11 (1889): 341–62, at 345–61.

7.   *Letter-book of Gabriel Harvey, A.D. 1573–1580*, ed. Edward John Long Scott (London: Camden, 1884), 65. For Spenser's French reading, see Anne Lake Prescott,

"French Renaissance Literature," in *The Spenser Encyclopedia*, gen. ed. A. C. Hamilton (Toronto: University of Toronto Press, 1990), 320–21 with bibliography; for Italian, Vesin Kostić, *Spensers Sources in Italian Poetry* (Belgrade: Filološki fakultet Beogradskog univerziteta, 1969).

    8.   See Raymond Gillespie, "The Book Trade in Southern Ireland, 1590–1640," in *Books beyond the Pale: Aspects of the Provincial Book Trade in Ireland before 1850*, ed. Gerard Long (Dublin: Rare Books Group of the Library Association of Ireland, 1996), 1–17; the quotation (from Barnaby Rich, 1578) appears on 1. London imports were not unheard of: "In 1545 [James Dartas of Dublin] is recorded as purchasing books from a London bookseller and shipping them to Ireland for retailing. These included primers, liturgical books, romance literature, and ballads." Colm Lennon, "The Print Trade, 1550–1700," in *The Irish Book in English: 1550–1800*, ed. Raymond Gillespie and Andrew Hadfield, The Oxford History of the Irish Book 3 (Oxford: Oxford University Press, 2006), 61–87, at 63.

    9.   Letter from the Lord Chancellor of Ireland to Lord Burghley, September 1594. Qtd., Henry R. Plomer and Tom Peete Cross, *The Life and Correspondence of Lodowick Bryskett* (Chicago: University of Chicago Press, 1927), 54.

10.   W. Mustard, "Lodowick Brysket and Bernardo Tasso," *American Journal of Philology* 35 (1914): 192–99.

LAUREN SILBERMAN

"Perfect Hole": Spenser and Greek Romance

When, at the conclusion of Book III of *The Faerie Queene*, Britomart rescues Amoret from Busirane, Amoret is described in Spenser's words as being restored, "perfect hole." A number of Spenser
critics, most notably Jonathan Goldberg and Maureen Quilligan,
have seen in the spelling of whole "H-O-L-E" the possibility of
a naughty pun. A. Kent Hieatt disallows the pun and cites the
Spenser Concordance to the effect that Spenser tends to use "hole"
and "holesome" to mean "healthy" (as in Amoret's case), but
"whole" to meant "entire." I argue that "perfect hole" is a bilingual pun that brings together both "healthy" and "entire" as
possible meanings. With the phrase "perfect hole," Spenser makes
reference to the Greek romance *Clitophon and Leucippe* by Achilles
Tatius. At one point in that work, the heroine Leukippe seems,
through a theatrical trick, to be eviscerated and then restored to
wholeness. The Greek word used to describe the transformation
is *holókleron* (ὁλόκληρον), or, *perfect whole*. This episode of *Clitophon and Leucippe*, which underlies Amoret's restoration, as she is
rendered "perfect hole," brings the role of drama and dramatists
in Spenser's rendition more clearly into focus. Busirane has traditionally been read as an artist figure and potential dark double of
Spenser, but Busirane's specific role as a dramatist merits further
attention in light of the Greek subtext, as do complex negotiations of page and stage in the scene of Busirane's castle.

NEAR THE CLOSE OF Book III of *The Faerie Queene*, Britomart
rescues Amoret from the enchanter Busirane by forestalling a repeat
performance of the Masque of Cupid. When the door out of which
the masquers issued on the previous night opens, Britomart boldly
enters to find Amoret bound to a pillar and Busirane "figuring

straunge characters of his art" (III.xii.31.2), writing in blood dropping from Amoret's wounded heart.[1] The Martial Maid forces the enchanter to reverse his spell, Amoret's chains drop away, her wound heals "as it had not been bor'd" (III.xii.38.5),[2] and she perceives herself, in Spenser's words, "perfect hole" (38.9). The spelling of whole "H-O-L-E" allows into this scene of rescue and restoration a naughty pun noted by a number of Spenser critics[3] and contextualized by Jonathan Goldberg as a key to a reading of the structure of desire and loss in Book IV of the *Faerie Queene*.[4] In her book *Milton's Spenser*, Maureen Quilligan cites approvingly Goldberg's point about the full ambiguity of being rendered "perfect hole" and thereby draws the ire of Kent Hieatt in his review of *Milton's Spenser* for *Milton Quarterly*, as Hieatt ascribes Quilligan's identification of the pun to memories of "rich gusts of liberating seminar-laughter" and dismisses it as mere lubricity and bathos.[5] (Parenthetically, I think that memories of student laughter are more likely to suppress than encourage a critic's awareness of indecorous and disruptive wordplay. It is with a pang that English professors of the post-war Baby Boom generation realize that they are the only ones in the classroom having to suppress giggles at references to either Shakespeare or Spenser's Claribelle.)

Hieatt brings the *Spenser Concordance* to bear against a possible reading of "perfect hole" as a pun. He states, "The concordance lists establish that Spenser tends to use 'hole' [h-o-l-e] and 'holesome' [h-o-l-e-s-o-m-e] to mean 'healthy' (as in Amoret's case), but 'whole' [w-h-o-l-e] to mean 'entire.' " His point is valid as far as it goes, but, of course, any argument from a concordance ultimately goes in a big circle. Any particular example may, by differing from the range of meanings given by a concordance, expand that range of meanings. In addition, by placing a given use of a particular word by a particular author in the context of work by that author, a concordance—or the *Oxford English Dictionary*, for that matter, which is a kind of language-wide concordance—will have nothing to say when Spenser, as I think he does on more than one occasion, makes a bilingual pun that alludes to another text. For example, when Spenser describes Acrasia, "greedily depasturing delight" (II.xix.73.4) as she hangs over the sleeping Verdant, his expression echoes and amplifies an analogous scene in Tasso's *Gerusalemme liberata,* which describes Armida bending over the sleeping Rinaldo, "e I famelici squardi avidamente / in lei pascendo si consuma e strugge" (*Gerusalemme liberata*, 16.19.1–2).[6] Fairfax translates this, "His hungry eyes upon her face he fed, / And feeding them so pin'd himself away" (16.19.1–2).[7] Tasso's word "pascendo" is the present participle of an Italian verb for eating that specifically connotes the eating done by animals.[8] Fairfax's rendering of "pascendo" as "feeding" is the more literal translation, but Spenser's elegantly Romance-Latinate "depasturing" calls attention to Tasso's text as much as to his meaning.[9]

I think that the description of Amoret "perfect hole" is another example of Spenser's making allusion to a text in another language by Englishing its words. The text is *Clitophon and Leucippe* by Achilles Tatius—a particularly disreputable example of a disreputable genre: Greek romance.[10] I stumbled on the reference while teaching the text in an undergraduate Great Books course. I have discovered that teaching texts that would never make it into the Norton Anthology is fun on a lot of levels and very useful for scholarship on such authors as Spenser and Shakespeare, whose idea of literary tradition was a good deal broader than that of the editors of anthologies. I was inspired to include Greek romance in my teaching by an NEH seminar organized by Professor Thomas Roche a number of years ago and have found it quite rewarding pedagogically. Technically, the texts are highly sophisticated—someone like Heliodorus, for example, probably forgot more about narrative technique than any present-day expert in narratology can ever hope to learn. At the same time, the content is at least superficially devoid of what looks like redeeming social value, so students are forced to consider issues of literary technique rather than being tempted to relate characters and events to their own experience and go on to share how they feel about it all.

The episode from *Clitophon and Leucippe* that provides one source for Amoret's wounding and restoration is a particularly lurid one, although, to be sure, it is not the passage infamously translated from Greek into Latin (2.37.6–38.5) in the 1917 Loeb edition of Achilles Tatius.[11] In the episode that inspired Spenser, the heroine, Leucippe has been abducted by brigands and separated from her lover and the forces of rescue by a deep trench. Her lover, Clitophon, narrates the scene that unfolds in pantomime before his eyes:

> We could in fact see brigands aplenty and fully armed standing on the opposite side of the trench. They had improvised an altar of earth and near it a coffin. Two of them were leading a girl to the altar with her hands tied behind her back. I couldn't see who they were in their armor, but I did recognize that the maiden was Leukippe. They poured a libation over her head and led her around the altar to the accompaniment of a flute and a priest intoning what I guessed was an Egyptian hymn—at

least, the movements of his mouth and the distention of his facial muscles suggested that he was chanting.

Then at a signal they all moved far away from the altar. One of the attendants laid her on her back and tied her to stakes fixed in the ground, as sculptors picture Marsyas bound to the tree. He next raised a sword and plunged it into her heart and then sawed all the way down to her abdomen. Her viscera leaped out. The attendants pulled out her entrails and carried them in their hands over to the altar. When it was well done they carved the whole lot up, and all the bandits shared the meal. . . .

When the ceremony was concluded, so far as I could tell, they placed her body in the coffin, covered it with a lid, razed the altar, and ran away without looking behind them.

(3.15)[12]

Although things look rather discouraging at this point for the lovers, Leucippe is restored to Clitophon as he makes ready to plunge his sword into his throat. Two friends interrupt him, open the coffin, and Leucippe emerges "the entire length of her stomach [hanging] open and the visceral cavity . . . hollow" (3.17) but otherwise quite lively.[13] It turns out that the friends had been captured by the afore-mentioned brigands and, as an initiation rite, were given the task of sacrificing Leucippe, cooking and eating her liver and then placing her remains in a coffin. It also turns out that the day before the sacrifice is to occur, the friends get hold of a stage sword with a disappearing blade, which had belonged to a professional stage actor killed by the brigands in another raid. They use the trick sword and animal viscera to fake the sacrifice. Having released Leucippe from the coffin, the friends instruct Clitophon to cover his eyes as they pretend to use magic so that "she will recover her innards, her frontal gash will grow together, and [he] will see her once more sound" (3.18, p. 218). When Clitophon uncovers his eyes, he sees Leucippe restored. The Greek word Achilles Tatius uses is ὁλόκληρον—"ent-ire," "complete in all its parts," in short: "perfect hole." Indeed, I asked my colleague, Prof. Christina Christoforatou—a scholar of Greek medieval literature—to verify my rendering of the Greek term and she said that perfect hole is a more faithful translation of ὁλόκληρον than what was given in the Loeb edition of Achilles Tatius, that is, "whole and restored" (3.18.4; Loeb, 172–73).[14]

If the Spenserian "perfect hole" does allude to the Greek term, then, *pace* Professor Hieatt and his concordance lists, here is one example in which *hole*, spelled H-O-L-E, does carry with it the meaning "entire," as in *hologram*—among any number of other meanings and referents, of course. What is more, sustained allusion to Achilles Tatius's infamous gross-out scene is, arguably, as indecorous a verbal gesture in this context as would be a glancing advertence to a bodily aperture. In his 1758 edition of *The Faerie Queene*, John Upton observed the similarity between the scene of Leucippe's mock-disembowelment and Serena's rescue from the cannibals in Book VI of *The Faerie Queene* (VI.viii.38ff). Subsequently, the venerable scholar Edwin Greenlaw made a point of rejecting *Clitophon and Leucippe* as a potential Spenserian source with the assertion that *Daphnis and Chloe* is "the only true Greek pastoral which influenced English literature," dismissing Achilles Tatius along with Heliodorus because they "stressed the wanderings of the lovers and introduced various other elements which are without significance in the present study [of Shakespeare's pastorals]." In his 1925 article, Merritt Y. Hughes contests Greenlaw's categorical exclusion of Achilles Tatius as a Spenserian source but tends to underplay Spenser's borrowing from the Greek author.[15]

Scholarly reluctance to emphasize *Clitophon and Leucippe* as a source, even of the indecorous episode of Serena and the cannibals is not surprising. Classicist B. F. Reardon adduces the scene in question, of Leucippe's apparent sacrifice, in comparing the lurid qualities of Achilles Tatius and Seneca. He observes acidly, "Achilles Tatius merely disembowels . . . his heroine in narrative; Seneca would have had it happen on stage, and another character would have tried to glue the pieces together again."[16] Whether or not Seneca's plays were in fact closet drama, Reardon is certainly being unjust to the Roman author; with regard to Achilles Tatius—maybe not so much. Nonetheless, Reardon identifies a link between Seneca and Achilles Tatius that goes far beyond a shared taste for lurid violence, and Spenser's imitation of the lurid scene from Achilles Tatius reflects a deeper connection between drama and romance set forth in that scene.

What appears in *Clitophon and Leucippe* as a theatrical trick—the mutilation and subsequent restoration of the heroine—manifests itself in *The Faerie Queene* as a matter of both magical and poetic power. Busirane enchants Amoret, and Britomart forces him to reverse his spell; Busirane creates an illusion with his words, and Britomart sees through the illusion in a symbolic act of reading. Nevertheless, despite the fact that the apparently magical restoration of Leucippe is so thoroughly demystified, the episode in Achilles Tatius is not without its own meta-discursive sorcery in the way it plays dramatic representation off against romance narrative. Although technically the disemboweling of Leucippe is a stage illusion and her restoration the result of a little tidying-up, the narrative effect—what is perceived by both the hero and the first-time reader as a shocking death and resurrection—is the product of a conspicuously improbable series of coincidences arranged by Achilles Tatius in blatantly artificial fashion—as the details of the convoluted back-story that account for the spectacular plot twist accumulate and strain credulity.[17] Romance overcomes drama in a tacit *paragone*, or contest between genres: the stage trick is eclipsed as the agent of Leucippe's restoration by the stereotypically outrageous romance plot twists that account for the trick and, as it were, put the stage trick in its narrative place. To add to the sense of generic meta-contest, the stage actor whose sword the romance characters appropriate fails to make successful use of his own props. Attacked by the brigands, the actor arms fellow passengers with stage weapons and leads a defense, with the predictable result that they are all slaughtered by the brigands. In a sense, Achilles Tatius has gleefully killed off a rival from a competing genre. In this context, the fact that Britomart attempts to kill Busirane but must be restrained from doing so acquires deeper significance. Busirane has traditionally been read as an artist figure and potential dark double of Spenser, but Busirane's specific role as a dramatist merits further attention, I think, as do complex negotiations of page and stage in the scene of Busirane's castle and in the rest of Spenser's oeuvre.[18] Taken as a figure of the artist, Busirane raises questions about sexual politics as mediated through the discursive resources available to poetry.[19] Taken as a dramatist, Busirane directs attention specifically to the role of artistic media in engaging these issues.

The resurrection of Leucippe celebrates the power of romance narrative as it reveals narrative coherence to be an artifice. As he echoes the episode from Achilles Tatius, Spenser gives more scope to narrative discontinuities. In the 1596 edition of *The Faerie Queene*, Spenser cancels the original conclusion to Book III in which the lovers are reunited and in Canto x of Book IV substitutes Scudamour's flashback account of winning Amoret for a description of the lovers' reunion. Thomas P. Roche, Jr. has commented that literary critics tend to be divided by temperament into the categories of tidyers-up and messers-up.[20] I like to imagine some critics raking the leaves of the Spenserian canon into a big, beautiful pile for other critics to jump into—so that another generation can come along and construct a different synthesis, and so on. In his groundbreaking study *The Kindly Flame,* Roche has taught us to see profound intellectual continuities and coherence of meaning in Books III and IV of *The Faerie Queene*.[21] It seems to me that there is a certain, undoubtedly misguided, temptation to tidy up after Roche and go from his insights about continuities between Books III and IV to an imaginative reordering of the conclusion of Book III and the opening of Book IV into a sequential narrative of one very outré wedding. James Nohrnberg, for example, flirts with this when he remarks of Amoret's torment at the House of Busirane, "The trouble begins on Amoret's wedding night," although he goes on to complicate his own conflation.[22] The intertextual hijinks underlying Amoret's "perfect hole," however, reveal narrative to be just part of the story in *The Faerie Queene*. Amoret's rescue from the wicked enchanter and her wondrous, mysterious restoration emerge from a complex and self-aware tradition in which wonder and aggression, high art and low-brow entertainment combine.

Baruch College, City University of New York

NOTES

1. Unless otherwise noted, Spenser quotations taken from *The Faerie Queene*, ed. A. C. Hamilton, Hiroshi Yamashita, and Toshiyuki Suzuki, 2nd ed. (Harlow: Longman, 2001).

2. In the second edition of the Longman Spenser, Yamashita and Suzuki render this "sor'd," after the 1590 *FQ*, rather than "bor'd," after the 1596 *FQ* and 1609 Folio.

3. See, for example, Tracey Sedinger, "Women's Friendship and the Refusal of Lesbian Desire in *The Faerie Queene*," *Criticism* 42 (2000): 91–113. Sedinger reads the pun on "perfect hole" as play on bodily integrity and nothingness in an indication of the problematic nature of representing chaste desire in the poem. See also Elizabeth J. Bellamy, "Waiting for Hymen: Literary History as "Symptom" in Spenser and Milton," *ELH* 64 (1997): 391–414.

4. Jonathan Goldberg, *Endlesse Worke: Spenser and the Structures of Discourse* (Baltimore: Johns Hopkins University Press, 1981), 3. Katherine Eggert describes how Spenser's "rapturous poetry lingers lovingly on the edge of hollow feminine enclosures" (14) and contests Goldberg's identification of such space as a place of loss (23–24).

5. Maureen Quilligan, *Milton's Spenser: The Politics of Reading* (Ithaca: Cornell University Press, 1983), 199. A. Kent Hieatt, review, *Milton Quarterly* 18 (1984): 95.

6. Torquato Tasso, *Poesie*, ed. Francesco Flora (Milan: Riccardo Ricciardi, 1952).

7. Torquato Tasso, *Jerusalem Delivered*, trans. Edward Fairfax (New York: Capricorn, 1963).

8. *Dizionario Inglese Italiano Italiano Inglese* (Trento: Paravia and Oxford University Press, 2001), s.v. "pascere," I.1, 2.

9. On Spenser's echo of Tasso, see A. Bartlett Giamatti, *The Earthly Paradise and the Renaissance Epic* (Princeton: Princeton University Press, 1966), 278. The earliest *OED* citation of *depasture* meaning "to graze" is 1586: "*Wills & Inv. N.C.* II Surtees (1860) 131 My cattell shall remayne and despasture, upon my grounds as they are at this instante." The earliest use of *depasture* as a transitive verb cited by the *OED* is by Spenser in 1596 ("*State Irel.* Wks. (Globe ed.) 630/1"), meaning "to consume the produce of the land by grazing on it." Ironically the *OED* misses the Spenser citation in the 1590 *Faerie Queene*. Tasso may be echoing Virgil. In *Aeneid* 1.464, Aeneas is described as poring over the pictures of the Trojan War on the walls of the temple of Juno at Carthage, "atque animum pictura pascit inani" (1.464), which Stanley Lombardo renders "And he fed his soul on empty picture" (1.570). See Virgil, *Aeneid*, trans. Stanley Lombardo (Indianapolis: Hackett, 2005).

10. It is likely that Spenser draws on the ekphrastic description of Europa and the bull from the opening of *Clitophon and Leucippe* (1.1.13, 8–9; 177) in *Muiopotmos* (289–91). Both the painting of Europa described in *Clitophon and Leucippe* and the scene rendered in Arachne's tapestry include a detail not found in Ovid's *Metamorphoses*: a winged Eros leading the bull. See David Rosand, "Ut Pictor Poeta: Meaning in Titian's *Poesie*," *New Literary History* 3 (1972): 527–46, esp. 544–45.

11. *Achilles Tatius*, trans. S. Gaselee (London: Heinemann, 1917). Clitophon has been attempting to cheer up his gay best friend Menelaus by engaging him in a favorite topic of debate: the relative merits of women and boys as objects of desire. In the passage translated from Greek into Latin, each friend describes the physical experience of loving his preferred object.

12. B. F. Reardon, ed. *Collected Ancient Greek Novels* (Berkeley: University of California Press, 1989), 217. I have included book and chapter references in my text. Although Reardon uses more closely transliterated spellings of the title and characters, I use the more common, romanized spelling of Clitophon and Leucippe in the text of this essay.

13. Reardon edition, 217.

14. *Achilles Tatius*, trans. S. Gaselee (Cambridge MA: Harvard University Press, 1984).

15. Edwin Greenlaw, "Shakespeare's Pastorals," *SP* 13 (1913): 122–54; Merritt Hughes, "Spenser's Debt to the Greek Romances," *MP* (1925). Hughes tack theorizes several intermediaries between *The Faerie Queene* and the Greek romance. Dorothy Woodward Culp takes up this matter in "Courtesy and Fortune's Chance in Book 6 of *The Faerie Queene*" *MP* (1971): 254–59. She observes, "Scholars are divided on whether the influence of the Greek romances on book 6 is direct or whether Spenser was influenced by intermediate works. . . . However, an examination of the number of editions of Longus, Achilles Tatius, and Heliodorus available prior to 1590 makes this a questionable assumption. There were at least three editions of *Daphnis and Chloe*, eleven of *Cliotphon and Leucippe,* and twenty-two of the *Aethiopica*." See also M. M. Grey, "The Influence of Spenser's Irish Experience on *The Faerie Queene*," *RES* 6 (1930): 413–28, esp. 421.

16. B. F. Reardon, 162[n]-163[n].

17.   Robert Durling's discussion of how Ariosto makes himself as poet evident as a Providential force as he disposes the convoluted elements of his narrative is classic in this regard. See *The Figure of the Poet in Renaissance Epic* (Cambridge, MA: Harvard University Press, 1965), 112–32.

18.   Patrick Cheney and John Watkins have recently done very interesting work in this regard, and it is a rich area of inquiry. See John Watkins, "Polemic and Nostalgia: Medieval Crosscurrents in Spenser's Allegory of Pride," *Spenser Studies* 18 (2003): 41–57; and Patrick Cheney, *Shakespeare, National Poet-Playwright* (Cambridge: Cambridge University Press, 2004) and *Marlowe's Counterfeit Profession: Ovid, Spenser, Counter-Nationhood* (Toronto: University of Toronto Press, 1997).

19.   For particularly astute observations in this regard, see Dorothy Stephens, "Into Other Arms: Amoret's Evasion," *ELH* 58 (1991): 523–44, esp. 526–28. She reads "perfect hole" as emblematic of the irreconcilable claims made on females as chaste objects of male desire. In "Of Chastity and Violence: Elizabeth I and Edmund Spenser in the House of Busirane," *Signs* 20 (1994): 49–78, Susan Frye identifies the House of Busirane as the scene of conflict between competing versions of chastity: the self-sufficient chastity that provided a basis for the authority of Elizabeth I and conventional chastity vulnerable to male violence. Amoret's being healed "perfect hole" signals the way the text inscribes and erases sexual violence against women. See also Kimberly Anne Coles, " 'Perfect Hole': Elizabeth I, Spenser, and Chaste Productions," *ELR* 32 (2002): 31–61.

20.   Personal comment.

21.   Thomas P. Roche, Jr., *"The Kindly Flame": A Study of the Third and Fourth Books of Spenser's* The Faerie Queene (Princeton: Princeton University Press, 1964).

22.   James Nohrnberg, *The Analogy of* The Faerie Queene (Princeton: Princeton University Press, 1976), 475.

WILLIAM E. BOLTON

Anglo-Saxons in Faerie Land?: A Note on Some Unlikely Characters in Spenser's *Britain moniments*

Within the historical sections of the *The Faerie Queene*, Anglo-Saxons represent negative, violent forces against which King Arthur's British forefathers must contend. This essay argues that as antagonists, Anglo-Saxons in the poem are a type of dramatic foil. They can be seen to represent the historical enemies of Queen Elizabeth, as well as the opposite of the allegory of temperance explored in Book II. These Germanic invaders are violent, rash, and treacherous—all characteristics at odds with the virtues and the monarch Spenser praises in the poem. Furthermore, in a complicated move Spenser uses the Anglo-Saxon, Angela, as the direct inspiration for both Britomart's transvestism and warlike prowess. By using a character whose kinsmen are described in strictly negative terms as inspiration for Britomart, Spenser underscores the transgressive and confused nature of the virgin knight's character.

*E*DMUND SPENSER'S *THE FAERIE QUEENE* seems like a rather unlikely place to find an Anglo-Saxon.[1] Nevertheless, a few of these early Englishmen and Germans do appear in the poem, showing up in the historical sections, Book II, Canto x, and Book III, Canto iii. Spenser does not dwell long on these Anglo-Saxon names and moves briskly through his British chronicle, clearly more interested in tracing the mythical lineage of Arthur and Arthegall back to Troy by way of Brutus than in them. A second look at the Anglo-Saxons who appear in the "historical" sections of *The Faerie Queene*, however, suggests that they do not appear haphazardly. In Spenser's version of British national history, Anglo-Saxons are complicating, oppressive, and violent characters whose rule constituted an unfortunate interlude between the idyllic Britton reign of Arthur and the contemporary rule of Elizabeth and who help to define the allegory of temperance in Book II as a foil of the virtue. Further, they also offer yet another complicating factor to Britomart by way of her emulation of the Saxon virgin Angela, mentioned at the end of the third canto of Book III.

Nothing has been written specifically about the Anglo-Saxons in *The Faerie Queene*, and what might be said about them appears in criticism on the *Britain moniments* sections of *The Faerie Queene*. Most scholarship on the subject is greatly indebted to Carrie Anna Harper's thorough and frequently mentioned 1910 monograph *The Sources of the British Chronicle History in Spenser's* Faerie Queene,[2] Harper shows that Spenser predominately used Geoffrey of Monmouth's *Historia Regum Britanniae* (*History of the Kings of Britain*) for his historical material.[3] Geoffrey's *Historia* is a natural source for Spenser. He is, after all, constructing a poem that is in many ways centered on King Arthur, of whose history Geoffrey gives a detailed and well-known account. It is initially unsurprising that Anglo-Saxons are not portrayed in a flattering light in Spenser's version of British history given his use of Geoffrey. Geoffrey was a Welshman and was interested in creating a history of the British that legitimizes native Britons who were antagonized and later conquered by Anglo-Saxon invaders. Arthur himself is also well known to have Welsh origins. This all culminates in a thoroughly Welsh-feeling account of history in *The Faerie Queene*, which turns out to be useful for Spenser, who was writing for a Tudor monarch of supposed Welsh origin. As Laurie A. Finke points out, Spenser's history is probably making an appeal to Elizabeth's lineage:

> From the accession of Henry VII, Tudor monarchs had exploited their links with Britain's Celtic pre-history as a means of bypassing the demands of [male] primogeniture and assuaging doubts about the legitimacy of their claim to the throne. Geoffrey of Monmouth had written that Cadwaller, the last British king, who fled from the Saxons to Brittany was told by an angel's voice that he should not return to Britain "for that God had willed that the Britons should no longer reign in Britain before the time should come whereof Merlin prophesized unto Arthur."[4]

When Richard III declared that Henry Tudor had no legitimate claim to the throne, Henry was quick to commission a Welsh genealogy that would show that he was a descendent of Arthur and therefore

Brutus in order to legitimize his right to rule by showing that it came from antiquity.[5] Further, Finke shows that Elizabeth too used the Arthur legend to legitimize her own rule: "poems like *The Faerie Queene*, created a political myth that helped Elizabeth to defuse anxieties about the succession. Arthurian legends provided Elizabeth with a political mystification that appeared to satisfy the demands of patrilineage while redefining those demands through an elaborate historical allegory of the monarch's immortal body."[6]

Invading and eventually conquering, the Anglo-Saxons are viewed by Spenser as representing an unfortunate interlude in Brittan between the rule of Arthur and Elizabeth. He does not mince words when expressing what a problem Anglo-Saxon dominance is for the Britons in the poem. In Book III, Canto iii, at the beginning of stanza 42, he writes of the Saxons' domination of Britain: "Then, woe, and woe, and euerlasting woe,/Be to the Briton babe, that shalbe borne,/To live in thraldome of his fathers foe."[7] The Anglo-Saxons continue to be a problem until the coming of William the Conqueror in stanza 47, ushering in Norman rule and further delaying the coming of a Briton monarch.[8] Before William's arrival, the Anglo-Saxons "ruled wickedly" and treated the Britons with "fell cruelty" (III.iii.46). Clearly, if Spenser is trying to praise the lineage of the queen, Anglo-Saxons must be portrayed as enemies. In this history, Anglo-Saxons stood directly in the way of the eventual accession to power of Elizabeth's family and did so, according to Spenser, brutally.

The strife the Anglo-Saxons cause for the Britons is also relevant to the way Spenser's account of history is read allegorically. Harry Berger, Jr., suggests that Spenser's vision of British history is not adequately understood "by referring to Renaissance and Tudor historiography alone, nor by a simple appeal to chronicle sources,"[9] and argues that it is part and parcel of Spenser's allegory of temperance in Book II. Berger claims that Spenser's chronicle of British history must be read in conjunction with his account of Faerie history. He argues that there is a lesson about temperance to be learned from these two accounts. The chronicle of British history illustrates the tumultuous problems of all leadership; it "presents the universal context—the problems of any ruler incurred because she is human and derived from earth."[10] Joan Warchol Rossi, arguing similarly, suggests that "the only way to understand Spenser's theme of Temperance in the Chronicle is to view the history in light of the allegory: to recognize that history here is transformed by poetic vision so that there is actually an interdependence between allegory and history."[11] Rossi

argues that within Spenser's British chronicle, temperance is manifested in a worldly setting and then is contrasted with Faerie chronicle. "Thematically, the Elfin Chronicle depicts the triumph of
Temperance in a world without sin, while *Briton moniments* depicts
the definition of Temperance in a sinful world."[12] She goes on to
argue that there is a type of "militant Temperance" working itself
out in Spenser's British chronicle that would be apparent to a Renaissance or medieval reader. The Faerie chronicle embodies temperance's "political and military triumph," and in the fallen world of
the British chronicle the triumph of temperance cannot always be assured.[13]

Allegorically, the Anglo-Saxons in *The Faerie Queene* clearly embody a sort of anti-temperance, or, at least, the things that temperance
must overcome. Assuming that the Britons have a divinely ordained
claim to England by way of their ancestor Brutus, the Anglo-Saxons
stand as a roadblock to and even usurpers of this divine will and
eventually drive the Britons out of what will become England. They
impede the process of governing with grace and temperance because
they expel the mythical ancestors of the Tudors and of Elizabeth,
who, by the logic presented in *The Faerie Queene*, must be successfully
temperate if they are in power now. In the world of historical Brittan,
the Anglo-Saxons are those who keep the island in a fallen state and
impede the process that will eventually result in Tudor rule.

Further, the Anglo-Saxons in Spenser's British history are themselves nearly pictures of anti-temperance or rashness. Spenser's inclusion of the story of Hengist and Horsa in Book II, Canto x, is
particularly telling. In Spenser's version of the tale, after usurping the
British throne, Vortiger sends to Germany for help defending himself
against the marauding Picts. Not long afterward, three small boats of
Saxons arrive commanded by two brothers, Hengist and Horsa.
Spenser describes them primarily by their prowess in war: "*Hengist*
and *Horsus*, well approu'd in warre, / And both of them men of
renoumed might" (II.x.65). In return for their help in the wars
against the Picts, Hengist and Horsa are both granted large parcels of
land. This is apparently not good enough for the brothers, who depose Vortiger. Vortiger soon regains the throne with help from his
son, however. Hengist, apparently in an attempt to salvage some of
his previously won power, flatters Vortiger and gives him his daughter's hand. Then, for unknown reasons, Hengist slays 300 British
lords whom he was entertaining. Ambrose and Uther, who fled the
country when their uncle, Vortiger, seized the crown, return to Britain and slay their guilty uncle. Hengist is soon afterward killed as
well. Vortiger's successor, Aurelius, rules for some time then, until he

is poisoned and entombed at Stonehenge (II.x.66). The monument Stonehenge, we are told in the previous stanza, symbolizes treachery because it is the very spot where Hengist slays the aforementioned British lords.

Spenser gives us this account in only four confusing and action-packed stanzas. What is clear from his rendition of the Hengist and Horsa story is that the characters are far from temperate. To begin with, they are mercenaries who come to England only to participate in a war they might benefit from. This evidences, secondly, their greed, a vice Spenser mentions often at other points in *The Faerie Queene*, such as when "greedy *Auarice*" appears in Book I.iv.26. They are also treacherous and disloyal, as illustrated by their betrayal of Vortiger. Further, in a monstrous breach of courtesy, which is the topic of the last book of the poem, Hengist murders 300 British lords at his own table. Spenser seems to be suggesting it as an ironic anti-pode for the dinner party later in Book II where presumably it would be considered atrocious to pick a fight, let alone kill anyone. We have in Hengist and Horsa the embodiment of two powerful leaders who were not temperate in the least and suffered because of it. They offer a dramatic foil for temperance and for the good and virtuous kings in the rest of the chronicle. In typical Spenserian fashion, the reader is presented with a picture of a virtue by means of its exact op-posite.

Another reading of Spenser's British chronicle brings us to the subject of Anglo-Saxons in *The Faerie Queene* in a roundabout fashion. In a short but insightful article, Jerry Leath Mills points out that there are significant numerological things happening in the historical sections of Book II and Book III.[14] Mills argues that the British chronicles are structured around the numerically significant numbers 7 and 9, "extending the numerological formulation of Temperance throughout and beyond Canto x and magnifying its significance to the level of history."[15] Using these numbers, Mills shows that Spenser constructed his British chronicle with specific proportions in mind. The numerological structure of the two chronicles ends at the end of stanza 47 in Book III, just before the introduction of the first Tudor monarch.[16] Mills makes a fairly convincing argument that Spenser's chronicle, beginning in Book II and carried through until Book III, is mathematically and thematically proportionate. Even if one is not convinced by the specifics of Mills's mathematical formula, Spenser clearly meant for his chronicle to have a certain size and proportion and did not just randomly include extraneous details. Not only is it clear from Mills's discussion that the chronicles have a very specific structure, but the text itself suggests the same. In Book III,

Canto iii, after the chronicle ends as Mills suggests with stanza 47, Merlin offers two stanzas prophesying the rise of the Tudors and the ascent of the "royall virgin," Queen Elizabeth. Merlin's speech, oddly, ends with the first half line of stanza 50: "But yet the end is not. There *Merlin* stayd," (III.iii.50). With this half line, Spenser seems to suggest either that the Queen will rule for some time in the future or signal the uncertainty of her succession. The half line transgresses the boundaries of the preceding stanzas and launches the "end" of Elizabeth's rule into the future and, literally, into a future stanza. At any rate, it is clear that when Merlin stops speaking, we have come to the definite end of the chronicle sections of the poem.

A small amount of historical material, however, exists just outside of Merlin's prophecy. In a strange turn, the nurse, Glauce, recounts historical information to Britomart that again contains the appearance of an Anglo-Saxon. At the top of stanza 52, the nurse begins to tell a story: "At last the Nourse in her foolhardy wit / Conceiu'd a bold deuise, and thus bespake" (III.iii.52). Glauce then explains that Uther, the father of Arthur, has recently won a battle against Octa, the son of Hengist, and his kinsman Oza. Although the chronicle seems to be over, Spenser takes us back to the historical information that he lays out in Book II, Canto x. We are reminded about the continuous struggle between the Anglo-Saxons and the Britons, and by implication, the allegorical struggle over temperance and the historical legitimacy of Elizabeth's rule. The nurse then suggests that the two of them dress up in armor and leave the castle disguised. In case Britomart is afraid of the idea, the nurse bolsters her courage with a speech about several women warriors, ending with "a *Saxon* Virgin," whom she reports having seen fight against Uther in a recent battle. Glauce goes so far as to suggest that Britomart should emulate this Saxon virgin:

> Ah, read, (quoth Britomart) how is she hight?
> Faire *Angela* (quoth she) men do her call,
> No whit lesse faire, then terrible in fight:
> She hath the leading of a Martiall
> And mighty people, dreaded more than all
> The other *Saxons*, which do for her sake
> And loue, themselues of her name *Angles* call.
> Therefore faire infant her ensample make
> Vnto thyselfe, and equall courage to thee take.

> (III.iii.56)

Britomart is thus convinced and dons the very same armor once worn by the fierce Angela herself.

In light of Mills's observations about the proportionate structure of the historical sections in *The Faerie Queene*, it is immediately apparent that this little story exists outside that structure. The story transgresses the mathematical proportions and limits because it is *about* a transgression. The point of the story is to explain the origins of Britomart's transvestism, and Spenser seems to be setting up this little episode to show that whatever Britomart's cross-dressing actually means, it is a transgression. Not only does the passage exist outside the borders of the other historical material, but it also comes from a feminine source, Glauce the nurse. In contrast, the earlier sources of history were the two books read by Arthur and Guyon, and the prophecy from Merlin.

But the most strikingly significant transgression in this story, in terms of Britomart's character and in light of the early British chronicle, is that Britomart takes the Saxon, Angela, as her model for being a warrior-woman. Angela is, as is Britomart, an allusion to Virgil's Camilla in the *Aeneid*. Like Camilla, Angela is a virtuous, powerful, virgin warrior-woman in the enemy's camp. Angela, however, is further complicated because of her origins. Spenser has Britomart take as her role model a member of a people fundamentally opposed to the history and virtue he was trying to suggest earlier. During the course of Spenser's version of British history, Anglo-Saxons are the antagonists of the historical and the allegorical virtues he is espousing. They are the people who depose the Welsh ancestors of his own monarch, and they are the antithesis of temperance. As Britomart takes up the arms of Angela, Spenser further confuses his already confusing character by having her emulate someone from a people that he has previously described in negative terms. The great irony of all of this is the two characters' names. For his Anglo-Saxon virgin, Spenser chooses the name "Angela," for whose honor the Saxons call themselves "Angles," and "for whom England was named."[17] Britomart's name, as John E. Hankins has shown, is a combination of "Mars" and "Britain."[18] It is obvious that Spenser is drawing a comparison between this Anglo-Saxon source for the name of England and his chaste knight of Britain. At the same time that Spenser uses the whole passage to show a type of transgression, he confuses the scene further by suggesting that his two women-warriors, Britomart and Angela, are, ironically, the same. In this context, Britomart can be read as combining the virtuous and historically legitimate Britons and the violent, anti-temperate, historically unfavorable Anglo-Saxons.

In Spenser's British history in Books II and III, it is easy to pass over specific names and events as they are abundant, convoluted, and rapidly mentioned, but I have tried to show that some of these obscure names and events contribute to the poem's meaning. The Anglo-Saxons who appear in Spenser's British history do not appear simply because they were on the island at the time. They also add a layer of meaning to the chronicle. They help to reinforce Spenser's historical arguments about the legitimacy of a monarch whose ancestral roots were in Wales and they help to illustrate more clearly the allegory of temperance in Book II by demonstrating how absolutely un-temperate a person can be. And most interestingly, an Anglo-Saxon helps to define, or perhaps further confuse Britomart, one of the most interesting characters in *The Faerie Queene*.

Arizona State University

NOTES

1. The term "Anglo-Saxon" is used throughout for the sake of simplicity and continuity with common modern usage. Spenser does not use the term, referring instead to "Saxons," although even his usage is confusing because of his inclusion of the Saxon virgin, Angela. My intent is to make a simple distinction between the "native" Celtic peoples of Brittan and the Germanic ones who invade and conquer them.

2. Carrie Anna Harper, *The Sources of the British Chronicle History in Spenser's Faerie Queene* (New York: Haskell House, 1964).

3. Harper includes John Hardyng's *Chronicle*, Raphael Holinshed's *Chronicles*, and John Stow's *Chronicles of England*, among others.

4. Laurie A. Finke, "Spenser for Hire: Arthurian History as Cultural Capital in the Faerie Queene," in *Culture and the King: The Social Implications of the Arthurian Legend*, ed. Martin B. Schictman and James P. Carley (Albany: State University of New York Press, 1994), 211–33.

5. Ibid., 212.

6. Ibid., 213.

7. All the quotations of *The Faerie Queene* follow Thomas P. Roche, Jr.'s edition (London: Penguin Books, 1978).

8. That Spenser covers Norman rule in such a small space is indicative of the complicated way that his contemporaries viewed England's historical relationship with France. For more, see Deanne Willliams, *The French Fetish from Chaucer to Shakespeare* (Cambridge: Cambridge University Press, 2004) and Andrew M. Kirk, *The Mirror of Confusion: The Representation of French History in English Renaissance Drama* (New York: Garland, 1996).

9.   Harry Berger, *The Allegorical Temper: Vision and Reality in Book II of Spenser's Faerie Queene* (New Haven: Yale University Press, 1957), 89.

10.   Ibid., 114.

11.   Joan Warchol Rossi, " 'Britons Moniments': Spenser's Definition of Temperance in History," *English Literary Renaissance* 15.1 (1985): 42–58.

12.   Ibid., 44.

13.   Ibid., 45, 47.

14.   Jerry Leath Mills, "Spenser and the Numbers of History: A Note on the British and Elfin Chronicles in the Faerie Queene," *Philological Quarterly* 55 (1976): 281–87.

15.   Ibid., 282.

16.   Mills's formula is fairly straightforward: "The British chronicle in Canto x begins with stanza 5 and continues through stanza 67, ending abruptly in the first line of stanza 68 with a mention of Uther Pendragon, Arthur's father and the currently reigning British monarch. We are thus presented with a complete history of 63 stanzas totaling 567 lines—in Bodin's terms the historically significant 'square of nine by the base seven.' . . . When the chronicle resumes in III.iii as part of Merlin's prophecy to Britomart, it begins in stanza 29 with the son of Britomart and Arthegall and continues through stanza 47 before introducing the first Tudor. This is a total of nineteen chronicle stanzas. But one of these, stanza 43, is an interruption in which Britomart halts the relation with a question about God's divine providence; Merlin does not speak. If we subtract this stanza we have eighteen chronicle stanzas between Britomart and the Tudors. Added to the chronicle stanzas of the British history in Book II this puts the prophecy of Henry VII immediately after eighty-one completed chronicle stanzas and 729 (9 cubed) completed lines" (283). Mills's omission of stanza 43 in the episode between Britomart and Merlin is excusable, as he points out, because there is so much going on mathematically in *The Faerie Queene*, Spenser had to have built in buffers so that everything would add up correctly.

17.   For possible sources for Spenser's story of Angela see Harper, 165–68.

18.   John E. Hankins, "The Sources of Spenser's Britomartis," *Modern Language Notes* 58.8 (1943): 607–10.

REBECCA OLSON

A Closer Look at Spenser's "Clothes of Arras and of Toure"

In *The Faerie Queene* III, Britomart encounters "clothes of Arras and of Toure" in the Castle Joyous (III.i.34.2). While "Arras" clearly refers to that city's great tapestry workshops, which made "arras" synonymous with high-quality hangings, Spenser's allusion to "Toure" is more mysterious—does this truncated word refer to the French city Tours or, rather, the Flemish Tournai? This short essay makes a renewed case for Tournai: I argue that Spenser's singular word "Toure" might in fact refer to the Tournai workshop's distinctive mark—a tower—and thus underscore his fictional tapestries' correspondence to those on display in Elizabethan courts.

AMONG THE MOST MEMORABLE objects in Spenser's *Faerie Queene* are the Ovidian tapestries, or arras hangings, that Britomart encounters in Book III's Castle Joyous and Hall of Busyrane. These lively examples of Renaissance ekphrasis helped to establish Spenser's reputation as a "painterly poet,"[1] and have provoked critical speculation that in these passages Spenser describes tapestries he himself had witnessed, either at Elizabeth's court or Leicester House.[2] However, our sense that Spenser's arras hangings are "real" tapestries may not derive from realistic detail as much as from strategically layered rhetorical techniques. As Claud A. Thompson points out, "We seem often to have an impression of more abundant visual detail than Spenser actually provides"; he attributes this to Spenser's striving for *energeia* and his use of such rhetorical techniques as apostrophe and exclamation.[3] In other words, the feeling readers have that Spenser is describing "real" tapestries does not mean that he actually *is*; nonetheless, that is exactly what he wants us to think.

I suggest that whether or not Spenser is working from specific contemporary models when he describes these Ovidian tapestries, his

allusion to the "clothes of Arras and of Toure" in the Castle Joyous
does indicate an up-close familiarity with these valued Tudor objects.
Although critics have, for the most part, assumed that Spenser's
clothes of "Toure" refers to tapestry hangings woven in Tours, I
argue that "Toure" could in fact be a strategically truncated word
for Tournai, one of the greatest tapestry centers in sixteenth-century Europe.

After Britomart defeats six guards on behalf of an outnumbered
knight in the first canto of Book III, she is invited inside the Castle
Joyous to meet its lady, Malecasta. The Castle's great chamber features
a dazzling display, including tapestries:

> The wals were round about apparelled
> With costly clothes of *Arras* and of *Toure*,
> In which with cunning hand was pourtrahed
> The loue of *Venus* and her Paramoure
> The faire *Adonis*, turned to a flowre,
> A worke of rare deuice, and wonderous wit.
>
> (III.i.34)[4]

The narrator goes on to describe the tapestries' depiction of Ovid's
story of Venus and Adonis, from Venus's wooing of the boy to the
moment she finds him languishing, gored by the boar, and transforms
him into a "dainty flowre" (III.i.38.8). Although the tapestries become directly involved with the mythological, the allegorical, and
the eternal (just as the garden itself is eternal), we should note that
they are first introduced with very time-specific place names; from
the start of the ekphrasis, Spenser overtly calls attention to the fictional tapestries' places of origin—cities that continued to produce
magnificent textiles throughout the sixteenth century. This did not
escape the eighteenth-century critic Thomas Warton, who considered the reference to "Arras and of Toure" to be one of Spenser's
most egregious "anachronisms" or "historical mistakes."[5] If Warton's
assumption that Spenser included the names "Arras" and "Toure"
in error seems naive, the anachronism itself—which escapes most
modern readers—is worth consideration. Here we are told explicitly
that the tapestries in Malecasta's castle are very much like—in fact,
woven at the same places as—those one would see in Elizabethan England.

By the second half of the sixteenth century, the city of Arras, now
French but then part of the Spanish Netherlands, had been known

as a prime center of weaving and tapestry production for two hundred years. The name of the city had, consequently, become synonymous with high-quality hangings.[6] The tapestry historian Thomas Campbell has argued that in sixteenth-century England, the term "arras" specifically referred to tapestries woven with gold or silver threads, not necessarily woven at the workshop of Arras; Spenser's ekphrasis of the tapestries in the Hall of Busyrane, which are "wouen with gold and silke so close and nere, / That the rich metall lurked priuily" (III.xi.28.2–3) support this claim.[7] "Clothes" of Arras clearly demanded respect, and editors of *The Faerie Queene* have consequently assumed that the reference to "clothes of Arras and of Toure" operates in the same way as Spenser's more ubiquitous "rich and costly"—that it is a conventional way of communicating the value of the object.[8]

While Spenser's reference to "Arras" is to be expected, there has been some critical disagreement over whether Spenser's "Toure" references Tours or Tournai—both cities were well known sites of tapestry production. In his edition of *The Faerie Queene* Thomas P. Roche identifies "Arras and Toure" as Arras and the French city Tours: "famous for their tapestries."[9] In terms of pronunciation, "Toure" does seem closer to "Tours" than "Tournai"—although it does seem a little odd that Spenser drops the final *s*, this can be reasonably explained by the constraints of the stanza.[10] However, we should not altogether discount Tournai as a possible alternative. Frances Stillman argues that Tournai would make more sense chiefly because Arras and Tournai were often spoken of together and were in closer physical proximity; Spenser may link them together, she maintains, to make it clear that the tapestries in Malecasta's hall were Flemish.[11] The explanation for his shortening of Tournai to "Toure" is, again, that he simply needed to fit the rhyme.[12]

In fact, the truncation of the word may be another clue to the identity of "Toure." In the early sixteenth century, the overwhelming popularity of Flemish tapestries led to hastened production, which in turn led to legislation passed by the Brussels tapestry guild in 1528 requiring tapestries of a certain size to bear woven marks that proved they had been inspected for quality.[13] The workshop of Tournai's mark was a tower—or, as it is spelled in some fourteenth-century manuscripts, "toure."[14] By shortening "Tournai" to "Toure," Spenser might therefore have seized an opportunity to both "antiquate" his language and, at the same time, make a clever pun.[15]

The critical difference between Tournai and Tours is that tapestries from Tournai were far more visible in English courts and noble homes, in part because the city was briefly under English control in the early sixteenth century. While Tours was a relatively small work-shop operating from the 1520s, Tournai was once the dominant tapestry center of the world, and many pieces woven there eventually came into the English Royal Collection.[16] It is therefore entirely possible that Spenser would have, in his own gazing upon court tapestries, encountered Tournai's distinctive mark. That said, tapes-tries from Tours were probably not entirely obscure in Elizabethan England—what seems important is not that we definitively identify "Toure" as either one city or the other, but rather acknowledge the way that in presenting these fictional arras hangings, Spenser underscores their resemblance to actual contemporary counterparts.

Oregon State University

NOTES

1. For an overview, see Rudolf Gottfried, "The Pictorial Element in Spenser's Poetry," *English Literary Renaissance* 19 (1952): 203–13.

2. As Frederick Hard argued in an influential 1930 essay, "Spenser's insistence on the reality of the tapestries described affords convincing evidence that he was writing with his mind's eye upon examples which he had actually seen" ("Spenser's 'Clothes of Arras and of Toure,' " *Studies in Philology* 27 [1930]): 176).

3. See Claud A. Thompson, "Spenser's 'Many Faire Pourtraicts, and Many a Faire Feate,' " *Studies in English Literature* 12 (1972): 23. See also Paul Alpers, "Narra-tive and Rhetoric in *The Faerie Queene*," *Studies in English Literature* 2 (1962): 37.

4. All *Faerie Queene* quotations are from A. C. Hamilton's edition (London: Longman, 1977).

5. See Thomas Warton, *Observations on the* Fairy Queen *of Spenser*, 2 vols. (Lon-don, 1762; rprt. Westmead: Gregg, 1969), 20–21.

6. See W. G. Thomson, *A History of Tapestry:From the Earliest Times until the Present Day*, ed. F. P. Thomson and E. S. Thomson, 3rd ed. (East Ardsley: EP Publishing, 1973) 40, 71.

7. For example, the most expensive category in the 1558 "Book of Rates" is "Tappestry with Golde called Arras"; see Thomas Campbell, "Tapestry Quality in Tudor England: Problems of Terminology." *Studies in the Decorative Arts* (Fall-Winter 1995–1996): 33.

8. *The Faerie Queene*, p. 311. Other tapestries in *The Faerie Queene* include the "costly arras" in the House of Pride (I.iv.6.6); the "royall arras" in Orgoglio's lair (I.viii.35.2); the "royall arras richly dight" in the House of Temperance (II.ix.33.7); and the "goodly arras of great maiesty" in the House of Busyrane (III.xi.28.2).

9. *The Faerie Queene*, ed. Thomas P. Roche, Jr. (London: Penguin, 1978), 1142n34.2. Spenser may even have known Tours first-hand from traveling to that city to convey letters from the English ambassador of France back to England: in

1569 an "Edmonde Spencer" brought from Tours letters from Sir Henry Norris to the Queen (see Hamilton's introduction to *The Faerie Queene*, viii). However, this date seems a little early: he did not receive his M.A. until 1576 and does not seem to have been officially employed as a secretary until 1577; see Richard Rambuss, *Spenser's Secret Career* (Cambridge: Cambridge University Press, 1993), 7.

10.   In late sixteenth-century inventories, Tours is spelled "Towers" or "towres," as in "towres taffata"; see *OED*, "Tours," def. a. An inventory from the Great Wardrobe (1586–89), for example, refers to "Towers ribon of sondry colours" (PRO LC 5/36, f. 65).

11.   See Frances Jennings Stillman, "Visual Arts in the *Faerie Queene*," Ph.D. diss. (City University of New York, 1971), 282. Tournai replaced Arras as the "principal center" of tapestry production in the second half of the fifteenth century, and was replaced in turn by Brussels in the sixteenth century.

12.   Stillman, "Visual Arts in the Faerie Queene," 282

13.   See Campbell, *Tapestry in the Renaissance: Art and Magnificence* (Metropolitan Museum of Art; New Haven: Yale University Press, 2002), 282.

14.   See *OED* definitions 1 and 3 of "tower." For two illustrations of Tournai's mark, which resembles the rook piece in a chess set, see Thomson, *A History of Tapestry*, 509. In *The Faerie Queene*, "towre" is Spenser's spelling for "tower," as in "king *Nine* whilome built *Babell* towre" (II.ix.21.6). In one instance, however, the plural form is spelled "toures": "Which they far off beheld from *Troian* toures" (III.ix.35.5).

15.   The pun could also refer to the Tower of London, which was the repository for a large number of the royal arras hangings. Paul Hentzner described entering the Tower in the late sixteenth century: "Upon entering the tower, we were obliged to quit our swords at the gate, and deliver them to the guard. When we were introduced, we were shewn above a hundred pieces of arras belonging to the crown, made of gold, silver, and silk . . ." (*Paul Hentzner's Travels in England*, trans. Horace, Earl of Oxford [London: 1797], 26).

16.   Campbell, *Tapestry in the Renaissance*, 459 and 31. See also Susan Groag Bell, *The Lost Tapestries of the City of Ladies* (Berkeley: University of California Press, 2004), 42. On the distribution of tapestries to the English after the capture of Tournai (and Cardinal Wolsey's involvement in particular), see Campbell, "The English Royal Tapestry Collection," Ph.D. diss. (Courtauld Institute, London University, 1998), 73.

FRED BLICK

Spenser's *Amoretti* and Elizabeth Boyle: Her Names Immortalized

On the evidence of *The Fairie Queene*, Spenser has long been recognized as a master of hovering puns and allusions. However, in the Amoretti he deployed this skill further by immortalizing the name of his bride to be, Elizabeth Boyle, by devices of word play. He appears to have fulfilled the promise of immortality for her name which he made in *Amoretti* sonnet 75. Spenser's ingenuity was such that, except for critical recognition of the references to "my Helice" (my Elise) in sonnet 34 and to "three Elizabeths" in sonnet 74, his loving but humorous name play has hitherto gone unnoticed. A consideration of new examples of name play enlivens a reading of the *Amoretti* and reveals how Elizabeth joined in the game by an allusive depiction of Spenser and of herself in a beautiful piece of her own drawn work embroidery.

*I*T IS VERY LIKELY THAT Edmund Spenser intended as a wedding gift to his second wife, Elizabeth Boyle, the sonnets entitled *Amoretti* and the *Epithalamion* printed with it in 1595.[1] It is to the period around 1592–94, which spans his courtship of Elizabeth, that most of the sonnets of the *Amoretti* appear to belong. When, in sonnet 75, he remarks that the tide has made her name its "pray" by erasing the letters he has written on the sand and he asserts that he will nonetheless make that "name" immortal, it is a conventional gesture, but he may have meant what he said quite literally. I intend to show how he observed that the "th" of Elizabeth and the "B" of Boyle could be elided in a lisping way as "thBoyle" or "spoyle" and how from this base he developed a punning chain of ideas on "Boyle/spoyle/prey/trophy/purchase" which were repeatedly expressed as name play in the *Amoretti*. Spenser might have found in Petrarch, Surrey,

Ronsard, and Sidney many precedents for the playing on a loved
one's name in verse, and he himself possessed a well recognized pro-
pensity for name play. [2] Presented with the name of Elizabeth Boyle
to play upon poetically, Spenser faced much greater difficulty than
most of his predecessors, but, with some humor, he did not flinch
from the task.

Spenser tells us in sonnet 74 why the name is "glorious": it is the
name of Queen Elizabeth, the "Gloriana" of *The Faerie Queene*, of
his mother Elizabeth, and also of his future wife Elizabeth. He prays
that the three beloved holders of the name would "for ever live."
But not content with naming her Elizabeth, he plays (unlike Petrarch
but like Sidney) with his beloved's surname.

> The famous warriors of the anticke world,
> Used Trophees to erect in stately wize:
> In which they would the records have enrold,
> Of theyr great deeds and valarous emprize.
> What trophee then shall I most fit devize,
> In which I may record the memory
> Of my loves conquest, peerelesse beauties prise,
> Adorned with honour, love and chastity.
> Even this verse vowd to eternity,
> Shall be thereof immortall moniment:
> And tell her prayse to all posterity,
> That may admire such worlds rare wonderment:
> The happy purchase of *my glorious spoile*,
> Gotten at last with labour and long toyle.
>
>   (69)

The concluding couplet of this immortalizing sonnet fulfils the purpose and meaning of the previous twelve lines. The couplet contains
her name, as promised—"Glorious," by association with the Queen,
suggesting "Elizabeth" and "glorious spoile," elided, sounding "Glorious Boyle." "Trophee" (l. 5) is defined in the *OED* (sb 2a and b)
as the "spoil" of hunting or war and a monument or memorial. In
"the antique world" of Greek and Roman times, the trophy often
included arms or other spoils of the vanquished and so, to be true to
the promise in lines 9 and 10 of this sonnet, Spenser had to include
in "Even this verse" something which belonged to his "loves conquest": the name Boyle, made glorious by its combination with

"Elizabeth." The tautology of "trophee," meaning spoil, "purchase," meaning captured prey or plunder (*OED*, sb. I.1), and "spoile," meaning the object of plunder, a prey (*OED*, sb. 4), signals the pun on "spoile"/Boyle —also the "pray" of the tide in sonnet 75.

Spenser had already punned on the name "Boyle" by using a similar warlike metaphor in sonnet 52. Here he depicts himself as a defeated prisoner and as a victim in the poetically conventional war of love:

> So oft as homeward I from her depart,
> I go lyke one that having lost the field,
> Is prisoner led away with heavy hart,
> *Despoyld* of warlike armes and knowen shield.

He complains that in having to quit his Elizabeth, he is a "prisoner," deprived of his desired conquest; he is "despoiled," that is, "dis-Boyled."

Initially, in the sequence, Spenser regards himself as Elizabeth's "pray," vanquished in love (see the final couplet of 20). Thereafter, he alternates between being hunter (or victor) and prey (or vanquished), as witness sonnets 11, 12, 23, 28, 37, 38, 41, 49, 53, 56, and 57. Eventually he definitely takes the part of the victor and allots Elizabeth the part of "pray" or "spoyle," now for obvious name-play reasons. Judging by the number of "victor" and "spoile"/"spoyle" sonnets, Spenser must have planned this as a persistent theme (and private joke) from the start. He gently eases her into the "spoyle" role in sonnet 65, where he suggests that she is nervous about losing her liberty in marriage. He assures her that "the gentle birde feeles no captivity / Within her cage, but singes and feeds her fill." In sonnet 67, she comes to him in the allegorical form of a long-hunted "gentle" deer / dear returning to drink in a nearby brook, and "Strange thing me seemd to see a beast so wyld, / so goodly wonne with her owne will beguyld." His willing "spoyle" is then and there trussed and trophied.

In sonnet 23, early in the sequence, Spenser compares Elizabeth's wiles to those of Penelope the wife of Ulysses, who delayed giving an answer to her suitors by saying that she must complete a shroud for her aged father-in-law before deciding among them. She then undid at night the weaving that she had done by day. Similarly, in this sonnet Elizabeth destroys the work of Spenser's wooing with "one looke" and "one word," so that he becomes a frustrated Spider whose tediously spun web is repeatedly blown away. Here Spenser is punning with false etymology on his own name, Spenser the spinster, spinner or "spider" (see the *OED*, 1 a and 1 b). Elizabeth, who as we shall see enjoyed needlework, seems to have taken this "spider" symbolism in good part, and to have known that she was the "spoyle" or "prey" to Spenser's "Spider" for reasons of name-play. From the evidence of sonnet 71 set out below, which was written after she had accepted him, it appears that at least one piece of her drawn-work embroidery depicted Spenser as the "Spider" and herself as a "Bee." It is probable that this embroidery contained their names or initials, "Sp" or "S" standing for Spenser the Spider and "B" standing for Boyle the Bee (a bee stings Cupid in the Anacreontic verses separating the *Amoretti* sonnets from the *Epithalamion*). Sonnet 71 makes the symbolism clear:

> I joy to see how in your drawen work,
> Your selfe unto the Bee ye do compare;
> And me unto the Spyder that doth lurke,
> In close awayt to catch her unaware.
> Right so your selfe were caught in cunning snare
> Of a deare foe, and thralled to his love;
> In whose streight bands ye now captived are
> So firmely, that ye never may remove.
> But as your worke is woven all about,
> With woodbynd flowers and fragrant Eglantine:
> So sweet your prison you in time shall prove,
> With many deare delights bedecked fyne.
> And all thensforth eternall peace shall see
> Betweene the Spyder and the gentle Bee.

If we recognize that the word "spoyle" equals "Boyle," the "prey" of Spenser the Spider and of Spenser the Hunter of a deer/dear in sonnet 67, we can see that in the erotic daydream of sonnet 76 he names her again. Here Spenser imagines his thoughts, which focus on Elizabeth's bosom: "diving deepe through amorous insight, /On the *sweet spoyle* of beautie they did *pray*." Line eight, appropriately elided sounds, "On the sweet'st Boyle of beauty they did prey." One can only hope that Elizabeth enjoyed the pair of sonnets 76 and 77, which have not always seemed to be entirely in good taste to some older or modern ears.[3]

In sonnet 41 Spenser plays upon the name more obscurely:

She meanes at last to make her *piteous spoyle.*
O fayrest fayre *let never it be named,*
   That so fayre beauty was so fowly shamed. [My italics]

The final couplet stresses that Elizabeth Boyle's, *"glorious* beauty"
(line 9) might be "fowly shamed" (line 14) if she were to make him
her "piteous spoyle" (line 12). By doing so she would risk gaining
in line 13 the name "piteous Boyle" ("make her piteous spoyle"
becomes "make her piteous Boyle"). The adjective "piteous" applied
to "spoyle" means either "pitiable" or "deplorable," but is punningly
transferred to the Lady whose willful behavior might make her "so
fowly shamed" that she might become the subject of pity herself,
that is, pitiable.

   Like many Renaissance poets, Spenser uses paradox to suggest his
mixed feelings that his love provokes. The paradox is sometimes
simple: Elizabeth is "cruell faire" (55). But he perceives in the burn-
ing heat of her name, Boyle, a Petrarchan opportunity for play on
her initial coolness to his advances. In sonnet 55 he says, "I marvaile
of what substance was the mould / The which her made . . . / . . . for
her love doth burne like fyre." That is, she is "full of the living fire"
(including the fire implied by "Boyle") inflaming his love with "these
flames in which I fry." Yet, he declares, "she frieseth in her wilfull
pryde" (32), and initially, she had been like ice to him in her response
to the "boyling sweat" of his advances. Sonnet 30 illustrates the
paradox clearly, and at the same time glances at her name:

My love is like to yse, and I to fyre;
How comes it then that this her cold so great
Is not dissolved through my so hot desyre,
But harder growes the more I her intreat?
Or how comes it that my exceeding heat
Is nor delayd by her hart frosen cold;
But that *I burne much more in boyling sweat,*
And feele my flames augmented manifold?
What more miraculous thing may be told
That fire which all thing melts, should harden yse:
And yse which is congeald with sencelesse cold,
Should *kind*le fyre by wonderfull devyse?

> Such is the powre of love in gentle mind,
> That it can alter all the course *of kynd*. [My italics]

The final couplet explains the paradox and the strenuous puns. She is Boyle of "*kynd*"— that is by name, kin, and descent (*OED*, sb. 1, 2, 3), yet she is "like to yse." He burns "in *boyling* sweat" undeterred by her "hart frozen cold" toward his "hot desire." "Such is the power of love" to "*kind*le fire" as well as alter the "course of *kynd*," that is, to alter the inflammatory nature of the "Boyle" *kind* (or kin) to "cold" or "ice." He complains that she blew hot and cold—a not very unusual circumstance in the trials of poets' courtships.

The "boyling" effect of Elizabeth upon him is worked into another elided pun in sonnet 33, addressed to his friend Lodowick Bryskett, in which Spenser excuses himself for not having completed his *The Faerie Queene,* blaming his failure on

> . . . a proud love, that doth my *spirite spoyle*.
> Ceasse then, till she vouchsafe to grawnt me rest,
> Or lend you me another living brest.

By elision, line 12 reads, "a proud love that doth my *spirits boyle*," which is akin to the line "but that I burne much more in boyling sweat" (30). The "boyling" unrest in his "living brest," inflamed by his "proud love," is vividly caught in the last four lines of sonnet 33 with the words "tost with troublous fit," the elided pun "my spirits boyle," and with the plea either "to grawnt me rest" or to give him the loan of "another living brest." These phrases clearly underscore the "spoyle"/Boyle pun. This pun, like the other puns noted in this analysis, provides additional and explanatory meaning to the context—a sure test for identifying deliberate, topical wordplay.

Spenser is generally considered to have had one of the best ears of any English poet, and *The Faerie Queene* has been described as "a collection of hovering puns."[4] It is inconceivable that he would have been oblivious to the wordplay perceived and explored in this analysis. Elizabethans were aware that, in emphatic enunciation, "p" could easily be substituted for "b," especially in Celtic-influenced pronunciation (Spenser, of course, wooed Elizabeth in Ireland). This is clear from the words of Shakespeare's Fluellen in *King Henry V*: "Kill the poys [boys]" and "Alexander the Pig [Big]" (IV.vii). It seems to me that Spenser planned his *Amoretti* with the intention to play on Elizabeth Boyle's name. Enclosing her names within the bounds of his sonnets was one way in which he might satisfy his urge to possess his "gentle deare" or deer, his "Helice" (his guiding star) who is also the Elise (Elizabeth) of sonnet 34.

Spenser's little allegory describing his betrothal after long wooing is set out in sonnet 67. The betrothal and the fiancée's name are immortalized two sonnets later in the "trophee" sonnet, 69. In both of these sonnets Spenser clearly records the taking "in hand" (sonnet 67's play on a formal betrothal) of his "trophee," "game," and "deare," or otherwise his "pray"/"spoile"/thBoyle. These examples, taken together, constitute persuasive evidence for how Spenser immortalized, as promised, the name of his beloved, Elizabeth Boyle.

Stafford, England

NOTES

1.   I follow the text of the *Amoretti* in *Edmund Spenser's Poetry,* ed. Hugh MacLean and Anne Lake Prescott, 3rd ed. (New York: Norton, 1993).

2.   A. C. Hamilton, ed., *The Faerie Queene* (London: Longman, 1977). 15–18.

3.   On Spenser's playful pragmatism in 76 and 77, see Edmund Spenser, *Selected Shorter Poems*, ed. Douglas Brooks-Davies (London: Longman, 1995), 203.

4.   Gordon Braden, "riverrun: An Epic Catalogue in *The Faerie Queene,*" *English Literary Renaissance* 5 (1975): 25–48.

Index

(Page numbers in italics represent illustrations)